Children's Rights in Ghana

Children's Rights in Ghana

Reality or Rhetoric?

Edited by Robert Kwame Ame,
DeBrenna LaFa Agbényiga, and Nana Araba Apt

LEXINGTON BOOKS
A division of
ROWMAN & LITTLEFIELD PUBLISHERS, INC.
Lanham • Boulder • New York • Toronto • Plymouth, UK

Published by Lexington Books
A division of Rowman & Littlefield Publishers, Inc.
A wholly owned subsidiary of The Rowman & Littlefield Publishing Group, Inc.
4501 Forbes Boulevard, Suite 200, Lanham, Maryland 20706
http://www.lexingtonbooks.com

Estover Road, Plymouth PL6 7PY, United Kingdom

British Library Cataloguing in Publication Information Available

Library of Congress Cataloging-in-Publication Data

Children's rights in Ghana : reality or rhetoric? / edited by Robert Kwame Ame, DeBrenna LaFa Agbényiga, and Nana Araba Apt.
p. cm.
Includes bibliographical references and index.
ISBN 978-0-7391-4800-6 (cloth : alk. paper)
1. Children's rights—Ghana. 2. Children—Social conditions—Ghana. 3. Child labor—Ghana. 4. Child abuse—Ghana. 5. Child welfare—Ghana. I. Ame, Robert Kwame, 1958– II. Agbényiga, DeBrenna LaFa, 1971– III. Apt, Nana A.
HQ789.C4643 2011
305.23086'94209667—dc22 2010040255

™ The paper used in this publication meets the minimum requirements of American National Standard for Information Sciences—Permanence of Paper for Printed Library Materials, ANSI/NISO Z39.48-1992.

Printed in the United States of America

Contents

Figures vii
Tables ix
Foreword xi
Honorable Justice Georgina T. Wood, Chief Justice of the Republic of Ghana
Acknowledgments xiii

Part I: Childhood and Identity 1

1 Introduction: Confronting the Challenges: Optimizing Child Rights in Ghana 3
Nana Araba Apt, DeBrenna LaFa Agbényiga, and Robert Kwame Ame

2 Defining Childhood: A Historical Development Perspective 15
DeBrenna LaFa Agbényiga

3 Controversies in Paternity: Who Is a Child's Father under Ghanaian Law? 37
Beatrice Akua Duncan

4 Bridging the Child Rights Gap in a Refugee Context: Survival Strategies and Impact on Inter-generational Relations 59
Kate Hampshire, Gina Porter, Kate Kilpatrick, Peter Ohene Kyei, Michael Kwodwo Adjaloo, and George Oppong Ampong

Part II: Children in Dangerous Circumstances: Exploitation and Abuse 75

5 Corporal Punishment in Ghana 77
Sylvester Kyei-Gyamfi

6 Child Labor in Ghana: Global Concern and Local Reality 99
George Clerk

7 Children's Rights, Mobility, and Transport in Ghana: Access to Education and Health Services 113
Gina Porter, Albert Abane, Kathrin Blaufuss, and Frank Owusu Acheampong

Part III: Policies, Laws, and Programs 129

8 Children's Rights, Controversial Traditional Practices, and the *Trokosi* System: A Critical Socio-legal Perspective 131
Robert Kwame Ame

9 Assessing the Progress of the 1998 Children's Act of Ghana: Achievements, Opportunities, and Challenges of the First Ten Years 151
Afua Twum-Danso

10 Situating CRC Implementation Processes in the Local Contexts of Correctional Institutions for Children in Conflict with the Law in Ghana 169
Lilian Ayete-Nyampong

11 Ghana's Education System: Where Rhetoric Meets Reform 193
Leah McMillan

12 Conclusion: The Future of Children's Rights in Ghana 215
Robert Kwame Ame, Nana Araba Apt, and DeBrenna LaFa Agbényiga

Appendices 223
A United Nations Convention on the Rights of the Child 1989 225
B The Children's Act, 1998 (Act 560) 245

Index 277
About the Contributors 291

Figures

5.1 Who Usually Carries Out Corrective Measure at Home 81

5.2 Who Usually Carries Out Corrective Measure in School 86

Tables

4.1	Failure of Child Rights within Buduburam	63
5.1	Types of Corrective Measures Used on Children in School and Home	84
5.2	Most Appropriate Way to Correct a Child at Home and School According to Children	84
5.3	Reasons for Which Children Are Punished in School	86

Foreword

By Honorable Justice Georgina T. Wood, Chief Justice of the Republic of Ghana

The United Nations (UN) Convention on the Rights of the Child (CRC) 1989, which enjoys almost universal ratification (only the United States and Somalia have not ratified it, even though the United States has signed), has become the benchmark against which children's rights issues are measured globally. Ghana was the first country to ratify the CRC in February 1990, an act that the government and people of Ghana take great pride in. The Convention guarantees children: (1) rights of provision (adequate nutrition, health care, education, economic welfare), (2) rights of protection (protection from abuse, neglect, violence, exploitation), and (3) rights of participation (a voice in decisions affecting the child). The Convention places an obligation on state parties to promote these rights.

Even though Ghana was the first country to have ratified this Convention, there is very little published material on children's rights in our jurisdiction. To date, Henrietta Mensa-Bonsu and Christine Dowuona-Hammond's *The Rights of the Child in Ghana—Perspectives*, which was published sixteen years ago, is the only book on children's rights in Ghana that we can boast of. Considering the paucity of literature on children's rights in Ghana, this book fills an important gap even as it provides the latest research findings and data on children's rights in Ghana.

This book seeks to find answers to the following questions: What does the ratification of this Convention mean to children in Ghana after eighteen years? Has it translated into a better quality of life for children? Have the government and people of Ghana lived up to their obligations under the Convention? How committed is Ghana to the CRC?

Additionally, this book aims at assessing Ghana's compliance with the CRC and commitment to children's rights by addressing a wide range of children's issues, including but not limited to controversial traditional practices (e.g., the *trokosi* system); a child's identity (e.g., ethnic definitions of a child and childhood, legal determination of paternity); violence against children and women (e.g., corporal punishment); child labor (e.g., in hazardous fishing and mining); and children in dangerous circumstances (e.g., refugees and victims of ethnic conflicts); children in conflict with the law (e.g., juvenile delinquency, youth justice); education (e.g., compulsory basic education; school feeding program); and access to health, decision making, and economic survival.

In Chapter 9, the authors of the book deal admirably with the "achievements and challenges" of the Children's Act 1998 (Act 560). This is the law that regulates the conduct of family courts/tribunals that deal with issues of paternity, maintenance, custody, and other ancillary matters related to the welfare and interest of children.

This book seeks to identify the main obstacles that hinder the full realization of children's rights in Ghana such as the lack of will, inadequate funding for implementing policies and programs, and harmful cultural, traditional, and religious practices. Accordingly, every chapter reflects the theme of compliance and commitment to the Convention. This is the common theme that runs through the book. The contributors to the volume are scholars, doctoral students, and human rights activists, working either with government or NGOs. Each contributor has done empirical work in Ghana on the topic of his/her choice.

It is in pursuit of these matters that the Ghanaian Judiciary has set up a cluster of specialized family courts in Accra, dedicated to the expeditious hearing and disposal of cases that impinge on the rights of children. It is my hope that in later editions of the book, the authors will find some space to comment on the impact of these courts on children's rights generally.

This book should be of great value to human rights students, child rights activists, NGOs, and donor agencies that fund children's programs in Ghana. By it, they would understand the motivation that led to the signing of the Convention and the challenges faced by the Government of Ghana in meeting the principles of the Convention.

I highly recommend it to all interested in children's rights issues in Ghana.

Acknowledgments

The editors are grateful to their respective institutions—Wilfrid Laurier University, Canada; Michigan State University, United States of America (USA); and, Ashesi University College, Ghana—for their support in the preparation of this book manuscript. We would also like to thank the numerous contributors to this volume; their dedication translated our vision into reality. We would like to express our sincere gratitude to Rose Homa for providing her professional and meticulous editing of this volume and preparing the camera-ready copy for the publishers. Michael Sisskin, our initial Acquisitions Editor at Lexington Books, Justin Race who took over from Michael, and Victoria Koulakjian, Assistant Editor of Production at Rowman & Littlefield Publishing Group were great people to work with. They always responded to our queries promptly providing useful information and guidance.

Robert Ame wishes to express appreciation to the Research Office at Wilfrid Laurier University (WLU) and the Tshepo Institute for the Study of Contemporary Africa and Laurier Brantford for their financial support that enabled him to co-organize a panel by the same title as this book at the Africa-Europe Group for Interdisciplinary Studies European Conference on African Studies at Leipzig, Germany, in June 2009 and for a book preparation grant from the Research Office in 2010. I gratefully acknowledge that the financial support that enabled me to attend the conference and to prepare the manuscript for publication was received from a grant partly funded by WLU operating funds and partly by the Social Sciences and Humanities Research Council Institutional Grant awarded to WLU. I also want to express gratitude to Professor Rhoda Howard-Hassmann, Canada Research Chair of International Human Rights at WLU, who recommended me to the organizers of the Undefended Childhood Conference at Michigan State University, East Lansing, Michigan, USA, where I participated in the meeting of the Ghana Interest Group at which the idea for this book was born. I wish to thank Drs. DeBrenna LaFa Agbényiga, Deborah J. Johnson, and Robert Hitchcock, the co-principal investigators for the Undefended Childhood Research Project, who invited me to participate at the conference in April 2008. I would like to extend another thanks to Dr. Agbényiga for hosting the Ghana Interest Group meeting where the idea for this book was developed and for her initial lead role in the development of this book project.

DeBrenna LaFa Agbényiga wishes to express a heartfelt thanks to the Center for the Advancement of International Development and the Women in International Development Center at Michigan State University for their funding support of the Undefended Childhood in a Global Context conference as part of the Global Area Thematic Initiatives. That funding support served as a foundation for this book project. I would also like to thank my colleagues in Ghana for their continued support during my numerous research endeavors. A most sincere thanks to the beautiful people of Ghana for always welcoming me into their communities to further understand their challenges and successes in various capacities. I would also like to thank my husband, Agbéko, for his unwavering support and encouragement throughout this process. Finally, I wish to thank my children—Isaac Kwaku, Foley Cyril Kokou, and Gabrielle Mama Aku Sika Agbényiga—for their constant reminder of the true meaning, importance, and value of having a childhood with all of the supported rights.

Nana Araba Apt wishes to place on record her gratitude to members of the Executive of Ashesi University College in Accra, Ghana, for their understanding and support in granting her leave of absence from the University to complete work on this book. Additionally, I would like to thank all members of Ashesi faculty and staff for keeping me informed and up to date on affairs of the University while away. I thank especially Dr. Nathan Amanquah, head of the Department of Computer Science, who filled in for me during my absence from Ashesi as Dean of Academic Affairs.

Part I
Childhood and Identity

Chapter 1

Introduction: Confronting the Challenges: Optimizing Child Rights in Ghana

By Nana Araba Apt, DeBrenna LaFa Agbényiga, and Robert Kwame Ame

Human rights violations concern everyone. The reach of issues affecting human rights—problems, concerns, and challenges—are great in Africa and extend well beyond children or any one age cohort. This book addresses the rights of children in Ghana. Generally, human rights violations occur at multiple levels in Ghana from birth to death, but in 1990 Ghana was the first country to ratify the 1989 United Nations (UN) Convention on the Rights of the Child (CRC). The Convention, which is now twenty years old, specifically guarantees the rights of children to:

- Adequate nutrition, health care, education, economic welfare;
- Rights to protection from abuse, neglect, violence, and exploitation; and
- Rights to participation in decisions affecting them.

Ghana's ratification of the Convention signifies her acceptance and obligation to provide and protect these rights, but in reality are children's human rights indeed protected? This book examines the extent that the Government of Ghana has been able to protect children's rights after her ratification of the Convention in 1990 as well as current efforts to rectify violations of the Convention. It does so by providing an understanding to these overarching questions: What are the issues in child rights? What impediments are hindering efforts at eliminating violations? Twenty years after Ghana's ratification of the Convention, we believe it is time for this assessment.

The idea for the book first came up for discussion at a Ghana Interest Group meeting during the Undefended Childhood Conference held at Michigan State University, East Lansing, Michigan, USA, in April 2008. This book is a review, first, of some of the programs and services of the governmental entities in whose institutional mandate the protection of children are placed. In this respect, it provides an overview of the context within which human rights violations occur in Ghana. Second, the review examines avenues for enhanced institutional processes and interventions that could promote the rights of children and minimize the impact of various life cycle risks that impact negatively on the well-being of children. Major life-cycle risk factors in Ghana include orphanage, disability, sickness, unemployment, and old age, most of which act often in various combinations to drive hordes of Ghanaian families onto the fringes of society. The negative impact on children raised on the fringes of society is great and well documented (Apt, 2006, 2007; GHDR, 2007; DSW, 2006; CSPS, 2001; Apt & Wilson, 1995). Third, the review seeks to explore ways for strengthening linkages to existing government programs and services through the identification of opportunities to support the implementation of social development interventions for families and children over the long term. Furthermore, it examines pertinent issues related to Ghanaian family life and the upbringing of children, the cultural and societal norms and acceptances that often place children in difficult circumstances and infringe on their human rights. In this respect, the government's role in promoting healthy family life and safeguarding children's welfare is examined.

Child Rights: Analysis

A number of factors tend to hinder the development and human rights of children in Ghana. Poverty is fundamental. In impoverished areas of Ghana, children are caught in a vicious cycle of poverty and are forced to live in risky and harmful conditions (GHDR, 2007). Poverty trends show that an estimated 40 percent of Ghanaians are "poor," referring to persons who have the capacity to meet their basic nutritional needs but are unable to provide for additional necessities such as health, shelter, clothing, and education (Apt, 2007). Furthermore, approximately 14.7 percent of the population are living in "extreme poverty" and are thus unable to provide for basic human needs, including their nutritional requirements, and additionally suffer from inter-generational poverty (GHDR, 2007). The proportion of Ghanaians living in absolute or extreme poverty has generally declined over the past fifteen years from 51 percent in 1992 to 29 percent in 2006.[1] However, poverty is the root cause of child neglect. At very young ages, children of the poor become their own agents of care and sustenance. Children from the more deprived Northern Ghana, for example, flock to the south to make a living for themselves on the streets of regional capitals (Apt, Blavo, & Opoku, 1992; Korboe, 1994; Apt & Greico, 1995). Despite the decline of poverty over the last fifteen years, gross inequality exists geographically in poverty trends (Ors, 2007). While Greater Accra, the region within which Ghana's capital is located, and many other southern sectors of the country have registered significant improvements in lowering its poverty levels, the three northern regions of the country have regressed in the arena of absolute poverty, rising from 33 percent in 1992 to 50 percent in 2006 (Ghana Statistical Service, 2007).

Other related factors accounting for the slow rate of development of children are of demographic significance. These include family size. Considerable differences exist among regions regarding family size preferences that vary because of diverse cultural values, traditions, and attitudes regarding reproduction and childcare.

In rural areas, especially in the north where traditional values are much more likely to be held and where poverty is rife, family sizes remain large, even while family poverty rises. More children are needed to work and bring food to the table because there is not enough on the table to feed large numbers of children—a chicken and egg situation. In general, the mean family size has dropped from 5.5 in 1984 to 4.7 in 2000, but family size remains larger in rural areas (Ghana Statistical Service, 2005). Women in rural areas have an average of 5.6 children compared to 4.7 for urban women. However, in the urban areas, economic considerations play a vital role in the determination of family size. For example, younger professional males and females are more likely to favor smaller families. This fact and the proven correlation between the educational status of a woman and family size (Ghana Statistical Service, 2005)—that is, the higher the educational status of a woman, the smaller the family size—is a clear indicator for gender and educational policy as well as population and poverty reduction strategies in Ghana.

Approximately 56 percent of Ghanaians reside in rural areas and engage mainly in agricultural pursuits. The majority farm on small tracts of land that do not exceed two hectares. Illiteracy levels are higher in rural areas where poverty is endemic. There are marked differences in the probability of children dying in rural and urban areas (GHDR, 2007). Mortality rates among children living in rural areas are higher than among children of urban residence; therefore, the chances of survival in early childhood are higher for urban children.

Women's poverty, in particular, reflects the social deprivations and early socialization of children into the world of work. Women constitute 50.5 percent of the population; however, one-third of all households are headed by females, a situation that reflects migration trends, divorce, single parenthood, and widowhood.[2] Women are particularly engaged in food crop production and are estimated to produce 70 percent[3] of subsistence crops in the country but are mainly poor; food crop farmers are listed among the poorest in Ghana (Apt, 2007). Therefore, child poverty is to a large extent a manifestation of the poverty of women. Female poverty entails further deprivations that become obvious in children's significant levels of care, malnutrition, and infant mortality. Infant and child mortality rates are basically the results of poverty, deprivation, malnutrition, and poor access to health and basic education (Asante & Asenso-Okyere, 2003).

Children comprise 47.5 percent of the population, with boys outnumbering girls until after age nineteen. Children under age fifteen continue to account for about half the population in Ghana (GHDR, 2007). Younger children, especially girls from low-income families, are socialized early into work and labor on the streets and in households, missing out in education and skills training opportunities. In times of crisis, poor families may withdraw their children from school to save on costs and for extra labor. Girls are typically withdrawn from formal education before boys. In addition, a growing number of young children are denied their basic rights due to abandonment or orphanhood early in life. The national Orphans and Vulnerable Children (OVC) policy document estimates that the number of OVCs is over 170,000. Many children are driven by poverty to migrate to cities and large towns to fend for themselves, leaving them on the margins of society without education, basic health care, and employable skills.

Consequently, child labor has emerged in Ghana as a major phenomenon, exposing young children to considerable risk of accidents as defined under the International Labor Organization (ILO) program on the Worst Forms of Child Labor (WFCL). Children engaged in hazardous work such as fishing, commercial sex, ritual and domestic servitude (Apt, 2006) have been found to be among the sites of WFCL. Sites for WFCL are common in Northern Ghana for gold mining, in Greater Accra for stone quarrying, in the Volta Region for fishing and ritual and domestic servitude, and commercial sex in the capital city and regional capitals.

Population growth is another factor of demography worth examining in the context of childcare and child rights. At an annual growth rate of 2.7 percent, the country has registered a population increase of 53.8 percent over the 1984 population. Though the average density is 79.3 persons per sq. km, the distribution shows that there is greater pressure on resources in the more prosperous south than the poorer north of the country. Other violations of children's rights occur in Ghana through certain traditional practices that do not bode well for healthy development of children. These include child betrothals, female genital mutilations, and *trokosi* practice.

Emerging social issues resulting from new epidemics such as HIV/AIDS leading to an escalation in orphanhood, migration to cities and other countries by the most economically active family members, particularly young fathers and increasingly mothers, has manifested in the phenomenon of aged grandparents caring for young people in communities. A common outcome of geographical mobility of parents in search of improved incomes is their inability to adequately provide the needed financial support to caregivers of dependents on a regular basis. This reality causes the family to become dependent on services of the Department of Social Welfare, the major arm of government overseeing the rights and welfare of children. Low educational attainment as well as lack of valuable employable skills, and in the case of external migration, illegal habitation, frequently results in incapacity to earn enough to provide for the upkeep of the sojourner, let alone save sufficient money for sending remittances to family members.

Émigrés who succeed in securing well-remunerated jobs usually contribute financially and materially to the upkeep of their dependents left behind. Anecdotal accounts show that such positive outcomes are more exceptional than the norm. Families left behind in rural areas without telephone and banking facilities frequently depend on intermediaries who sometimes exploit the communication gap between senders and beneficiaries of remittances. Glamorization of outward migration, particularly where children have lost one parent, increases the vulnerability of children left behind, especially when they are in the care of aged grandparents who have traditional skills in childrearing with little understanding of intergenerational culture. Older guardians' difficulty in controlling children, especially teenagers, usually predisposes children to vagrant behavior, including truancy and the irrational desire to also migrate through any means offered by predatory adults.

Government's Role

The Department of Social Welfare (DSW) derives its original mandate from statutory orders dating from 1944 that made it responsible for social services encompassing health, housing, education, and agriculture. With the establishment of specific ministries for these sectors, the DSW mandate has been redefined to make it responsible for policy development, regulation, and supervision of social welfare practice as it relates to justice administration, particularly for juveniles. It is also responsible for the establishment and operation of orphanages as well as community care of disadvantaged children, youth, elderly populations, and people with disabilities.

In the past three decades, Ghana has demonstrated commitment to numerous human rights treaties that reorient the outlook of state actions toward opportunity creation for socio-economic autonomy. Most of these international human rights impinge on the mandate of the DSW; for example, the following:

- UN Declaration on Human Rights (UNHDR 1948)
- UN International Convention on Peoples' Rights
- UN Covenant on Economic, Social and Cultural Rights (1966)

- UN Minimum Rules for the Administration of Juvenile Justice
- The Convention on Intercountry Adoption (The Hague Convention)
- UN Standard Rules for Children Deprived of their Liberty (Beijing Rules)
- Convention on the Elimination of All Forms of Discrimination Against Women (CEDAW) 1979
- UN Convention Against Torture and Other Cruel and Inhuman Treatment or Punishment (1984)
- Convention on the Rights of the Child (CRC) 1989
- UN/ILO Convention on the Worst Forms of Child Labor (1999)
- Optional Protocol to the CRC on the Sale of Children and Child Prostitution (2000)

In furtherance of its avowed belief in human rights, Ghana has sought to comprehensively translate international legislation into various domestic laws, including:

- Criminal Code (Amendment) Act 1994 (Act 484)
- Criminal Code (Amendment) Act 1998 (Act 554)
- The Children's Act 1998 (Act 560)
- The Labor Act 2003 (Act 651)
- Juvenile Justice Act 2003 (Act 653)
- The Child Rights Regulations 2003 (Legislative Instrument 1705)
- Human Trafficking Act 2005 (Act 694)
- National Disability Act 2006 (Act 715)
- The Domestic Violence Act 2007 (Act 732)

Furthermore, policies addressing poignant social issues such as disability, orphans, vulnerable children, and HIV/AIDS are operational. The above catalog of legislation and policies notwithstanding, the national agency, the Department of Social Welfare, mandated for providing social welfare services to prevent segments of the Ghanaian population, in particular children, from social exclusion and the stigma of poverty, is unable to guarantee social protection due to inadequate budget allocation and staffing (DSW, 2006; Apt & Akuffo-Amoabeng, 2007). Reliance of the DSW on previous strategies that were created from inadequate human and financial resources available must be rectified for the nation to attain the objectives of the Growth and Poverty Reduction Strategy (GPRS) and Millennium Development Goals (MDG), which support the goals of the CRC.

In 2007, the National Social Protection Strategy (NSPS) developed by the Ministry of Labor and Social Welfare received approval from the Cabinet and thereafter from Parliament, showing an unequivocal demonstration of the Government of Ghana's commitment to equitable human development. The NSPS contains measures for addressing extremely poor individuals, households, and communities, including those needing special care but lacking access to basic social services. The framework goes beyond income support to the indigent and seeks to strengthen social cohesion, human development, and livelihoods, as well as protection of rights and entitlements of populations on the fringes of society. Furthermore, it seeks to propel the DSW into a pro-active institution that provides access to all social protection opportunities available to communities. The initial platform for launching the NSPS is the Livelihood Empowerment Against Poverty (LEAP) program, which provides cash grants to extremely poor individuals, households, and communities, including those needing special care but lacking access to basic social services. Four types of subprograms are planned under LEAP; namely:

- *Livelihood Creation*—Non-contributory schemes to support those who are unable to meet their basic survival needs. Targets for this would be persons living in extreme poverty, such as OVCs, debilitated elderly, seasonal agricultural groups who experience chronic hardship, and persons with severe forms of disability. Interventions for these categories include cash transfers, supplementary feeding, and disaster relief.

- *Livelihood Protection*—These measures are contributory programs such as social security, health insurance, micro-insurance, and crop insurance programs based on the principle of risk mitigation. The measures ensure stability and prevent people from sliding into unacceptable levels of need or penury. They include contributions to insurance and pension programs as well as legislation in the arena of labor market and land reforms.

- *Promotion of Equal Opportunities*—Access to programs that offer livelihood-enhancing opportunities for target populations.

- *Social Empowerment*—Through social policy development for inclusion and national cohesion that takes into cognizance gender equity throughout the life cycle; access to information on government policies, the justice system, and other social services. Examples include protection of the rights of socially vulnerable populations through measures such as law reform, enforcement, and attitudinal and behavioral change through public education.

It is anticipated that considerations of the NSPS will provide an investment in families and individuals whose disability or vulnerability can be effectively harnessed to culminate in improved socio-economic autonomy with respect to children in their care. When NSPS is well implemented by the DSW, poverty need not be an impediment to children's access to social services such as schools and medical care that promote their human rights and well-being.

Chapter Content

In this book, authors provide analysis and vibrant discussion regarding various child rights issues, while critically examining human rights violations that impact negatively on the development of children in Ghana from the family to societal levels. Each contributor has done empirical work in Ghana on the topic of their chapter. To ensure conformity with the book's mission, each contributor was required to follow R. B. Howe & K. Covell's (2007:9–11) approach to evaluating compliance with the CRC. To this end, each contributor identifies and explains Ghana's commitment to the rights of children on the issue of their research topic as reflected in her actions through legal reform, policies, program development, and supportive institutional and services structures; wherever appropriate, authors sought to address the following broad questions: (1) Has the Convention been incorporated into Ghana's laws and public policy? (e.g., What children's laws and public policies have been made since Ghana ratified the convention? Do these laws and policies incorporate the standards of the Convention and how? Have the new laws made any difference in the situation of children?) (2) Have special institutions in support of children's rights been created? (e.g., children's ombudsman or commissioner, minister); (3) Are there effective coordinating and monitoring mechanisms for children's rights? (e.g., district, regional, and national monitoring mechanisms); and (4) Have substantive results been achieved in implementing specific articles of the CRC?

The book has three parts, covering: (1) childhood and identity, (2) children in dangerous circumstances: exploitation and abuse, and (3) policies, laws, and programs safeguarding child rights.

In part 1, dealing with childhood and identity, DeBrenna LaFa Agbényiga leads with a historical and cultural definition of childhood, pinpointing where and why violations occur. In her introduction, she postulates that the primary emphasis on issues relating to the definition of childhood includes the tension between the universal definition of childhood and the socio-cultural milieu that challenges child development and protection. She argues that of critical analytical focus is the relationship between economic difficulties and long-term welfare goals of governments. She further explains "questions about prioritization among issues related to indebted government, high unemployment rate, developing infrastructure, and public section provision are ultimately raised as a significant aspect of childhood and the rights of children."

Following, Beatrice Akua Duncan examines some of the tenets of traditional law on paternity rights and discusses the controversies surrounding the definition of a child's father asking the question: Who is a child's father under the law? She develops this question, pinpointing the inherent implications of conflicts between modern and traditional law, which often trample on the rights of the child. She decries the operation of a pluralistic legal system that has had a tendency to undermine these rights and discusses the implications of a customary law that has received limited visibility in the field of child rights: "Prevailing in many Ghanaian societies, the rule has the effect of denying paternity to the biological father of a child born out of an adulterous union." Kate Hampshire et al. conclude the first part of the book with a review of the gaps in child rights in a refugee setting and raise other issues of childhood identity. They describe the ways in which children and young people have sought strategies that enable them to obtain access to "rights" that have been taken away through war and displacement and examine how these processes led to a re-negotiation of intergenerational roles and relations. They note that there may be costs attached, in terms of negative consequences, to very rapid social change.

In part 2, dealing with children in dangerous circumstances: exploitation and abuse, Sylvester Kyei-Gyamfi discusses the problem of violence against children. Based on his recent research, he highlights an aspect of child torture in Ghana, focusing specifically on corporal punishment. His basic premise is that in Ghana, most modes of discipline, whether in domestic or educational settings, are corporal in nature. This premise is further strengthened by his research reports on the practice of corporal punishment in the home, community, and educational settings. Sylvester Kyei-Gyamfi gives an account of children's own perceptions of the use of corporal punishments by parents, family members, and school authorities and makes a number of suggestions as to how best to address corporal punishment in Ghana.

George Clerk reviews child labor, a widespread and growing phenomenon in the exploitation of children. In a review of the effectiveness of government laws, policies, and programs that incorporate the CRC principles toward the protection of children from exploitation, he concludes that there is a gap between official policies and local reality, making implementation largely ineffective. Following, Gina Porter and associates present an interesting review of children's patterns of access to motorized transport, arguing that children's mobility, wherever they may live, is crucial in their access to health and basic education. Drawing principally on field evidence from four off-road villages in Gomoa District in Southern Ghana, they review children's patterns of access to education and health services, the implications of child poverty for access to motorized transport, limitations imposed by physique and smaller stature on ability to walk long distances, and associated vulnerability to traffic accidents. They argue that because young people commonly lack power and access to decision-making processes in Ghana, their transport and mobility needs are even less likely to be met than those of others, although young people's input into the transport arena could have enormous potential for improving lives.

Finally, part 3 mostly reviews policies, laws, and programs instituted to benefit children's rights. Authors discuss the challenges inherent in their implementation and propose ways to overcome them. Robert Kwame Ame takes up the issue of child rights with respect to harmful traditional practices in a sociolegal discussion and analysis of the *trokosi* system and bemoans the failure of governments, traditional councils, and civil society organizations to propose credible alternatives to the practice. He argues that beyond the law, more resources should be invested in research that seeks a better understanding of harmful traditional practices, with the goal of finding effective ways of transforming them. Afua Twum-Danso assesses the progress of the 1998 Children's Act of Ghana. This Act, which came into force in January 1999, is the major legislation protecting children in Ghana. It aims at ensuring that children's rights to protection, development, and care are provided by families, communities, and the state through its institutions and structures. Afua Twum-Danso explores the progress of this Act through her most recent research undertaken in two communities in the capital city of Accra. From her work experience with the national human rights institution in Ghana, Lilian Ayete-Nyampong writes regarding children in conflict with the law in correctional institutions in Ghana. In her observation, the pre-occupation of lawyers, human rights officers, and related actors with compliance and implementation of standards and laws causes them to be professionally blinded from seeing the social persons behind the legal label. She makes a case for examining daily experiences of juvenile offenders, inspiring discussions that go beyond the role of the criminal justice system and the single definition of crime. Leah McMillan's chapter closes this final part of the book. Focusing on Ghana's educational system, she analyzes the varying policies and reforms to the education system, questioning whether these have been coupled with appropriate implementation mechanisms. She poses the central question to her chapter's discussion: Has the rhetoric of better education, with impetus from the CRC, resulted in an actual improvement to the Ghanaian school system?

Concluding, this book is about Ghana's efforts toward meeting the tenets of the 1989 United Nations Convention on the Rights of the Child, which she was the first country to ratify in 1990. What is being done or has been done to implement the human rights of children in Ghana is this book's main concern. It is a book worth reading by all and sundry persons and organizations interested in child development issues in Ghana.

Notes

1. Ghana Statistical Service, *Patterns and trends of poverty in Ghana, 1991–2006; 2007.*

2. Ghana Statistical Service, *Population data analysis report,* vol. 2, 2005.

3. Ministry of Food and Agriculture, *Gender and agriculture development strategy,* 2001.

References

Apt, N. A. (2006). *Child domestic work and fosterage in Northern and Upper East regions.* UNICEF, Accra.

———. (2007). *Learning How to Play to Win.* London: Motjuste.

Apt, N. A., and B. Akufo-Amoabeng. (2007). *Department of Social Welfare assessment report.* Ministry of Manpower Youth and Employment, Accra.

Apt, N. A., E. Q. Blavo, and S. Opoku. (1992). *Street children in Accra.* Social Administration Unit, University of Ghana, Legon.

Apt, N. A., and M. Grieco. (1995). *Listening to girls on the street tell their own story.* UNICEF, Accra.

Apt, N. A., and S. Wilson. (1995). *Children in difficult circumstances: Ghanaian children in institutions.* UNICEF, Accra.

Asante, A. F., and K. Asenso-Okyere. (2003). *Economic burden of malaria in Ghana.* A technical report submitted to the World Health Organisation, Africa Regional Office.

Center for Social Policy Studies (CSPS). (2001). *Child domestic workers in Accra.* Unpublished document, Center for Social Policy Studies, University of Ghana, Legon.

Department of Social Welfare (DSW). (2006). Annual evaluation report. Department of Social Welfare, Accra.

Ghana Human Development Report (GHDR). (2007). Social exclusion. In *Ghana Human Development Report.* United Nations Development Program, Accra.

Ghana Statistical Service (GSS). (2005). *Population data analysis report 2.*

———. (2007). *Pattern and trends of poverty in Ghana, 1991–2006.*

Growth and Poverty Reduction Strategy (GPRS) (2006–2009). Government of Ghana, Accra.

Howe, R. B., and K. Covell. (2007). *Children's Rights in Canada: A Question of Commitment.* Waterloo, ON: Wilfrid Laurier University Press.

Korboe, D. (1994). *Street children in Kumasi.* UNICEF, Accra.

Ministry of Food and Agriculture (MOFA). (2001). *Gender and agriculture development strategy.* Ministry of Food and Agriculture, Accra.

National Social Protection Strategy (NSPS). (2006). Ministry of Manpower, Youth and Employment, Government of Ghana, Accra.

Chapter 2
Defining Childhood: A Historical Development Perspective

By DeBrenna LaFa Agbényiga

As the first country to ratify the United Nations (UN) Convention on the Rights of the Child (CRC) in 1990, Ghana made a statement on its image of childhood. This statement has been expanded through the 1994 and 1998 amendments to the Criminal Code, the passage of the Children's Act 1998, the Juvenile Justice Act 2003, the Human Trafficking Act 2005, the Domestic Violence Act 2007, and finally, the endorsement of the International Labor Organization's (ILO) Convention on the Worst Forms of Child Labor (WFCL) 1999. In the legal definition of childhood in Ghana, the core elements define a child as every person under the age of eighteen years, regardless of their age, gender, religion, and regional and social origin. They have the inherent rights of survival, protection, and development, and Ghana recognizes its legislative, administrative, and other measures to protect the rights of a child for his or her best interests. The establishment of the Ghana National Commission on Children is one of the administrative actions to illustrate its responsibilities for the rights of children in Ghana.

There is a general consensus on the necessity and importance of legislation for aspects of the provision and protection of the rights of children (Mensa-Bonsu & Dowuona-Hammond, 1994; Veerman, 1992), but legislative changes in the definition of childhood are not viewed as progress in the discourse of defining childhood in Ghana, in particular, and in developing countries, in general (McCreery, 2001; Twum-Danso, 2005, 2008; Windborne, 2006). In her child labor study conducted at Yindure, a northern village, Bruscino (2001) examined the image of childhood from the eyes of children, parents, and officers at the Ghana National Commission on Children, which has questioned the gap between hope and the reality of childhood. First, "Nobody was asking the children for their input, and they were the ones who were actually being affected by the Convention." Second, "What Ghana needs as a developing country is a piece of legislation which would allow children to work but under certain conditions" (Bruscino, 2001).

The competing images of childhood between legislation of children's rights and children's everyday experiences reflect the dynamic nature of perceived childhood and children's treatment in the society. Veerman (1992) first demonstrated that there has not been a static and singular image of childhood even in American history, that the image of childhood has been changed during the last century, and that it has varied in different parts of the world. Veernman's conceptual framework of the changing image of childhood provides necessary "vertical and horizontal modes" (Jenks, 2004) to elucidate children's rights and patterns of their change and continuity in different eras of Ghanaian history and in different regions of Ghana. By analyzing the images of childhood in indigenous readings of the everyday experiences of Ghanaian children and their families and historical evidence documented in interdisciplinary research, this chapter intends to answer these critical questions: What is the image of childhood in Ghana? Has the image of childhood changed in Ghana since the pre-colonial era and, if so, how has it changed?

Images of Childhood in the Pre-colonial Era

An undated Akan lullaby sings an image of an infant in a rural family in which the child is valued and cared for by women in the household:

> Why do you cry?
> You are the child of a yam farmer,
> Why do you cry?
> You are the child of a cocoyam farmer.
> Why do you cry?
>
> Someone would like to have you for her child,
> But you are my own.
> Someone wishes she had you to nurse on a good mat,
> Someone wishes you were hers.
> She would put you on a camel blanket,
> But I have you to rear on a torn mat.
>
> (David & Harrington, 1971:29–30)

This lullaby shows how traditional Akan children are valued and cared for within the household setting. Studies have supported this kind of care of children in large domestic groups, often in a polygamous and multi-household compound organized by the matrilineal or patrilineal family structure where children are cared for by the birthmother and other women in the household (Nkrumah, 1971; LeVine, Dixon, LeVine, Richman, Leiderman, Keefer, et al., 1994). According to the informant of Allman (1997), about a week after a child is born, a father names the child. Child naming usually depends on the gender of the child and the day of the week on which the child is born (Nkrumah, 1971). LeVine and colleagues (1994) observed that the mother and the family organize child-care around a birth interval of two to three years of age, with intensive breast-feeding and undivided attention to each infant during this period. Research has linked prolonged breast-feeding to healthcare in tropical Africa because it provides the infant with protein and antibodies against prevalent infection; however, this process is also linked to the mother-child bond. This lullaby presents the pride of the mother, as traditional Ghanaian society values the social placement of children as a blessing from the gods and ancestors (Caldwell & Caldwell, 1987; LeVine et al., 1994; Mends, 1994). More importantly, children also often define their parents' adulthood. Two pieces of cultural evidence have supported this statement: the notion of "spirit child" (Caldwell & Caldwell, 1987) and the termination of childhood. Nsamenang (1992) has pointed out that age was not the sole determinant of the division between childhood and adulthood in traditional African societies. In Northern Ghana, girls entered adulthood once they became mothers (Goody, 1982), while boys entered into adulthood only when they could acquire a wife and build their own compounds. Anthropological research has reached the conclusion that the fundamental purpose of marriage is having children, comforting and supporting aged parents, and maintaining the future of lineage and community ties (Fortes, 1936; McCaskie, 2000).

Hake (1972) stated that children are social and economic assets that function as a central aspect of the family:

> They help with the chores in the house and on the farm, they serve guests, they become the form of "social security" for the parents in old age, and they serve as a source of family prestige. They also represent the continuation of the lineage, which is of great importance to Ghanaian families (Hake, 1972:5).

The self-awareness of the differences in lives of children in the pre-colonial era articulates the variability in the image of childhood in a traditional society, which Jenks (2004) calls "many childhoods." The notion of many images of childhood is especially helpful to understand children's different everyday experience and treatment in approximately one hundred distinct and similar ethnic and cultural groups. In a diverse country such as Ghana, the variation of childhood in the traditional society could relate to ethnicity, linguistics, social position, and region the child belongs to or identifies with. The Akan lullaby uses "a torn mat" to refer to the perceived poverty of the Akan loving mother. In this popular Fanti and Yoruba Rhyme, an image of childhood is illustrated by the way a group of young children are cooperating for survival.

Fanti version:

Iyi se ngaa ngaa	The first one (baby) says (crying) ngaa ngaa.
Iyi se den na oye wo?	The second says, what is the matter?

Iyi se gyama okom a	The third one says, perhaps it is hunger.
Iyi se kefa ma yendzi	The fourth says, take the food so we can eat.
Iyi se mennye oo	The fifth says, I won't do it oo.
Iyi se mena ba mebeka	I'll tell mum when she comes home.

Yoruba version:

Èkin ni ebi pa mi,	The first one says, I'm hungry.
Èkeji ni iya ɑsi ńilè,	The second says, mother is not home.
Èketa ni jè ka ji nka loko,	The third one says, let's get something at the farm.
Èkeri ni bi oloko ba mu è?	The fourth one says, what if the farmer catches us?
Èkarùn ni ma wò ibòmi.	The fifth one says, I'll look the other way.

(Benjamin, 2007:19)

There are five children left for the day, with an absence of adults and lunch or breakfast. Schooling or education is not in the picture. They could be siblings, half-siblings, or cousins. Research has found that in the traditional Ghanaian families, sibling childcare often occurs after the infant reaches five months of age, and there are variations in the amount of sibling care, the activities, and the extent of adult supervision (LeVine et al., 1994). It is evident that sibling care-giving is beneficial for lifelong emotional attachment between siblings (1994). Some have pointed out the importance of Ghanaian traditional family structure for understanding the prevalence of child fosterage, which is an important aspect of childhood image in traditional Ghana (Isiugo-Abanihe, 1985). Caldwell & Caldwell (1987) suggested that child fosterage reduces the long-term net cost of children in the face of high fertility, and it fits the perceived weak linkage between biological parents and the number of children being raised.

The above Yoruba Rhyme that is sung among the Fanti shows no concern about child safety or adult supervision. It shows children exploring and learning problem solving skills within the societal cultural context. Whiting, Whiting, & Longabaugh (1975) compared children of six cultures and found that children from collective cultures are more responsible, more willing to offer help and support, and less likely to seek attention and help than American children. In a pre-colonial Adeɛbeba study (McCaskie, 2000), the author argues that although the evidence is limited concerning the specifics of childhood in pre-colonial Adeɛbeba, an Ashanti village, it is evident that education or training takes different forms in traditional Ghanaian society: "Playing, exploring, learning, and helping in the house or on the farm were staples of an Asante childhood in Adeɛbeba as elsewhere." Through Asante's recollections, McCaskie documented a different form of socialization or education from the modern concept of education. This form of education or training is collective activities. One particular Adeɛbeba game called "*ahenahene*," meaning "who is the king?" mirrors the larger worlds of adult power and behavior at pre-colonial Adeɛbeba, and the experience was widely remembered by children and adults. One informant recalled:

> All the time we played "Ahenahene." Everyone in the village took part. Some were chiefs, linguists, and "Asafohene," whilst others were servants and stool carriers. I once "married" a young girl to whom I gave crabs and meat, and in return I was given dishes of Fufu in the evenings. It was the common practice of village children to organize miniature courts for the trial of cases and the punishment of offenders. Sometimes we chose an elderly man who was made the chief and to him we brought out cases for settlement. The children met and all the complaints were gone into. The guilty were fined—sometimes they had to go to tap a pot of palm wine. This was useful training and most children desired to have their cases tried instead of fighting or taking vengeance on their enemies. We played at this from morning to night or any time when were able. It was a thing children liked to do (McCaskie, 2000:55).

Through games and activities, children at Adeɛbeba learned social norms, gender roles, and everyday skills. Ewe poet Geormbeeyi Adali-Mortti interpreted socialization in childhood as "becoming," a process which involved everyone in the immediate family, the clan, the village, and the natural environment (Adali-Mortti, 1971). Ahenahene not only contextualizes how a village rears, but also tells us that pre-colonial Adeɛbeba did not specify differences between infants, children, and adolescents in the process of becoming an adult. All children learned from the game and from each other, and all liked the way to learn. Available indigenous readings suggest that the role of adults in the learning process varies at the tribe, community, clan, family, and personal levels. The significant roles of mothers and grandmothers in children's lives generally are norms in the pre-colonial images of children, but fathers are not always distant as they are often portrayed as being in the context of African families. In *Palm leaves of childhood*, Adali-Mortti (1971) recognized his father as an intimate and fun role model in his childhood:

> When I was very small indeed,
> and Joe and Fred were six-year giants,
> my father, they and I, with soil
> did mix farm-yard manure.
> In this we planted coconuts,
> naming them by brothers' names.
> The palms grew faster far than I;
> and soon, ere I could grow a Man,
> they, flowering, reached their goal!
> Like the earrings that my sisters wore
> Came the tender golden flowers.
> I watched them grow from gold to green;
> then nuts as large as Tata's head.
> I craved the milk I knew they bore.
> I listened to the whispering leaves:
> to the chattering, rattling, whispering leaves,
> when night winds did wake.
> They haunt me still in work and play:
> Those whispering leaves behind the slit

On the cabin wall of childhood's
dreaming and becoming.

(Adali-Mortti, 1971:31–32)

Although Ghana experienced urbanization before the arrival of Europeans (Ofori-Attah, 2007), no competing images of childhood had been documented until Christian missionaries and the Portuguese and the Dutch traders made the first attempt to establish European formal schools in Gold Coast's Golden Triangle (Accra-Kumasi-Cape Coast/Takoradi). Kimble (1963) documented the statement made by the Asantehene in 1842 in a letter to Rev. Picot:

> We will not select children for education; for the Ashanti children have better work to do than to sit down all day idly to learn hoy! hoy! hoy! They have to fan their parents, to do other work, which is much better (Kimble, 1963:75).

The statement emphasizes that the image of childhood in Ghana traditionally was depicted through the child's personal relationship with parents and other members in the household, by his or her extended family group, clan, community, and tribe. It also supports the observation that "helping in the house or on the farm" was engraved in the image of childhood as McCaskie (2000) observed from the pre-colonial Adeɛbeba. Meanwhile, the historical context of this statement adds another layer in the multifaceted image of childhood in pre-colonial Ghana: children and their families and communities were forced to face imperial culture on issues of childhood, education, and employment. The 100-year conflict between Ashanti and the British before 1902 presented the first competing image of childhood in pre-colonial Ghana: one is communal and agricultural oriented, and another is individual and industrial oriented. It also is the first time in Ghanaian history that the meaning of childhood and rights of children was politicized.

It is important to recognize that the notions of "child" and "childhood" have different meanings as defined by the CRC and other international documents on children's universal rights. First, the image of childhood in the pre-colonial era was defined by its collective identity, including family, community, tribe, and nationality (McCaskie, 2000; Whiting et al., 1975). Second, childhood is terminated by economic independence and parenthood rather than the nineteenth birthday because the core meaning of childhood is understood as the state of dependence (Goody, 1982; Nsamenang, 1992). Despite noticeable differences in the images of childhood across regions, tribes, communities, and family, the pre-colonial image of childhood is understood to be associated with play and work (Ofori-Attah, 2007; McCaskie, 2000). Poverty in childhood was openly recognized by individuals, and children were not independent from household survival (Benjamin, 2007; David & Harrington, 1971).

Images of Childhood in the Colonial Era

Although literature has suggested that by the end of the eighteenth century many children were enrolled in school, and there were 139 small schools in 1881 in urban centers, the Christian missionaries and the British colonial government did not establish schools until the British colonized Ghana entirely. This establishment reached its peak in 1951 when the Accelerated Development Plan for Education, a universal six-year primary education plan for all children in Ghana, was proposed (Graham, 1971). Ghana's first president, Kwame Nkrumah (1971) recalled that in the colonial era, formal education was viewed as a necessity for a child, and as an Akan boy, that is how schooling became a critical part of his childhood. When he was about 9 years old, his mother quietly but determinedly dragged him by the arm each morning and deposited him in the schoolroom. At age 17, after eight years at the elementary school, he became a pupil-teacher for one year at Half Assini.

Throughout 1902–1957, the British colonial government was the main administrator of education in Ghana. Thomas (1974) and Ofori-Attah (2007) argued that education administered by missionaries and the government's administration was the major force for social change in colonial Ghana. It is commonly agreed that the images of childhood were changed by colonial schools in three ways. First, Ofori-Attah (2007) argued that curricula offered by colonial schools were linked to commercial and governmental activity and led children and parents to see education primarily as a pathway to employment, which permitted alienation from the rural economy and from the local image of childhood. Thomas (1974) recorded a 1907 report from a northern district commissioner that confirmed this fear of cultural colonization of children: all twenty-three students in the district could "answer questions intelligently in English, can tell the time, and understand that the British government looks after the country." The tone in the report underlines a European-centered evolutionary lens and a total dismissal of indigenous knowledge on collective education as a value among the indigenous people of Ghana.

Second, 90 percent of colonial-era schools were located in the Gold Coast. This area was defined by the British colonial rule for its natural resources—such as gold, metal ores, diamonds, ivory, pepper, timber, grain, and cocoa—thus, the British colonizers built railways and other transport systems in addition to schools. Ultimately, this created a regional gap of educational development between Northern, Southern, and Ashanti regions. Thomas (1974) depicted the uneven and inadequate spread of schools in Northern Ghana, which caused low enrollment and high rates of leavers. Studies on colonial education have revealed that different administrative strategies were operated in different regions and shaped children's relationship with traditional institutions and values by regional differences. For example, when Kwame Nkrumah's mother dragged him to school every morning in the south, the northern chiefs and other elites were reluctant to send their children away to school, so they sent their domestic servants' sons to school (Nkrumah, 1971; Thomas, 1974). Another regional difference was the role of traditional institutions (Fortes, 1936; Thomas, 1974). In the north, the protectorate tended to control social change through traditional institutions. One example of retaining power of traditional institutions was that commissioners and chiefs worked as a team to select prospective students, and only boys were eligible for schools (Thomas, 1974).

Finally, schooling broadened the gender gap between male children and female children. Parents generally assigned them different roles: male children to school and female children to duties of porters and farmhands. Thomas (1974) recorded that there were twenty-six students in a new northern mission school in 1907, and all were boys, and schools only recruited boys. According to Graham (1971), 68,900 boys and 20,500 girls were in primary schools in 1941. Although the colonial government enacted a law, Ordinance 19 of 1940, to prohibit the employment of children under age twelve years in any occupation except if the employment was with the child's own family, the image of gender inequality in childhood was not ended by the law. Thomas (1974) argued that labor migration in childhood became a habit among Northern Ghanaian families in the colonial era. There was counter-evidence of Thomas's habit hypothesis in several studies. Caldwell & Caldwell (1987) linked rural-urban migration to accusations of witchcraft. Akurang-Parry (2002), on the other hand, connected forced female child labor and migration with colonization. Although female child labor was practiced in the pre-colonial tribes, the exploitative aspects of child labor were exacerbated by colonial labor ordinances and by-laws because the colonial state depended on female child labor for road building, the maintenance of government buildings, and the cleaning up of colonial administrative towns (2002).

Beyond the emergence and establishment of colonial institutionalized schools (majority were mission schools), churches, hospitals, and administrative networks, research has reflected other fundamental changes in the image of childhood during the colonial era. The emerging concept of adolescence and organized humanity involvement in the protection and treatment of children in colonial era are few among these changes, and the early scientific inquiry on the images of childhood in Ghana (Fortes, 1967; Hall, 1904).

Fortes (1936) used "adolescents" to refer to a different subgroup of children in fieldwork in the Northern Territories of the Gold Coast. In his observation of everyday social life, Fortes (1936) documented how missionaries devoted their energies principally to children and adolescents. In a northern commissioner's report documented by Thomas (1974), a distinction was made between children and adolescents, and the latter was called "nearly grown men" and "youths." Alternative approaches were used to dispose of adolescents who were viewed as "idle" (Thomas, 1974). Occupational training and football were two of these examples.

Another change during this era was the increasing international influence in recreating the image of childhood. In 1920, the Save the Children International Union (SCIU) started to promote children's rights beyond and above all considerations of race, nationality, or creed. SCIU organized the Conference on the African Child of 1931 in Geneva to work for the increase of African interest and help, gradually bringing the universal rights of the child into a national and international movement for the care and protection of the African child (Marshall, 2004). Although there were only five Africans among 200 attendants, this conference reconstructed the images of childhood in Africa among missionaries, child welfare humanitarians, and social scientists and had a long-term influence on the knowledge of rights and welfare of the child in Ghana. The conference contributed to the following construction of knowledge about the African child by: (1) the effort to collect scientific knowledge for a comprehensive view of the situation of African children in the years of conference preparation, and (2) assisting with the development of child protection institutions and child welfare agencies following the conference, with an emphasis on the rights and welfare of the African child (Marshall, 2004). Perhaps Emily Torday's statement is the best evidence as to how the 1931 conference contributed to fundamentally change the conversation on children's rights in Africa:

> We can and must take these sentiments (i.e., religious sentiments) into account whenever we seek Africans' advice on how to save the children. Far be it from me to suggest that the African parent needs encouragement to give his child the best care he or she can conceive, but advice on the best methods will be welcomed, though perhaps it is not quite as necessary as some well-meaning people unacquainted with African conditions, or imbued with their own infallibility, may think. There is more wisdom in the African matron's head than they dream of in their philosophy. . . . But there is no doubt that there is great scope in many directions. Let those who wish to achieve them realize that they will hopelessly fail if they do not take the deeply religious sentiments of the Negro into account and forget that the African soul like any chord vibrates only in sympathy. (Torday quoted in Rattray, 1933:471).

Although Ordinance 19 of 1940 and the Accelerated Development Plan for Education in Ghana of 1951 indicate the emergence of written provisions for child rights protection in the colonial era, a more fundamental change occurred in knowledge building of children's social and cultural context and child psychological development. In a child-rearing study among the tribes of the Northern and Ashanti regions, Rattray (1933) collected invaluable local knowledge on child-training through study of proverb, folklore, and interviews. The informants in the Northern Territory described how a girl-training takes place:

> A male child will learn how to herd livestock, to follow sheep and cattle. A girl child must learn to work in the house, learn how to grind flour, sweep up refuse, get grass for mats, and do other women's work. When a boy has followed the sheep and next the cattle and learned how to do work other than the following of animals, he will turn to farming with his father. He will have his own small plot for grain crops, his own ground-nut plot, and his own plot for potatoes. He will also learn hunting with his neighbors (Rattray, 1933:468).

The child-training includes sex education:

> About eight years of age when a girl can work and use reason, her mother is always showing her how to sweep out the rooms and yard, and how to wash plates and calabashes. When she nears puberty and "strikes" having breasts, she learns how to weave and wear visi in place of always wearing leaves. If her mother is a potteress or a basket-maker, the girl will sit and watch her mother at work and the mother will also instruct her little. She will follow her mother in the rainy-season time, when the shea-butter trees bear fruit, and learn how to collect the nuts and make shea-butter oil. She learns how to grind corn and fetch water; the making of grain foods, and how to make soup stews, in order to know how to do all these things in the future. Her mother shows her how a girl should sleep on a mat with a boy who is not her husband (Rattray, 1933:467).

The following is instruction given to a young boy of the leopard clan on nearing puberty:

> When a child is old enough, he will be told the clan secrets by his father in the night. He (the father) will say, "My son, come hither, and sit down here. Have you not got hairs in front? Do you not see that I have something to tell you? Know my Kyisiri (avoidance, totem) is a leopard. Some day when you go into the long grass and see a leopard, do not kill it. If you kill it you have killed me, myself, who am sitting here (Rattray, 1933:468).

In summary, during the colonial era, the image of children became more dynamic and complicated as a result of the hegemony of missionary and British colonial approaches to children's rights and treatment in Ghana. Beyond the region, tribe, community, clan, and family that the child came from, the images of childhood were heavily defined by colonialism. Allman (1997) documented how this change happened in colonial Asante through an *ntamoba* case in 1921. The nature of changes that occurred in the era was rather exploitive and evangelical. For example, although child welfare agencies, formal schools, and hospitals have benefited children to enhance existing means of education and healthcare, mission schools and governmental schools dismissed traditional child-training and collective wisdom and redefined the meaning of childhood based on colonial beliefs and values. For female children, especially female adolescents, they experienced double exploitation of gendered traditional institutions and colonial economy, as Akurang-Parry (2002) observed. One progressive change in the image of childhood in the colonial era was that research began to sincerely inquire into the real image of childhood in Ghana and discovered the diverse and changing image of childhood. These progressive studies were rare (Rattray, 1933; Fortes, 1936). Rattray's contribution was to read proverbs and folklore through the eyes of children's rights and to advocate for a children's rights campaign in Ghana with respect to culture and identity of the child.

Images of Childhood in the Post-colonial Era

In the Immediate Post-colonial Era

A poem titled "The Mosquito and the Young Ghanaian" documented that children were involved in the Declaration of Independence in 1957 (Nyako, 1971). From the perspective of the image of childhood in the post-colonial Ghana, there were two distinct periods, divided by the ratification of the CRC in 1990. Immediately after the Declaration of Independence in 1957, children's education rights were a high national priority on the government's agenda. The Education Act of 1960 called for free compulsory basic education of all children in Ghana. As a result, the enrollment of elementary and secondary schools was increased dramatically during Kwame Nkrumah's administration, 1957–1966. A 1988 education reform cut pre-university education from seventeen years to twelve years: six years of primary, three years of junior secondary, and three years of senior secondary. In response to high school dropout rates, a national literacy campaign called for non-formal education in 1987. In 1996, the Free Compulsory Universal Basic Education (FCUBE) was implemented to continue Kwame Nkrumah's agenda on basic education access and quality for every child.

The single most important socioeconomic change that significantly impacted the treatment of children in the post-colonial era was that Ghana became independent from the British colonial administration, while it also became economically dependent on foreign countries and international banks due to an ever-growing foreign indebtedness. Research shows that the total external debts increased from US $600 million in 1965 to US $3,521 million in 1990 (Osei, 1995). Ghana was classified as a severe indebted low-income country in 1983, down from a low-income country at the end of the 1970s and from a medium-income country in the 1960s (Osei, 1995; Verlet, 2000). Although United Nations data shows that infant mortality in Ghana has decreased consistently since independence, its infant mortality rates (83.3) and under-five mortality rates (110) during 1985–1990 have remained higher than the world levels of 65.1 and 85 respectively (UN, 2008). Research has found that structural adjustment policies have increased inequality and poverty in indebted low-income countries and have disproportionately harmed children because of fewer resources for immunization, general health maintenance, prenatal care, nutrition, and other programs that have an impact on children's development (Bradshaw, Noonan, Gash, & Sershen, 1993; Easterly, 2005). UNICEF (1986) reported on the severity of child malnutrition in Ghana in 1982 and 1983 and stated that the caloric and protein intake of children was below 69 percent and 87 percent of requirements, respectively, and that 5 percent of children under five years of age were severely malnourished, and 50 percent were under 90 percent of the standard weight for their age. By 1989, Ghana was still listed as a county with per capita calorie intake below minimum standard (Njoku, 1993).

The immediate post-colonial era not only witnessed continuous crises of high child mortality, child malnutrition, and child labor, but also witnessed unprecedented changes in provisions of children's rights and protection. These changes included, but were not limited to, the establishment of child protection institutions, the visibility of international development organizations, and local awareness.

Children were valued as the future of the country and became a subject of social protection in this era. Compulsive basic education policies, the Labor Decree of 1967 (NLCD 157), and the establishment of the Ghana National Commission on Children in 1979 and the Department of Social Welfare were institutional efforts made to legitimize childhood as a structural stage of development. They were also viewed as an aspect of building institutional infrastructure that was intended to ensure children's educational and survival rights and to protect children from inappropriate economic exploitation. These institutional shifts in Ghana occurred in the context of Western research that not only experienced a new ontology era that questioned the basic assumptions on childhood and social realities (Jenks, 1982) but also discovered "child abuse" (Parton, 1985). The fundamental shift of the image of childhood in Ghana echoed this broader change indirectly through concepts and standards contained in United Nations, International Labor Organization (ILO), and other international entities' documents, and directly through international non-governmental organizations (NGOs) and programs in Ghana (ILO, 1973; Laird, 2008; UN, 1959).

As a result of the World Bank and International Monetary Fund (IMF) loans, international NGOs became the necessary alternative mechanisms in child protection service delivery. In 1960, the first ten registered NGOs emerged in Ghana. By 1990, this number had increased to 350 (Laird, 2008). In addition, international development projects and interventions were active and influential in health, education, and social protection sectors. Among these interventions, the Expanded Program on Immunization (EPI) and Malnutrition Rehabilitation Centers (NRCs) were two international child survival and development interventions initiated in the 1970s and became part of the community health infrastructure to reduce child protein-energy malnutrition (PEM) and to increase child immunization coverage (Bosu, Ahelegbe, Edum-Forwe, Bainson, & Turkson, 1997; Colecraft, Marquis, Bartolucci, Pulley, Owusu, & Maetz, 2004) and family planning services (Benefo & Schultz, 1996).

Research has responded to the visibility of international NGOs in the protection and treatment of children with unprecedented independent thinking and critique. This change was integrated into research methods. For example, when Benefo & Schultz (1996) chose five-year-old child survival rates instead of infant mortality rates for a 1987–1988 Ghana infant mortality study, the decision was not determined by measures commonly used internationally. Rather, it was based on the high level of child mortality between the ages of one and five in Ghana. The most crucial change in the public conversation on the rights of the child was the effort that was made to articulate the danger of imperialist culture in constructing the image of childhood in Ghana, in particular, and in Africa, in general. This change was most noticed in the individual versus collective rights debate led by Asmorom Legesse (1980). Legesse (1980) deconstructed the

Western individualism base of "human rights" through his famous "the concept of the sacralized individual whose private wars against society are celebrated." Legesse (1980) claimed that if Africans are "the sole author of the Universal Declaration of Human Rights, they might have ranked the rights of communities above those of individuals." This argument laid out the foundation for the conceptualization of the promotion for children's rights in Ghana and other non-Western countries. When the United Nations adopted the CRC in 1989, the conversation about universal rights of the child and social-cultural traditions became essential for defining the image of childhood in Ghana.

Images of Childhood Since 1990

The debate over universal rights of the child and social-cultural traditions has continued and deepened since 1990. During this time, two events have significantly impacted the images of childhood in the new era. The first event was that Ghana ratified the CRC, which defined the child as any person under age of eighteen and recognized that all children as individuals have specific rights attached to this stage of life course—rights to survival, education, to leisure, recreation, and cultural activities, to be protected from economic exploitation, to name a few. Another event was that the Organization of African Unity (OAU, later becoming the African Union) adapted the African Charter on the Rights and Welfare of the Child (ACRWC, or the African Charter), which required "every child shall have responsibilities towards his family and society, the State and other legally recognized communities and the international community" (OAU, 1990).

Research has interpreted the differences and tension between the CRC and the African Charter in socially constructing childhood (Grover, 2004; Machel, 1996, 2006; Rwezaura, 1998). The significance of these differences is recognized at many theoretical and practical levels. At the theoretical level, the differences lay on whether there are universal rights that the child is entitled to without distinction of race, color, sex, language, religion, political, or other opinion, national or social origin, property, birth, or other status (UN, 1989). If the answer is yes, the ultimate question is whether this means that there is a "good" and "normal" childhood for all children in the world, and therefore, other kinds of childhood are problematic (Rizzini, 2001; Twum-Danso, 2005). Furthermore, do characteristics of the child and diversity in the image of childhood across culture and societies play a role or not in defining childhood (Rizzini, 2001; Twum-Danso, 2005)? At the practical level, the differences have to do with defining the problem and the interventions related to child poverty, child labor, child soldier, and other images of childhood that are socially and economically constructed. Some push further and think that the differences could determine which option puts the best interest of the child first regardless of whether or not the focus is on promise or implementation (Grover, 2004; Lloyd, 2002). Bühler-Niderberger & Krieken (2008) argued that promise without implementation brings more harm than protection for children's rights.

Although Ghana ratified the CRC immediately but did not ratify the African Charter until 2005, the importance and impact of the CRC and its universalism can be viewed as being very influential and visible in the legislative and political language about the image of childhood in contemporary Ghana. McCreery (2001) linked child labor in Ghana and the successful performance of the Government of Ghana in reform program implementation. The metaphor of children "from street to stage" indicates that children and childhood have become highly visible as a public issue, but children's lives and everyday experiences have not changed.

It is evident that politicizing the image of childhood in contemporary Ghana has raised public awareness of children's rights. A UNICEF-sponsored study surveyed ten children's rights recognized by the CRC among eighty students and 111 educators in forty-eight selected basic schools (Asiegbor, Fincham, Nanang, Gala, & Britwum, 2001). The findings indicated that the majority of school children were aware of their rights to education, to rest and recreation, to think independently, to his/her own religious beliefs and freedom of religious expression, to privacy and freedom of correspondence, and to the freedom of association, and freedom of speech. Meanwhile, the findings suggested that: (1) some students viewed children's rights as linked to children's gender, ethnicity, region, and religion; (2) students who perform manual work were viewed as normal by peers, parents, and teachers; and (3) students who have suffered physical and emotional abuse from peers, parents, and teachers were viewed as having experienced a normal part of the child rearing development stage (Asiegbor et al., 2001). The study also found a severe shortage of learning materials in public schools and that educators generally believed the shortage was caused by some parents' prioritizing marrying new wives and performing funeral rites over their children's education (Asiegbor et al., 2001). McCreery (2001) also found shortages of learning material at Accra schools as a part of his study and suggested that the shortage was due to the wrong priorities of the Government of Ghana.

The disconnection between promised children's rights and the reality of severe child poverty as revealed in research on child mortality, child malnutrition, education, and child labor made a case that local institutions for promotion and protection of children's well-being and social-cultural traditions in constructing the image of childhood has been long marginalized (Agarwal, Attah, Apt, Grieco, Kwakye, & Turner, 1997; Beauchemin, 1999; Colecraft et al., 2004; Gyimah, 2006). Laird (2008) recorded a rapid expansion in the numbers and influence of NGOs since the 1990s, and by 2004 there were 3,000 NGOs in Ghana, up from over 300 in 1990. Unfortunately, the underlying issues can be reflected in the fact that the government social welfare agencies are a low priority in the promotion and protection of children's rights to survival, to education, and to protection from economic exploitation (Laird, 2008), while NGOs play a more critical role in promotion and protection of children's rights. For example, McCreery (2001) documented how Street Girls' Aid and Catholic Action for Street Children have benefited many individual children in a period of their childhood by getting them off of the streets and providing them with educational and employment training opportunities.

While the aforementioned organizations are making some progress, others are more interested in why parents, local communities, or children have different priorities or wrong priorities from the CRC and the state so that the government and the international community could better serve the needs of children and their families and communities (Agarwal et al., 1997; Grover, 2004; Twum-Danso, 2005, 2008). Windborne (2006) argued that the distance between universal promise and social-cultural tradition has resulted in local resistance to children's rights. The study drew the conclusion that state mandates could not realize children's rights until the historical, political, and economic conditions in Ghana are in line to have the same agenda for children and communities. Veerman & LeVine (2000) call for implementation of children's rights on a local level. Twum-Danso (2005, 2008) examined constructing childhood in traditional African societies and challenged the fixed image of childhood by age and the nature of incompetence. She pointed out that chronological age was not an indicator of the termination of childhood in traditional Africa and that a useful concept for defining a child or an adult is whether or not one has the physical capacity to perform tasks reserved for adults (Twum-Danso, 2005).

Twum-Danso's framework explained controversies around child labor and child soldiers, especially child domestic work, and was instrumental for future exploration in images of childhood in Ghana. Many take a more moderate stance to advocate for the integration of universal promise and cultural fit implementation. The World Declaration on the Survival, Protection and Development of Children in 1990 is an example of this appeal (WSC, 1990). It promises and hopes "to give every child a better future" and believes that childhood "should be one of joy and peace, of playing, learning, and growing," but it faces a different reality of childhood from promise (WSC, 1990).

Continuity of the Image of Childhood in Ghana

The past few centuries have witnessed significant changes in the images of childhood in Ghana (Mensa-Bonsu & Dowuona-Hammond, 1994). Compared with the pre-colonial era, contemporary Ghanaian children are more likely to survive due to better infant mortality rates, under-five mortality rates, and life expectancy at birth (UN, 2008; WHO, 2006). All children have state-mandated rights to basic education as it is demonstrated by school enrollment and adult literacy rates (WHO, 2006). The image of childhood has became a public agenda such that children, parents, extended family, communities, governmental organizations, and international NGOs are stakeholders of promotion and protection for children's rights. Under the pressure of the United Nations, World Bank, IMF, ILO, WHO, and other international entities, Ghana has developed an institutional infrastructure for the promotion and protection of children's rights in the form of legislation, governmental organizations, international NGOs, and interventions (Asiegbor et al., 2001; Aidam, Pérez-Escamilla, Lartey, & Aidam, 2005; Oheneba-Sakyi & Takyi, 1991). Although children's rights are a controversial concept for Ghanaian children and communities and in the international arena, the social position of children became highly visible due to the debate over universal children's rights and socio-cultural traditions.

Changes in images of childhood in Ghana have been viewed in terms of the inconsistency between the reality of children's everyday experience across gender, religion, and class and the promise in policy (Agarwal et al., 1997; Dawes & Cairns, 1998; Murray, 2004; Oheneba-Sakyi & Takyi, 1991), which is interpreted to bring more harm than progress (Pare, 2003; Twum-Danso, 2005; Windborne, 2006). For example, the CRC and other international conventions on children's rights recognize children's rights to their own identity, which is interconnected to their nationality and cultural heritage; however, educational language policy has delivered messages different than the definition of children's rights indicated in the CRC. Asiegbor et al. (2001) found that school language policies forbade basic school students to use local languages in school settings. Throughout the history of education language policy from 1529–2002 in Ghana, Owu-Ewie (2006) revealed that there was no consistent correlation between sovereignty and English-only language policy.

Veerman & LeVine (2001) noted that different approaches regarding changes in images of childhood over time will determine future efforts to promote children's rights. They called for changes on the local level so that the gap in images of children between Geneva and Ghana could be narrowed to the level of what Windborne (2006) interpreted as the local framework for the realization of children's rights. It is worth recognizing that although change in image of childhood has happened in Ghana, Ghana has experienced different transformations in the images of childhood from Western countries as well as other countries in the South (Hernandez, 1993; Tomes, 1986).

At the local level, continuity of the image of childhood has been a consistent theme in Ghana. Continuity means that children have been special social assets of family, community, and nation. Play, learn, and work have been three aspects of childhood in Ghana. Beliefs of the spirit child, children's duties to parents, extended family and communities, and reciprocity continue to influence perceptions of childhood and children's treatment in the society (Allotey & Reidpath, 2001; Douglass & McGadney-Douglass, 2008; Twum-Danso, 2005, 2008). More importantly, continuity means that transformation of images of childhood and children's rights in Ghana could contribute greatly to transformation in other parts of the world through the competing images of childhood between the past and present and between international and local settings.

While Ghana can and should be commended for the work that has been done to improve the lives of children, we must be reminded that more is yet to be done. As a country, the transformation of children rights can be seen throughout the various regions. However, consistency and impact are not unilateral in the country. As the country moves forward, this is an imperative aspect to ensure that the rights of children are respected and held by all children, regardless of where they live in the country. The current work in the country can certainly serve as the foundation for unifying the rights of children and moving forward to include all children, while creating a sense of equilibrium for the country's most vulnerable citizens.

References

Adali-Mortti, G. (1971). Palm leaves of childhood. In J. David and H. Harrington (eds.). *Growing Up African*, 51–52. New York: William Morrow and Company.

Agarwal, S., M. Attah, N. Apt, M. Grieco, E. A. Kwakye, and J. Turner. (1997). Bearing the weight: The kayayoo, Ghana's working girl child. *International Social Work* 40, 245–263.

Aidam, B. A., R. Pérez-Escamilla, A. Lartey, and J. Aidam. (2005). Factors associated with exclusive breastfeeding in Accra, Ghana. *European Journal of Clinical Nutrition* 59 (6), 789–796.

Akurang-Parry, K. O. (2002). The loads are heavier than usual: Forced labor by women and children in the Central Province, Gold Coast (colonial Ghana), c.a. 1900–1940. *African Economic History* 30, 31–51.

Allman, J. (1997). Fathering, mothering and making sense of Ntamoba: Reflections on the economy of child-rearing in colonial Asante. *Africa* 67 (2), 296–321.

Allotey, P., and D. Reidpath. (2001). Establishing the causes of childhood mortality in Ghana: The "spirit child." *Social Science & Medicine* 52 (7), 1007–1012.

Asiegbor, I., K. Fincham, M. Nanang, E. E. K. Gala, and A. O. Britwum. (2001). *Rights and equity in the classroom: A case study of classroom interactions in basic schools in Ghana.* Accra: Ghana Education Services.

Beauchemin, E. (1999). *The exodus: The growing migration of children from Ghana's rural areas to the urban centres.* Accra, Ghana: Catholic Action for Street Children (CAS) and UNICEF.

Benefo, K., and T. P. Schultz. (1996). Fertility and child mortality in Côte d'Ivoire and Ghana. *The World Bank Economic Review* 10 (1), 123–158.

Benjamin, F. (2007). *Skip Across the Ocean: Nursery Rhymes from Around the World.* London: Frances Lincoln.

Bosu, W. K., D. Ahelegbe, E. Edum-Forwe, K. A. Bainson, and P. K. Turkson. (1997). Factors influencing attendance to immunization sessions for children in a rural district of Ghana. *Acta Tropica* 68 (3), 259–267.

Bradshaw, Y. W., R. Noonan, L. Gash, and C. B. Sershen. (1993). Borrowing against the future: Children and Third World indebtedness. *Social Forces* 71 (3), 629–656.

Bruscino, A. (2001). Child labor in Ghana: An analysis of perceptions and practices. *African Diaspora SIT Graduate Institute/SIT Study Abroad Digital Collection.* Retrieved on June 20, 2008, from http://digitalcollections.sit.edu/african_diaspora_isp/77/.

Bühler-Niderberger, D., and R. V. Krieken. (2008). Persisting inequalities: Childhood between global influences and local traditions. *Childhood* 15 (2), 147–155.

Burman, E. (1996). Local, global or globalized? Child development and international child rights legislation. *Childhood* 3 (1), 45–66.

Caldwell, J. C., and P. Caldwell. (1987). The cultural context of high fertility in sub-Saharan Africa. *Population and Development Review* 13 (3), 409–437.

Canagrajah, S., and H. Coulombe. (1997). Child labor and schooling in Ghana. *World Bank Working Paper 1844.* Washington, DC: World Bank.

Colecraft, E. K., G. S. Marquis, A. A. Bartolucci, L. Pulley, W. B. Owusu, and H. M. Maetz. (2004). A longitudinal assessment of the diet and growth of malnourished children participating in nutrition rehabilitation centres in Accra, Ghana. *Public Health Nutrition* 7 (4), 487–494.

David, J., and H. Harrington (eds.). (1971). *Growing Up African*. New York: William Morrow and Company.

Dawes, A., and E. Cairns. (1998). The Machel study: Dilemmas of cultural sensitivity and universal rights of children. *Peace and Conflicts* 4 (4), 335–348.

Douglass, R. L., and B. F. McGadney-Douglass. (2008). The role of grandmothers and older women in the survival of children with Kwashiorkor in urban Accra, Ghana. *Research in Human Development* 5 (1), 26–43.

Easterly, W. (2005). National policies and economic growth: A reappraisal. In P. Aghion and S. Durlauf (ed.). *Handbook of Economic Growth* 1A (15), 1015–1059.

Fortes, M. (1936). Culture contact as a dynamic process: An investigation in the Northern Territories of the Gold Coast. *Africa* 9 (1), 24–55.

———. (1967). *An Analysis of the Social Structure of a Trans-Volta Tribe*. New York: Humanities Press.

Goody, E. (1982). *Parenthood and Social Reproduction: Fostering and Occupational Roles in West Africa*. Cambridge: Cambridge University Press.

Graham, C. K. (1971). *History of Education in Ghana.* Tema, Ghana: Ghana Publishing Cooperation.

Grover, S. (2004). On recognizing children's universal rights: What needs to change in the Convention on the Rights of the Child. *The International Journal of Children's Rights* 12, 259–271.

Gyimah, S. O. (2006). Cultural background and infant survival in Ghana. *Ethnicity & Health* 11 (2), 101–120.

Hake, J. M. (1972). *Child-rearing Practices in Northern Nigeria*. Ibadan: Ibadan University Press.

Hall, G. S. (1904). *Adolescence: Its Psychology and Its Relations to Physiology, Anthropology, Sociology, Sex, Crime, Religion, and Education*, 2 volumes. New York: Appleton.

Hernandez, D. J. (1993). Historical transformation of childhood, children's statistics and social policy. *Childhood* 1 (4), 187-201.

International Labour Organization (ILO). (1973). Minimum Age Convention, 1973 (No. 138) report form. Retrieved on April 15, 2008, from http://www.ilo.org/ilolex/ english/reportforms/pdf/22e138.pdf.

Isiugo-Abanihe, U. C. (1985). Child fosterage in West Africa. *Population and Development Review* 11 (1), 53–73.

Jenks, C. (1982). *Sociology of Childhood*. London: Batsford Academics and Educational.

———. (2004). Many childhoods? *Childhood* 11 (1), 5–8.

Kimble, D. (1963). *A Political History of Ghana*. Oxford: Oxford University Press.

Laird, S. E. (2008). African social services in peril: A study of the Department of Social Welfare in Ghana under the highly indebted poor countries initiative. *Journal of Social Work* 8 (4), 377–389.

Legesse, A. (1980). Human rights in African political culture. In K. W. Thompson (ed.). *The Moral Imperatives of Human Rights: A World Survey*, 123–138. Lanham, MD: University Press of America.

LeVine, R. A., S. Dixon, S. LeVine, A. Richman, P. H. Leiderman, C. H. Keefer, et al. (1994). *Child Care and Culture: Lessons from Africa*. New York: Cambridge University Press.

Lloyd, A. (2002). Evolution of the African Charter on the Rights and Welfare of the Child and the African Committee of Experts: Raising the gauntlet. *International Journal of Children's Rights* 10, 179–198.

Machel, G. (1996). *The impact of armed conflict on children*. New York: UN.

———. (2006). *The Machel Review 1996–2000: A critical analysis of progress made and obstacles encountered in increasing protection for war-affected children*. New York: UN.

Marshall, D. (2004). Children's rights in imperial political cultures: Missionary and humanitarian contributions to the Conference on the African Child of 1931. *International Journal of Children's Rights* 12, 273–318.

McCaskie, T. C. (2000). *Asante Identities: History and Modernity in an African Village, 1850–1950*. Bloomington, IN: Indiana University Press.

McCreery, K. (2001). From street to stage with children in Brazil and Ghana. *Annals of the American Academy of Political and Social Science* 575, 122–146.

Mends, E. H. (1994). The rights of the child in Ghana: The socio-cultural milieu. In J. A. N. Mensa-Bonsu and C. Dowuona-Hammond (eds.). *The Rights of the Child in Ghana: Perspectives*, 3–9. Accra: Woeli Publishing Services.

Mensa-Bonsu, J. A. N., and C. Dowuona-Hammond (eds.). (1994). *The Rights of the Child in Ghana: Perspectives*. Accra: Woeli Publishing Services.

Murray, U. (2004). A comparative analysis: Girl child labour in agriculture, domestic work, and sexual exploitation: The cases of Ghana, Ecuador, and the Philippines. *Girl Child Labor Studies* 2. Geneva: International Labor Office.

Njoku, J. E. E. (1993). *African childhood: Poor social and economic environments*. Edwin Mellen Press.

Nkrumah, K. (1971). Ghana: The autobiography of Kwame Nkrumah. In J. David and H. Harrington (eds.). *Growing Up African*, 215–218. New York: William Morrow and Company.

Nsamenang, A. B. (1992). *Human development in a cultural context: A Third World perspective*. Newburry Park, CA: Sage.

Nyako, K. A. (1971). The mosquito and the young Ghanaian. In J. David and H. Harrington (eds.). *Growing Up African*, 219–220. New York: William Morrow and Company.

Ofori-Attah, K. D. (2007). Urbanization and schooling in Africa: Trends, issues, and challenges from Ghana during the colonial era. In W. T. Pink and G. W. Noblit (eds.). *International Handbook of Urban Education*, 23–47. Springer.

Oheneba-Sakyi, Y., and B. K. Takyi. (1991). Sociodemographic correlates of breast feeding in Ghana. *Human Biology* 63 (3), 389–402.

Organization of African Unity. (1990). African Charter on the Rights and Welfare of the Child, July 11, 1990, CAB/LEG/24.9/49 (1990). Retrieved July 12, 2009, from http://www.unhcr.org/refworld/docid/3ae6b38c18.html.

Osei, B. (1995). Ghana: The burden of debt service payment under structural adjustment. *Research Paper 33*, Africa Economic Research Consortium.

Owu-Ewie, C. (2006). The language policy of education in Ghana: A critical look at the English-only language policy of education. In J. Mugane et al. (eds.). *Selected Proceedings of the 35th Annual Conference on African Linguistics*, 76–85. Somerville, MA: Cascadilla Proceedings Project.

Pare, M. (2003). Why have street children disappeared? The role of international human rights law in protecting vulnerable groups. *International Journal of Children's Rights* 11 (1), 1–32.

Parton, N. (1985). *The Politics of Child Abuse*. London: MacMillan Publishers Ltd.

Rattray, R. S. (1933). The African child in proverb, folklore, and fact. *Africa: Journal of the International African Institute* 6 (4), 456–471.

Rizzini, I. (2001). On cultural diversity and childhood adversity. *Childhood* 8 (3), 315–321.

Rwezaura, B. (1998). Competing "images" of childhood in the social and legal systems of contemporary sub-Saharan Africa. *International Journal of Law, Policy, and the Family* 12, 253–278.

Thomas, R. G. (1974). Education in Northern Ghana, 1906–1940: A study in colonial paradox. *International Journal of African Historical Studies* 7 (3), 427–467.

Tomes, N. (1986). From useful to useless: The changing social value of children. *Reviews in American History* 14 (1), 50–54.

Twum-Danso, A. (2005). The political child. In A. McIntyre (ed.). *Invisible stakeholders: Children and war in Africa*, 7–30. Pretoria: Institute for Security Studies.

Twum-Danso, A. (2008). A cultural bridge, not an imposition: Legitimizing children's rights in the eyes of local communities. *Journal of the History of Childhood and Youth* 1 (3), 391–413.

United Nations. (1959). United Nations Declaration of the Rights of the Child. Geneva: UN. Retrieved on April 12, 2008, from http://www.canadiancrc.com/UN_CRC/UN_Declaration_on_the_Rights_of_the_Child.aspx.

———. (1989). United Nations Convention on the Rights of the Child. Geneva: UN.

———. (2008). *World population prospects*. New York: UN.

United Nations Children's Fund (UNICEF). (1986). *Ghana: Adjustment policies and programmes to protect children and other vulnerable groups*. Accra: UNICEF.

Veerman, P. E. (1992). *The Rights of the Child and the Changing Image of Childhood*. Norwell, MA: Martinus Nijhoff Publishers.

Veerman, P., and H. LeVine. (2000). Implementing children's rights on a local level: Narrowing the gap between Geneva and the grassroots. *The International Journal of Children's Rights* 8, 373–384.

Verlet, M. (2000). Growing up in Ghana: Deregulation and the employment of children. In B. Schlemmer (ed.). *The Exploited Child*, 67–82. New York: Zed Books.

Whiting, B. B., J. W. M. Whiting, and R. Longabaugh. (1975). *Children of Six Cultures: A Psycho-Cultural Analysis*. Harvard University Press.

Windborne, J. (2006). New laws, old values: Indigenous resistance to children's rights in Ghana. *Atlantic Journal of Communication* 14 (3), 156–172.

World Health Organization (WHO). (2006). *Country Cooperation Strategy at a glance: Ghana.* Geneva: WHO.

World Summit for Children. (1990). *World declaration on the survival, protection and development of children.* New York: World Summit for Children.

Chapter 3
Controversies in Paternity: Who Is a Child's Father under Ghanaian Law?

By Beatrice Akua Duncan

The question, "Who is a child's father under Ghanaian law?" would strike many as mischievous or even superfluous. Paternity is defined through biological connections and other modern and traditional methods. These include adoption and child fosterage within the Ghanaian context countries. This chapter addresses the implications of an existing customary law prevalent in many Ghanaian societies that denies the right of paternity to the biological father of a child born out of an adulterous union by conferring such a right on the legally recognized husband of the child's mother. Among other human rights infringements to be discussed below, the connotation arising from this norm is that a child is potentially denied the right to know and be cared for by his or her natural father.

The question cuts across a range of social and legal domains: First, it is closely connected to the question of sexuality and reproduction inside and outside of marriage. The wide-ranging, social, civil, and criminal sanctions against extra-marital relationships such as incest, pre-marital sex, and adultery are commonplace across both traditional and modern systems. The discussions demonstrate that traditional views of marriage as the acceptable framework within which reproduction is expected to take place potentially result in differentiation between children, men, and women based upon the circumstances of the birth of the child and the reproductive context in which it takes place. Second, we are also dealing here with the question of the parental rights of children born out of wedlock and the corresponding rights and obligations of the adults involved in their procreation. An opportunity is presented to compare and contrast traditional and modern interpretations of paternity and paternal responsibility based on the type of sexual relationship existing between a man and a woman who are identified as responsible for the birth of a child. Third, the specific issue at hand can be addressed from the perspective of a traditional practice. Some traditional practices in Ghana are yet to be discovered or fully ascertained. Over the years, the focus of attention has tended to be on what may be termed the "major" or "inimical" issues of female genital mutilation, early marriage, *trokosi,* and discriminatory inheritance practices. Falling outside of this typical domain, this chapter attempts to kindle discussion around what may be termed a "non-traditional" traditional practice that has received only cursory or no attention at all. Its basis lies, therefore, in the need to generate knowledge, discussion, and debate on a question of custom that has caught the limited attention of Ghanaian literature and case law. The final thrust of this chapter demonstrates that while children's rights are to be considered unique and distinct, they are closely and inevitably interwoven into that of adults, especially those to whom they are socially and biologically connected.

The methodology deployed in the analysis of the problem involves a comparative review of Ghanaian and other African case law, customary law, legislation, international treaties, and secondary literature.[1] The issue under discussion has been inspired by the author's exposure to a number of case materials during her co-compilation of the first *Case Book on the Rights of Women in Ghana*, which unearthed a rich and wide range of judicial case material impacting on rights of both women and children.[2] Among these were some reported cases (albeit negligible) that depicted the existence of this traditional norm in some Ghanaian communities. As noted previously, the question has not been hotly contested or debated in the public domain. But the fact that the issue has gained more judicial visibility compared to that of research, advocacy, and policy suggests that there must be a semblance of concern, however minute, to tackle as part of Ghana's pursuit to respond to its local and international obligations toward all children.

The Legal Context of Ghana

Sloth-Nielsen's (2008:4) assertion that "considerable progress has been made toward making children's rights visible in a variety of domains on the continent since the entry into force of the African Charter on the Rights and Welfare of the Child (ACRWC)" is true of Ghana. It may only be added in the case of this country, that the United Nations (UN) Declaration of the International Year of the Child in 1979, in addition to the country's punctual ratification of the Convention on the Rights of the Child (CRC) in 1990, constituted the most essential catapulting ingredients that brought child rights to the front burner of national affairs.

This period and the years immediately thereafter witnessed the creation of an independent Commission on Children in 1979 (The Ghana National Commission on Children) and the commencement of a law reform process, which resulted in a comprehensive overhaul of child rights laws. More importantly, the two events also influenced the formulation and integration of children's rights as human rights within the 1992 Constitution of the country. The period following ratification also saw the flourishing of a number of civil society organizations such as the Ghana non-governmental organization (NGO) Coalition on the Rights of the Child, enhanced awareness of child rights issues across the length and breadth of the country, and the formulation of policies and programs in the fields of child survival, development, protection, and participation. In more recent times, an important milestone occurred in 2000 with the establishment of a cabinet-level Ministry of Women and Children's Affairs. It is also critical to note that Ghana has submitted progress reports to the Committee on the Rights of the Child on two occasions in line with Article 44 (1) of the CRC. Its initial report was submitted in 1995, and following that a combined first, second, and third report was submitted and considered in 2005. These events and processes, in addition to many others, have demonstrated an overt willingness on the part of relevant partners to push the child rights agenda forward.

Underpinning this discussion is the legal environment in which child rights is located in Ghana. An overview of the legal system and constitutional and legal texts relevant to the issue at stake is, therefore, critical. The legal system of Ghana may metaphorically be described as "polygamous" in scope and nature. This is embedded in the fact that the laws of the country, as well as their formulation, interpretation, implementation, and even the character of institutions involved in law making and enforcement derive their content and practice from traditional, colonial, post-colonial, and international experiences. Post-independence constitutions of 1969, 1979, and 1992 reflect this intermingling in terms of law and policy formulation, in addition to the structures that oversee their implementation and enforcement.

The sources from which laws are derived in Ghana reflect its plural base. Article 11 (1)–(5) of the 1992 Constitution defines the laws of Ghana in the following manner:

1. The laws of Ghana shall comprise—
   a) This Constitution;
   b) Enactments made by or under the authority of the Parliament established by this Constitution;
   c) Any Orders, Rules and Regulations made by any person or authority under a power conferred by this Constitution;
   d) The existing law; and
   e) The common law.
2. The common law of Ghana shall comprise the rules of law generally known as the common law, the rules generally known as the doctrines of

equity *and the rules of customary law including those determined by the Superior Court of Judicature.* (emphasis added)

3. *For the purposes of this article, "customary law" means the rules of law, which by custom are applicable to particular communities in Ghana.* (emphasis added)
4. The existing law shall, except as otherwise provided in clause (1) of this article, comprise the written and *unwritten laws* of Ghana as they existed immediately before the coming into force of this Constitution, and any Act, Decree, law or statutory instrument issued or made before that date, which is to come into force on or after that date.
5. Subject to the provisions of this Constitution, the existing law shall not be affected by the coming into force of this Constitution.

The plural dimensions of the law potentially generate complexities in the process of interpretation (Ncube, 2008:9) as well as implementation and fulfillment of non-discrimination provisions (Molokomme & Mokobi, 1998:183) of legal texts. This is because the circumstances call for paying attention to law sources that are more divergent than convergent. The constitutional provisions cited above give prominence to the operation of community-specific customary law, received law from the colonial past of Ghana, statutory laws of the post-independent state, and the interpretation of the law by the courts of Ghana.

However, the definition of the law is not the only fundamental provision in so far as the question being addressed in this chapter is concerned. The subject under discussion inevitably calls for mention to be made to the chief cornerstone and reference point of child rights protection, survival, and development in Ghana. Article 28 of the 1992 Constitution, which deals specifically with the rights of the child and is of particular relevance to this article, partly states:

(1) Parliament shall enact such laws as are necessary to ensure that:
   a) every child has the right to the same measure of special care, assistance and maintenance as is necessary for its development *from its natural parents,* except where those parents have effectively surrendered their rights and responsibilities in respect of the child in accordance with law; (emphasis added)
   b) *every child, whether or not born in wedlock,* shall be entitled to reasonable provision out of the estate of its parents; (emphasis added)
   c) *parents undertake their natural right and obligation of care, maintenance and upbringing of their children* in co-operation with such institutions as Parliament may, by law, prescribe in such manner that in all cases the interests of the children are paramount. (emphasis added)

These provisions were crafted in general response to a range of international human rights standards acceded to by Ghana. The 1991 Constitutional Commission, which was constituted to draft the Constitution, was careful to draw on the provisions of a range of human rights sources such as the International Bill of

Rights (comprising the Universal Declaration of Human Rights (UDHR), the International Covenant on Civil and Political Rights (ICCPR), and the International Covenant on Economic, Social, and Cultural Rights (ICESCR), and the Convention on the Rights of the Child (CRC). In addition to these, Ghanaian child rights law formulation and implementation have also been shaped by the Convention on the Elimination of All Forms of Discrimination Against Women (CEDAW), the ACRWC, and the Protocol to the African Charter on Human Rights on the Rights of Women (the African Women's Protocol), among other instruments.

Accessions to these instruments, however, can by no means be considered an end in themselves. After two decades of ratification of the CRC, the business of ensuring that the right of every child is respected and fulfilled remains unfinished. As already indicated, the Committee on the Rights of the Child, to which Ghana has reported on two occasions, has stressed the important need of addressing critical issues affecting children. Of particular relevance to this chapter, the Committee's 1997 Concluding Observations and Recommendations to Ghana noted "certain traditional practices and customs, prevailing particularly in rural areas, hamper the effective implementation of the provisions of the Convention."[3] An important specific remark made in its 2006 Concluding Observations and Recommendations was:

> Notwithstanding the positive steps taken by the State Party in the context of the comprehensive legislative reform, the Committee remains concerned about the insufficient implementation creating a gap between law and practice (Ghana: CRC/C/GHA/CO/2/2006. Para. 9).

In the next sections, an attempt is made to explore the length and breadth of the traditional practice under discussion and how it potentially impacts on implementation of the rights of the child in Ghana.

Perspectives on the Changing Character of the Family

Appreciating the centrality of the family is important because it is within its confines that the norms and values affecting the conception of childhood, its entitlements, and obligations affecting adults are defined (Ncube, 1998:13). Given the natural and other diverse circumstances under which children are born, the family has been accorded immense attention and space in local and international legal texts. This section compares and contrasts international, regional, and national provisions pertaining to the family and how they impact on the rights of the child. Existing literature on the role of the family in this respect is extremely diverse. Emphasis on the significance of wider family and kinship networks on rights, roles, responsibilities, and obligations in African countries have been highlighted by writers such as Busia (1951) and Nukunya (1992), both writing in the specific context of Ghana, and Verhoef (2005) with respect to that of Cameroon. It was out of deference to this situation that the CRC makes express reference to the potential roles of the extended family in the protection and well-being of the child. Article 5 embodies this ideal:

> States Parties shall respect the responsibilities, rights and duties of parents or, where applicable, the members of the *extended family* or community as provided for by local custom, legal guardians or other persons legally responsible for the child, to provide, in a manner consistent with the evolving capacities of the child, appropriate direction and guidance in the exercise by the child of the rights recognized in the present Convention. (emphasis added)

However, roles and responsibilities of the extended family, in addition to obligations placed on its members toward it, have shifted in response to socio-economic change. The emergence of cash crop economies in many African countries has resulted in a demand for a steady supply of labor that can be secured on a long-term basis by the nuclear family. With respect to the Ghanaian context, researchers such as Austin (1987, 2005), Duncan (2009), Mikell (1975), and Okali (1983) demonstrated how the introduction of the cocoa cash crop economy resulted in the narrowing of importance of the extended family and a widening of influence and recognition of the nuclear family. However, by the time the CRC was in place, linkages between the nuclear and extended families had taken shape in many African countries. Sloth-Nielsen (2008:56) asserted there has been, in general, a legislative response in Africa to the changing nature of family forms as a consequence of the transformation from a rural, communitarian, agrarian, and subsistence society to a vastly more urbanized, diverse population, moving steadfastly toward a cash-based economy. This shifting position of the family and the rise in prominence of nuclear family responsibilities have been reflected in other international and regional provisions, which tend to integrate provisions on the family with those that deal with marriage relations and parental responsibilities. Articles 16 (3), 10 (1), 23 (1), and 18 (1) of the UDHR, ICESCR, ICCPR, and the ACRWC are cases in point, and by way of illustration, the relevant provisions of the ACRWC are set out as follows:

> *Article 18: Protection of the Family*
>
> 1. The family shall be the natural unit and basis of society. It shall enjoy the protection and support of the State for its establishment and development.
> 2. States Parties to the present Charter shall take appropriate steps to ensure equality of rights and responsibilities of spouses with regard to children during marriage and in the event of its dissolution. In case of the dissolution, provision shall be made for the necessary protection of the child.
> 3. No child shall be deprived of maintenance by reference to the parents' marital status.

The passage of the Intestate Succession Law of Ghana (Provisional National Defense Council Law (PNDCL, 111) in 1985, affirmed the emerging importance of the nuclear family within the framework of the inheritance rights of children and adults. Contrasting the present-day situation with the past, in which the communal involvement of the extended family was critical to the upbringing and care of children, the Memorandum to the Law makes the following explicit statement of justification for the radical shift in emphasis from the extended family to the nuclear family:

> The present law on intestate succession appears to have been overtaken by changes in the Ghanaian family system. The nuclear family (i.e., husband, wife and children) is gaining in importance, which is not reflected in the current laws of succession. There is a tension between this smaller group and the traditional family unit as to the appropriate line of devolution of property upon the death intestate of a member of both units.

The shedding of extended family influence and the growing importance of the nuclear family are not the only changes to have occurred in family relations. Interrelated to this, has been the rapid wave of change taking place in the meanings and makings of marriage (Allman & Tashjian, 2000), which has traditionally been regarded as the appropriate setting for reproduction. In their case study of the Tswana of Botswana, Molokomme & Mokobi (1998:183) indicated that it is on this basis that traditional law distinguishes between children born within and outside of marriage. A review of their discussions shows a link between a valid marriage and paternal rights and responsibilities. They noted that the rules of traditional Tswana family law were primarily geared toward ensuring male control over productive resources, female sexuality, and production (1998:186). The transfer of *bogadi* (bridewealth) had the effect of transferring the woman's reproductive capacity from her lineage to that of her husband. Since *bogadi* was one of the requirements of a valid marriage, the right of a man to guardianship or his duty to maintain his children depended on whether the children were born within or outside of marriage. They further assert that a man, who fathered a child outside or within marriage without producing *bogadi*, was deprived of rights of guardianship. Instead, such a child was affiliated to its mother's lineage because her reproductive capacity had not been transferred from her family to that of her husband. A similar situation pertains among the Krobo of the Eastern Region of Ghana, although the affiliation of such children to the lineage of their mothers leads to shirking of responsibility of maintenance on the part of the fathers, resulting in extreme situations of deprivation of mothers and children. Also significant about Molokomme & Mokobi's analysis is their observation as with most African traditional societies that children who were born outside of the confines of marriage were stigmatized. They suggest that since reproduction was permissible only within the context of marriage, such situations were rare at least within the context of Tswana, and where they did occur, such children were killed and tagged as *bana ka dikgora* (children whose fathers had crept surreptitiously through the fence) (1998:187).

It would appear, however, that the negative connotations of child illegitimacy might have been different in some parts of pre-colonial Ghana. Rattray (1927:95) noted that "illegitimacy" was hardly accepted in Ashanti, except in respect to a child born to a slave woman. He asserted, by contrast, that children born to an unmarried woman were always absorbed into the lineage of their mother.

In support of Rattray's observation, the 2007 Namibian case of *Frans v. Paschke and Others*,[4] underscored the significant influence of colonialism in the fostering of legitimacy within the context of marriage. The case examined and dealt with the rule that an illegitimate child cannot inherit intestate from his father. The court used the following common law rule as the basis of its decision:

> But those who are born of a union which is entirely odious to us, and, therefore, prohibited, shall not be called natural children and no indulgence whatever shall be extended to them. But this fact shall be punishment for the fathers, that they know that children who are the issue of their sinful passion will inherit nothing, and that in the case where a mother of two children, one legitimate and the other illegitimate, died, the illegitimate one could not inherit, either through will or intestacy, if the legitimate child was still alive at her death. The reason for this rule was given as:
>
> > For the preservation of chastity is the first duty of freedom of an illustrious woman and because it would be unjust, and very oppressive and unworthy of the spirit of our age, for bastards to be acknowledged.
>
> It is debatable whether or not the above statements were only applicable to children born out of an incestuous relationship. Nevertheless, Dutch writers such as Voet, regarded adultery not a less heinous crime than incest. Accordingly, the sins of fathers who committed adultery were also visited upon their children. They could also not inherit intestate from their fathers.

In line with the point made earlier that family relationships and their significance have been more of a shifting terrain in response to socioeconomic change, researchers such as Brydon (1979) and Sloth-Neilsen (2008) were in accord with the view that the question of illegitimacy may be a thing of the past.

In her piece, Brydon (1979:320–329) presented the case that among the patrilineal Amedzofe-Avatime of the Volta Region of Ghana, children born outside of wedlock are not by any means stigmatized, but absorbed into the lineage and household of their maternal grandfathers. Similarly, Sloth-Neilsen (2008:56) asserted that there is "a diminishing concern for the status of illegitimacy" among a host of other issues within the context of socio-economic transformations taking place in African countries. A recent study conducted by Faryorsey (2003) in the patrilineal Ga South of Ghana to assess the changing nature of marriage relationships indicated that an estimated one in every four urban women lives in an informal union and that the customary requirement that formal marriages are the expected confines within which procreation should take place is fast eroding. Against the background that children born out of wedlock in Ghana have a tendency to be disinherited, both the Children's Act and the Constitution of Ghana place their provisions on children born out of wedlock within the context of inheritance. It is instructive that their respective provisions read in similar manner:

> *Section 7 of the Children's Act:*
> No person shall deprive a child of reasonable provision out of the estate of a parent whether or not born in wedlock.
>
> *Section 28 (1) (b) of the 1992 Constitution:*
> Every child, whether or not born in wedlock, shall be entitled to reasonable provision out of the estate of its parents.

These provisions reflect others specified under international law, for example, Article 25 (2) of the UDHR. However, while current legal provisions appear to be sufficiently broad enough to cover all "children born out of wedlock," it is the contention of the author that researchers and advocates of children's rights may be overlooking the potentially precarious situation of "children born out of adultery," which is specifically discussed in the next section.

Children Born Out of Adulterous Unions

Discussions around the status of children born out of adultery are also to be situated in the customary marriage and family context. Critical to this is the fact that customary marriages are regarded as potentially polygamous, meaning that men possess an unlimited freedom to marry an unlimited number of women. This extends to loose consensual unions (*mpena aware* in Twi)[5] that do not generally involve the performance of marriage rites. Women are, however, not given the same measure of freedom of choice in the number of spouses or partners; therefore, any attempt by a woman to forge a relationship (sometimes, no matter how close) with a man outside of marriage is labeled as adultery. By contrast, the only situation in which a man may be deemed to have committed adultery in customary context is where he engages in sexual relations with another man's wife.

The import of adultery has several implications on the status of women and, therefore, children born out of such relationships. First, flowing from the just preceding, the customary law position in most communities in Ghana is that the husband of a woman possesses exclusive sexual rights over her (Manuh, 1995). The woman is deemed to be a jural minor under the guardianship of her husband (Grier, 1992; Opoku, 1976) and, therefore, remains under his economic, social, and sexual control.

Consequently, the literature suggests that the commission of adultery is an act that offends the husband of the married woman as opposed to the wife of the other married man with whom the act has been committed. Hence, McCaskie (1981:489) noted that adultery is interpreted substantially in terms of a transaction between two males, while totally ignoring the rights of the woman/women affected. This is clear from his following observation:

> Adultery was strictly defined as importuning or having sexual connection with a married woman; it was literally understood as a theft, requiring compensation of one man's property by another man. . . . Commonly, adultery located woman as a convertible economic good—infidelity having a monetary equivalence always payable by the offending male to the injured husband, in the relations of power between man and man.

Both McCaskie (1981) and Manuh (1995) demonstrated how different adultery fees (*ayefre*) were chargeable for and against different classes of men within Ashanti. More recent studies (for example, Duncan, 2008) have tended to show that the customary positions of men and women in situations of adultery have not changed in modern times. The observations of McCaskie, therefore, remain relevant and are an open demonstration of the tendency for women to be objectified within the context of marriage.

It is on the basis of this understanding of the customary implications of adultery that three reported cases on the subject have arrived at conclusions that have implications for rights of both the parents and children involved.

One of the early cases to establish the nexus between adultery and paternity was *Nyarkoa v. Mansu* (1967) GLR 523. In this case, the parties to the marriage (W and H) were customarily married for fourteen years until its dissolution in 1966. At the time of the trial, H was seventy years of age, and there had been four children of the marriage. H instituted an action to claim custody of the two younger children whom W took away when she was leaving the matrimonial home to live with D. W, however, contended that the two children were the issues of an adulterous association with D while her marriage with H was subsisting and insisted that D was the father of the children. She maintained that after seven years of marriage, when the first two elder children had been born, H became impotent, and by mutual agreement, he entreated her to stay in the matrimonial home and call him "uncle" and presumably, with unbridled license to her to have sexual relations outside of the marriage. In determining paternity of the two children, the court made the following pertinent observations:

> The established principle of customary law that a husband was entitled to any children born in adultery to the wife during the subsistence of the marriage was not invariable or inviolable.

This position of custom was questioned in the case of *Abangana v. Akologo* (1977) 1 GLR 382, in which the plaintiff and his wife were both Frafra citizens, married under Frafra customary law. The wife left the husband not long after the marriage and cohabited for about five years with the defendant, also a Frafra citizen. The defendant and the plaintiff's wife had two children during their illicit cohabitation. Subsequently, the husband sued for the return of his wife and the two children and damages for seduction. The trial magistrate held as follows:

> Now the custom as it stands is to the credit of the plaintiff, in that the plaintiff has paid full dowry, and secondly did not divorce the woman whom the defendant alleged he married. The defendant cannot be the father of the children when they are born from an unbroken marriage as the custom stands. I therefore find the plaintiff's case proved to my satisfaction and enter judgment in his favour. This plaintiff is to collect his wife and the two children.

On appeal by the defendant to the High Court, one of the issues to be determined was whether a custom that deprives a person of his or her natural child is to be regarded as repugnant to the principles of equity, good conscience, and natural justice. In reversing the decision of the trial court to hand over his two children to the plaintiff, the High Court noted that the latter was a stranger to the union and that the existing Frafra customary rule of practice was unsustainable, it being repugnant to the principles of equity, good conscience, and natural justice in addition to the well-founded duty of the court to take account of the paramount welfare of the children in child custody matters.

This is to be contrasted with the outcome of the third case, *Ibrahim v. Amalibini* (1978) GLR, 368, in which the respondent sought an order against the appellant for the return of a woman he alleged to be his wife and also the custody of the child of the said union. His case was that he had married the woman in accordance with Frafra customary law and that the appellant, an uncle of the said wife, had persuaded her to leave him. The appellant on the other hand, denied that the respondent had been married to the woman and insisted that the woman became pregnant before she met the respondent. The trial judge found as a fact that the respondent had not fully performed the essential marriage custom and, accordingly, held that there was no valid marriage. The judge, however, held that the respondent was the father of the child and, therefore, granted him custody. All the parties involved in this action belonged to the Frafra tribe. In determining the appeal, the appellate court had to consider whether the respondent was under customary law entitled to the custody of a child born out of wedlock. It used the opportunity to make a pronouncement on the question of illegitimacy, stating that under Frafra customary law a child born by an unmarried woman was not illegitimate. Such a child was considered as the legal child of the maternal grandfather and his family who were entitled to the custody of the child. The putative father had no right to the custody of the child. Similarly, the right to the custody of a child born out of an adulterous union was vested in the husband and the adulterer was given no rights whatsoever. Consequently, the order of the District Court Grade II, ignoring the customary law and giving custody of the child to the respondent merely on the grounds that he was the natural father, was erroneous in law.

Based on the trend of limited decision-making with respect to the paternal status of children born out of adultery, it would be accurate to suggest that the law is presently in disarray and completely unsettled. This has been aggravated by the fact that the highest judicial bodies in all instances have been High Courts, which are not bound by each other's decisions. It would have taken a higher court, such as the Court of Appeal or the Supreme Court to bring the matter to rest. More importantly, it is to be observed that none of the judges in these cases made reference to local or international legal texts on children. Although by the time these cases were initiated, the CRC, CEDAW, and ACRWC were not yet in place, other legal texts such as the International Bill of Rights and the Declaration on the Rights of the Child of 1959 could have informed the judicial decision-making process. At a local level, the 1969 Constitution, which made pioneering reference to children, could have been used as an important resource to tackle the issue once and for all. To the extent that the issue remains unresolved, it becomes important to analyze how the issue of adultery and procreation impact upon the legal rights of the affected children and adults in the light of the legal frameworks cited in preceding sections.

Human Rights Implications

The first observation to be made is that the custom under discussion and the judicial decisions reached in relation to it are at variance with the 1992 Constitution, the 1998 Children's Act (Act 560), the CRC, ACRWC, CEDAW, and the International Bill of Rights. An analysis of case law and the literature shows that the rights of both the child and his or her natural parents are at stake. Regardless of whether the birth took place in a pre-marital or adulterous context, the consequences tend to be the same, given that in each case fathers are prevented from enjoying full parental rights and automatic rights of access and custody. By implication, it suggests that the actors involved are being treated differently from other children and parents by virtue of the circumstances of reproduction. This sins against Article 2 of the CRC, which states:

> 1. States Parties shall respect and ensure the rights set forth in the present Convention to each child within their jurisdiction without discrimination

of any kind, irrespective of the child's or his or her parent's or legal guardian's race, colour, sex, language, religion, political or other opinion, national, ethnic or social origin, property, disability, birth or other status.

2. States Parties shall take all appropriate measures to ensure that the child is protected against all forms of discrimination or punishment on the basis of the status, activities, expressed opinions, or beliefs of the child's parents, legal guardians, or family members.

McCaskie's contention that adultery is treated as a transaction between two men leads to an objectification of the children and women involved. Any norm that objectifies a person or group of people is to be examined since it potentially contradicts a basic human rights principle that women and children are subjects and not objects of rights. In their analysis of the Botswana situation, Molokomme & Mokobi (1998:194–195) demonstrated how all the parties of non-marital situations are discriminated against:

> Before the best interest principle statute became law in Botswana in 1969, the common law rule which favoured mothers of non-marital children over their biological father was applicable. This reflected the different treatment of children based on their birth status, which . . . was in violation of Article 2 of the Convention. It also reflects discrimination against the biological fathers of non-marital children because, while the common law required them to maintain their children, it did not give them automatic rights of access to them.

It discriminates against women in matters of marriage, family, and in the upbringing of their children. To the extent that the practice honors men by making it permissible for them to enter into multiple relationships with women in the name of polygamy, while penalizing women for engaging in extra-marital affairs, it also specifically contravenes Article 16 (1) (d) of CEDAW, which states as follows among others:

> States Parties shall take all appropriate measures to eliminate discrimination against women in all matters relating to marriage and family relations and in particular shall ensure, on a basis of equality of men and women: (d) The same rights and responsibilities as parents, irrespective of their marital status, in matters relating to their children; in all cases the interests of the children shall be paramount.

That African customary jurisprudence generally tends to discriminate against women, is supported by Molokomme & Mokobi (1998:187), who demonstrated that in matters of divorce, the conduct of a wife would be central to determining whether she would have custody of her children. The conduct of the man, apparently, would not come into play, since he is assumed to be the guardian of the child. Furthermore, Manuh (1984) has shown that among some ethnic groups in Ghana, a woman who initiates divorce could lose rights to alimony settlements. It may also be argued that the rule contained in most Matrimonial Causes legislation in Africa and elsewhere—that children of tender years must of necessity be placed in the custody of their mothers—is an extension of the view that the primary role of women is connected to reproduction.

In some cases, it has even been shown that a working woman could be deprived of the opportunity of taking custody of such children as it is assumed that she may not be able to balance her maternal and professional responsibilities. In the Botswana case of *Isaac v. Issac*, for instance, the court was faced with the dilemma of granting custody of a young child to a mother who apparently led a busy life. The judge in that case ruled "young children below the age of 7 ought normally to be in the custody of their mother. However, as I said, the mother is a working woman."[6]

Himonga (2008:83), however, presented a different perspective by noting that the customary law practice of payment of damages by a man for the extra marital pregnancy intersects with a number of rights of children, particularly the right to parental care and the right to grow up with one's parents. This point is debatable, however, since it could also be argued that the damages are being offered to defray the "cost" of the dishonor, which is perceived to have fallen on a disaffected father and husband.

Legal texts of some African countries have tended to reflect this discriminatory tendency against men. Section 24 of the Children Act (2001) (Cap 586 Laws of Kenya), states that "where a child's father and mother were married to each other at the time of his birth, they shall have parental responsibility for the child and neither the father nor the mother of the child shall have a superior right or claim against the other in exercise of such parental responsibility." However, if the father and the mother of the child were not married at the time of birth, the same section provides that the mother has parental responsibility at the first instance, and the father can only acquire it after signing a Parental Responsibility Agreement with the mother or if he gets a court order upon application. Civil society organizations such as CRADLE–The Children's Foundation have been concerned about the fact that responsibility for the maintenance of the child tends to fall on the mother, whereas it becomes optional for the father of the child.[7] In its recent Concluding Observations and Recommendations to Kenya, the Committee on the Rights of the Child had occasion to express concern at the *de facto* discrimination faced by children born out of wedlock.[8]

The influence of the common law in the shaping of African legislation in this respect cannot be underestimated. Taking the situation of Jersey, a crown colony of Britain practicing the common law, Section 5 of its Law on Children (2002) has the following provision in relation to children born out of wedlock:

> *Acquisition of parental responsibility by father*
>
> (1) Where a child's father and mother were not married to each other at the time of the child's birth—

(a) the court may, on the application of the father, order that he shall have parental responsibility for the child; or
(b) the father and mother may by agreement provide for the father to have parental responsibility for the child.

(2) Where a child is treated in law as legitimate the court may—
(a) on the application of a person claiming to be the child's biological father; and
(b) where the court is satisfied he is the child's biological father, order that he shall have parental responsibility for the child notwithstanding that he is not in law the child's father.

In a comparative study on consolidated children's statutes initiated by UNICEF, Duncan (2008:48) noted that the above provisions are discriminatory toward children and their natural fathers. The extent to which the norms affecting children born out of adulterous relationships impact on the human rights of the actors involved is, however, of much wider significance. In addition to the rights of the child and father, those of the mother are also affected. The general outcome of these cases raises a number of questions, among which include who constitutes the parents of a child born out of an adulterous relationship. In as much as the wide-ranging provisions on the family assist in ensuring that the child is not displaced, section 4 of the Children's Act of Ghana affords additional protection that must be considered. Whereas the CRC and ACRWC express parents in general terms, Article 28 (1) (a) of the Constitution (already quoted) places this within the context of the natural family. However, section 4 of the Children's Act provides more holistic provisions in so far as they endorse the rights and obligations of both natural parents and the extended family:

> Section 4. *Right to name and nationality.*
> No person shall deprive a child of the right from birth to a name, the right to acquire a nationality or the right as far as possible to know his *natural parents and extended family* subject to the provisions of Part IV, Sub-Part II of this Act. (emphasis added)

At the same time, we are also compelled to consider Article 41 (a) of the CRC, which cautions that "nothing in the present Convention shall affect any provisions which are more conducive to the realization of the rights of the child and which may be contained in the law of a State Party." The contention being made is that Article 28 (1) (a) of the Constitution in addition to section 4 of the Children's Act present more conducive channels through which the rights of children born out of adultery may be fully addressed, and they should, as such, be the primary basis for any reform that is being contemplated in this area of the law.

There are indications that African courts are beginning to respond positively to their constitutional and international obligations toward children. In the Namibian case of *Frans v. Paschke and Others*, already cited, the rule that an illegitimate child cannot inherit intestate from his father was called into question. The plaintiff contended that the common law rule was unlawful and invalid by virtue of the Namibian Constitution of 1990, that it violated its various provisions, such as non-discrimination [Article 10 (2)], equality before the law [Article 10 (1)], the right to be accorded dignity [Article 8 (1)], the right to know and to be cared for by both parents [Article 15 (1)], and the right to acquire property [Article 16 (1)]. The court declared the common law rule unconstitutional and was not deterred by the possibility that this would lead to a floodgate of other cases at its door steps, declaring:

> The Constitution is the supreme law. Inevitably, consequences will result upon a declaration of unconstitutionality, be it in respect of common law rules or legislation. But the concern should not be the consequences. With that, the law must deal in due course. "*Floodgate-litigation-arguments*" cannot cause an unconstitutional rule to survive. Sometimes, as in this case, it is indeed necessary to open the floodgates to give constitutional water to the arid land of prejudice upon which the common law rule has survived for so many years in practice. (emphasis added)

The relevant constitutional provisions in relation to children under Article 28 of the 1992 Constitution of Ghana have already been cited. However, it also becomes clear that the implications of the discriminatory tendencies underlying procreation in adulterous circumstances will also not be tolerated under Article 17, which deals with the following all-encompassing definition of discrimination:

> 1. All persons shall be equal before the law.
> 2. A person shall not be discriminated against on grounds of gender, race, color, ethnic origin, religion, creed or social or economic status.
> 3. For the purposes of this article, "discriminate" means to give different treatment to different persons attributable only or mainly to their respective descriptions by race, place of origin, political opinions, color, gender, occupation, religion or creed, whereby persons of one description are subjected to disabilities or restrictions to which persons of another description are not made subject or are granted privileges or advantages which are not granted to persons of another description.

Looking for a Solution

The discussions thus far have revealed that the customary norm regarding the paternity of children born out of adultery is potentially discriminatory in content, purpose, and effect and violates the rights of all actors concerned. A response has, however, been provided under the constitutional and legislative frameworks that protect children born out of wedlock in general. This is bolstered by complementary provisions regarding non-discrimination in other regional and global treaties. The recognition given to the nuclear family as the ideal family situation by frameworks such as the ACRWC was applicable in general situations. The fluid approach enjoined by the CRC, the more specific indications provided by the Children's Act of Ghana, and the CEDAW provisions on the equal rights of women and men in marriage render modifications in the definition of a parent in a manner that would ensure that a child is not deprived of knowing and being cared for by his or her natural father. Other mediating provisions, such as those on the child's best interest (Article 3 of the CRC) and the conditionality of protecting the child from an abusive parent (Article 9 of the CRC), the child's right to participate in the decision-making process (Article 12 of the CRC) exists to ensure that appropriate decisions are made.

While this discussion is not instigating a break up of marriages, it becomes clear the basis upon which a natural father is potentially excluded from the upbringing of his child procreated out of adultery, itself, lacks the legitimacy of agreed upon local and international human rights frameworks. To the extent that the issue has been mainly contested at the level of the judiciary (and even so, through very limited case law), it can be contended that proactive measures would have to be taken by this institution if this customary anomaly is to be dealt with. In line with the legal developments of the 1990s, Ghanaian judges are to be encouraged to apply and deploy all the legal resources at their disposal. The judicial experience of Ghana shows that judges are yet to exercise a full-fledged application and utilization of the international human rights law such as the CRC, CEDAW, and the ACRWC. The Committee on the Rights of the Child has commented on the role that is expected of the judiciary in the implementation of the principles and provisions of the CRC. In its General Comment No. 5 of 2005, which deals with the General Measures of Implementation for the Convention on the Rights of the Child,[9] the Committee indicated that "the development of a children's rights perspective throughout government, parliament and the *judiciary* is required for effective implementation of the whole Convention" (Paragraph 12, with emphasis added). More revealingly, Paragraph 20 spells out the trusting and expectant role of the judiciary with respect to CRC implementation:

> Incorporation should mean that the provisions of the Convention can be directly invoked before the courts and applied by national authorities and that the Convention will prevail where there is a conflict with domestic legislation or common practice.

These developments are to operate in tandem with other provisions of the Constitution that mandate the courts to give due deference to other factors in their interpretation of the law. The most important ones are Article 11 (6) and 26, which state as follows:

Article 11 (6)
The existing law shall be construed with any modifications, adaptations, qualifications and exceptions necessary to bring it into conformity with the provisions of this Constitution, or otherwise to give effect to, or enable effect to be given to, any changes effected by this Constitution.

Article 26
1. Every person is entitled to enjoy, practice, profess, maintain and promote any culture, language, tradition or religion subject to the provisions of this Constitution.
2. All customary practices which dehumanise or are injurious to the physical and mental well being of a person are prohibited.

These provisions and others point to the need for a "judicial revolution" in favor of the Ghanaian child, involving a rigorous engagement with the Constitution, the CRC, the ACRWC, CEDAW, and other relevant instruments in matters affecting children, including those related to them. Not only is the proactive role of the judiciary required in this respect. The strategic importance of civil society groups and legal practitioners cannot be ignored in the light of constitutional provisions that permit specific questions of unconstitutionality to be tackled in the Supreme Court. Article 2 (1) of the Constitution lays the basis for the submission of constitutional cases in favor of children by its following provisions:

(1) A person who alleges that—
    (a) an enactment or anything contained in or done under the authority of that or any other enactment; or
    (b) any act or omission of any person;
    is inconsistent with, or is in contravention of a provision of this Constitution, may bring an action in the Supreme Court for a declaration to that effect.

Some African countries such as South Africa may be better placed to develop a body of jurisprudence on constitutional issues affecting children, based on the existence of specific constitutional courts. This has facilitated the hearing and disposal of a number of child-related cases (for example, *Fraser v. Children's Court Pretoria North and Others*).[10] The absence of a specific constitutional court in Ghana should not, however, prevent the development of constitutional child rights law. The mandate provided under Article 2 (1), coupled with the range of other ingredients under local and international law are sufficient to assist the judiciary as it presently exists to begin the process of responding more rigorously to violations of the rights of the child.

Conclusions

This discussion presents a road map and justification for tackling an otherwise obscure aspect of child rights in Ghana. It may have dealt with a minor aspect of the law in relation to children but has, nevertheless, touched upon a number of issues that impact on the implementation of local and international laws overall. It has shown that some children could be potentially excluded from knowing and being cared for by their natural parents on the basis of the sexual decisions and choices of the latter. On the thrust of the interpretation of the law in its totality, it does not seem appropriate to deny a child any right accorded them only by reason of the actions of adults. From this observation, we also appreciate the degree to which human rights treaties are interdependent. As a case in point, the provisions of the CRC and CEDAW intersect in so far as they relate to the prevention of discrimination and the promotion of equal rights between men and women in marriage. The article has articulated the important role that can be played by the judiciary in the advancement of children's rights in Ghana. Ingredients afforded under the Constitution, Children's Act, and General Comment No. 5 of the Committee on the Rights of the Child lay the foundation for engendering a body of constitutional jurisprudence in favor of children. Last but not least, developments across other parts of Africa, particularly in countries that also operate under the influence of plural legal systems, demonstrate that positive change is possible. In particular, special mention may be made of the Namibian constitutional case of *Frans v. Paschke and Others* in which the court wasted no time declaring the common law rule on illegitimacy unconstitutional.

Notes

1. The dearth of existing information (judicial and non-judicial alike) on the specific issue of the status of children born in adulterous situations in Ghana is a basic weakness of this research. The chapter, therefore, explores existing information on a similar issue of children born out of pre-marital situations in addition to literature emerging from other African countries on questions of illegitimacy and paternity to illustrate the problem statement being advanced.

2. See Duncan & Kingsley-Nyinah (2006). *A Casebook on the Rights of Women in Ghana (1959–2005)*. Produced by the Ghana Literacy and Resource Foundation.

3. See *Concluding observations of the Committee on the Rights of the Child: Ghana*. 18/06/97. CRC/C/15/Add.73. Para. 6.

4. (PI1548/2005) (2007) NAHC 49 (July 11, 2007).

5. Twi is a generic language of the Akan ethnic group in Ghana and is spoken by people of other ethnic categories.

6. See MC/F21/1990. High Court, unreported and cited in Molokomme & Mokobi (1998:192).

7. See http://www.pambazuka.org/en/category/rights/26624.

8. See CRC/C/KEN/CO/2/2007. Para. 24 (unedited version).
9. See CRC/GC/2003/5. *General Comments.*
10. (CCT31/96) (1997) ZACC 1; 1996 (8) BCLR 1085; 1997 (2) SA 218 (February 5, 1997).

References

Abangana v. Akologo. (1977). 1 GLR 382.

Allman, J., and V. Tashjian. (2000). *I Will Not Eat Stone: A Women's History of Colonial Asante.* In A. Isaacman and J. Allman (eds.). Portsmouth: Heinemann; Oxford: Curry; and Capetown: Philip.

Austin, G. (1987). The emergence of capitalist relations in South Asante cocoa-farming, c. 1916–1933. *Journal of African History* 28, 259–279.

———. (2005). *Labour, Land and Capital in Ghana: From Slavery to Free Labour in Asante (1807–1956).* New York: University of Rochester Press.

Brydon, L. (1979). Women at work: Some changes in family structure in Amedzofe-Avatime, Ghana. *Africa* 49 (2), 97–111.

Busia, A. K. (1951). *The Position of a Chief in the Modern Political System of Ashanti: A Study of the Influence of Contemporary Social Changes on Ashanti Political Institutions.* Oxford University Press.

Concluding observations and recommendations of the Committee on the Rights of the Child. (1997). Ghana: CRC/C/15/Add.73.

———. (2006). Ghana: CRC/C/GHA/CO/2.

———. (2007). Kenya: CRC/C/KEN/CO/2/2007.

Duncan, B. (2008). Global perspectives on consolidated children's rights statutes. *Legislative Reform Initiatives Paper Series.* Division of Policy and Practice, UNICEF, New York.

———. (2009). *Gender, land and cocoa in Ghana: Changing access rights in matrilineal and patrilineal communities.* PhD thesis submitted to the University of Birmingham.

Duncan, B., and D. Kingsley-Nyinah. (2006). *A Casebook on the Rights of Women in Ghana (1959–2005).* Accra, Ghana: Ghana Literacy and Resource Foundation.

Faryorsey, C. (2003). *Polygamy and plural marriages: Legal implications for inheritance rights, property rights and childcare and maintenance.* The Legal Pluralism and Gender Project, Accra.

Frans v. Paschke and Others. (2007). (PI1548/2005) NAHC 49 (July 11, 2007).

Fraser v. Children's Court Pretoria North and Others. (CCT31/96) (1997) ZACC 1; 1996 (8) BCLR 1085; 1997 (2) SA 218 (February 5, 1997).

General comments of the Committee on the Rights of the Child. *General Comment No. 5 of 2005: General Measures of Implementation for the Convention on the Rights of the Child.* CRC/GC/2003/5.

Grier, B. (1992). Pawns, porters, and petty traders: Women in the transition to cash crop agriculture in colonial Ghana. In J. Boetcher and B. Laslet (eds.). *Signs* 17 (2), 304–328.

Himonga, C. (2008). African customary law and children's rights: Intersections and domains in a new era. In J. Sloth-Nielsen (ed.). *Children's Rights in Africa: A Legal Perspective,* 73–90. University of Western Cape, South Africa.

Ibrahim v. Amalibini. (1978). GLR 368.

Intestate Succession Law of Ghana (Provisional National Defense Council) Law 111, 1985.

Isaac v. Issac. MC/F21/1990. High Court, unreported.

Manuh, T. (1984). *Law and the Status of Women in Ghana.* Addis Ababa: ECA.

———. (1995). Changes in marriage and funeral exchanges among the Asante: A case study from Kona, Afigya-Kwabre. In J. Guyer (ed.). *Money Matters,* 188–201. London: Heinemann and Portsmouth: Currey.

McCaskie, T. (1981). State and society, marriage and adultery: Some considerations toward social history of pre-colonial Asante. *Journal of African History* 22 (4), 477–494.

Mikell, G. (1975). *Cocoa and social change in Ghana: A study of development in the Sunyani District.* PhD thesis, Columbia University.

Molokomme, A., and K. Mokobi. (1998). Custody and guardianship of children in Botswana: Customary laws and judicial practice within the framework of the children's convention. In W. Ncube (ed.). *Law, Culture, Tradition and Children's Rights in Eastern and Southern Africa,* 182–202. Ashgate, Darmouth.

Ncube, W. (1998). Prospects and challenges in Eastern and Southern Africa: The interplay between international human rights norms and domestic law, tradition and culture. In W. Ncube (ed.). *Law, Culture, Tradition and Children's Rights in Eastern and Southern Africa,* 1–10. Singapore: Ashgate Darmouth.

———. (2008). The African cultural fingerprint? The changing concept of childhood. In W. Ncube (ed.). *Law, Culture, Tradition and Children's Rights in Eastern and Southern Africa,* 11–27. Singapore: Ashgate Darmouth.

Nukunya, G. K. (1992). *Tradition and Change in Ghana: An Introduction to Sociology.* Accra: Ghana Universities Press.

Nyarkoa v. Mansu. (1967). GLR 523.

Okali, C. (1983). *Cocoa and Kinship in Ghana: The Matrilineal Akan of Ghana.* International African Institute. London, Boston, and Melbourne: Kegan Paul International.

Opoku, K. (1976). *The Law of Marriage in Ghana: A Study of Legal Pluralism.* University of Hamburg.

Rattray, R. S. (1927). *Religion and Art in Ashanti.* Oxford: Clarendon Press.

Sloth-Nielsen, J. (2008). Children's rights and the law in African context. In J. Sloth-Nielsen (ed.). *Children's Rights in Africa. A Legal Perspective,* 3–12. University of Western Cape, South Africa.

———. (2008). Domestication of children's rights in national legal systems in African context: Progress and prospects. In J. Sloth-Nielsen (ed.). *Children's Rights in Africa. A Legal Perspective,* 53–72. University of Western Cape, South Africa.

Verhoef, H. (2005). A child has many mothers: Views of child fostering in northwestern Cameroon. *Childhood* 12, 369–390.

Chapter 4

Bridging the Child Rights Gap in a Refugee Context: Survival Strategies and Impact on Inter-generational Relations

By Kate Hampshire, Gina Porter, Kate Kilpatrick, Peter Ohene Kyei, Michael Kwodwo Adjaloo, and George Oppong Ampong

Conflict and displacement have the potential to threaten almost every one of the rights enshrined in the United Nations (UN) Convention on the Rights of the Child (CRC) 1989. As we shall see, Liberian children and young people who were forced to flee their country and are now residing in Buduburam refugee settlements in Ghana, are deprived of all three basic rights of the child: right of provision (adequate nutrition, healthcare, education, and economic welfare), right of protection (protection from abuse, neglect, violence, and exploitation), and right of participation. As refugees, children can "slip through the net" of the CRC. In the case of Buduburam, it has often been unclear who, if anyone, is responsible for upholding the rights of children—the Ghanaian government, the United Nations High Commission for Refugees (UNHCR), or welfare authorities within the camp.

Over recent years, there has been a shift within the literature to focus on the resilience of children affected and displaced by war and their ability to overcome adversity, despite their apparent lack of rights (Boydon, 2003). Young people may be more adaptable than their elders to rapid social change and better able to take up new livelihood opportunities, sometimes reversing inter-generational flows of wealth and support (Vincent & Sorenson, 2001; Chatty & Hundt, 2001; Swaine, 2004). Such transformations may have important consequences for inter-generational relations. Supporting elders economically can enable young people to establish a role for themselves within a community and become adults (Hinton, 2000; Mann, 2004). Conversely, older people may feel threatened by inter-generational role reversals, which challenge social norms around relations of authority and respect between young people and their elders (Swaine, 2004; Kaiser, 2006).

This chapter describes the ways in which children and young people have sought strategies that enable them to obtain access to some of the things that would normally be regarded as "rights" for children, but which have been taken away through war and displacement. The authors then examine how these processes led to a renegotiation of inter-generational roles and relations, arguing that there may be costs attached in terms of negative consequences of very rapid social change.

Researching Youth: Methodological Approaches

Intensive fieldwork was conducted in the Buduburam Refugee Settlement over a four-month period (January–May 2005), largely by three experienced Ghanaian researchers, with short visits from United Kingdom (UK) researchers.[1] The goal was to generate refugees' own perspectives on social change. The definition of youth was left unspecified deliberately to elicit local interpretations and meanings. It emerged that youth is a contingent category and that the experience of conflict and becoming refugees has shaped social and generational categories.

A multi-method, qualitative approach was adopted in order to facilitate crosschecking and triangulation of data to increase reliability. Nineteen focus group discussions were held, twelve with groups of young people and seven with elders. Groups were composed of six to ten people and were in most cases homogeneous with respect to generation and gender. Thirty individual interviews were conducted: ten semi-structured interviews with young camp inhabitants, eight life history interviews with older Liberians, and twelve key informant interviews with representatives of camp-based organizations and local government. In addition, two Senior Secondary School students kept 24-hour photo-diaries, using disposable cameras, and one other kept a detailed daily diary for two months. The three Ghanaian researchers participated in daily life and took detailed field notes in the form of an ethnographic diary based on detailed observations (Geertz, 1973; Sanjek, 1990).

All interviews and focus groups were conducted in English and were fully transcribed and coded for topics (Miles & Huberman, 1994). Subsequent analysis used grounded theory: theory generated from the data rather than imposed (Glaser & Strauss, 1967). The coded data were searched for emergent patterns, using a series of validity checks (Miles & Huberman, 1994). Throughout the research process, regular meetings were held with a small consultative group of key stakeholders and camp residents. Additionally, two workshops were held for camp inhabitants, which enabled people to comment on, and make changes to, the findings and analysis.

This study was given ethical approval by the Durham University Ethics Advisory Committee. There are clearly serious ethical implications of conducting research with young people who have lived through conflict and displacement, in particular the possibility of re-evoking emotional and psychological trauma and falsely raising hopes and expectations. These concerns were discussed at the consultative group meetings before research commenced, and mitigating steps were taken.

Life in the Buduburam Settlement: The Struggle for Basic Needs and Rights

The conflict that led to Liberians fleeing to Ghana and other West African countries began in December 1989, although it had its roots in the last 150 years of Liberian history, since the founding of the country in 1821 as a colony for slaves freed from the United States. By the official end of Liberia's war in 1996, there had been some 200,000 casualties, approximately 750,000 refugees, as well as 1.4 million internally displaced persons (out of a pre-war population of 2.8 million).

When the first wave of refugees arrived in Ghana, a National Reception Committee was quickly constituted, made up of the Ghanaian Ministry of Mobilization and Social Welfare, along with several non-governmental organizations (NGOs). Accustomed to dealing with much smaller numbers of refugees, Ghana was unprepared to handle the great influx of Liberians and called upon the UNHCR for assistance. To accommodate the refugees, the Ghanaian government made land available at Buduburam in the Gomoa District, situated some 35 km west of Accra. The majority of Liberians were settled in Buduburam, with smaller numbers going to live in Accra and other towns, as well as at the much smaller Krisan camp in Senzulle, near the border with Côte d'Iviore (Dick 2002a, b).

At the request of the Ghanaian government, material assistance was provided under the UNHCR's administrative direction, in partnership with a variety of NGOs. Food rations were provided, and tents were distributed for shelter. The Ghana Red Cross set up a clinic, World Relief provided water, and other aid agencies participated in relief efforts. In the early 1990s, educational assistance was also provided. A Ghanaian NGO, the Christian Council, became the UNHCR's implementing partner responsible for supporting education within the camp. The Christian Council oversaw the development of primary schools that had been set up by the refugees themselves: building new classrooms, providing a small stipend for teachers, and providing basic materials. By 1991, there was a junior high school, and in 1996, Buduburam Secondary School, BuduSec, opened. In 1993, the International Rescue Committee (IRC) began vocational skills training, including construction, carpentry, sewing, soap-making, and community health. Also in 1993, the UNHCR initiated an agriculture and micro-credit program in an attempt to promote self-reliance (Dick, 2002b). The basic needs of the Liberian refugees arriving in Ghana were, thus, largely met until 1997 (Dick, 2002b).

In 1997, the UNHCR began withdrawing humanitarian support, as it was deemed safe to return to Liberia. By 2000, all UNHCR assistance had been withdrawn, as part of a regional policy (Dick, 2002a, b). However, as it became clearer that the situation in Liberia was far from stable, the UNHCR reintroduced limited support for "vulnerable groups," but were focusing largely on promoting community self-reliance rather than providing humanitarian assistance to individuals. By 2005, when this study was conducted, the focus had again shifted to repatriation. The population of Buduburam was now greater than ever: the UNHCR reported a total of over 41,000 Liberian refugees and asylum seekers residing at Buduburam (UNHCR Ghana, 2005). The gap left by the gradual removal of refugee status and UNHCR support had not been filled, since the residents of Buduburam were not Ghanaian citizens and, as such, had few rights and limited access to services. Many complained that they could not work formally outside the camp without a work permit, which was very difficult to obtain, and that this pushed people into insecure, informal sector work.

Since our fieldwork occurred, repatriation has accelerated. UNHCR withdrew from the camp in 2007, and refugee status has since been removed from those Liberians remaining in Ghana. However, the repatriation process has not gone smoothly, with substantial delays having been reported. Many Liberians have complained about the terms of repatriation, particularly the baggage restrictions (50 kg, clothes only), which are hard on those who have been residing in Ghana for many years (Swen, 2008). For those Liberians remaining in Buduburam, life has become increasingly difficult, and there have been several reports of violence and raids by the Ghanaian police (Chester, 2008).

Thus, Buduburam has had a rather checkered history with regard to the provision of basic needs and human rights. Without exception, our informants, both young and old, pointed to the day-to-day difficulties experienced by those living in Buduburam. The major problems identified by those under age 18 included: very limited educational and livelihood opportunities; high living costs (accommodation, education, healthcare, food, water, and sanitation); insufficient external support and loss of family members; risks associated with the need to engage in dangerous or illegal livelihood activities (prostitution, drug trafficking, armed robbery); perceived lack of control over their lives and future prospects.

These problems strongly reflect the failure of child rights legislation to penetrate the camp. For example, while the right of every child to education is enshrined in Article 28 of the CRC, most young Liberians to whom we spoke in

Buduburam reported that their education had been curtailed because they could not afford to pay for school fees and examination fees, while others talked about the lack of vocational training opportunities. Similarly, access to healthcare (CRC Article 24) is extremely difficult and, therefore, rather patchy for young people in Buduburam, with fees for consultations and prescribed drugs beyond the reach of many. There were many cases where mothers said they had not been able to afford hospital treatment for their children, and had needed to go around the camp begging for money in the case of serious illness. Even basic sanitation is beyond the reach of many, who cannot afford the (300 cedi) charge for using a Kumasi Ventilated Improved Pit (KVIP) latrine. Instead, many of the young people we interviewed reported defecating in plastic bags, which were then thrown on rubbish heaps, an option which also carried risks of being fined by the camp authorities.

The situation is particularly difficult for children separated from their families who, under Article 20 of the CRC, should be entitled to special protection and assistance. According to the Camp Welfare Council, the majority of young people living in Buduburam have experienced the death or disappearance of close family members, and many are living alone and unsupported. The majority of such children reported having had to cope and grow up alone. As one twenty-four-year-old man, who had come to Ghana alone fifteen years earlier, put it: "I'm a self-grown child." And, as we shall see, even those children who have family members in the camp cannot always rely on their support (material or emotional). Table 4.1 provides a summary of the discrepancies between the UNCRC ideal and the lived reality of young people living in Buduburam in the mid 2000s.

Table 4.1. Failure of Child Rights within Buduburam

Articles from the UNCRC (OHCHR, 1989)	Children's lived realities in Buduburam
Article 2: States Parties shall respect and ensure the rights set forth in the present Convention to each child within their jurisdiction without discrimination of any kind, irrespective of the child's . . . national, ethnic . . . or other status.	Liberian children living in Buduburam do not enjoy the same rights as Ghanaian children.
Article 6: States Parties recognize that every child has the inherent right to life.	Lack of adequate healthcare and nutrition endangers children's right to life.
Article 20: A child temporarily or permanently deprived of his or her family environment . . . shall be entitled to special protection and assistance provided by the State.	A high proportion of children in Buduburam are separated from their families and yet do not enjoy "special protection."
Article 22: A child who is seeking refugee status or who is considered a refugee in accordance with applicable international or domestic law and procedures shall . . . receive appropriate protection and humanitarian assistance in the enjoyment of applicable rights set forth in the present Convention.	Many children in Buduburam have "slipped through the net" of humanitarian assistance.

Continued on next page

Table 4.1—Continued

Articles from the UNCRC (OHCHR, 1989)	Children's lived realities in Buduburam
Article 24: States Parties recognize the right of the child to the enjoyment of the highest attainable standard of health and to facilities for the treatment of illness and rehabilitation of health. States Parties shall strive to ensure that no child is deprived of his or her right of access to such health care services.	The limited provision of health services in the camp and the high costs of seeking treatment restrict children's access to healthcare.
Article 26: States Parties shall recognize for every child the right to benefit from social security, including social insurance.	There is no "safety net" for children in Buduburam, forcing many into hazardous livelihood strategies.
Article 27: States Parties recognize the right of every child to a standard of living adequate for the child's physical, mental, spiritual, moral and social development.	Lack of basic needs is a key concern for children in Buduburam. These include: accommodation, nutrition, health, education and security.
Article 28: States Parties recognize the right of the child to education, and with a view to achieving this right progressively and on the basis of equal opportunity.	The lack of schools in Buduburam severely restricts access to education for most children.
Article 31: States Parties recognize the right of the child to rest and leisure, to engage in play and recreational activities.	Many children in Buduburam have very little leisure time, due to the pressing demands of securing a living.
Article 32: States Parties recognize the right of the child to be protected from economic exploitation and from performing any work that is likely to be hazardous or to interfere with the child's education, or to be harmful to the child's health or physical, mental, spiritual, moral or social development.	Many children in Buduburam are forced to engage in dangerous livelihood activities in order to meet basic subsistence needs. These activities include: armed robbery, drug trafficking, commercial sex work, as well as carrying very heavy loads.
Article 33: States Parties shall take all appropriate measures, including legislative, administrative, social and educational measures, to protect children from the illicit use of narcotic drugs and psychotropic substances as defined in the relevant international treaties, and to prevent the use of children in the illicit production and trafficking of such substances.	Drug trafficking is an important source of livelihood for children in Buduburam.
Article 34: States Parties undertake to protect the child from all forms of sexual exploitation and sexual abuse . . . [including] [t]he exploitative use of children in prostitution.	Prostitution is an important source of livelihood for children in Buduburam.
Article 39: States Parties shall take all appropriate measures to promote physical and psychological recovery and social reintegration of a child victim of: any form of neglect, exploitation, or abuse; torture or any other form of cruel, inhuman or degrading treatment or punishment; or armed conflicts. Such recovery and reintegration shall take place in an environment which fosters the health, self-respect and dignity of the child.	Recovery and re-integration is restricted by lack of access to basic needs, as well as a failure on the part of UNHCR and the Ghanaian government to create sufficient opportunities for long-term refugee children to integrate in Ghanaian society.

Because of their marginal status (living temporarily in Ghana, but not being Ghanaian citizens), young refugees appeared to have "slipped through the net" in terms of child rights legislation. Indeed, their status in Ghana has been highly ambiguous. The 1992 Constitution of Ghana (amended 1996) extended to "every person in Ghana" its fundamental individual rights, including life, dignity, and protection from torture and slavery, freedom of movement, and the right to work. It did, however, allow the government to pass laws restricting the rights to own property and free movement for foreigners and allowed limitation of the right to work for national security reasons (USCRI, 2008). Ghana's Second State Report to the UN in relation to the UNCRC (UNCRC, 2005) stated that refugee children in Ghana are entitled to rights in accordance with UN protocol and Ghana Refugee Law (1992). In particular, the report asserts that special protection is given to refugee children in relation to the provision of shelter, food, counseling, and emotional support, and Ghana's Department of Social Welfare sent social workers to major refugee camps, including Buduburam. However, the UNCRC's (2006) response to Ghana's report contains a recommendation that Ghana should "increase its efforts to meet the specific protection needs of refugee children in the refugee settlements," in relation particularly to sexual and gender-based violence and unaccompanied refugee children (UNCRC, 2006:13).

This effective denial of basic rights to children and youth underpins many of the tensions and ambiguities in inter-generational relations that are described below. Children and young people have been obliged to adopt a range of strategies to secure access to those things that would normally be regarded as "rights." Although many have been successful in their endeavors, the successes came at a cost in terms of rapid, and often unwanted, social changes.

Coping Strategies Adopted by Children and Young People: Livelihoods

Resilience and coping were prominent themes in the narratives of children and young people in Buduburam. Examples of this included informal peer support to make up for loss of family and helping in the process of rehabilitation (psychological recovery and social reintegration) following the conflict and flight from Liberia (UNCRC Articles 20, 22, 39), and making contacts abroad to provide a source of economic security (Article 26). In this chapter, we focus particularly on the ways in which children and young people have sought to cope with the struggle to meet basic needs necessary to have an adequate standard of living (Article 27).

Finding work was absolutely crucial for almost all young people living in the camp (Porter, Hampshire, Kyei, Adjaloo, Rapoo, & Kilpatrick, 2008). Many were living on their own, with no assistance whatsoever, like the young girl we interviewed whose sister had left her alone in the camp when she was age fourteen. In other cases, young people had to work to support their parents:

> My mother, she begged people for food and I was ashamed so I decided to work to bring money in (girl, age 19).

> When I lost my mother, I started being adult because my father was having to support three children. I was 15 (girl, age 17).

As noted above, making a living proved very difficult for many children in Buduburam. Interruptions to, and early curtailment of, education (academic and skills training) were widespread, due primarily to a lack of funds and age limits for scholarships. Lack of educational and training opportunities was perceived to be a serious barrier to getting skilled work for young people. However, even those who had skills thought their routes to formal sector employment were blocked by the difficulties in obtaining work permits and, in some cases, by a feeling that their Liberian nationality would disqualify them from skilled work. One specific example was cited by a man who heard a few boys arguing:

> I advised [one of the boys] . . . to go to computer school. The boy said, 'I'm in Ghana so I can't do a job with skills' (man, late 20s).

Most young people (and older people), therefore, sought informal sector work within Buduburam. Some managed to earn income by growing crops for sale (such as potato green, a product much favored by Liberians) on Ghanaian-owned land near the camp, although lack of land seriously limited opportunities for earning a living through farming. Other areas of work ranged from running small after-school study classes for children, to renting bicycles (men), carpentry and masonry work (men), plaiting hair (girls), retailing goods (e.g., soft drinks, enamelware) for others or on their own account in the camp, or simply selling well water or washing clothes. Some of the hardest physical jobs included working as porters and wheelbarrow pushers on construction sites, carrying ice blocks and brick making: "I must push before I eat" (girl, age 19).

Many school children worked selling things after school. Even very young children helped their parents by pushing heavy wheelbarrows at the camp market and at construction sites to earn money for the family. The camp market was another potential area for earning income, although the opportunities for making a living through trade were inevitably limited, given the numbers of would-be traders involved and the very low average income (and thus purchasing power) of camp inhabitants. The main regional market at Kasoa was inaccessible to most camp inhabitants as traders, reportedly due to disputes with the Kasoa market association.

Access to livelihood opportunities varied substantially by age (as well as gender). Many older women in the camp made small sums by trading charcoal, water, and other basic items. The ability to speak some Twi (the *lingua franca* in this part of Ghana) was probably an important factor enabling most to do so. By contrast, most young people were unable to speak Twi and had little or no experience of trading. Some of those whose education had been disrupted or curtailed thought that older people had better access to skilled jobs than they did, having had the opportunity of completing their education before the war.

Other livelihood opportunities, however, were widely seen to be more accessible to young people, particularly those who depend on physical strength. Many young men and women worked as porters, pushing trucks, making bricks, etc. Remittances from family members abroad—particularly in the United States—were a very important source of financial support for many camp inhabitants. Young people were often pivotal in maintaining links with family abroad, through mobile phones and the Internet. Many young people spent a lot of time in the many Internet cafés in the camp, soliciting new sponsors from abroad and keeping in contact with existing ones. However, such reliance was risky and liable to break down:

> I have seven brothers and sisters in America, but when I call, they don't respond. They even tell me on the phone they don't know me. So I decided not to call them again and am making it alone in Ghana (woman, age 40).

Other livelihood strategies adopted by young people involved harmful and illegal activities, notably: prostitution, selling drugs, robbery (including armed robbery), illegal electrical connections, and gambling. "I call this Camp Sodom and Gomorrah," said a middle-aged woman. For many young girls, the only solution in the face of the pressures on them to support parents (and possibly children, too) seemed to be sex work:

> Now 16-year-old girls are supporting their parents, and parents don't want to know where they get the money because they use it. It was different before the war (woman, age 31).

Sex work ranged from accepting "gifts" from "boyfriends" to various other forms of prostitution. In some cases, girls were involved in prostitution with the agreement/acceptance of their partners and families because of the necessity to buy food. One volunteer with the HIV/AIDS outreach program recounted the story of how he encountered a woman who would not let them meet with her girls, "because we may be preventing them from going for money for her through prostitution."

Impact of Young People's Coping Strategies: Changes in Inter-generational Roles and Relationships

As well as the direct harm that may be caused by young people engaging in risky and illegal livelihood strategies such as those outlined above, there have been some apparently negative social impacts of young people's adoption of certain economic survival strategies. Here, we explore one of these: impacts on inter-generational roles and relations.

There was a strong consensus in the camp (across generations and ethnic groups) that conflict and exile resulted in major changes in inter-generational relations and often an increase in inter-generational conflict. One of the most widely expressed concerns, both of young people and elders, was the inability of parents, and the older generation more widely, to provide materially for their children and the impacts of this on social authority. As noted above, many of the livelihood opportunities on the camp were seen to be more accessible for young people than for elders, including sex work, heavy manual labor, violent crime, and soliciting remittances through information/communication technologies. There were many accounts of inter-generational role reversals within the household, in which children were now providing for parents, rather than the other way around, with elders becoming increasingly dependent on youth incomes for their own survival:

> Now a 50-year-old man may be depending on a 20-year-old boy because he gets remittances from the USA (young man).

> Back home, we didn't have the system of young people working—the parents were responsible for their upkeep, but here you can't provide for them (elderly man).

It was the widespread view of camp inhabitants, both young and old, that the apparent economic role reversals have led to a breakdown of the usual relationships of authority and respect between young and old. "In the camp, the young people are not respecting older people. If you call a young person to offer some advice, they will insult you—they will shout, 'Is it your concern?'" explained an old woman—a view echoed widely in interviews and focus groups. The breakdown in respect and authority was generally blamed on parents' inability to support their children materially. As one old woman explained:

> As conditions deteriorated and started getting harder . . . things changed, and the respect got lost because you can't feed your children. The children go out for food themselves. The respect has been eroded. You can't even reprimand someone's child.

Experience of the conflict was also seen to have contributed to changes in inter-generational relations: "During the war, children had guns, so they had power over older people," explained one elderly man.

The increased control that children and young people had over household resource decisions, as a result of becoming the major breadwinners, led to a process of "infantilization" of elders. Many elders were, in their own terms, losing their adult status through becoming obliged to depend on their children for support:

> My daughter from London sends me money and gives me instructions as to what to use the money for. She is making decisions for me.

> This is exactly what is happening. They decide what the money should be used for. My daughter sends $50 and dictates for us how long the money should last, and what we should eat and buy (focus group of elderly women).

Many believed that old age was no longer valued, while youth had become prized. Addressing someone as an old woman or man used to be seen as a mark of respect; now some saw it as an insult, as one older woman explained:

> Some old women now refuse to be called old women. You want to give them respect by calling them old woman, but they are angry.

Changes in inter-generational relations were not without ambiguity. As we have argued elsewhere (Hampshire, Porter, Kilpatrick, Kyei, Adjaloo, & Rapoo, 2008), it would be wrong to portray all inter-generational relations in Buduburam as fraught with difficulty and mutual hostility. Many young people expressed the importance of advice and emotional support provided by elders in their families and the wider community. "The old people have experience. They can counsel you and give you the encouragement to continue in life" (young woman in a focus group). In turn, many elders understand and are extremely sympathetic for the plight of young people in Buduburam: "If I were a younger person in this camp where my parents don't support me financially . . . it would be difficult. It is more difficult to be a youth now in this camp [than it was for us when we were young]" (older woman). Nonetheless, most people interviewed, both young and old, regretted the perceived negative changes in inter-generational relations.

Summary

Young people in Buduburam are "slipping through the net" of child rights. As Liberian nationals in exile in Ghana, there is no clear legislative framework to ensure the operation of a realistic and realizable child rights framework. As such, children and young people (and, indeed, all the refugees) have been subject to the vagaries of changing UNHCR policy.

As we have seen, young long-term refugees have demonstrated a strong degree of resilience and resourcefulness, overcoming the challenges they face in the absence of many rights that would, in "normal" circumstances, be taken for granted. Many have taken up the mantle in terms of becoming the major breadwinners within their families, resorting to a range of livelihood strategies, often at some risk to themselves.

It is, however, important to recognize that there is sometimes a price to be paid for this in terms of social consequences, many of which are felt to be negative by the refugees themselves. Although we would not argue that changes in inter-generational relations have come about purely as a result of the conflict and forced migration, it is likely that the experience of conflict, exile, and concomitant economic hardship has accelerated processes of social change (Kaiser, 2006). Thus, particularly in protracted refugee situations, more thought needs to be given, not just to supporting young refugees' struggle for self-reliance, but to helping people cope with the wider consequences of very rapid, and often unwanted, social change.

Looking Outward: Implications for Policy and Practice

We have shown that children in Buduburam have suffered because of the failure of child rights to penetrate the camp adequately. There is a huge gulf between the rights that children might expect under the UNCRC and the lived reality in Buduburam, where the majority of children and young people have woefully poor access to healthcare, shelter, education, sanitation, and livelihoods, and where there is little or no special protection for those separated from their families. We argue strongly that, in the case of Buduburam, the UNHCR's policy of promoting self-reliance through a withdrawal of humanitarian assistance has not been a success. Indeed, by effectively denying basic rights and needs to large sectors of the population in Buduburam (including children and their parents), it has been impossible for many to work toward self-reliance in ways that do not carry serious dangers and other costs to well-being. Instead, the promotion of self-reliance needs to run alongside humanitarian assistance and needs to take place within a rights-based framework in which the upholding of child rights (as well as human rights more broadly) is central. The focus needs to be not just on what happens within the camp, but on facilitating long-term refugees to integrate into Ghanaian society, particularly in terms of education and livelihoods.

However, in making these suggestions, it is important not to ignore the wider context in Ghana. Gomoa District, in which Buduburam is located, is one of the poorest areas of Ghana. Elsewhere (Porter et al., 2008), we have discussed the already problematic relations between camp inhabitants and local Ghanaians, many of whom have resented the assistance given to Liberians when they were also struggling with poverty. As demonstrated by Porter & Abane (Ame, Agbényiga, & Apt, 2010), many local Ghanaian children also suffer from lack of basic rights, including access to education, health facilities, and secure livelihoods. In other words, it is important to see "child rights" as situated within the economic and social realities that prevail in countries like Ghana.

There is no easy solution, since widespread poverty and livelihood insecurity underlie much of the failure of child rights both within Buduburam and in the surrounding Gomoa District. Part of the solution might, therefore, lie simply in people from within and outside the camp coming together to address common concerns. One positive outcome of our research was a partial bridging and addressing of misunderstandings between local Gomoans and Liberians. For example, because it is culturally very important for Liberians to dress well and look good, many Buduburam inhabitants prioritized purchasing new clothes over eating. Seeing well-dressed Liberians gave local Ghanaians the impression that they were wealthier than they were, leading to resentment. Conversely, many Liberians saw local Ghanaians as unwelcoming (for example, at Kasoa market), without fully appreciating the livelihood difficulties they were experiencing. Many such misunderstandings were at least partially corrected through a coming together of Ghanaian researchers, local inhabitants, and Liberian refugees in our project research and associated consultative group meetings.

What lessons can be learned for other situations in which long-term refugee children settle in a country in which local people are also experiencing hardships that impinge on child rights? We offer the following tentative suggestions:

- bring the child rights agenda to the center of UNHCR policy and practice;
- establish a clear framework among the UNHCR, the national government, and other relevant agencies, in which it is clear who has responsibility for upholding the rights of child refugees;
- establish dialogue, at an early stage, between refugees and host communities, in order to pre-empt misunderstandings and to encourage an integrated approach to child rights; and
- build on and support children's strengths and capabilities, in addressing refugee children's rights, but provide a "safety net" for children who are not able to secure their rights without external assistance.

Notes

1. This study was funded by the Nuffield Foundation. We thank Penny Nagbe, Morris Kormazu, and Kester Miller, our camp-based research assistants, for their invaluable contribution to the project. We also wish to acknowledge the enormous assistance given by the Liberia Welfare Council, the Camp Commandant, CBOs and NGOs, which are based or work in the camp, and the very many other individuals within the camp who made this study possible.

References

Boyden, J. (2003). Children under fire: Challenging assumptions about children's resilience. *Youth, Education and Environments* 13 (1).

Chatty, D., and G. Hundt. (2001). *Lessons learned report: Children and adolescents in Palestinian households: Living with the effects of prolonged conflict and forced migration.* Refugee Studies Centre, Oxford University.

Chester, P. (2008). Buduburam Refugee Concerns International calls for action to protect the human rights of refugees in Ghana. *New Liberian.* Retrieved March 26, 2009, from http://newliberian.com/?p=329#respond.

Dick, S. (2002a). Liberians in Ghana: Living without humanitarian assistance. *New Issues in Refugees Research, Working Paper No. 57.*

——— (2002b). *Responding to protracted refugee situations: A case study of Liberian refugees in Ghana.* Geneva: UNHCR Evaluation and Policy Analysis Unit.

Geertz, C. (1973). *The Interpretation of Cultures.* New York: Basic Books.

Glasser, B. G., and A. L. Strauss. (1967). *The Discovery of Grounded Theory: Strategies for Qualitative Research.* New York: Aldine.

Hampshire, K. R., G. Porter, K. Kilpatrick, P. Kyei, M. Adjaloo, and G. Rapoo. (2008). Liminal spaces: Changing inter-generational relations among long-term Liberian refugees in Ghana. *Human Organisation* 67 (1), 25–36.

Hinton, R. (2000). Seen but not heard: Refugee children and models for intervention. In C. Panter-Brick and M. Smith (eds.). *Abandoned Children.* Cambridge: CUP.

Kaiser, T. (2006). Songs, discos and dancing in Kiryandongo, Uganda. *Journal of Ethnic and Migration Studies* 32 (2), 183–202.

Mann, G. (2004). Separated children: Care and support in context. In J. Boyden and J. de Berry (eds.). *Children and Youth on the Front Line.* Oxford: Berghahn.

Miles, M. B., and A. M. Huberman. (1994). *Qualitative Data Analysis.* Newbury Park, CA: Sage.

Office of the High Commissioner for Human Rights (OHCHR). (1989). Convention on the Rights of the Child. Retrieved March 26, 2009, from http://www2.ohchr.org/english/law/crc.htm.

Porter, G., A. Abane, K. Blaufuss, and F. O. Acheampong. (2010). Children's rights, mobility, and transport in Ghana: Access to education and health services. In R. K. Ame, D. L. Agbényiga, and N. A. Apt (eds.). *Children's Rights in Ghana: Reality or Rhetoric?* Lanham, MD: Lexington Books.

Porter, G., K. Hampshire, P. Kyei, M. Adjaloo, G. Rapoo, and K. Kilpatrick. (2008). Linkages between livelihood opportunities and refugee-host relations: Learning from the experiences of Liberian camp-based refugees in Ghana. *Journal of Refugee Studies* 21, 230–252.

Sanjek, R. (ed.). (1990). *Fieldnotes: The Makings of Anthropology.* Ithaca: Cornell University Press.

Swaine, A., with T. Feeney. (2004). A neglected perspective: Adolescent girls' experiences of the Kosovo conflict of 1999. In J. Boyden and J. de Berry (eds.). *Children and Youth on the Front Line.* Oxford: Berghahn.

Swen, J. (2008). Repatriation process frustrates Liberian refugees in Ghana. Retrieved March 26, 2009, from http://newliberian.com/?p=446.

United Nations Commission on the Rights of the Child (UNCRC). (2005). *Second Periodic Reports of State Parties: Ghana.* Retrieved September 14, 2009, from http://www.unhchr.ch/tbs/doc.nsf/898586b1dc7b4043c1256a450044f331/cb2ade967 9679 dccc1257077005462b1/$FILE/G0542738.pdf.

———. (2006). *Consideration of reports submitted by state parties under Article 44 of the Convention: Concluding observations: Ghana.* Retrieved September 14, 2009, from http://www.unhchr.ch/tbs/doc.nsf/898586b1dc7b4043c1256a450044f331/ba9ccae3e901b5f4c125716200435cea/$FILE/G0640957.pdf.

United Nations High Commission for Refugees (UNHCR). (2000). *UNHCR policy on older refugees: Older refugees a resource for the community.* Geneva: Health and Community Development Section, UNHCR.

United Nations High Commission for Refugees (UNHCR) Ghana. (2005). Statistical report of asylum seekers and refugees in Ghana, January 1, 2005.

United States Committee for Refugees and Immigrants (USCRI). (2008). *World Refugee Survey: Ghana.* Retrieved March 26, 2009, from http://www.refugees.org/countryreports.aspx?id=2141.

Vincent, M., and B. R. Sorensen (eds.). (2001). *Caught Between Borders: Response Strategies of the Internally Displaced.* London: Pluto Press.

Part II
Children in Dangerous Circumstances: Exploitation and Abuse

Chapter 5
Corporal Punishment in Ghana
By Sylvester Kyei-Gyamfi

Violence takes place when a person applies force to another person or uses position of power to purposely cause injury to someone else. It includes threats of violence and acts that have the potential to cause harm as well as those threats and actions that actually do. The harm involved can be to a person's mind or to his or her general health and well-being as well as to his or her body. Violence also includes deliberate harm people do to themselves as in the case of suicide. Children are the most susceptible to violence because they have no way to protect themselves, and it is often the people who are entrusted with the care of the children who perpetrate the violence. Violence against children occurs almost everywhere around the world, but the prevailing socio-cultural, economic, and political factors determine the nature of the violence children face (UN, 2006).

In 2001, the United Nations (UN) General Assembly requested that the Secretary General conduct an in-depth study on violence against children. The purpose of the study was to present strategies aimed at effectively preventing and combating all forms of violence against children (VAC) around the world. It identified various types of violence perpetrated on children throughout the world and categorized them into five settings: home and family, schools and educational settings, care and justice systems, work settings, and in the community. Children in Ghana also face violence in the five settings categorized in the UN report. Children are subjected to all kinds of abuses in the home, at school and in other settings responsible for childcare. Between 2002 and 2006, the Domestic Violence and Victim Support Unit (DOVVSU) of the Police Service reported 12,212 assault cases against children (MOWAC, 2007). Even though there is not much data on the actual number of abuses that occur in care institutions, Ghanaian media has reported varying examples of abuse perpetrated against children in children's homes, shelters, and orphanages in the country (MOWAC, 2008).

Corporal or physical punishment is the use of physical force intended to cause some degree of pain or discomfort for discipline, correction, control, changing behavior, or in the belief of educating/bringing up the child (Save the Children, 2003). It may occur anywhere and typically takes the form of striking through specific methods such as whipping, beating, paddling, and flogging. Such treatment of anyone is harmful, abusive, and an infringement on fundamental human rights. This statement is even truer when dealing with children; it has negative effects on children's education, health, and social welfare. Indeed, it has no positive value on the upbringing and development of children (Kyei-Gyamfi, 2008).

In 1979, Sweden became the first country to ban all corporal punishment of children, setting a positive example for other countries to follow. Since then, significant strides have been made by other countries such as Austria, Bulgaria, Croatia, Cyprus, Denmark, Finland, Germany, Greece, Hungary, Israel, Iceland, Italy, Latvia, Norway, Romania, Ukraine, and Netherlands (EPOCH–USA, 2007a) to also ban the phenomenon. To date, only twenty-three countries have declared a total ban on corporal punishment in all settings (Plan, 2008).

Although the Government of Ghana has made important strides to protect children from corporal punishment, the phenomenon is still applied. Media reports have shown that children are traumatized, maimed, beaten, and even killed as a result of harsh punishment meted out to them by their parents, siblings, teachers, and other persons in charge of their care and protection. Significantly, these reports indicate that corporal punishment is still in practice, almost twenty years after Ghana's ratification of the United Nations Convention on the Rights of the Child (CRC).

In some countries, laws have been enacted regarding the kinds of discipline that are considered excessive or abusive and how they are to be administered. Ghana's compliance with the CRC led to the passage of the Children's Act 1998 (Act 560), which sets the tone for the protection of children from unreasonable punishment. Act 560 was the most visible outcome of the CRC, which brought together laws on children previously scattered within Ghanaian statute books (UNICEF, 2000).

This chapter examines the use of corporal punishment on children in Ghana. It also highlights efforts made to address corporal punishment, in light of Ghana's ratification of the CRC. Specifically, the chapter:

- examines the nature of corporal punishment as applied in the home and school settings;
- ascertains children's and adult's perceptions of corporal punishment;
- identifies steps undertaken by government and other civil society groups to address issues relating to the use of corporal punishment in Ghana; and

- suggests ways in which corporal punishment could be minimized or eliminated completely.

Three methods were employed to gather information for this chapter: document review, in-depth interviews, and focus group discussions. Literature and information from official sources such as government ministries, departments, and agencies (MDAs), international organizations and non-governmental organizations (NGOs) were used for the compilation of the chapter. Secondary material on the Internet was also retrieved to serve as additional source of documentary information.

The interview method was also utilized to gather relevant information for the chapter. Interview sessions were held with key officials of the following agencies:

- Ghana Education Service (GES);
- Department of Social Welfare (DSW);
- Domestic Violence and Victim Support Unit (DOVVSU) of the Police; and
- Department of Children (DOC) of the Ministry of Women and Children's Affairs (MOWAC).

All officials contacted answered specific questions about their roles in the application and regulation of corporal punishment in the home and within educational institutions.

Community interviews and focus group discussions were also held to gather firsthand information as input for the chapter. Community members interviewed included both adults and children from selected households in the Ashanti, Western, Central, Northern, and the Volta regions. A group of teachers was also interviewed and asked to express their opinions on corporal punishment.

It is very common for children to be subjected on a daily basis to different types of physical beatings for various wrongdoings. Significantly, this practice seems to have become a norm that is accepted by the majority of Ghanaians, both children and adults. Indeed, corporal punishment has been accepted to the point that parents who fail to apply it to their recalcitrant children are seen to be too soft in their parenting methods. In effect, punishing a child is generally seen as a way to correct and instill discipline into wayward children (Kyei-Gyamfi, 2008).

In Ghana, children are caned, slapped, hit, flogged, or subjected to other forms of physical punishment by biological parents, family members, educational authorities, siblings, peers, and other adults who are generally close to them. Subjecting children to any form of corporal punishment may be a deliberate act for corrective purposes or a reactive act of an angry parent or teacher venting his or her anger on a child for a wrongdoing. In whatever form it is administered, corporal punishment breaches the tenets of the CRC, which Ghana is signatory to. Incidentally, even though the act is in violation of universal human principles, Ghanaian social and legal systems accept it.

The use of corporal punishment by educational authorities and family members has generated controversial public debate in Ghana. Many Ghanaians—young and old—believe that when children do wrong, they ought to be corrected. What has led to this debate is the appropriateness of the mode of correction to be applied. The debate is usually split along two standpoints: one side arguing that corporal punishment should be banned and an alternative corrective method put in its place, while the other emphasizes that the practice be maintained but controlled in its application. The diversity in public opinion indicates that an exact and definite position has not been taken on the phenomenon in society, and this clearly indicates that a lot more work needs to be done on the issue of corporal punishment, especially since Ghana has ratified the CRC. When a government ratifies a convention, it is bound by international law to create the necessary conditions to ensure realization of the rights spelled out in that convention. Preventing children from violence and abuse is a critical area covered by the CRC, and twenty years after ratifying the CRC, Ghana has yet to create the necessary environment that protects children from the application of corporal punishment.

Corporal Punishment in the Home and School

Corporal punishment is used in many households in Ghana, and there is no law that bans its use. At home, parents, guardians, siblings, and other members of households are free to punish children when they misconduct themselves without being questioned. At school, the use of corporal punishment is limited by regulations in the Ghana Education Code of Discipline for second cycle schools.

Home

Corporal punishment of children is socially acceptable in many Ghanaian homes, and caning remains the most common form of punishing children in the home. According to the 2006 Multiple Indicator Cluster Survey (MICS) in Ghana, 89 percent of children ages two–fourteen years were subjected to at least one form of psychological or physical punishment by their mothers, caretakers, or other household members (GSS/UNICEF/MOH, 2006). In another field study of children ages six–seventeen conducted by the Department of Children (DOC) and the Children and Youth in Broadcasting (CURIOUS MINDS),[1] 81 percent of children indicated that they are punished when they do something wrong (DOC/CURIOUS MINDS, 2008). The findings of these two studies indicate that punishing children for wrongdoing is very common in Ghana.

Children are punished when they are considered to have committed acts that require disciplinary action as a result. In an interview, an elderly man in Kumasi indicated, "No elderly person in his right mind would beat a child when he or she has not done anything wrong. We punish our children to instill discipline in them."

Although this opinion is shared by many Ghanaians, there is no denying that children are subjected to differing forms of corporal punishment at home. The MICS study showed that 43 percent of mothers or caretakers believe that children should be physically punished to correct them (GSS/UNICEF/MOH, 2006). This suggests a general acceptance that children have to be beaten in order to correct them, and this is in clear violation of the CRC, which Ghana has ratified and agreed to its tenets of protecting children from abuse and all forms of degrading treatments.

At the household level, corporal punishment can be administered by any elder member of the family. However, if the act committed by the child is considered too severe, an elderly person who the child respects or fears most carries out the punishment. The DOC/CURIOUS MINDS study on corporal punishment showed that more women (47 percent) than men (31 percent) carry out corporal punishment at home (Figure 5.1).

Figure 5.1. Who Usually Carries Out Corrective Measure at Home

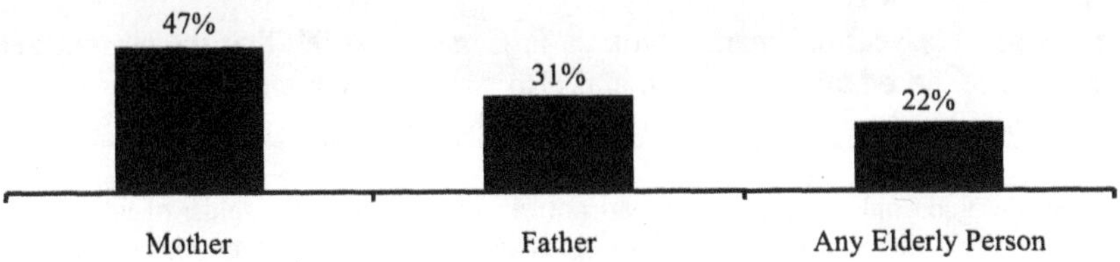

The study findings reflect the caregiving roles played by women in the early childhood development of children. As more women than men spend time with children, there is a higher likelihood that incidents of children's misdeeds will occur in the presence of women than men. It is important to note, however, that women caregivers only punish children for trivial misdeeds, while grievous ones are punished by men. It is a common perception in Ghana that when a child does something wrong, the child is corrected at the very moment of wrongdoing. Punishment is only postponed when the child has done something considered bad enough that a father, uncle, or any other male relative is called in to administer the corrective measure.[2]

Some of the offenses for which a child would be severely punished at home include stealing, engaging in pre-marital sex, insulting an elderly person, being disobedient, or telling lies (DOC/CURIOUS MINDS, 2008). Even though children are punished for various reasons, the nature of the punishment varies. The more grievous a misdeed, the more corporal its mode of correction becomes. For instance, among some Akans,[3] girls who engage in premarital sex are punished by females, usually grandmothers. The most popular punishment, though very crude, is the insertion of ground ginger mixed with pepper into the vagina of the girl who has done the wrong thing. This method is occasionally applied to boys, but in their case, insertion is done in the anus. While this corrective method may also be performed for medicinal purposes, whenever it is applied as punishment, hot pepper is added to increase pain. As Ghana is becoming more and more urbanized, this mode of correction is gradually fading out, though evidence abounds that it is still practiced in some homes.

After ratifying the CRC, Ghana positioned itself as a country committed to ensuring the realization of children's rights. Almost two decades later, many adults in Ghana still believe that children should be punished when they get out of line, and for them, punishing children severely is the best way of "teaching them a good lesson," as put by a seventy-year-old woman in Apremdo.[4] Even though there is not much evidence, many people seem to believe there is moral decadence in Ghana because parents do not punish their children well enough. Interactions with some adult community members in Akwadum,[5] Cape Coast,[6] and Ho[7] showed adults have varying opinions regarding child correction. In the Akwadum community, a forty one-year-old carpenter who felt that children of the present generation do not respect because they are not corrected by their parents, expressed, "Children of today do not respect because their parents do not straighten them when they go wrong. They are pampered and so have no respect for authority."

A seventy-year-old market woman in Cape Coast felt that the current generation of children talks too much and also strives to share the same space with adults. She expressed her disappointment in the following words:

> In the good old days, a child could not raise his voice in the midst of adults. My own children ask too many questions and talk even when they are not supposed to express an opinion.

Some adults have sufficient knowledge of children's rights but would not abide by them because they find it an alien concept. In Ho, a retired head teacher expressed:

> I am a Presbyterian, and as a Presbyterian I believe in strong ethics. In the past, children of Presbyterians were brought up on the church's principles, and these were passed on to many generations. Something is not right with child upbringing lately. I believe this so-called Children's Rights is an alien concept, which seems to have taken over the best of all our culture and religion. It is time we go back to the past.

The sentiments expressed in the community interactions indicate that some adults believe that punishment is good for children and do not see it as abuse. Indeed, many adults in Ghana hold the view that they were beaten or psychologically punished as children and seem to think that since it was for their own good, in the same way it should be good for their own children. There are some parents in Ghana who do not know of any other disciplinary measures than the application of corporal punishment.[8] For some parents, their being law abiding, respectful, virtuous, and morally upright in their adult life is because they were brought up by their parents in an atmosphere of beatings, punishment, and fear. Though this assertion may be just a perception, many believe in it. It is also important to note that even though the present can be measured, the past cannot. In this way, there will always be a clash of opinions between adults and young people because the adults feel that child rearing was best in their time.

The adults' perceptions and opinions about the effectiveness of corporal punishment is linked to old Ghanaian traditions and customs. In the past, most Ghanaians lived in small communities, shared common value systems, religious beliefs, and sets of practices to express these values and beliefs. A child in the community belonged to every member of the community, so when a child did something wrong, it was in the community's best interest to correct that child. As a result of close interaction through community living, everyone was another's keeper. The community kept a watchful eye on the behavior of young people, thereby reducing the number of deviant behaviors among children. Today, Ghanaian social norms, practices, and structures have revolutionized, transforming from small mechanical societies into organically structured societies with contemporary features. Many people have moved from their communities of origin to settle in urban areas and have changed lifestyles in the process. There seems to be a clash between tradition and modernity, and the clash has had a major effect on the upbringing of children by their parents. Adults with changed lifestyles inculcate modern ideals into the upbringing of their children, and these are opposed by adults with conservative mentalities.

Even though most children accept the cane as the most commonly used corrective method in Ghanaian homes and educational institutions, the majority of them, irrespective of age, would prefer their parents to advise them at the first instance and apply the cane when committing the same offense a second time or a more severe offense (GNCC, 2004). According to the Ghana National Commission on Children (GNCC) study findings in 2004, which sampled the opinions of 4,507 boys and girls ages eight–seventeen in forty of the 110 districts[9] in Ghana, about 90 percent of the children felt that the caning method was the most frequent disciplinary measure used at school. Other methods mentioned included performance of chores on school grounds, physical drills, and carrying of stones. The children expressed their preference for the cane, which they felt was effective because of the lasting effect of pain. The study also showed that for children older than age thirteen, counseling was thought to be the most appropriate corrective method.

Table 5.1. Types of Corrective Measures Used on Children in School and Home

Home	School
Caning and whipping	Caning and whipping
Denial of food and freedoms	Verbal abuse
Verbal abuse	Physical abuse (slapping, beating, pulling of ear)
Physical abuse (slapping, beating, pulling of ear)	Denial of freedoms to participate in games and leisure activities
Carrying loads of heavy objects	Carrying loads of heavy objects
Kneeling down	Kneeling down, standing for long hours
Assigned duties/chores to perform (washing of utensils, sweeping, fetching water, etc.)	Assigned duties/chores to perform (weeding, sweeping, digging, fetching water, etc.)
Pep talk	Pep talk
Putting pepper/ginger in eyes and other private parts	Suspension and dismissal from school
	Writing lines, copying notes on chalkboard

Source: DOC/CURIOUS MINDS Fieldwork, October–November 2008

Almost a decade after the GNCC national survey, the perception of most Ghanaian children on corporal punishment had not changed. Many children still perceived the cane as the main corrective measure at both the home and in school as indicated in Table 5.2.

Table 5.2. Most Appropriate Way to Correct a Child at Home and School According to Children

Response	Percent	
	Home	School
No response	4.2	25.9
Advice/counsel	39.8	22.7
Left alone	1.6	2.0
Pulling of ear	1.2	1.9
Kneeling down	3.4	4.7
Caning	44.5	35.6
Weeding	.3	1.8
Fetching water	.2	.6
Sweeping	.4	.9
Picking/dumping rubbish		1.1
Shout at		.1
Running around the compound	.1	.2
Talked to	3.5	2.0
Scrubbing	.1	.5
Don't know	.6	.1
Total	100.0	100.0

Source: DOC/CURIOUS MINDS Fieldwork, October–November 2008

School

In Ghana, school officials routinely use corporal punishment (refer to Table 5.1) to maintain classroom discipline and punish children for poor academic performance or stepping out of line with school regulations.

The Ghana Education Code of Discipline for second cycle schools provides for corporal punishment in very rare cases but on the condition that a head teacher of the school is the person to give authorization or the one to administer the punishment. The *Head Teacher's Handbook* (GES, 1994:260–261), outlines certain offenses that justify corporal punishment after an initial strong warning. These offenses include: fighting, quarrelling, stealing, squandering of school fees, using drugs, drinking alcohol, smoking, flouting authority, assaulting colleagues, and assaulting staff, among other offenses.

The acceptable rule for using the cane in educational institutions is that caning should be administered by the head of the school in his or her office; the act should not exceed four strokes at the basic education level; the stroke should be recorded in the logbook and put under lock and key; and at the secondary level, the strokes should not exceed six. In spite of this regulation, the use of the cane in schools is very common, even though there is evidence that the practice has diminished in urban schools. The use of the cane is also common in other training institutions such as apprenticeships and vocational training settings. As indicated in Table 5.1, other types of corrective methods used in Ghanaian schools include: physical abuse (slapping, beating, pulling of the ear); denial of freedom to participate in games and leisure activities; carrying loads of heavy objects; kneeling down; standing for long hours; assigning duties such as weeding, sweeping, digging, and fetching water; suspension and dismissal from school; writing lines and copying notes on the chalkboard.

Many educational authorities in Ghana perceive that the use of corporal punishment enhances teaching and learning.[10] On the contrary, research has shown that excessive use of the cane turns children away from school if they cannot stand the lasting physical and psychosocial effect (Brown, 2002). It also puts fear into children, results in other physical injuries, and turns innocent children into pathological liars. Children may believe telling lies is the only viable option when their only inhibition against a misdeed is the fear that they will be caught and punished. In this way, children may be strongly tempted to lie in order to avoid detection rather than correct wrong behavior (MOWAC, 2008).

As already stated, efforts made to reduce the use of corporal punishment in school administrations have not yielded the desired results in educational and training institutions in Ghana. The majority (72 percent) of children interviewed in the DOC/CURIOUS MINDS study indicated that when they do something wrong in school, they are punished. When asked who doles out the punishment, 69 percent indicated their class teachers, 3 percent mentioned the head teacher, 1 percent said the class prefect, and slightly over 1 percent indicated a senior pupil as indicated in Figure 5.2.

Figure 5.2. Who Usually Carries Out Corrective Measure in School

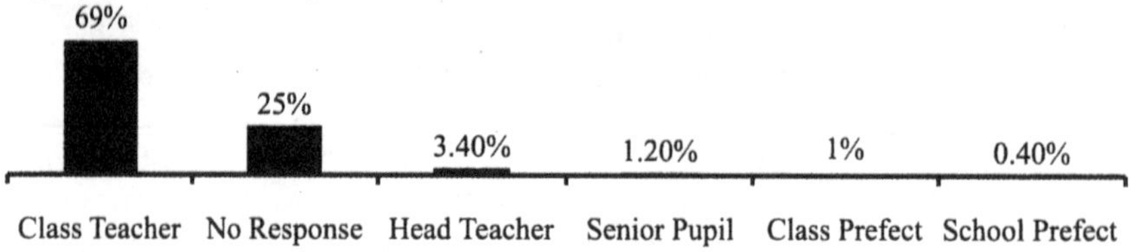

Incidentally, head teachers, who are mandated by law to administer punishment, constituted just 3 percent of the above-stated responses, which indicates that class teachers have taken over the responsibilities of head teachers, or some head teachers delegate teachers to administer punishment in school. The use of corporal punishment by class teachers has serious implications for learning and teaching. The findings of the study indicate that most schools in Ghana are flouting rules regulating the use of corporal punishment with impunity. Furthermore, since almost every class teacher punishes, it is almost impossible for the strokes teachers give out to children to be recorded, let alone monitored.

However, children are not punished arbitrarily in school. Punishment is meted out to children when they flout school regulations.[11] In certain schools, children are not punished during instructional hours. It is only when the child has done something to show extremely bad behavior that he or she is punished during instructional hours. Some of the reasons for which children are punished in school are indicated in Table 5.3.

Table 5.3. Reasons for Which Children Are Punished in School

Reasons
Arriving at school late or getting back to class from break late
Getting an answer wrong in class
Fighting in class
Being absent from school without permission
Being disobedient or breaking school regulations
Casting insinuations at mates
Not submitting homework
Telling a lie
Not concentrating in class or playing while lessons are ongoing
Playing in class
Disturbing in class
Cheating in class
Not paying studies or school fees
Performing poorly in class
Improper dressing
Stealing
Speaking vernacular
Talking in class

Source: DOC/CURIOUS MINDS Fieldwork, October–November 2008

Even though children are punished for the reasons listed in Table 5.3, the severity of the punishment varies according to the severity of the misdeed. For example, a child who steals does not receive the same punishment as one who talks in class. Again, because the list is not properly regulated, a child who steals in a class may be suspended, while a child in another school could be caned for the same offense.[12] It must be noted, however, that few schools have taken steps to regulate who punishes a child for a wrongdoing. On a broader level, there are no equal rules governing the type(s) of punishment to be meted out to children.

It is worthwhile acknowledging that sometimes teachers' behaviors are controlled by the challenges they face in particular circumstances. In a situation where the teacher's coping capabilities are low, there is no guarantee that in the face of children's misconduct in the classroom such a teacher will have the patience to let an incident go. For instance, a teacher in Apowa, a community in the Western Region, intimated that there are times when monthly salaries are delayed, and handling up to sixty pupils in a class, he "gets into class already constrained and sometimes is easily provoked by the children in the class." Another teacher in Dwomo (also in the Western Region) indicated that he lives about six kilometers from the school where he teaches and commutes to school every day. As a result, before he even gets to the school, he is already tired, angry, and "ready to pounce on any child who misbehaves." These statements suggest that sometimes teachers go to school already provoked and vent their anger on naughty but innocent children.

Teachers at a school in Cape Coast expressed that many of the children in their class are so naughty that one has to be extremely cautious and patient in handling them. One of the participants in the group discussion summed it up in the following words:

> My brother, you have no idea how difficult it is to handle the children. Can you imagine teaching about forty naughty boys from different homes? Sometimes I regret choosing the teaching profession because it is so difficult to teach in Ghana.

During the discussion, some teachers expressed that throughout their teaching career they have used the cane as an educational aid in correcting the behavior of their students, but the punishment has never worked. The children who usually get punished for a wrongdoing are the same ones beaten the next time around, an indication that the cane is not an effective tool for teaching good behavior.

Consequences for Teachers Applying Corporal Punishment in School

As already discussed, any teacher who applies corporal punishment on any child without explicit instruction from a head teacher, violates GES policy. The discussions in this chapter indicate that class teachers in many schools in Ghana use corporal punishment during school instructional hours. As a result of overstepping their duties, teachers are occasionally reprimanded by school authorities for applying corporal punishment. There are reported instances where teachers' conduct was deemed unacceptable, and consequently, they were warned, dismissed, demoted, or transferred. Generally, however, most teachers punish children and receive no negative consequences.[13]

Severe and unreasonable use of the cane has caused serious trouble for some teachers. The Ghana News Agency (GNA) published a story on Sunday, August 12, 2007, about an incident concerning an increasing rate of brutalities and hostile attitudes of some communities toward teachers in Nkawie in the Ashanti Region. According to the story, some youth in the community assaulted teachers from Atwima-Mim Junior High School because the teachers were alleged to have inflicted corporal punishment on recalcitrant pupils for examination malpractices.

In a March 15, 2009, publication, the Ghana Media Advocacy Program (G-MAP), an NGO for children's rights, urged the Government of Ghana as a matter of urgency to enact a law to abolish corporal punishment of children (Ghana News Agency 2009). This call was made because the NGO felt the practice was affecting the development and well-being of children in the northern part of Ghana, where children were abandoning the classroom and roaming the streets as a result of corporal punishment. The statement was also linked to an incident in which a teacher of Oda Nkwanta Local Authority Primary School was facing charges of provisional murder in a magistrate's court at Akim Oda for allegedly administering two strokes of cane on a fourteen-year-old pupil, which resulted in the child's death.

These may be a few isolated cases, but they have significant implications for children's education, health, and welfare. Where children feel threatened because of abusive use of the cane, they lose concentration in class or stop going completely. At the same time, when teachers remain in fear of constant threats of community hostilities, the quality of teaching suffers, and children are the ones who face the brunt of poor teaching.

National Response

Legislation, regulations in the *Head Teacher's Handbook*, and awareness programs in the media and other governmental and civil society engagements form part of the national response to the phenomenon.

Legislation

The first step that a government can take to protect children from violence is to have a legal framework that offers protection to children and reflects international standards. Ghana ratified the CRC on February 5, 1990, the first country to do so. After ratification, Ghana took steps to consolidate its laws on children in order to conform to the CRC. The process of law reform, which constituted the first major step in the consolidation and harmonization of laws, began in 1995. The Children's Bill was drafted through the revision of all existing laws relating to children and the provision of proposed amendments to ensure conformity of national legislation with principles of the CRC.[14] In Article 19 of the CRC, provisions are made for the protection of children from harm, stating that:

> States Parties shall take all appropriate legislative, administrative, social and educational measures to protect the child from all forms of physical or mental violence, injury or abuse, neglect or negligent treatment, maltreatment or exploitation, including sexual abuse, while in the care of parent(s), legal guardian(s) or any other person who has the care of the child.

This provision serves as a reference point for lawmakers and policymakers to legislate and formulate policies to protect children from harm.

Any punishment meant to cause physical and emotional stress on the child is a crime under the Children's Act (Act 560). Section 13 (2) of Act 560 stipulates that no correction order is justifiable which is unreasonable in kind or in degree according to the age and physical and mental condition of the child, and no correction order is justifiable if the child, by reason of tender age or otherwise, is incapable of understanding the purpose of the correction. Similar wording is captured in 41 (e) of the Criminal Code, 1960 (Act 29). Even though the provisions in the acts do not necessarily state that corporal punishment is illegal, they prohibit assault and other physical actions intended to cause harm to any person, including children.

Section 41 of Act 29 permits corporal punishment for children depending on the capacity of the child to understand the reason for the punishment and with the intention of correcting the child in conflict with the law. The Criminal Code Amendment Act 1998 (Act 554) and the Juvenile Justice Act 2003 (Act 653) state the corrective measure for such children. These children are placed in correctional institutions and given livelihood and vocational skills as part of their reform process.

In Ghana, corporal punishment cannot be used as a sentence for a crime. The 1992 Constitution of the Republic of Ghana states in Article 28 (3) that: "A child shall not be subjected to torture or other cruel, inhuman or degrading treatment or punishment." Article 15 (2) of the Constitution also states that: "No person shall, whether arrested or not, restricted or detained, be subjected to (a) torture or other cruel, inhuman or degrading treatment or punishment, (b) any other condition that detracts or is likely to detract from his dignity and worth as a human being."

Again, Article 15 (1) provides that the dignity of all persons shall be inviolable. The administration of juvenile justice is governed by the Juvenile Justice Act 2003 (Act 653). The Children's Act specifies the judicial measures to which a child may be subjected by a Child Panel, and these do not include corporal punishment (Articles 31 and 32).

Corporal punishment is also applied in other childcare institutions such as children's homes and orphanages. There are 153 children's homes and orphanages in the Department of Social Welfare (DSW) database. The Children's Act makes provisions for foster care, adoption, and institutionalized care and permits the use of "reasonable" and "justifiable" punishment under the transfer of parental responsibility. The Daycare Center Decree 1978 (SMDC 144) applies to the establishment and operation of registered daycare centers and crèches, though many unregistered centers also operate. The provisions in the Criminal Code against unjustifiable force also apply in these situations.

Section 4 of the Criminal Code (Amendment) Act stipulates that any person above the age of 12 may be deemed criminally responsible and, hence, may be deprived of their liberty in accordance with the Juvenile Justice Act. Children convicted of offenses may be detained in borstal institutions and industrial institutions.

Ghana Education Service: *Head Teacher's Handbook*

As already stated, as part of efforts to reduce the administration of corporal punishment, the Ghana Education Service (GES) has made provisions for regulating the use of the cane in the *Head Teacher's Handbook*. The introduction of the *Handbook* has not had a major impact on the use of corporal punishment, but some significance has been realized in some urban schools where the use of the cane has been abolished. The GES itself has come under attack concerning the arbitrary use of the cane, especially, in public schools in the country. Even though the UN Committee on the Rights of the Child acknowledged Ghana's efforts to prohibit the use of corporal punishment in educational settings through prohibitions outlined in the *Head Teacher's Handbook*, it also expressed serious concerns that Ghana should find a more practicable way of addressing the issue. The Committee was concerned that the Children's Act allows for a degree of "reasonable" and "justifiable" punishment. The Committee urged Ghana to institute measures explicitly to suppress all forms of corporal punishment in the family, schools, and other institutional settings and alternative care systems as a matter of priority. The Committee also recommended intensification in awareness creation and sensitization to educate parents, guardians, and professionals working with and for children by carrying out public educational campaigns.[15]

Role of the Media

In the absence of comprehensive research, the media has served as an important source of information on the nature and prevalence of corporal punishment. Both state- and privately-owned electronic and print media have reported incidents of corporal punishment of children, some of which have been reported as criminal cases to the DOVVSU.

The role of the media has been instrumental in focusing public awareness on corporal punishment. Currently, there are about 120 private FM radio stations nationwide, and these stations have specific programs on issues related to child protection, including: corporal punishment, child labor, pornography, pedophilia, and abusive traditional practices. Many of the stations establish advocacy programs at the national, regional, and district levels to disseminate information through a cross section of stakeholders and civil society groups.

Both the state and private television media have also contributed immensely through the broadcast of news items, announcements, movies, and other forms of entertainment that focus on corporal punishment in educational institutions and homes. These programs have increased public awareness and help shape opinions on the phenomenon.

The print media also publish stories on VAC, while other publications such as newsletters, magazines, and books carry stories with a specific focus on children as victims of abuse and exploitation. Concisely, media reportage has been very instrumental in leading to the identification, arrest, and prosecution of parents, guardians, and officials who have subjected children to corporal punishment.

Role of Non-governmental Organizations

The campaign to abolish VAC is complemented by the immense support from donor partners and NGOs. NGOs constitute the largest group in the private sector in the campaign against child rights violations such as child pornography, sexual exploitation, trafficking, and other abuses against children. The NGOs are located in almost every part of the country and operate in various child rights areas. Most have educational programs that sensitize the public regarding child abuse, including the use of corporal punishment as a corrective measure in homes and educational institutions. Leading NGOs in the campaign against corporal punishment include Plan Ghana, Children and Youth in Broadcasting (CURIOUS MINDS), and Child Rights International (CRI).

Role of Faith-based Organizations

Faith-based organizations (FBOs) also play very important roles in educating and informing the public through their members on corporal punishment and other acts of aggression that hinder the development of children. Some FBOs provide financial, human, and material support to development partners in order to suppress VAC. Some FBOs have established institutions to focus on child-related violations in some communities, and these institutions receive their funding from the FBO. There have also been many instances where themes related to corporal punishment have been used in sermons and captions for special occasions dedicated to child welfare and development.

One conflicting issue, however, is the stand of the church on corporal punishment. Even though some Christian groups frown on VAC, many believe in punishing children for doing something wrong. The biblical saying, "He who spares the rod hates his son, but he who loves him is careful to discipline him" (Holy Bible, Proverbs 13:24),[16] has often been the point of reference. Interaction with community members indicates that a lot of Christians misconstrue the real meaning of this biblical statement, which intends that a child should be corrected if that child is wayward to mean beating children in order to correct them.

In spite of the position of the church, the contribution of FBOs has helped in changing behaviors and attitudes of many who have subjected children to different types of abuse.

Role of United Nations Children's Fund

The United Nations Children's Fund (UNICEF) office in Ghana has played a supportive role in building capacities of government agencies to implement their mandates. UNICEF was very instrumental in providing support to the GES for the review of the *Head Teacher's Handbook*. UNICEF also has a program component for advocating for the eradication of corporal punishment in schools in its Child Abuse Network (CAN), which was introduced in the early part of 2008.

UNICEF has also supported MOWAC in the development of a five-year action plan on VAC, spanning the period from 2008 to 2012. The Five Year Action Plan on VAC is a comprehensive plan for suppressing violence, with measurable targets and indicators in which every Ghanaian at every level has a role to play. The aim of the plan is to create a safe environment that protects children from all forms of violence wherever they occur.

Programs and Projects by Ministries, Departments, and Agencies

Programs and projects organized to end corporal punishment include ongoing community sensitization programs through forums, workshops, media programs, capacity building, posters, and advertisements. These are organized with support from the government, philanthropists, and donor partners such as UNICEF, Danish International Development Agency (DANIDA), World Vision International, Save the Children, United States Agency for International Development (USAID), United Nations Development Program (UNDP), and International Labor Organization (ILO), among others.

Conclusion

In spite of the Government of Ghana's efforts at making legislation to suppress violence, many children still face various degrees of violence in Ghana. This may be because legislation does not necessarily guarantee social and behavioral changes. There seems to be a gap between law and practice concerning the use of corporal punishment in educational institutions. While the Children's Act prohibits the use of mental and physical torture or other inhuman or degrading treatment or punishment against children, the practice of corporal punishment in schools is a prescribed measure in the *Head Teacher's Handbook*, albeit in a supervised environment.

The Children's Act does not prohibit corporal punishment of children; indeed, it allows for a degree of "reasonable" and "justifiable"[17] punishment, an issue that was raised by the UN Committee on the Rights of the Child in its observation of Ghana's second periodic report to the Committee. This suggests that legislation on corporal punishment is not adequate in explicitly prohibiting all forms of corporal punishment in Ghana.

A number of programs and projects have been organized by MDAs and civil society groups to train, sensitize, and advocate regarding issues of violence against children at the national, regional, and district levels. These programs have created general awareness on the effects of corporal punishment. However, they seem not to have the commensurate level of compliance in the practice of removing the use of corporal punishment on children. In other words, many people have become aware of the ill effects of using corporal punishment but have not changed their behaviors.

Studies conducted on corporal punishment show that there is general acceptance of the use of corporal punishment by both children and caregivers in Ghana, suggesting that, in general, Ghanaians believe in beating children in order to correct them. Subjecting children to beatings is in clear violation of their rights, indicating that twenty years after ratifying the CRC, Ghana has not done much to improve people's perception of appropriate ways to correct children for wrongdoing.

There are few schools in Ghana, especially among the private ones in urban areas, where steps have been taken to regulate who punishes a child for a wrongdoing. On a broader perspective, most schools in Ghana are flouting rules regulating the use of corporal punishment with impunity. Children are punished in school by school authorities, especially class teachers, thus making it impossible for the strokes administered to children to be regulated. This situation indicates some weaknesses in the mechanisms in place in Ghanaian schools for checking the use of corporal punishment, thus having serious implications for the safety of children in school.

Even though teachers use corporal punishment, it is done so in violation of the GES policy on punishment. There have been few occasions when teachers have been reprimanded by school authorities for applying corporal punishment.

Such teachers are warned, dismissed, demoted, or transferred. Generally, however, most teachers punish children without being reprimanded, suggesting a weakness in the system.

The use of corporal punishment causes more harm than good to child development. It has negative implications and deleterious effects for children's education, health, and welfare. Children live in constant fear, their concentration and participation in school is affected, and teachers' lives are also threatened by community members because of the abusive use of the cane. The cumulative effect is that quality of teaching suffers, and children are the ones who face the brunt of poor teaching.

There is very little data on corporal punishment in Ghana. Apart from the recent national study on corporal punishment carried out by the DOC and CURIOUS MINDS, no major study has been conducted on the phenomenon. At present, the only reliable source of data on abuse, assault, and other domestic violence against women and children is the DOVVSU database. Thus, the lack of reliable data on corporal punishment affects government efforts in formulating policies in this area. The detrimental issues arising from children facing violence in the home and at school may also not be properly addressed, and the problem of violence against children may not receive the appropriate attention, time, and focus that are needed to help make the home and school a safer, more prosperous environment for Ghana's children.

The media is an important channel for awareness raising and consensus building on the use of corporal punishment and other forms of VAC. Incidentally, in spite of the significant contribution of both state and private-owned electronic and print media in reporting incidents of corporal punishment of children, the phenomenon is still in practice. The continuous use of corporal punishment indicates an unchanged attitude of Ghanaians.

Suggestions for Change

In spite of legislation, regulation, and advocacy work done at the national, regional, and district levels to change people's attitudes and perceptions of corporal punishment, the phenomenon is still in use. Discussions with both children and adults indicate that many people have flawed knowledge on what constitutes a corrective method. While adults seem to think that corporal punishment is an effective method, children think it is the only means through which a child could be made to conform and reform. A significant number of community adults and children endorsed caning as the appropriate means of discipline, according to the interactions with groups of adults and children. It may be assumed that the cane has been a symbol for correction in Ghana for a very long time such that many people see it as the only effective means of correction. This notion has to be corrected and a more humane method discussed. This requires much more work regarding the appropriate or suitable methods to apply in situations where children need to be corrected. Intensive awareness raising and implementation of policy actions could also help. Parents, educational authorities, and community people must be sensitized that the appropriate corrective method is one that reforms and not deforms. For example, in the home children could be denied certain privileges such as not being allowed to watch a favorite TV program or movie, and parents should explain to the child that he or she is being denied these privileges because of wrongdoing. At the school, a recalcitrant child could be prevented from taking part in social events, and as mentioned earlier, the child must be made to understand the reason for this action.

The fact that many parents believe in punishing children as a corrective measure is a disturbing revelation, which ought to be checked by providing appropriate protective mechanisms that will prevent children from abuse at home, and the government must lead the way. Intensification of raising awareness on the effects of corporal punishment and the need to introduce alternative non-violent types of corrective measures at the national, regional, district, and community levels will also be required. The media should continue to be an important channel for carrying relevant messages to parents, guardians, and other caregivers about these non-violent methods.

It is also very disturbing to note that in school, it is the class teachers (instead of the head teachers) who administer the cane. This is against the principles of the GES. This, therefore, could be an indication that teachers are abusing this principle, perhaps out of ignorance. It may also mean that teachers are fully aware of the implications of the violation of this principle but are doing so with impunity. Efforts have to be made to ensure that the principle is adhered to in schools, and this can be done effectively through regular monitoring visits by Educational Circuit[18] supervisors.

There is very little impact to be made in actions taken that are not backed by sufficient and reliable data. Lack of a reliable and relevant database on corporal punishment is problematic, and steps have to be taken to improve the current situation. Government could encourage research and academic institutions through grants and resources to carry out more surveys on corporal punishment and other child-related emerging issues. The Ghana Statistical Service should be motivated to include issues that relate to VAC in its routine data collection activities in order to improve child-related statistics.

Notes

1. CURIOUS MINDS is an NGO in Ghana run by very young people.
2. Interview with the director of the Department of Social Welfare, November 2008.
3. The Akan people are an ethnic linguistic group of West Africa. They speak the Akan languages and have the most dominant culture in present-day Ghana. The Akans constitute the largest ethnic group in Ghana.
4. A community in the Western Region of Ghana.
5. A community in the Eastern Region of Ghana.

6. Regional capital of the Central Region in Ghana.

7. Regional capital of the Volta Region in Ghana.

8. Interview with a police officer at DOVVSU Head Office, March 23, 2009.

9. At the time of study, Ghana had 110 administrative districts. At present, the number is 170.

10. Interview with a director of Ghana Education Service (GES), March 24, 2009.

11. Interview with a director of GES, March 24, 2009.

12. Interview with a director of GES, March 24, 2009.

13. Interview with a director of GES, March 24, 2009.

14. GOG/UNICEF (2002), *Situation analysis of children and women in Ghana 2000*, p. 15.

15. CRC/C/GHA/CO/2, March 17, 2006.

16. New International Version (Holy Bible).

17. Quotes in parenthesis were taken from the Children's Act, 1998 (Act 560).

18. For administrative and supervisory purposes, every district in Ghana is divided into educational circuits, and each circuit has a circuit supervisor whose duty is to supervise the administration of the circuit and report to the district director of education.

References

Brown, C. K. (2002). A study on sexual abuse in schools in Ghana, Accra.

Department of Children (DOC)/CURIOUS MINDS. (2008). *Children's perceptions on the use of corporal punishment in Ghana.* Unpublished.

End Physical Punishment of Children (EPOCH–USA). (2007a). *Laws: Legal reforms worldwide.* Retrieved from www.StopHitting.org.

Ghana National Commission on Children (GNCC). (2004). *Republic of Ghana's Report to the UN Committee on the Rights of the Child 1997–2003.*

Ghana News Agency (2009) 'G-MAP calls for abolition of corporal punishment'. Posted on GhanaWeb's General News website http://ghanaweb.com/GhanaHomePage/NewsArchive/artikel.php?ID=159060 on Sunday, 15 March 2009. Retrieved on the same date.

Ghana Statistical Service/United Nations Children's Fund/Ministry of Health (GSS/UNICEF/MOH). (2006). *Multiple indicator cluster survey: Monitoring the situation of children, women and men.*

Government of Ghana. (1992). Constitution of the Republic of Ghana.

———. (1998). The Children's Act, 1998 (Act 560). Assembly Press.

Holy Bible. (1984). The New International Version, International Bible Society, Colorado Springs.

Kyei-Gyamfi, S. (2008). Speech presented at the Regional Dissemination on Violence Against Children.

Ministry of Women and Children's Affairs (MOWAC). (2007). *A review of child trafficking, sexual exploitation and pornography in Ghana.* Unpublished.

———. (2008). *Five-year national action plan on violence against children (2008–2012).* Unpublished.

Plan. (2008). *The global campaign to end violence in schools.*

Save the Children. (2003). *Corporal punishment: International Save the Children Alliance position on corporal punishment.* Retrieved from www.savethechildren.net.nz/alliance/resources/corporal_punish.pdf.

United Nations. (2006). Child friendly version of *Report on Violence Against Children.*

United Nations Children's Fund (UNICEF). (2000). *Situation analysis of children and women in Ghana 2000*, Accra.

Chapter 6
Child Labor in Ghana: Global Concern and Local Reality

By George Clerk

The adoption of the United Nations (UN) Convention on the Rights of the Child (CRC) 1989 has shaped our notion of childhood and reinforced the idea that child labor is a problem. Since the CRC, there has been a trend toward a globalized notion of childhood, which has been driven by such ideas as our innate humanness and common humanity, in line with the universalist principle of human rights (Leonardo, 2006:155).

This chapter acknowledges the importance of the CRC as a global standard for protecting children from economic exploitation and guaranteeing their welfare. It explores the reality of child labor in Ghana and attempts to make sense of the application of global notions of children's rights and welfare, which are not easily translated or applied meaningfully in local contexts. The child labor situation in Ghana would, therefore, be evaluated using the CRC as the global standard. It establishes that globalization of international law and standards have coerced countries around the world into recognizing and maintaining international standards for the welfare of the child to the extent that child labor is now perceived as a problem. However, there are problems implementing the CRC in Ghana because there is no consensus on a key concept such as childhood, which is fundamental to understanding child labor. While the law in Ghana reflects international law by defining a child as anyone under age eighteen, customary law does not have such a clear-cut age definition of the child. The choice of age eighteen, therefore, can be described as arbitrary.

Considering the trend toward universalizing children's rights and the acknowledgment of child labor as a problem, the central questions of this chapter are: How did this concept of child labor as a problem come to be adopted all over the world and, indeed, in Africa, and why is child labor so persistent in spite of the laws and policies put in place to tackle it? In order to address these questions, this chapter will look briefly at the globalization process and the acknowledgment of child labor as a problem. This chapter will then progress into a discussion on child labor in Ghana and how it is being tackled.

Internationalization of Child Labor As a Problem

To understand the nature of current global developments in child labor law and policy, it is important to understand the globalization phenomenon and its impact on social norms. Global concern for child labor has grown since 1919 when the International Labor Organization (ILO) adopted the Convention on Minimum Age, which included proposals for child work. This was followed by the adoption of a number of other international treaties by the ILO and other agencies, including ILO Convention 138 (1973), ILO Convention 192 (1999), the 1924 Declaration of the Rights of the Child by the League of Nations, and the 1959 Declaration on the Rights of the Child, which specifically stipulated that:

> The child shall be protected against all forms of neglect, cruelty and exploitation. He shall not be the subject of traffic in any form. The child shall not be admitted to employment before an appropriate minimum age; he shall in no case be caused or permitted to engage in any occupation or employment, which will prejudice his health or education or interfere with his physical, mental or moral development.

The CRC, one of the most universally ratified international conventions, was adopted in 1989. It provides appropriate penalties to deal with the violation of its provisions and imposes an obligation on signatory states to adopt and implement the principles in the Convention. The CRC universalizes rights and projects the idea of a shared global notion of rights for children; hence, children's rights has ceased to be a local issue; it has become a global issue. At the regional level, this culminated in the adoption of the 1990 African Charter on the Rights and Welfare of the Child and further led to the 1998 Children's Act in Ghana. Developments in international law and policy, therefore, have had a trickle-down effect from the global to national and regional levels, resulting in the enactment of laws upholding the principles established in the CRC.

The CRC established a principle in Article 32 that requires states to protect children from economic exploitation. Since its adoption, there has been an increasing trend toward globalizing child labor as a problem. The critical point here is that through multilateral agencies such as the UN and the World Bank, member states are obliged under the influence of these organizations and the other powerful northern member states to adopt and implement international conventions, which are believed to be an essential standard for our "common good." It is simply based on the premise and idea of a global community with shared goals and aspirations.

There is, however, a major weakness in the globalization process: the agenda is set from above, but the implementation occurs from below. This process generates many problems, including the discord between the perceptions at the global level and reality at the local level. In effect, child labor continues to persist in countries like Ghana notwithstanding efforts in place to stop it. This discord derives from the different understandings of key concepts such as childhood, which influences the attitudes of local people toward children and the place of children in society.

The global notion of childhood denotes a stage of vulnerability, a lack of maturity, and a need for special protection from exploitation. International law, therefore, reinforces the general notion that a child lacks both physical and mental maturity and is unable to make sound judgment. This notion underlies the concept of child protection, and this has far reaching implications for the well-being of children. Hence, through the same legal guarantees, childhood, which on one hand is empowered by law, is on the other hand disempowered by the underlying notion that children do not have the mental capacity to assert or enforce these rights. Liebel (2004) noted that such Western notions of childhood were developed in industrial societies of Europe from the eighteenth century onward but have now become the bedrock of the global policy agenda through multilateral agencies such as UNICEF and the ILO. Such notions of childhood have also been the driving force behind the artificial division between education and work. The current emphasis on education generally exempts children from the world of work altogether until they are at least 16, when they are expected to have completed their basic education. Although there may be exceptions, the formal sector does not generally offer children work; however, in traditional societies, children are socialized through work. There is no clear-cut division between education and work in traditional society.

Children are members of society, with privileges that increase with increasing responsibilities. Customary law and practice do not aim at disempowering, separating, or distinguishing children from adults; rather, they increasingly empower children as they mature and assume more responsibilities in their households.

Child Labor in Ghana

Historically, in Ghana, as in much of Africa, children's labor has been an essential element in the socioeconomic development of the country. Van Hear (1982) argued that child labor was particularly crucial to the development of capitalist agriculture in Ghana following the introduction of cash crops like cocoa, which is still the leading export crop for the state. He observed that with the revival of the cocoa industry in 1935, more women and children were migrating from northern Ghana with the laborers (1982). These children worked on cocoa farms as members of sharecroppers' families and were, therefore, not employed by the farm owners. Van Hear also noted that children also cultivated sharecroppers' food farms, thus freeing them for cocoa work and helped to transport cocoa to the marketing points. As members of sharecroppers' families, children also suffered the ill effects of fluctuating cocoa prices, which left them worse off.

The involvement of children in the cultivation and headloading was fraught with abuse and exploitation, however, Van Hear (1982:501) argued that the colonial administration made little attempt to investigate the conditions of employment of children, with interventions only occurring when the demands of African cocoa entrepreneurs threatened labor supply to expatriate concerns in, for example, mining. Child labor continues to be very important to agriculture, and part of the reason behind the continuing importance is "the 'nimble finger,' the 'small physical structure,' and 'thin arms' are additional justifications for the suitability of the children for other types of activities" (Adamassie, 2002:261).

Children also have a long history of domestic work and generally working as part of household production in Ghana. For example, Tallensi children start having economic duties as early as age five or six, and though there is no structured approach to doing this, such duties are an integral part of their play and other activities such as assisting their parents, so that by the time they have reached age twelve, they are fully responsible for some tasks (Bass, 2004:21). Further research also showed that children often perform such tasks as baby-tending and bird-scaring on farms, which enabled parents to pursue other interests (Oppong, 1973:51). Domestic work has been defined as "children under the age of eighteen who work in other people's households, doing domestic chores, caring for children, and running errands, among other tasks" (*Innocenti Digest*, 1999:2).

The ILO-IPEC (2004:9) emphasized the fact that child domestic labor is not the ordinary tasks that children perform at home. It is the domestic tasks that children perform in the homes of third parties under exploitative conditions. This is a highly unregulated, hidden, dispersed, and informal area of employment, with no stipulated hours of work and no minimum wage (Adamassie, 2002:257). Furthermore, many child domestics are not paid wages and cannot claim any rights but are saddled with duties and obligations (2002). It involves, for example, children and grandchildren of elderly relatives, caring for and doing tasks such as washing clothes, bringing food, running errands, carrying water to the bathroom, and sweeping the room for the elderly relatives (Van Der Geest, 2002:24). These practices have historically been underpinned by a culture of intergenerational obligation of support and reciprocity (Ncube, 1998:18). To this end, children have a sense of obligation to support their parents, and parents have a sense of entitlement to this support.

Another type of child labor that has gained publicity more recently is fishing.[1] Although it employs relatively fewer children, it is still an area of concern that has received a lot of attention because it highlights a cultural practice that directly forces children into one of the worst forms of child labor. Children in

Ghana have historically been involved in fishing; however, due to modernization and the decline in the fishing industry, their participation has significantly declined over the years (FAO, 2003; UNODC, 2010). Villages along the banks of the Volta River, however, have maintained the practice of child labor in the fishing industry.

Unfortunately, this practice has been fed through trafficking children, who are forced to work in the fishing industry.[2] Children are generally leaving the fishing industry because of depleting stocks and the effect it has on income; however, the same conditions have made child labor invaluable to this sector around Lake Volta. The construction of the Akosombo Dam and Lake Volta in the 1960s opened up the fishing business; however, with depleting stocks, fishermen have sought other means of earning extra income (FAO, 2003; UNODC, 2010). While searching for other sources, they have resorted to using the cheap labor of trafficked children, who have nimble fingers useful in releasing fish from smaller nets. Also, these children perform diving to release fishing nets that are stuck to tree stumps in the lake. In effect, they are exposed to the double jeopardy of death by drowning or diseases such as bilharzia or guinea worm. This practice violates section 91 of the 1998 Children's Act because these are children under age eighteen being exposed to serious hazards. Article 32 of the CRC also provides that children must be protected from economic exploitation and from any work that would affect the health and well-being of the child.

Child labor in artisanal and small-scale mining is considered one of the worst forms of child labor, considering that these children are exposed to chemicals, explosives, and crude machinery that could cause potential hazards. Here also, Article 32 of the CRC provides that children should be protected from economic exploitation and from performing any work that is potentially hazardous to the education and health of the child. Exploitation connotes power relations that allow some to take surplus value from other people's labor, typical of the capitalist system. The exploitation of children in child labor, however, is reinforced by cultural practices that emphasize duties, reciprocity, and rigorously enforced obedience, particularly from children.

I spent some time in the mining village of Mapatuam in the Ashanti Region and interviewed twenty child laborers as well as adults in the community. Mining activities in Mapatuam were illegal and on a small scale. This contrasted with the large scale and highly mechanized mining activities in the neighboring village, which was the result of foreign direct investment. The illegal miners in Mapatuam complained that their plight was a direct result of their vast farmland having been given to large companies. They felt they had been deprived of land and were forced to resort to illegal mining for survival.

The ages of the children in mining ranged from four to sixteen years, with fourteen girls and six boys. The girls engaged in activities such as washing and sifting sand deposits in water, while the boys engaged in digging and excavation, using shovels and pickaxes. The illegal activities of these children exposed them to some serious risks. Respondents indicated that one of the greatest dangers they faced was the risk of the ceiling of the tunnel collapsing on them while down in the tunnel. They recounted some tragic incidents; however, they were buoyed by the prospect of finding a huge amount of gold, which would change their livelihoods completely. The majority of the children claimed they were compelled to work because of poverty and deprivation.

Child prostitution is rife in Ghana and particularly so in urban areas like Accra, especially around the Kwame Nkrumah Circle. It was hard to find child prostitutes in a particular location because, according to some adult prostitutes, no landlord is willing to rent out a property to child prostitutes because, apart from prostitution being illegal, child prostitutes are also minors. In interviews with child prostitutes, poverty was named as major cause of child labor. However, they identified truancy as a major cause of prostitution. None of the prostitutes had completed secondary school or were attending school. A significant number of them were absent from school repeatedly, spending time with older friends who encouraged them to get into prostitution. They emphasized that they were involved in prostitution out of their own free will without the knowledge of their parents or family members.

They claimed that they were involved in prostitution not because they were from deprived families but because of truancy. Martha was a dropout from a secondary school in the Central Region of Ghana. She was very articulate and explained that her parents were indeed well off and capable of looking after her. However, she left home to fend for herself because she liked working as a prostitute. She explained how she got involved in prostitution:

> A senior student promised to look after me and protect me from the bullies. As my protector and mentor I learnt many things from her, including prostitution. Because she was a senior student, and she looked after me, she was like a "school mother" to me. She managed to convince the school authorities that her mother was ill so they allowed me to accompany her home to spend weekends, so that I would help her look after her mother. Once we left the boarding school and went to her house, she introduced me to men and encouraged me to have sexual intercourse with them. This became a regular practice and eventually I got lured unto the streets of Accra soliciting for sex as I began to enjoy it. It was hard for me to concentrate in school so much that I decided to give up school completely. My "school mother" who later died advised me to give up prostitution and go back to school, but I am finding it difficult to go back.

Martha's story captures a situation that in the past had been common in secondary schools in Ghana. In many schools, senior students and sometimes teachers exploited vulnerable junior students, a situation that called for concerted efforts particularly to protect the girl-child.[3] If the rights of the child were recognized and properly monitored, it is unlikely that teachers would, for example, ask students to perform tasks such as work on the teacher's farm, go shopping for the teacher, or do other chores for the teacher's private benefit.[4]

Prostitution and mining are among the worst forms of child labor as provided in ILO Convention 182 (1999). However, an activity such as sales, which is prevalent in urban areas, is not one of the worst forms of child labor. It is, however, an activity that potentially distracts children from schooling, hence, it requires equal attention. Many children in sales refused any suggestion that their activities constituted work. There was a common suggestion among these children that they were only helping and not working. The concept of child labor was unfamiliar to them. Sala explained:

> I am helping my mother because she doesn't have money and she asked me to help her. As a child you have to help your parents. It's not good for a child to be idle when your parents are struggling to look after you. My mother is very happy that I am helping her. She thinks I am a good child.

Tackling Child Labor

While the survey gives perspective to the number of economically active children, it is worth noting the government has initiatives in place to tackle child labor. One of the major steps taken after the CRC in Ghana was the adoption of the Children's Act 1998. This brought together all laws prohibiting child labor and protecting children from exploitation, outlined in sections 87–91. These sections deal with the prohibition of exploitative child labor, minimum age for child labor, and hazardous child labor. Article 32 of the CRC highlights the fact that children are rights-bearing individuals and provides that states parties recognize the right of the child and provide protection from exploitation. However, it is not clear how the state empowers children to seek protection from economic exploitation as a right.

The CRC clearly states in Article 32: "State Parties shall recognize the rights of the child to be protected from economic exploitation." Sections 1–15 of the Children's Act are subtitled "Rights of the Child and Parental Duty," and section 12 specifically provides that no person shall subject a child to exploitative labor; however, it does not seem to clearly state that such protection is in recognition of the rights of the child. The child, therefore, is not presented as a rights-bearing individual who is entitled to such protection. Ghanaian society traditionally cherishes children and places a high social value on their advancement (Mends, 1994:3). However, without empowering children with the rights in the CRC, it is unclear who has a duty to provide when the family/household fails to provide the safeguards enshrined in law.

There is a general perception that child labor is encouraged because there is poor access to education, and idle children occupy their time with work to benefit themselves and their families, especially in poor countries. "Children with little or no access to quality education have little alternative but to enter the labor market where they are often forced to work in dangerous and often exploitative conditions (ILO, 2006)." It is not only economic activity but also household chores performed by children that impact schooling.

In addition, parents as consumers have to make a choice about whether the gain of having their children in school is more than the loss to both children and family as a whole. If the cost of sending the child to school outweighs benefits such as better employment, then parents are likely to choose the immediate income from child labor—hence, the persistence of child labor in Ghana.

Domestic work is one form of labor that has the potential to interfere with the education, health, and welfare of children. The difficulty here is that household production is not counted as production in the calculation of gross domestic product (GDP), so although children engage in such tasks as fetching firewood, water, cooking, and childcare, such household chores do not fall under the definition of work (Guarcello, Rosati, & Lyon, 2008:2). In discussing child labor, it is worth noting that reference is made to work, which is generally detrimental to the well-being of the child. If household chores or domestic work can be detrimental to the child's education, then that is a matter of concern. One way to overcome this problem is to focus on educational achievement, which would expose even further the problem of child labor in areas where it is often overlooked, as demonstrated by Bhalotra & Heady (2003).

Children's continued participation in child labor, notwithstanding the efforts to combat it, is due to the fact that while it has been acknowledged as a problem by the international community and increasingly by the Government of Ghana in policy terms, local communities still do not see it as a problem. There remains a general perception among both children and adults in the community that children are simply engaging in work, which is essential for their socialization. In focus group discussions with adults in the community conducted in 2007,[5] participants agreed that work was necessary because it equipped children for marriage and adulthood. The absence of this notion in the everyday language of local people leaves a gap in official policy and local reality. In a personal interview with the police, officers argued that child labor has been part of our culture, so no one reports a child for engaging in some form of child labor. Also, to suggest that a child has a right to be protected from exploitation did not make sense to the local person. The language of rights is not spoken locally, so there is no sense of entitlement to resources for the upkeep of children, which would make child labor unnecessary.

An interesting pattern that emerged from the interviews I conducted was the lack of understanding of what children's rights meant. When the question, "What do you think of children's rights?" was asked, there were blank expressions on the faces of many respondents. There was, however, a desire to know more. Many claimed they had never heard about it, with the exception of a few. They were generally of the opinion that children's rights meant that children were free to do whatever they wanted to do. It was particularly difficult explaining the concept to children in their local languages. Since respondents did not understand the expression "children's rights," I proceeded to ask the same question in Twi. The difficulty faced was how to translate into Twi for the understanding of respondents without losing the essence, so I used expressions that had been suggested by some officials such as "*Nkolaa fawuhundie*," which literally means children's emancipation, *nkolaa yie die*, which means children's well-being, and "*mmofra ndinuaa*," which also means children's well-being.

None of the children interviewed had heard or used these expressions before, and they tried to interpret it in different ways.

Kwaakyewaa (silent initially) stated, "I don't know what children's rights mean. *Nkolaa fawuhundie* means (pause) *nkolaa* (children) can do whatever they want to do (laughter). I haven't heard about it, but I think it would like the government to look after us and help us to learn some skills so that we can get good jobs when we grow up."

Children interviewed generally interpreted the concept of children's rights as freedom to do whatever they want to do, but it is inaccurate to translate children's rights as "children having the freedom to do whatever they want." This further illustrates the difficulty of defining the concept of rights in our traditional languages. Yet even then, nearly 90 percent of them indicated that it was not right to let children do whatever they wanted to. This was, however, no surprise as even adults in the community were largely unaware of the concept children's rights and did not understand it.

The language of rights is used by officials in law and policy; however, lack of local understanding of the concept in the local languages makes communication flow between officials and the people difficult. Officials are often educated elites interconnected with global society and attuned to global discourse. The official view, therefore, conveys the principles of the CRC, which positions children as rights-bearing members of society. When confronted with local reality, some officials acknowledged that it was an uphill task conveying those principles in practice.

Under the socioeconomic circumstances in which most children in Ghana grow up, what sort of intervention is needed to deal appropriately with child labor? Considering that many children are involved in domestic work, which is not considered one of the worst forms of child labor, it is important to direct efforts toward the protection of children, not from their families, but from the socioeconomic circumstances that conspire against effective familial support (Laird, 2002:899). Poverty reduction in Ghana, therefore, needs to be addressed by mainstreaming social protection to alleviate the plight of the very vulnerable. Social protection may come in the form of social insurance, social assistance, and child protection. However, investing specifically in child protection under social protection may prove to be one of the most efficient and most sustainable steps to poverty alleviation (Crawford, 2001:543).

In Africa, typified by the Ghanaian case, social protection arrangements such as pensions are beneficial to a small minority who work in the formal sector. This is changing with the new pension program recently established in Ghana. However, it is worth noting that tier three offers a voluntary option for private contributions from the formal and informal sectors, a situation which does not offer guaranteed protection to informal sector workers, leaving them insecure. Not intervening beyond the early years risks compounding early social disadvantage because many children from deprived backgrounds may be denied the opportunity to start on an even plane. It is, therefore, not only an obligation to protect children through interventions but also the only way in which cost benefit can be achieved and economic security for future generations advanced (Crawford, 2001:522). The introduction of the Livelihood Empowerment Against Poverty (LEAP) social grants pilot implementation program is a step in the right direction. LEAP, a program introduced by the Department of Social Welfare since 2008, supports poor families and enables children to go to school. LEAP is a cash transfer program that benefits the most vulnerable in Ghana.[6]

A program that has been used in other countries is cash transfers. Taking a cue from these programs, Ghana has also adopted a cash transfer system.[7] It is estimated that in a pilot study on the capitation grant program, there was a 14.5 percent increase in enrollment figures in pre-school in forty of the most deprived districts in 2004 (Adamu-Issah, Elden, Forson, & Schrofer, 2007:13). The success of this program led to the adoption of the capitation grant program in 2005 with a multi-sectoral focus. Under the capitation grant program, schools receive a grant per pupil to cover their fees. It intervenes simultaneously in education, health, and nutrition because it replaces school fees with the capitation grant,[8] which is also complemented by a school feeding program (Adamu-Issah, et al., 2007).[9] Improved nutrition has the potential to indirectly impact on education through improved attendance and performance, and poor nutrition has the potential to result in the reverse. Skoufias & Parker (2001:54) admitted many questions remain unanswered. For example, they asked, "Is it not possible that cash transfers (conditional or unconditional) have a negative effect on the work incentives of adults?" They claimed that from a welfare perspective, it is questionable whether poor families really benefit in the long run from working less and having their children attending school. Battle, Torjman, Mendelson, & Tamagno (2007) referred to this problem as the "welfare wall," which suggests that welfare is a poverty deepening program that makes it difficult for some recipients to leave and move into the workforce. I contend that this is a challenge that all governments face and should not be the basis for ending such programs. The effectiveness of an education system is a different issue altogether but should be aimed at making children functionally literate.

Despite unanswered questions the idea seems laudable, as it suggests cash transfers targeting children in poor households are an effective way of tackling poverty, but they are currently underused in developing countries as a means to reduce poverty. The fear of abusing the system does not merit the denial of a lifeline through cash transfers. Cash transfers do not only reduce poverty but also support household consumption and investment, increased enrollment in school, reduced child labor, and benefit the household (Barrientos & DeJong, 2006:542).

Ghana's second state party report to the Committee on the Rights of the Child (CRC/C/65/Add.34, July 14, 2005) discussed in detail the impact Ghana's new education policy (including the capitation grant, school feeding program, etc.) has had on child labor in the country. It notes that the enrollment numbers have increased significantly in the three northern regions since the introduction of the school feeding program and attributes this increase to the introduction of this program. However, it also identifies retention of pupils in the school system as a major area of weakness. This requires innovative approaches to the problem in order to address the specific needs of families and households in different context. The Mills government has since added free school uniforms, shoes, and textbooks, therefore covering a wider area of need. Such efforts are commendable because it is another serious step toward tackling poverty, which seems to be the main reason for child labor. Also, though not enough, it is an indication of the seriousness the state attaches to the welfare of children.

Conclusion

Child labor in Ghana is not a hidden phenomenon. Its obvious nature goes to show that it is largely an acceptable way of life for the ordinary Ghanaian. In this chapter, an attempt has been made to outline some of the common types of child labor, some of which have been a direct response to globalization. It establishes the fact that child labor is indeed rife in agricultural and domestic work. The state has adopted a rights approach toward the elimination of child labor. This approach is mainly influenced from above, with no reference to the reality below. As a result, child labor still remains very visible in Ghana today. There is merit in the rights approach to combating child labor albeit because, in theory, children are empowered to claim what they are entitled to. The CRC provides that states must take measures to ensure that children are protected from economic exploitation. It provides in Article 20 that children who are deprived of their family environment or in whose own best interest cannot be allowed to remain in that environment, shall be entitled to special protection and assistance provided by the state. It imposes on the state a duty to provide alternative care arrangements for children under such circumstances. Without such provisions in law, efforts to deal with child labor remain cosmetic because there are no guarantees for protecting children who, for example, report cases of exploitation. The implementation of a rights-based child protection agenda requires financial resources, and the UN Committee on the Rights of the Child in their response to Ghana's 2005 report expressed concern about the lack of adequate financial and human resources for a successful realization of these rights (UNHCR, 2006).

The police expressed concern about prosecuting adults who were reported by children for any form of exploitation because they feared there were no alternative care arrangements for such children.[10] As Ghana marches toward children's rights, emphasis must be placed on poverty alleviation, and the preferences of children, who are actors and not mere objects in need of protection, must be taken into account. Instead of spending money on huge campaigns trying to change perceptions, money should go toward "up-skilling" and social mobility through education (Bass, 2004:187). This will ensure that the need for cash immediately does not compromise their future earnings and leave them in a cycle of poverty and denying their children of the rights they are often deprived of due to circumstances beyond their control.

Notes

1. See website for news report on children in fishing: http://www.irinnews.org/report.aspx?reportid=40703.

2. http://www.unodc.org/newsletter/en/perspectives/0601/page002.html.

3. See http://www.sussex.ac.uk/education/documents/ghana_.pdf.

4. See http://www.ghanadistricts.com/news/?read=8750.

5. I conducted focus group discussions for my PhD thesis in 2007.

6. See http://www.ipc-undp.org/ipc/PageAfrica-Brazil.do?id=11.

7. Cash transfers are a safety net system for social protection, which provides cash to families and households (Adamu-Issah, Elden, Forson, and Schrofer, 2007).

8. The capitation grant was a grant given to kindergartens, nursery, primary, and junior secondary schools that was instituted in 2005 by the Government of Ghana to avoid replacing school fees and levies.

9. The World Food Program's (WFP) Ghana country program for 2006–2010 has, for example, a school feeding program particularly in the north. See http://www.wfp.org/country_brief/indexcountry.asp?country=288.

10. Clerk, G. (2008). *Child labor in Ghana: A study in the context of globalization.* PhD thesis (unpublished).

References

Adamassie, A. (2002). Explaining the high incidence of child labor in sub-Saharan Africa. *African Development Review* 14 (2), 251–275.

Adamu-Issah M., L. Elden, M. Forson, and T. Schrofer. (2007). Achieving universal education in Ghana by 2015: A reality or a dream. *Working Paper*, UNICEF.

Barrientos, A., and J. DeJong. (2006). Reducing child poverty with cash transfers: A sure thing? *Development and Policy Review* 24 (5), 499–624.

Bass, L. E. (2004). *Child Labor in Sub-Saharan Africa.* Boulder: Lynne Rienner Publishers.

Battle, K., S. Torjman, M. Mendelson, and E. Tamagno. (2007). *Caledon response to liberal poverty strategy.* Caledon Institute of Social Policy.

Bhalotra, S., and C. Heady. (2003). Child farm labor: The wealth paradox. *The World Bank Economic Review* 17 (2).

Crawford, P. I. (2001). Child protection: A theoretical background. In I. Ortiz (ed.). *Social Protection in Asia Pacific.* Asian Development Bank.

Food and Agriculture Organization (FAO). (2003). *Cultural perception module Ghana.* Role of Agriculture Project International Conference. Retrieved on March 16, 2010, from ftp://ftp.fao.org/es/ESA/roa/pdf/7_Culture/Culture_Ghana.pdf.

Guarcello, L., F. C. Rosati, and S. Lyon. (2008). Child labor and education for all: An issue paper. *Journal of the History of Childhood and Youth* 1 (2), 254–266.

Hilson, G. (2001). A contextual review of the Ghanaian small-scale mining industry. *Mining, Minerals and Sustainable Development (MMSD)* 76.

Innocenti Digest. (1999). Child domestic work. Retrieved June 25, 2006, from http://www.unicef-icdc.org/publications/.

International Labor Organization (ILO). (2006). *What is the global march and its message?* Retrieved January 1, 2008, from http://www.ilo.org/public/english/comp/child/download/pdf/global.pdf.

International Labor Organization-International Program on the Elimination of Child Labor (ILO-IPEC). (2004). *Helping hands or shackled lives? Understanding child comestic labor and responses to it.* Geneva. Retrieved June 26, 2006, from http://www.ilo.org/public/english/standards/ipec/publ/download/cdl_2004_helpinghands_en.pdf.

Laird, S. (2002). The 1998 Children's Act: Problems of enforcement in Ghana. *British Journal of Social Work* 32 (7).

Leonardo, E. K. (2006). Globalization and the construction of universal human rights. *Human Rights and Human Welfare* 6, 151–163.

Liebel, M. (2004). *A Will of Their Own: Cross-Cultural Perspectives on Working Children.* London: Zed Books.

Mends, E. H. (1994). *Rights of the Child in Ghana.* Edited by H. Mensa-Bonsu and Dowuona-Hammond. Accra: Woeli Publishing Services.

Ncube, W. (ed.). (1998). *Law, Culture, Tradition and Children's Rights in Eastern and Southern Africa.* England: Ashgate.

Oppong, C. (1973). *Growing Up in Dagbon.* Accra: Ghana Publishing Company.

Skoufias, E., and S. Parker. (2001). Conditional cash transfers and their impact on child work and schooling: Evidence from PROGRESA a program in Mexico. *FCND Discussion Paper No. 123.* International Food Policy Research Institute. Retrieved August 16, 2005, from http://www.ifpri.org/divs/fcnd/dp/papers/fcndp 123.pdf.

United Nations High Commission for Refugees (UNHCR). (2006). *UN Committee on the Rights of the Child: Concluding observations, Ghana.* Retrieved March 16, 2010, from http://www.unhcr.org/refworld/publisher,CRC,CONCOBSERVATIONS,GHA,45377ed30,0.html.

United Nations Office on Drugs and Crime (UNODC). (2010). *Child trafficking in Ghana.* Retrieved March 16, 2010, from http://www.unodc.org/newsletter/en/perspectives/0601/page002.html.

Van Der Geest, S. (2002). Respect and reciprocity: Care of elderly people in rural Ghana. *Journal of Cross-Cultural Gerontology* 17.

Van Hear, N. (1982). Child labor and the development of capitalist agriculture in Ghana. *Development and Change* 13, 499–514.

Chapter 7

Children's Rights, Mobility, and Transport in Ghana: Access to Education and Health Services

By Gina Porter, Albert Abane, Kathrin Blaufuss, and Frank Owusu Acheampong

As noted elsewhere in this volume, Ghana was the first country to ratify the United Nations (UN) Convention on the Rights of the Child (CRC) in 1990. Subsequently, Ghana's 2003 Poverty Reduction Strategy confirmed the significance of the CRC by including a commitment to intensify awareness of the CRC and the Children's Act, especially regarding child labor. The Strategy also incorporates associated commitments to free basic primary education, alternative education for children out of school, and streamlining the legal system to protect children. Over the last decade, the CRC has arguably been the impetus for a range of activities in Ghana by non-governmental organizations (NGOs), community-based organizations (CBOs), and government to address child rights issues, including child trafficking, girls' urban migration for child porterage work, and violence against women and children.[1] In this chapter, we examine commitment to children's rights in a mobility and transport context, an area commonly overlooked in the context of child rights. Our specific focus is on children's physical mobility and the implications this has for their rights of access to health and education services. It is important to point out that there are also mobility-related implications for children's widespread obligations as head-loaders, filling the family transport gap. The time-poverty this induces can further substantially constrain children's access to education, health, and associated livelihood options, while infringing upon their rights to protection from economic exploitation as set out in Article 32 of the CRC. Child porterage as a topic, however, is considered only briefly.[2]

While physical mobility per se is not an explicit component of the "child rights package," and, thus, this chapter cannot assess specific elements of compliance in this field, we argue that the opportunity to be mobile, in order to access services not available in close vicinity to the child's place of residence, is crucial to many of the formal rights of the Convention, just as it is to many of the Millennium Development Goals (MDGs), which are also disturbingly silent on issues of mobility and transport. In particular, mobility potential may affect a child's rights to health and basic education set out, respectively, in Articles 24 and 28 of the CRC.

In a mobility context, six key points are particularly pertinent to children's circumstances, as opposed to those of other vulnerable groups:[3]

- *Education*—Children and young people need to be able to access basic education on a regular basis to obtain the skills (especially basic literacy and numeracy) they will need for their future lives and livelihoods. Mobility and transport constraints may make this impossible.

- *Health*—Vulnerability to rapid disease progression is particularly high among very young children. Where access and transport to health centers is poor, this will have potentially fatal implications, especially in the case of diseases like malaria and meningitis, where even a few hours delay in obtaining treatment can cause severe, possibly fatal, complications. Timely vaccination against major diseases in early childhood is vital.

- *Poverty*—Children tend to be among the poorest members of households and communities and, thus, may lack the funds to pay transport fares to schools and health centers (and any other key services they need to access) even when transport is available.[4]

- *Physique and mode of transport*—In rural areas, the majority of people are dependent on their own feet for transport. This raises particular difficulties for young children and physically disabled children who may have limited capacity to walk very long distances to school and health centers. Moreover, young children's small physical stature may make journeys over difficult terrain hazardous.

- *Traffic accidents*—Linked to the point above, young children are likely to be particularly vulnerable to traffic accidents as they negotiate busy roads on their way to school, health centers, and other services, due to their small physical stature.

- *Power and voice*—While young people are now widely recognized by Western academics as independent social actors rather than merely passive victims of social change, in Ghana they frequently appear to lack power and access to wider decision-making processes because they tend to occupy the bottom rung of household and community hierarchies. Consequently, their views are less likely to be heard, and their transport and mobility needs are even less likely to be met than those of other groups.

Drawing on these six points, this chapter explores the transport and mobility obstacles that children face in realizing their rights of physical access to education and health services in Ghana. We base our discussion principally on a series of field research projects conducted in coastal Ghana starting in the mid-1990s. This work commenced with environmentally focused studies across four districts in three regions, including Central Region during 1996–1999, followed by a study of market access in five selected off-road villages in the Central Region in 1998–1999, and an in-depth action research study in the same villages in 2001–2003. The length and breadth of the fieldwork has allowed us to site young people's mobility issues more securely within the broad socioeconomic and cultural contexts of the study communities. In 2005, the authors took this work forward with a small pilot study focused specifically on developing an innovative, child-centered approach to understanding children's transport needs through collaboration with child researchers (Porter & Abane, 2008). Again, the field research took place in the Central Region, where further studies are still ongoing.

A Brief Review of Relevant Key Literature

Child and youth studies focused on mobility are somewhat sparse in Ghana, as elsewhere in sub-Saharan Africa. For rural southern Ghana, a preliminary study by Porter & Blaufuss (2002) indicated some of the difficulties faced by both school children and those children not attending school in accessing transport from off-road villages and small rural centers. It emphasized the vital importance of setting mobility and transport within broader socioeconomic, cultural, physical, and environmental contexts. Cultural context, in particular, can play an important role in shaping gendered patterns of spatial autonomy, for instance, with reference to issues such as girls' access to and use of bicycles and the age at which children are considered safe to travel alone. This study complemented earlier work in Ghana's capital city, Accra, where the interconnections between young people's transport and mobility and the broader socioeconomic and cultural context were strongly established (Grieco, Apt, & Turner, 1996; Grieco,

Turner, & Kwakye, 1995; Turner & Kwakye, 1996). The urban research showed how timing of school shifts had become crucial because of the impact on children's ability to perform work; how school-age girls played a significant income role through their work in petty trading outlets and acted as domestic anchors, compensating for the absence of other household members delayed in distant markets by transport problems, and how all of these factors could impact severely on girls' access to education. An ongoing study of child mobility in eight sites across Ghana will add substantially to this evidence base (www.dur.ac.uk/child.mobility).

The education and health literature on Ghana is similarly limited in terms of analyses incorporating mobility issues. There are relatively few published studies that give specific attention to transport time, cost, and effort as factors influencing access. From this perspective, papers by Abane (1993; in press), Avotri, Owusu-Darko, Eghan, & Ocansey (1999), and Fentiman, Hall, & Bundy (1999) are particularly valuable. Fentiman et al. (1999) drew on field data collected from rural areas of three regions across Ghana. Respondents suggested that distance from household to primary school was a significant factor in late or delayed enrollment in basic education. They also found that the distance to school and poor nutrition/stunted growth may have been interrelated as contributing factors for late enrollment (Fentiman et al. 1999). Avotri et al. (1999), in an extensive review of literature relevant to education in Ghana, noted the particular difficulties faced by girl children. If children arrived late, they would be punished, and the punishment was often caning. The long distance to school may have also promoted truancy among girls, in particular, since especially girls would rather miss school than be caned when they are late (1999:51). They also observed that parents tended to spend more on transportation for girls than for boys because of concerns about their daughters' safety (1999:49).

Health research in Ghana has provided some evidence of the way poor access to health services, especially in remoter rural areas, may impact directly on children's lives but also indirectly through mothers' poor maternal health care. The consequences for young children of failure to immunize or delayed treatment (commonly associated with long distance to available health services and transport failure) are potentially severe and often fatal (Cullinan & Pieterick, 1998; Bossyns, Abache, Abdoulaye, Miye, Depoorter, & Van Lerberghe, 2006). In Ghana, Lavy, Strauss, Thomas, & de Vreyer (1996) observed that children under age 5 comprised about 19 percent of the population but accounted for almost half the reported deaths; at least 75 percent of those deaths were the result of preventable infectious and parasitic diseases. A study by Bosu, Ahelegbe, Edum-Fotwe, Bainson, & Turkson (1997) observed that childhood Expanded Program on Immunization (EPI) coverage remained well below target. In a rural area of coastal Ghana not far from our study sites, researchers found that seventy-four of 380 mothers interviewed had never attended an immunization clinic. The transportation difficulties faced by mothers were reported by community leaders as one of the key factors contributing to non-attendance at clinics. Ministry of Health staff members were also found to be affected by transport availability. When Ministry transport was unavailable, they were prevented from undertaking outreach visits. If they hired private transport, they risked not being paid. Subsequent research in Ghana's Volta Region (Tolhurst, Amekudzi, Nyonator, Squire, & Theobald, 2008) showed the complexity of decision-making where health-seeking treatment for children was concerned and how cash for transport was among the important influences affecting whether and when formal treatment for fever was sought. As noted above, failure to access that treatment can be fatal.

Children's Physical Mobility and Access to Health and Education Services: A Review of Field Evidence

In this section, drawing on field evidence, we examined, in turn, each of the key themes noted above that we considered particularly pertinent to children's mobility circumstances and constraints (as opposed to points also widely applicable to other vulnerable groups such as women) in the context of the child rights issue. We focused mainly on field research in four villages situated within the coastal savanna district of Gomoa, one of the poorest districts in Ghana. The villages, which varied in size from approximately 260 to 2,000 people, were primarily Fante villages, though stranger farmers from other Ghanaian regions also resided there. They were located at distances from 3 km to 8 km from the paved road. These were by no means remote settlements, but all were considered relatively disadvantaged (by comparison with settlements along the paved road) both by the district administration and by the villagers themselves. At the start of our studies in the mid-1990s, all faced considerable access problems, and not one had a regular transport service. This can be attributed at least in part to the poor quality of their access roads. Transport fares per km on the rough laterite roads to these villages were approximately double those along the paved roads in the same district. Vehicles were rarely found and even more rarely based in these settlements: one village had a taxi based there at night, one had three minibuses and a taxi (but these often operated elsewhere in the daytime), two other villages had no transport based there.

Health and Access to Health Services

Article 24 of the CRC observes the right of the child to "the enjoyment of the highest attainable standard of health and to facilities for the treatment of illness and rehabilitation of health. States Parties shall strive to ensure that no child is deprived of his or her right of access to such health care services." The states parties are expected to take a range of measures, including the following: to diminish infant and child mortality; to ensure provision of medical assistance and health care to all children, with specific emphasis on primary health care; to combat disease and malnutrition through provision of adequate nutritious foods and clean drinking water; to ensure pre-natal and post-natal care for mothers; and to develop preventive health care, including family planning information. When we examined conditions in our four Gomoa study villages, the significance of physical access as a constraint on achievement of these objectives was readily apparent.

In all four Gomoa villages, many children suffered from health problems associated with a range of water-borne and other diseases because locally available water supplies were poor and health services inadequate. Guinea worm incidence appeared to be relatively low, but chronic diarrhea was widespread among young children. A substantial proportion of children in the villages, possibly a majority, did not have access to clean drinking water. In three of the four villages, there were boreholes, but in two of three villages these were locked, and the charge made for water, though small, was prohibitive for many families, especially where there were large numbers of children. Consequently, children in particular spent much of their time, especially in the early morning and evening, carrying home buckets and bowls of water from nearby ponds and rivers where livestock were also watered.

In the context of widespread recourse to potentially contaminated water, the fact that vaccination coverage also appeared unsatisfactory, especially in some of the remoter hamlets associated with these villages, was especially disturbing. Vaccinations were administered by the community health nurses, who had to walk to the villages from the paved road when official transport was unavailable. Consequently, they often only had time to visit the main village center. In one hamlet, women suggested that it had been over two years since the vaccinator had visited the village. This accorded with observations about low rates of immunization in remoter locations noted by Bosu et al. (1997) mentioned above.

Usually, it was only when villagers considered their children seriously sick that they would try to access state health care services. Their first resort was commonly home herbal remedies, patent medicines available from the local market or the hawker who traveled around the villages on foot or bicycle, or perhaps to a village herbalist or spiritual healer. One of the reasons for not accessing state clinics was distance. Not one of the villages had a health post or clinic. Distances to the nearest basic facility varied between 5 km and 9 km by road. For Abora, the smallest village, the nearest health center was 5 km away along a narrow footpath, or about 8 km by road, though a private mobile clinic visited occasionally. Despite the charge for drugs, this was a popular facility precisely because it came to the village. For Lome, the largest village, the nearest clinic was 5 km away at a roadside settlement; however, drug stocks and equipment were limited there. Consequently, villagers who could afford transport tended to trek 5 km to the paved road with their sick child and then traveled by vehicle to the nearest town 23 km away (unless it was market day, in which case a local minibus [*tro-tro*] or taxi came into the village with traders from nearby towns). Preventive care and family planning services were similarly only available at distant facilities. So far as maternal health was concerned, the situation was slightly better in that three of the four villages had at least one traditional birth attendant, but the services provided could not be said to constitute adequate pre-natal and post-natal care for mothers who experienced anything other than a very straightforward pregnancy and birth.

The long-term implications of poor sanitation and poor physical access to health services in childhood are substantial. Poor health and delays in treatment raise child morbidity and mortality rates substantially. Chronic illness, in particular, is likely to impede school attendance, damage school performance, and reduce livelihood and life chances in the longer term.

Accessing Education

Article 28 of the CRC observes the right of the child to education, particularly primary education, which is to be "compulsory and available free to all." Measures are to be taken to encourage regular attendance at school. Secondary and vocational education is also to be made "available and accessible" to every child. "Access" in the CRC obviously implies more than physical access, but physical access can be a key issue affecting school enrollment and attendance, especially when considered in conjunction with other factors such as requirements to purchase uniforms, books, and other items, even when schooling is, in theory, free. Whereas Article 28 focuses on education for all, Article 29 (d) specifically notes that the education of the child shall be directed to preparation for responsible life in a free society, including equality of the sexes. Gendered access to education is a very significant issue so far as child rights are concerned in sub-Saharan Africa. Enrollment and attendance figures for primary education have risen rapidly in recent years, as efforts were made to reach MDG targets in this area, but many girls, in particular, continue to face substantial constraints in their access to regular education.

In our four Gomoa study villages, the requirement of free basic access to primary education set out in Article 28 was met. Indeed, there were nursery, primary, and junior secondary schools (JSS) in each village area. However, in the case of one village, there was no school at the main site, and children had to travel on foot 2–3 km or to other villages. In a few satellite settlements associated with one of the villages, some children had to walk up to 4 km to the primary school. Few of the children progressed to senior secondary school because this required travel beyond the village area to one of the four senior secondary schools in the district. Only a few boys (no girls) had bicycles and were able to travel daily to secondary school. One eighteen-year-old boy we met cycled each Monday to his school about 15 km away and returned for the weekend; he could not afford the 3,000 cedi *tro-tro* journey and had won the cycle in a lottery. Simon's weekly visits home were necessary because his parents could not afford to pay for his term expenses in one lump sum. For most families who wished to send a child to secondary school, the options were to find a relative for the child to stay with during the school term or to rent a room near the school unless the secondary school had affordable boarding facilities. However, the cost of secondary school fees and other incidental costs (such as uniforms and books) were usually prohibitive, especially when transport costs also had to be met.

Children—both boys and girls—were commonly enrolled at primary school because it was free. But pupils' attendance figures were well below enrollment due to the fact that children were needed to help with many tasks during the day, especially since there was a shortage of labor in this region. This was particularly the case on local market days when parents regularly took their children out of school to assist with family transport of goods, in the absence of cheap reliable motorized transport services. For girl children, such labor demands were especially high since they were expected to play a particularly substantial role in both headloading goods and domestic work, in general (Porter, Blaufuss, & Owusu Acheampong, in press). One young teacher complained, "The children come when they want," but attendance seemed to be more a factor of family demands than the children's preferences. He estimated there were probably over one hundred children in the village where he taught, but only fifty-four children were enrolled. At another village, the primary school headmaster observed that boy and girl numbers enrolled were roughly equal, but many didn't come to school because they had to carry firewood to market. Although schooling was free, the District Assembly (DA) assessed a small charge (2,200 cedis in 1998). Many children were unable to pay, but the headmaster didn't stop them from coming to school "because it's been difficult to get them to school in the first place." He complained that the DA had put an embargo on his salary because of his failure to collect sufficient payment. For boy and girl children in the satellite settlements, the long walk to school (usually preceded by long walks to obtain water) was a further disincentive to attendance throughout the school week. Where secondary school was concerned, we observed that the distances and associated costs involved in attendance usually prohibited enrollment. The number of girls enrolled in secondary schools in the four study villages could have been counted on one hand.

Transport-related issues not only affected children's attendance at school but also impacted on school quality within the four study villages. Teachers were extremely reluctant to work in these schools: off-road villages were commonly perceived as punishment postings. Consequently, many of the teachers in the study villages were untrained teachers or probationers who were required to work where the Ministry of Education posted them. As soon as the two-year probationary period was complete, they would apply for a posting elsewhere. They found village life uncomfortable in the absence of electricity, reliable potable water, and other urban amenities: "You don't get access to anything you want. You have to go and buy everything and bring it down," according to a JSS teacher in Sampa. Teachers' response was usually either to travel to town every weekend or to live permanently out of the village at the nearest roadside settlement (from which they would trek or cycle to work daily in the absence of regular motorized transport). In Adabra village, of the six (untrained) primary teachers and four (trained) JSS teachers, only one lived in the village. Another lived in the next village, but the remainder all lived at the paved road. Transport from the paved road was only available on two days each week; the remaining days they had to walk the 40–60 minutes to school each day; only one had a bicycle. Frequent teacher absences and late arrivals for lessons were inevitable.

Despite the provision of free primary education, it was clear that children in the study villages were unlikely to benefit to the degree one might anticipate. Enrollment had increased, but attendance figures remained substantially lower, especially for girls. As we have shown, low attendance was, in part, a factor of transport and accessibility issues, not only with respect to children but also to teachers. In the case of senior secondary schools, distance when coupled with fees and associated costs was a key factor inhibiting enrollment.

Child Poverty and Access to Transport

Although Articles 24 and 28 of the CRC observe the right of the child to health and education, respectively, we have observed that distance to health centers and to schools can be an important contributing factor inhibiting children's use of services. In the case of clinics, hospitals, and secondary schools, the location of facilities is substantially restricted by the availability of state funds for infrastructure and staff. Most are sited in accessible centers, principally larger villages or towns. Off-road villages are unlikely to be selected as appropriate locations. Consequently, in remoter areas it is often necessary to travel on foot, by bicycle, or by motorized transport to access them. Where distances are long, pedestrian travel becomes difficult, especially in the case of sick children where they may need to be carried. Bicycles or motorized public transport may be available for at least part of the journey, but their use generally implies access to funds to purchase or rent a bicycle or to pay fares for the journey on motorized transport. In the case of healthcare, children rarely travel to clinics and hospitals unaccompanied, so a parent or other family member will usually expect to pay the costs of the journey, but in the case of travel to school, children may have to pay the fare themselves or walk. Since children tend to be among the poorest members of households and communities and, thus, lack the funds to pay transport fares even when transport is available, this further constrains their access to distant facilities, notably senior secondary school.

In the four study villages, many children were expected to contribute to family income. While parents widely recognized their "primary responsibility to secure [within their abilities and financial capacities] the conditions of living necessary for the child's development," in accordance with Article 27, the difficulties of securing an adequate income in poor rural areas like Gomoa were substantial. Consequently, girls and boys may have needed to help their parents to earn money to pay for key items such as schoolbooks. Boys often wanted to earn money so that they could hire and, thus, learn to ride a bicycle. These bicycles for hire were sometimes available on weekends in the villages when they were brought in from nearby roadside centers. Few girls learned to cycle because they tended to have less opportunity to earn money to hire a bicycle and, in any case, risked disapprobation from community members when they cycled.

At least a portion of the work that children in the study villages undertook to earn money for transport was likely to contravene Article 32 of the CRC, which observes the right of the child to be protected from economic exploitation and "from any work that is likely to be hazardous or to interfere with the child's education, or to be harmful to the child's health." As we discussed above, such work prevents many children from regularly attending school, is likely to reduce effective performance at school, and where it involves carrying heavy loads, may be particularly harmful to children's health in the longer term. As one government review of child labor issues observed (Government of Ghana, 1992:xii), children are often regarded as an economic asset and security for old age. The arguments around exploitation versus socialization continue, but the review noted that it is necessary to be aware that socialization can camouflage or degenerate into exploitation. Given that fostering was a common practice in the study area, the danger of exploitation of foster children was especially great. Research in the Upper West Region of Ghana suggested that school dropouts were often girls who worked as house-helps for foster parents (Avotri et al., 1999:102).

Children's Physique, Mode of Transport, and Associated Road Safety Issues

Walking is the principal transport mode for the majority of people in Gomoa District, as in the rest of Ghana. This is the case especially in rural areas (Abane, 1982). However, young children, in particular, have limited capacity to walk very long distances to school and health centers, and their small physical stature may make journeys over difficult terrain particularly hazardous. For this reason, if the distance to school is great, children may be enrolled only when they are considered old and strong enough to make the journey regularly. Avotri et al. (1999) (citing Boakye, 1997), noted the high proportion of late-enrolled and non-enrolled children ages six–seven in the Afram Plains area of Ghana where access to schools was difficult. For disabled children, the likelihood of school enrollment in such circumstances was extremely low.

Children are likely to be particularly vulnerable as they negotiate busy roads on the journey to school, health centers, and other services, in part because of their relatively small stature, in part because they may be less aware of traffic and the dangers it presents, perhaps also because they have difficulty assessing speed of vehicles (Ghana Ministry of Transport and Communications, 2001). For the world as a whole, it is sobering to note that road crashes are now reportedly the leading cause of death for children and young people ages ten–twenty-four years (IRAP, n.d.). Accident fatality rates are high in Ghana (seventy-three reported fatalities per 10,000 vehicles), and pedestrians are at particularly high risk of fatal accidents (Ghana Ministry of Transport and Communications, 2001; Jorgensen & Abane, 1999). Many accidents—possibly four of five—are not reported. "Children, although they represent a relatively small road user group, have an alarmingly high fatality rate" (Ghana Ministry of Transport and Communications, 2001:14). A study by Mock, Forjuoh, & Rivara (1999) in Kumasi and the Brong Ahafo Region of Ghana, north of our study area, found both urban and rural children particularly vulnerable to traffic accidents. In Kumasi, 52 percent of injured pedestrians and 33 percent of injured cyclists were children up to fifteen years old. In their rural study area, 46 percent of injured pedestrians and 30 percent of cyclists were children. Many children are injured while buying and selling along busy roads, as Adesunkanmi, Oginnib, Oyelamic, & Badrub (2000) also reported in a Nigerian study. Deficient road safety measures can, in part, be blamed for the high level of injuries observed.

Interviews in Accra with donor agencies in 2002 suggested that the Ghana Road Fund has an obligation to release money for road safety, but one frustrated donor staff member observed, "It's the last priority!" Insufficient attention to implementation of road safety measures could arguably infringe upon Article 6 of the CRC, which observes that "State Parties recognize that every child has the inherent right to life," and "State Parties shall ensure to the maximum extent possible the survival and development of the child," and perhaps even Article 3 that "State Parties shall ensure that the institutions, services, and facilities responsible for the care or protection of children shall conform with the standards established by competent authorities, particularly in the areas of safety." A number of initiatives have been implemented in recent years, including plans for a nationwide road safety education program for school children ages eight–nine and twelve–thirteen within the life skills curriculum, engineering interventions of traffic calming on roads near schools, and preparation of safer crossing points as components of Ghana's 2001–2005 National Road Safety Strategy. An umbrella NGO focused on road safety, the Global Road Safety Partnership (GRSP), was also established in Ghana in 2000. These developments seem to have had some positive impact, but it must be noted that the education strategy will not reach out-of-school children. A traffic education strategy is probably most crucial for this group, given the fact that they are likely to be exposed to longer hours on the street since they are not attending school and especially dangerous contexts where they are engaged in roadside trading.

We undertook preliminary inquiries in Gomoa District in 2002 concerning the incidence of traffic accidents and road safety teaching. In our study's four off-road villages, there were virtually no reports of conventional road accidents involving children occurring within the village boundaries, although children had had accidents while headloading and cycling. The only cases we came across related to an eleven-year-old girl hit by a motorbike during a visit to her sister in Accra and a school party that had been traveling in an open lorry to a football match. The lorry was overloaded, and three children from the village were hurt when the lorry tire burst and the vehicle overturned. Even in the remotest of the off-road study villages, however, mothers said they taught basic principles of crossing the road to their children.

In and around the small towns of Gomoa, children were at greater risk of traffic accidents. Motorized traffic was sporadic along the often-potholed secondary paved roads, and there were no designated pedestrian areas. National speed restrictions were not widely enforced, and many vehicles were badly maintained and operated with inadequate brakes and faulty tires. Apam police headquarters reported that most accidents were caused by vehicle mechanical faults. Police in Ghana, however, were commonly lax in their attitude to traffic offenses, and small bribes were reportedly often sufficient to avoid further proceedings. Drivers (who frequently operated without a driving licence) avoided reporting accidents if at all possible, in order to avoid encounters with the police (Ghana National Road Safety Commission, 2001; author interviews, road safety officials, Accra).

In Dawurampong, a small town close to two of our study villages, 189 children were interviewed about road accidents. Sixteen of the 118 boys interviewed (13.5 percent) had experienced a road accident, as had six of the seventy-one girls (8 percent). These road accidents ranged from serious injury to minor cuts and bruises. An examination of the data by age suggested that the incidence of accidents among boys increased with age, particularly in the age range sixteen or older, whereas with girls the incidence was more even across the age groups. However, the total number of cases in each age set was insufficiently large to allow any reliable interpretation of this data. The issue needs further investigation with a larger data set. At nearby Apam's senior secondary school, very similar accident rates were found: seventeen of 116 boys (14.7 percent) and ten of 103 girls (9.7 percent) had experienced an accident. Discussions with teachers and others supported the view that boys were more likely to have road accidents than girls, both as pedestrians and cyclists: "Boys are always on the street . . . in most cases, girls are in their kitchens," said a teacher in Lome village.

Investigations into road safety education at the various schools where we conducted interviews in 2002 suggested that road safety was often taught merely as an adjunct to normal lessons at primary and JSS levels. It commonly included training about crossing a busy road and a jingle about traffic lights. The fact that this was a non-examined subject seemed to contribute to its low profile. None of the teachers we interviewed had received specialized road safety training.

Power and Voice

While young people are now widely recognized by Western academics as independent social actors rather than merely passive victims of social change, in Ghana they frequently appear to lack power and access to wider decision-making processes. Children tend to occupy the bottom rung of household and community hierarchies, and girls face particular constraints because women's place in the social hierarchy is below that of men. A child's place is to be respectful and obedient: to be seen but not heard (Lamptey, 1998; Appiah & Cusack, 1999; Twum-Danso (2009). Where initiatives had been introduced to support children, they often appeared paternalistic and essentially welfarist in approach. Child rights were perceived to be an issue for adults, not youth. When we interviewed parents about child-related mobility issues in the study villages, there was a tendency for parents to tell the children to go elsewhere if they were within earshot of the conversation; children were not expected to be party to adult discussions.

In these circumstances, young people's views were less likely to be heard and their transport and mobility needs even less likely to be met than those of other groups. In 2003, two of the authors conducted a small pilot study to see whether we might increase the input of children into transport planning in Ghana (Porter & Abane, 2008). We worked with a small group of twelve young people, seven boys and five girls between the ages of eleven and nineteen, who were trained in some basic methods for researching transport and mobility issues. They then interviewed their peers in a test site, a peri-urban settlement in Central Region, not far from the four study villages discussed above. The findings from this small project were extremely interesting, covering some of the issues we have raised above, such as long walks to school, but also drawing attention to problems which young people were probably rather reluctant to discuss with stranger adults or thought were likely to seem insignificant and foolish to adults. These included being frightened by taxis that hooted at them suddenly, having a precious school uniform drenched and dirtied by passing traffic in the rains, having to negotiate open drains and potholes (especially difficult in the case of children of small stature), and girls being propositioned by taxi drivers.

Getting these findings onto adult agendas and acted upon, however, is a harder task. This is especially the case in the transport world, where male civil engineers trained in road construction and maintenance are key decision-makers and tend (with a few notable exceptions) to resist the incorporation of road transport user needs and associated social issues in transport planning. For this reason, a Country Consultative Group was established at the start of the study, with representatives from two local children's NGOs and one national NGO, schoolteachers, the regional offices of relevant key ministries (women and children's affairs, education, agriculture, health, road transport, urban roads), the Ghana Private Road Transport Union (GPRTU), and the police. The positive feedback that the young researchers received from the consultative group, and the workshop we held for a wider audience of policymakers and practitioners at the end of the pilot, was sufficient to encourage the researchers of all ages to consider pursuing this work further in order to build a broader evidence base. We have done so in an ongoing research program covering eight sites in two different regions of Ghana, with both young people and adult researchers participating (www.dur.ac.uk/child.mobility). Hopefully, the new findings will give young people a greater voice in an area where children's input has potentially great significance for improving lives.

Conclusion: The Reality of Mobility Constraints

In a child rights context, little attention has been paid to mobility. This is unfortunate since, as we have shown in this chapter, improving mobility constraints is fundamental to achieving many children's rights. The constraints faced by girl children in this respect need particular attention. As Cornwall & Molyneux (2006) observed, governments tend to be selective in their promotion of rights. Citing Croll, they noted that in an Asian context, attention to the rights of girls has tended to be concentrated on just one dimension: education. Croll's view (2006), that girls' rights need to be highlighted in a more holistic way to confront deeper issues of discrimination and neglect, is arguably also relevant to the Ghanaian context. Education is certainly of vital importance, but access to healthcare and contraception are equally crucial. Discrimination against girls, in particular, in terms of participation and voice must also receive greater attention. As Croll emphasized, girls' interests may be quite different and possibly conflict with those of both women and boys: in many Ghanaian homes, the domestic burden placed on girl children, including their role as pedestrian transporters in particular, is an important factor impeding their independent mobility and access to a range of key services.

Greater recognition by the Ghanaian government of the mobility and transport constraints faced by girls, in particular, in realizing their rights of physical access to education and health services and specific efforts to address those constraints is essential. There are many transport and non-transport interventions worthy of consideration, including, for instance: bicycle hire centers based in schools; training of girls in cycle riding (to encourage a critical mass that would make girls' cycling more culturally acceptable); training of girls (and boys) in cycle maintenance and repair; training programs to sensitize teachers to children's lateness issues associated with domestic work demands and travel distance to school; improved water supplies and village fuel wood reserves to reduce children's time spent on long walks collecting water and wood and the potential effects of carrying heavy loads; and more efficient wood or solar stoves to reduce the volume of wood required by households each day. The potential of individual initiatives in different parts of Ghana would depend in part, of course, on local context (for instance, topographic conditions in the case of bicycles).

Although Ghana has achieved some progress in its attention to children's rights, there is clearly considerable room for further improvement. A stronger recognition of the role of physical mobility in achieving many of the formal rights of the CRC and appropriate interventions to address children's current mobility and access constraints would be a significant step forward.

Notes

1. However, the 2006 CRC State Party report review for Ghana (CRC/C/GHA/CO/2) indicates that broad problems around young people's lack of voice, limited funding for CRC implementation, and the still relatively restricted role played by NGOs and CBOs in promoting children's rights, remain a serious hindrance to improved conditions for children.

2. For further discussion of children's headloading, see Porter, Blaufuss, and Owusu Acheampong (2007, in press); further research is currently in progress: www.dur.ac.uk/child.mobility.

3. These points are made in Porter, in press, with reference to youth mobility and the MDGs.

4. This child poverty problem connects us to the vexed issue of child work, a complex child rights issue discussed in chapter 11 of Porter, in press. Children and young people often work hard at a range of domestic tasks in Ghana, for which they are unpaid. If they do obtain paid work, children's wages are usually lower than for adults.

References

Abane, A. M. (1982). *Roads and footpaths network analysis of the central northeast of the Upper Region, Ghana.* Unpublished MA thesis, University of Cape Coast, Ghana.

———. (1993). Mode choice for the journey to work among formal sector employees in Accra, Ghana. *Journal of Transport Geography* 1 (4), 119–129.

———. (in press). Travel behavior in Ghana: Empirical observations from four metropolitan areas. *Journal of Transport Geography.*

Adesunkanmi, A. R. K., L. M. Oginnib, O. A. Oyelamic, and O. S. Badrub. (2000). Road traffic accidents to African children. *Injury* 31, 225–228.

Appiah, D. C., and K. Cusack. (1999). *Violence against women and children in Ghana: Report of a national study on violence.* Accra: Gender Studies and Human Rights Documentation Centre.

Avotri, R., L. Owusu-Darko, H. Eghan, and S. Ocansey. (1999). *Gender and primary schooling in Ghana.* Sussex: Institute of Development Studies, October 1999.

Bossyns, P., R. Abache, M. S. Abdoulaye, H. Miye, A. M. Depoorter, and W. Van Lerberghe. (2006). Monitoring the referral system through benchmarking in rural Niger: An evaluation of the functional relation between health centers and the district hospital. *BMC Health Services Research* 6, 51, April 12, 2006.

Bosu, W. K., D. Ahelegbe, E. Edum-Fotwe, K. A. Bainson, and P. K. Turkson. (1997). Factors affecting attendance to immunization sessions in Ghana. *Acta Tropica* 68, 259–267.

Convention on the Rights of the Child (CRC). (2006). *Consideration of reports submitted by state parties under Article 44 of the Convention: Concluding observations: Ghana.* CRC/C/GHA/CO/2, March 17, 2006.

Cornwall, A., and M. Molyneux. (2006). The politics of rights—dilemmas for feminist praxis: An introduction. *Third World Quarterly* 27 (7), 1175–1191.

Croll, E. (2006). From the girl child to girls' rights. *Third World Quarterly* 27 (7), 1285–1297.

Cullinan, T. R., and C. Pieterick. (1998). Packaged treatment for first line care in cerebral malaria and meningitis. *Bull WHO* 76 (3), 257–264.

Fentiman, A., A. Hall, and D. Bundy. (1999). School enrolment patterns in rural Ghana: A comparative study of the impact of location, gender, age and health on children's access to basic schooling. *Comparative Education* 35 (3), 331–349.

Ghana Ministry of Transport and Communications. (2001). *National Road Safety Commission: National road safety strategy 2001–2005.* Republic of Ghana, July 2001.

Government of Ghana (GOG). (1992). *The child cannot wait: A national program of action on the follow-up to the world summit for children.* Accra, June 1992.

Grieco, M., N. Apt, and J. Turner. (1996). *At Christmas and on Rainy Days: Transport, Travel and the Female Traders of Accra.* Aldershot: Avebury.

Grieco, M., J. Turner, and E. Kwakye. (1995). A tale of two cultures: Ethnicity and cycling behavior in urban Ghana. *Transport Research Record 1441*, Washington, DC.

International Road Assessment Program (IRAP). (n.d.). *Vaccines for roads: The new IRAP tools and their pilot application.*

Jorgensen, S. H., and A. M. Abane. (1999). A comparative study of urban traffic accidents in developing and developed countries: Empirical observations and problems from Trondheim (Norway) and Accra (Ghana). *Bulletin of the Ghana Geographical Association* 21, 113–127.

Lamptey, A. (1998). Children creating awareness about their rights in Ghana. In V. Johnson, et al. *Stepping Forward: Children and Young People's Participation in the Development Process.* London: Intermediate Technology Publications.

Lavy, V., J. Strauss, D. Thomas, and P. de Vreyer. (1996). Quality of health care, survival and health outcomes in Ghana. *Journal of Health Economics* 15, 333–357.

Mock, C. N., S. N. Forjuoh, and F. P. Rivara. (1999). Epidemiology of transport-related injuries in Ghana. *Accident Analysis and Prevention* 31, 359–370.

Porter, G. (in press). Transport planning in sub-Saharan Africa III: The challenges of meeting children and young people's mobility and transport needs. *Progress in Development Studies.*

Porter, G., and A. Abane. (2008). Increasing children's participation in African transport planning: Reflections on methodological issues in a child-centered research project. *Children's Geographies* 6 (2), 151–167.

Porter, G., and K. Blaufuss. (2002). Children, transport and traffic in Southern Ghana. International workshop on transport and children, Copenhagen, May 2002.

Porter, G., K. Blaufuss, and F. O. Acheampong. (2007). Youth, mobility and rural livelihoods in sub-Saharan Africa: Perspectives from Ghana and Nigeria. *Africa Insight* 37 (3), 420–431.

———. (in press). Filling the family's transport gap in sub-Saharan Africa: Young people and load carrying in Ghana. In L. Holt (ed.). *Geographies of Children, Youth and Families: An International Perspective.* London: Routledge.

Tolhurst, R., Y. P. Amekudzi, F. K. Nyonator, S. B. Squire, and S. Theobald. (2008). He will ask why the child gets sick so often: The gendered dynamics of intra-household bargaining over healthcare for children with fever in the Volta Region of Ghana. *Social Science and Medicine* 66, 1106–1117.

Twum-Danso, A. (2009). Reciprocity, respect and responsibility: The three Rs underlying parent-child relationships in Ghana and the implications for children's rights. *The International Journal of Children's Rights*, 17(3), 415-432.

Turner, G., and E. Kwakye. (1996). Transport and survival strategies in a developing economy: Case evidence from Accra, Ghana. *Journal of Transport Geography* 4 (3), 161–168.

Part III
Policies, Laws, and Programs

Chapter 8

Children's Rights, Controversial Traditional Practices, and the *Trokosi* System: A Critical Socio-legal Perspective

By Robert Kwame Ame

Negative or controversial traditional practices are practices justified on grounds of culture or religion but which violate international human rights norms. Under international law, these practices fall under the rubric of contemporary forms of slavery.[1] This chapter examines children's rights and negative traditional practices, with focus on the *trokosi* system from a critical socio-legal perspective. It discusses the nebulous concept of human rights, its application to negative traditional practices, using the *trokosi* system to illustrate the complications entailed in transforming such practices. The chapter argues that recognition of traditional practices and religious rites in domestic law, acquiescence of parents and other close relatives, high patronage in practicing communities, the sanctimonious attitude of Ghanaians towards these practices, and failure of governments, traditional councils, and civil society organizations to propose credible alternatives to these practices have all worked together to complicate efforts to transform these practices.

In Ghana, controversial traditional practices include widowhood rites, female circumcision, child marriages, and the *trokosi* system. *Trokosi* practice is actualized when a female child, sometimes as young as three years, is abandoned at a shrine to serve in atonement for a crime committed by other family members, usually, males. But in so far as *trokosi* practice is part of the traditional religious and crime control system of the Ewes of Ghana, Togo, and Benin, it constitutes female ritual servitude (Ame, 2010). While it is predominantly an aspect of the traditional Ewe crime control system, the Dangmes of Ghana also indulge in the practice, calling it *woryokwe*. In theory, these girls and women are supposed to serve in the shrine for only a few years, but in practice, it becomes a lifetime of servitude as families are reluctant to perform the rituals that would liberate the girls from the shrines. With thousands of girls and women involved, *trokosi* practice falls within the domain of children's rights. The controversy over the *trokosi* system in Ghana has largely been set within the context of international human rights discourse whereby the practice is seen as violating the rights of the girls and women involved, while proponents of the practice disagree with this view (Ababio, 1995, 2000; Ameh, 2001, 2004a, 2004b; Bilyeu, 1999; Short, 1995, 1997, 1998a, 1998b, 2000, 2001; Dartey-Kumordzie 1995, 2000, n.d.; Addo, 1994, 1998). Thus, a good starting point for our discussions would be to grapple with the concept of human rights.

What Are Human Rights?

The concept and practice of human rights mean different things to different people and societies. Some scholars define rights as entitlements due a person simply for being human. Rights are, thus, defined as "the basic standards of equity and justice without which people cannot live in dignity." From this perspective, rights are seen as inherent, universal, and inalienable as they are deemed as emanating from nature. In this sense, they are god-given. It was in this vein that Darren O'Byrne (2003:26–27) defined human rights as "a universal set of ethical principles which seek to ensure the equal worth of each individual life and which are applicable to all peoples at all times and in all places." This definition underscores the idea that human rights are universal, incontrovertible, and subjective.

Others like Gary Teeple (2004) have, however, argued that human rights did not emerge in a vacuum and that they are products of social and political struggles that led to the granting of human rights first to white middle class property owners, then to all white males, before women and minorities. In this vein, Michael Goodhart (2009) argued that rights are inherently revolutionary and have never been given on a silver platter. Similarly, Norberto Bibbio (1996: xi–xii) rejects the idea of innate, pre-social rights and argued that human rights are and always have been historical rights and that different rights emerged at different times as a result of different social conflicts. There seems to be agreement in the literature that contemporary rights originate from the struggles that emerged around the liberal ideals of freedom and equality in Western societies. Starting from the Magna Carta (1215) and the English Bill of Rights (1688–1689) through the American Declarations of Rights (1776–1789) and the French Declaration of the Rights of Man and the Citizen (1789), rights have been products of social conflicts (Goodhart, 2009; Teeple, 2004; Smith, 2005; O'Byrne, 2003). These struggles culminated in the adoption of the Universal Declaration of Human Rights (UDHR) in 1948 and the subsequent Covenant on Civil and

Political Rights and Covenant on Economic, Social, Cultural Rights in 1966, the trio regarded today as the International Bill of Rights. Thus, as Goodhart (2009) rightly pointed out, the appeal of human rights lies in its revolutionary character and opposition to subordination, subjugation, and oppression of any kind.

However, some have argued that human rights can only flourish in societies ruled by the liberal ideals of individual autonomy, equality, and free market (Howard, 1986, 1992, 1993, 1995; Howard & Donnelley, 1986). Such scholars argue that human rights are, nevertheless, universal, as all contemporary states have given their consent to the current regime of international human rights as represented in the International Bill of Rights. Relativists retort by arguing that at the end of the day, human rights have to do with human dignity, and that every society of the world, whether liberal or not, has some conception of human dignity. Consequently, they argue, human rights did not originate with Western liberal societies and are subject to each society's values (Motala, 1989; wa Mutua, 1995; Nhlapo, 1989). Goodhart (2009:2–5), however, pointed out that the type of dignity entailed in human rights does not support subordination and injustice of any kind no matter its source, be it traditional, cultural, or religious. Goodhart (2009:1–5) and Anthony Langlois (2009:18–19) have convincingly argued that the core elements of modern human rights are human dignity, rationality, autonomy, equality, needs, and capabilities.

Yet, other scholars such as Hannah Arendt (1951:290–302) have also argued that however good rights are, they are meaningful only to the extent that states are capable and willing to enforce them. In essence, rights are simply entitlements states are prepared to grant their citizens or people within their jurisdiction. Arendt's assertion establishes a strong link between human rights and the political and legal structures of a state for the realization of human rights. "In that respect," as pointed out by Darren O'Byrne (2003:17), "the state—in its political, judicial, or military manifestations—is still central to the [human rights] debate." In effect, human rights are intricately linked to the politics, legal structures, and coercive apparatus of a state in a particular jurisdiction (Goodhart, 2009; Langlois, 2009; Cardenas, 2009). It then stands to reason that despite the popularity of the claims of the UDHR (1948) to the effect that all men are born equal, whatever rights one enjoys in practice depends on the state in which one resides and the rights that particular state offers and protects for people living within its jurisdiction. Even though the state plays a central role in the realization of human rights, it is important not to forget that that many negative traditional practices do not always involve state actors but non-state actors such as parents, other relatives, and ethnic, religious, cultural, and economic leaders in the local community. Consequently, rights are not limited to entitlements against the state but also non-state actors. This view of rights casts doubt on the idea of rights being inherent, inalienable, universal, incontrovertible, and indivisible.

While human rights may mean different things to different people, they have, nevertheless, become the predominant moral standard in international law and international relations and are constantly invoked in domestic affairs, as well. As pointed out by Goodhart (2009:3–5), its appeal lies in its revolutionary character and emancipatory logic that makes it attractive to people struggling against domination and oppression everywhere in the world. Human rights are attractive because of their opposition to subordination and subjugation, be it cultural, religious, or political, which has made it a rallying cry for the oppressed and excluded people wherever they are found all over the world.

Children's Rights in International Law

One group of rights bearers in international law is children. The first children's rights legal instrument was the Declaration of the Rights of the Child 1924, also referred to as the Geneva Declaration. It established the claim that "mankind owes to the child the best it has to give" and that the child must be given the material and spiritual means required for its normal development. It asserted that the child must be the first to receive relief in times of distress, put in a position to earn a livelihood, be protected against every form of exploitation, and be brought up in the consciousness that its talents must be devoted to the service of its fellow men. It specified that the needs of the sick, backward, orphan, poor, and hungry must be provided, thus creating a welfare principle in the protection of children.

Geraldine Van Bueren (1998:8) argued that this Declaration established the concept of the rights of the child internationally and laid the foundation for future work on children's rights, making false the contention that children's rights is a new development in international human rights law as it preceded the UDHR by twenty-four years. As she rightly pointed out, the Declaration was not only concerned with political and civil rights but also economic and social rights and, thus, provided the first international acknowledgment of the link between child welfare and the rights of the child. Mark Ensalaco (2005:10) also observed the significance of the link between meeting the needs of the child and its development in this Declaration and the connection between needs and the full development of the child in subsequent international instruments. However, neither the preamble nor the text placed any binding obligation on states parties to provide for the child. Rather, they placed a duty on "men and women of all states" to provide the child with "the best it has to give" and by so doing regarded children as the recipients of treatment (objects) rather than as bearers of specific rights and, therefore, not as subjects of international law (Van Bueren, 1998).

Declaration of the Rights of the Child 1959

Building on the principle of the 1924 Declaration that "mankind owes the child the best it has to give," the 1959 Declaration introduced the principles of "special protection" and "the best interests of the child" into international law. It acknowledged that children are equally entitled to rights in their own accord, making them subjects of international law rather than objects to be protected by others. Thus, unlike the 1924 Declaration, it placed an obligation on governments to implement the Declaration through legislative and other measures and also called on non-governmental organizations (NGOs) to observe the Declaration. It expanded the scope of rights listed in the 1924 Declaration by adding specific rights such as name and nationality, adequate nutrition, housing, medical services, education, play and recreation, special needs of the disabled, and required children's protection from all forms of exploitation, neglect, and trafficking (Van Bueren, 1998:10–11; Ensalaco 2005:12). As Van Bueren (1998:12) pointed out, the 1959 Declaration played a significant role in the promotion of children's rights around the world and set the stage for subsequent events that led to the drafting and adoption of the Convention on the Rights of the Child in 1989.

United Nations Convention on the Rights of the Child 1989

The United Nations (UN) Convention on the Rights of the Child (CRC) expanded on the welfare principles in the 1924 and 1959 Declarations. Three key principles for the interpretation of the CRC are "the best interests of the child," "the evolving capacities of the child," and "non-discrimination" by which it accords the same rights to all children everywhere in the world regardless of race, class, nationality, and family background. The Convention guarantees children: (1) rights of provision (adequate nutrition, health care, education, economic welfare), (2) rights of protection (protection from abuse, neglect, violence, exploitation), and (3) rights of participation (a voice in decisions affecting the child), and places an obligation on states parties to provide and protect these rights. Ghana ratified the CRC in February 1990, making it the first country to do so. The CRC has become so popular that it enjoys almost universal ratification (only the United States and Somalia have not ratified it even though both countries have signed it).

Harmful Traditional Practices

Harmful traditional practices is a broad term that encompasses all those practices outlined in the 1986 report of the Working Group on Traditional Practices Affecting the Health of Women and Children.[2] The list includes practices such as female circumcision, various forms of mutilation, including facial scarification, forced or early marriage, ritual killings, forced feeding of women. Van Bueren (1998:307) pointed out that Article 24 (3) of the CRC was the first binding international instrument to prohibit these practices, urging states parties to "take all effective and appropriate measures with a view to abolishing traditional practices prejudicial to the health of children."

Several problems have emerged, however, regarding the implementation of the article.

First, whereas many of the CRC articles point to support for cultural, religious, and local customs [e.g., Article 5 (respect for parents and family as provided for by local customs); Article 29 (c) (respect for cultural identity and values); Article 30 (right not to be denied enjoyment of a child's culture, to profess and practice one's own religion); and the preamble (emphasizing the importance of the traditions and cultural values for the protection and harmonious development of the child)], the overall import of the CRC is support for the individual rights of children. John Tobin (2009:374) described this as a dilemma in international law between "the need to accommodate and respect cultural differences and at the same time protect the internationally recognized rights of individuals." Similarly, Van Bueren (1998:310) argued that this situation presents a conflict between the desire to eliminate harmful practices on the one hand, and on the other hand, "the desire to preserve traditional lifestyles undergirded by traditional values, aspects of which are prejudicial to the health and development of children."

Second, many harmful traditional practices are done with the consent of victims, parents, other relatives, and community members and are, therefore, not state-sponsored, and in light of the desire to accommodate and respect family institutions and cultural differences (Articles 5, 29c, 30, and preamble of the CRC), this could lead to conflict. Under such a situation, Van Bueren (1998: 307–308), for instance, pointed out that harmful traditional practices such as female circumcision may not qualify as torture under international law. Within this context, Van Bueren rightly opined that the concept of harmful or negative traditional practices is a cultural minefield (p. 309).

Third, the obligation on states to abolish harmful traditional practices under Article 24 (3) of the CRC is a weak one. John Tobin (2009:375–377) and Van Bueren (1998:307) pointed out that the obligation under Article 24 (3) of the CRC is a progressive one that only requires states to make progress towards effective abolition. They argued that even though states parties are required under Article 24 (3) "to take 'all effective and appropriate measures,' this is effectively weakened by the qualifier 'with a view to' abolishing such traditional practices" (Van Bueren, 1998:307; Tobin, 2009:375–377).

Harmful traditional practices in Ghana illustrate these problems well. The practices known in Ghana include female genital mutilation, other forms of mutilation such as facial scarification, early and forced marriages, levirate and sororate marriages, widowhood rites, inheritance practices, witch villages,[3] and ritual servitude such as the *trokosi* system. While none of these practices is common to all the ethnic groups or regions in the country, each region and ethnic group has its share of them. Hence, the problem of harmful traditional practices is not peculiar to any particular ethnic group or region in Ghana. However, because the author has extensively researched the *trokosi* system and is, therefore, more familiar with it than any of the other practices,[4] the *trokosi* system will be used to depict the problems and dilemmas associated with implementing Article 24 (3) of the CRC as discussed above.[5] The rest of this section will depict how *trokosi* practice and the anti-*trokosi* campaign capture problems associated with implementing Article 24 (3) of the CRC (harmful traditional practices).

Key questions in the *trokosi* debate include whether the practice is slavery or a cultural and religious practice. The latter is addressed in a recent paper of the author,[6] so this chapter will only address the question as to whether *trokosi* is slavery. It is important to first briefly make the following two points. First, the 1992 Ghanaian Constitution recognizes customary law, which regulates customary practices in Ghana, as one of the laws of the land. Like the CRC, it guarantees Ghanaians the enjoyment of their culture and traditional religion. Second, even though *trokosi* girls and women are sent to *troxorvi* shrines[7] without their consent, it is parents and families who select and take them into servitude in the shrines. In fact, a priest once argued during one of my interviews that to effectively abolish the *trokosi* problem, parents must be asked to stop bringing their women and girls to the shrine. Further, while many in the practicing communities today do not favor the practice (Ameh, 2001), a significant segment of the population does. Generally, people in the practicing communities believe that as a traditional crime detection and control mechanism, the institution of *troxorvi*, that gave rise to the *trokosi* system, is more effective than the Western-imported criminal justice system, and the former must, therefore, be preserved (Abotchie, 1997).

Is *Trokosi* Slavery?

This has been one of the most contentious questions in the *trokosi* debate in Ghana. Similarly, in the scholarly literature, the definition of "slavery" has generated a lot of heated debate as slavery manifests itself in a wide variety of forms and practices (Turley, 2000; O'Byrne, 2003). David Weissbrodt and Anti-Slavery International (1999:10),[8] after reviewing a wide variety of definitions, identified the concept of ownership and control as the crux of slavery in the international context. They argued that ownership and control result in an individual losing all control over his or her own life and labor. Consequently, Weissbrodt and Anti-Slavery International maintained that, "the circumstances of the enslaved person are crucial to understanding and identifying what practices constitute slavery" (1999:10). They identified three main conditions that distinguish slavery from other practices and institutions:

> (i) "the degree of restriction of the individual's inherent right to freedom of movement; (ii) the degree of control of the individual's personal belongings; and (iii) the existence of informed consent and a full understanding of the nature of the relationship between the parties" (1999:10).

They maintained that, "These elements of control and ownership, often inflicted with the threat of violence and accompanied by ongoing abuse, are central to identifying the existence of slavery" (1999:10). They, however, argued that violations of other fundamental rights associated with slavery are aggravating circumstances, which provide "indication that slavery or forced labor is likely to be occurring but by itself is not sufficient evidence that slavery is taking place, just as its absence should not be interpreted as evidence that slavery is not taking place" (1999:12). Such violations included: beatings and other corporal punishment; keeping victims in chains; branding or other forms of mutilation; giving them no payment or giving them just enough to pay for meals and accommodation; giving them a new name; obliging them to speak a new language; or forcing them to change their religion; and preventing them from owning property (1999:11–13).

The first definition of slavery in an international legal document, and one that seems to be accepted internationally, is from the Slavery Convention of 1926. Article 1 (1) of the Convention defines slavery as "the status of or condition of a person over whom any or all of the powers attaching to the right of ownership are exercised."[9] The Supplementary Convention on the Abolition of Slavery, the Slave Trade, and Institutions and Practices Similar to Slavery (1956)[10] augmented the definition of slavery by adding slavery-like institutions and practices termed "servile status." Institutions and practices analogous to slavery were identified as: debt bondage, serfdom, different types of forced marriages including sale of wives, levirate and sororate, and child exploitation and servitude. The Rome Final Act (1998), establishing the International Criminal Court, added trafficking in persons, particularly in women and children, to the list of practices that constitute slavery and declared slavery a crime against humanity.[11]

How Does the Practice of *Trokosi* Compare with These Distinguishing Features of Slavery?

Restriction of Freedom of Movement

The element of control applies to the practice of *trokosi*. Once a *trokosi* goes through the ritual of initiation, her movements are restricted. Usually, there is an initial period (which varies from one shrine to another) when an initiated *trokosi* cannot leave the shrine. Thereafter, she can only leave the shrine with the permission of shrine functionaries. However, there is no element of ownership. A *trokosi*, even while serving at a shrine is considered a member of her family. Ideally, her family is even responsible for her feeding and general upkeep in the shrine.

Control over Personal Belongings

Decisions about what to do on a daily basis and what to do with their lives in general become the prerogative of the shrine functionaries. When *trokosis* work, eat (if food is available at all on some days), sleep, and wake-up are at the whims and caprices of shrine functionaries. Not surprisingly, most *trokosis* are denied basic education, healthcare, and sometimes even food. *Trokosis* and *fi-*

asidis[12] wear distinctive clothing: a blue or black piece of cloth, must go barefoot, and always wear their famous necklace made of *seshi*.

Consent

All *trokosis*, and some *fiasidis*, are sent to the shrines without their consent. However, it is parents and other family members who make the decision and actually send the girls and women to serve in the shrines. Several *trokosis* have reported being asked by their parents to accompany them on an errand[13] only to be abandoned at a shrine.

Thus, all three main conditions for identifying slavery are present in the practice of *trokosi*. Similarly, some of the "aggravating factors" of slavery identified by Weissbrodt and Anti-Slavery International (1999) constitute part of *trokosi* practice. Unruly *trokosis* are made to undergo all sorts of ill-treatment, including beatings and other corporal punishment such as kneeling down on palm kernel or broken bottles, and are made to drink ritual concoctions supposedly to make them corrigible. All *trokosis* in Tongu must have sex with the Shrine Priest after their third menarche. Consequently, most *trokosis* become pregnant and have children at an early age. *Trokosi* initiates are given a new name associated with the religion and must become adherents of the deity for the rest of their lives. Most *trokosis*, and all *fiasidis*, carry distinctive physical marks on their face. *Fiasidi* initiates are taught to speak a new language. *Trokosis* do not own property, but *fiasidis* are given land property by their families for becoming initiates (Dovlo & Adzoyi, 1995; Ameh, 1998, 2001, 2004a, 2004b; Greene, 1996).

Considering that ownership is absent in *trokosi* practice, even though control is almost absolute, and the girls and women serve for a set period of time after which they could be liberated by their families ("liberation rites" constitute a core component of the formal process of the *trokosi* system), it would seem that *trokosi* practice does not fall under the rubric of slavery as understood in the traditional use of the concept in the literature on the "old slavery." *Trokosi* practice may, however, better fall under the rubric of practices and institutions defined as contemporary forms of slavery—those slavery-like institutions and practices termed "servile status" that fall under the Supplementary Convention on the Abolition of Slavery, the Slave Trade, and Institutions and Practices Similar to Slavery (1956). These practices are today referred to as contemporary forms of slavery. Whatever one's opinion on *trokosi*, it definitely qualifies as a contemporary form of slavery, what Kevin Bales (2004) termed the "new slavery."

In defining slavery as a "person held by violence or by threat of violence for economic exploitation" (2004:5 and 280), Bales argued that the "new slavery" is different from the "old slavery" in that complete control over people without being responsible for them, rather than ownership, is the key defining characteristic. The new slavery then, as he points out, is "the total control of one person by another for the purpose of economic exploitation" (2004:6), with the key issue being vulnerability and desperation of large segments of the population who are extremely poor and are disposable due to the explosion of the world's population. Bales identified types of the new slavery as chattel slavery, debt bondage, contract slavery, child domestic servants, war slavery (including child soldiers), and ritual slavery, citing *trokosi* practice as an example (2004:19–22). Bales' "new slavery" actually described contemporary forms of slavery.

Like Bales, Suzanne Miers (2000) defined contemporary forms of slavery as all the exploitative and cruel practices that fall between that continuum with chattel slavery of ancient times at one end, and freedom at the other. These are institutions of slavery or slavery-like practices found in contemporary times that are regarded as vestiges of slavery of earlier periods. They include modern forms of chattel slavery, debt bondage, forced prostitution, sexual slavery, forced and servile marriage, forced or compulsory marriage, and ritual marriage and cults such as the *trokosi* system (Miers, 2000). Thus, both Bales and Miers firmly placed *trokosi* practice under the rubric of contemporary forms of slavery. Anti-Slavery International (1995, 1998) has equally labeled *trokosi* as a contemporary form of slavery. Note that shrine priests have absolute control of *trokosis* but no responsibility for their upkeep. While this responsibility falls on the families of *trokosi* girls and women, the families equally shirk their responsibilities, leaving the girls and women to a life of abject deprivation and loss of human dignity. However, economic exploitation per se is not the main goal of the *trokosi* system; it seems that this type of female ritual servitude best falls under the category of "harmful traditional practices" or "traditional practices prejudicial to the health of children" as captured by Article 24 (3) of the CRC as discussed above.

In Ghana, however, a complication in describing harmful traditional practices as slavery or considering them as criminal is the fact that the Constitution upholds customary practices and traditional religion and guarantees the rights of citizens to enjoy, practice, profess, maintain, and promote them. According to Article 11 (2) of the 1992 Constitution, the laws of Ghana include "customary law," which is defined as "the rules of law, which by custom are applicable to particular communities in Ghana" [Article 11 (3)]. Basically, these are the laws and customary practices applicable to specific ethnic groups in the country. Article 21 (c) guarantees "freedom to practice any religion and to manifest such practice," while, according to Article 26 (1) "Every person is entitled to enjoy, practice, profess, maintain, and promote any culture, language, tradition, or religion subject to the provisions of this Constitution." Thus, like the CRC, the Constitution of Ghana accords the people protection and lends support to the practice of customary and religious rites and the values upon which they are founded. Even though the same Constitution states in Article 26 (2) that "All customary practices which dehumanize or are injurious to the physical and mental well-being of a person are prohibited," and Article 16 (1) states that "No person shall be held in slavery,"[14] yet section 314 (2) of the Criminal Code (Act 29) exempts coercion based on parental, family, and customary reasons from slavery:

> This section does not apply to any such coercion as may lawfully be exercised by virtue of contracts of service between free persons, or by virtue of the rights of parents and other rights, not being contrary to law, arising out of the family relations customarily used and observed in Ghana.

So basically, under the laws of Ghana, slavery excludes acts that result from customary practices, including harmful traditional practices such as *trokosi* that involve parents and other family members taking girls and women to serve a lifetime of servitude in the shrines.

According to a report of the Ghana Law Reform Commission (1995), the courts in Ghana have been through a dilemma when dealing with cases concerning traditional religious practices. In the report that highlighted the legal constraints involved in addressing ritual servitude in Ghana,[15] the Commission stated that "The law prior to 1960 provided that the existence or otherwise of an alleged customary law was a question of fact and had to pass the test of whether it was not repugnant to natural justice, equity and good conscience" (Anti-Slavery International, 1995:28). Thus, while the courts could not automatically stop ritual practices nor prevent people from seeking recourse to them, findings from traditional religious practices were not legally acceptable evidence in the law courts, except in situations when their practices caused harm to someone and could, then, form a basis for criminal prosecution. The report argued that since 1960, however, customary laws and practices have been regarded as part of the laws of Ghana (1995:28). Under this circumstance, and in the absence of specific laws, the protection of individual rights depended on judicial interpretation of the scope of the respective rights (1995:29).

The report, however, cited several cases that show the judicial interpretations were mixed, as the court's rulings did not give any clear direction regarding the status of harmful customary practices and traditional religious rules in respect to the rights of Ghanaians. For example, the report cited *Atomo v. Tekpetey* (1980), a case that directly relates to *trokosi* practice (1995:13–15). The court was called upon to decide whether the *woryokwe* custom (as the *trokosi* system is called by the Dangmes) of considering all children born to a *woryokwe* during and after the lifetime of a shrine priest as children of the priest and, hence, not eligible to inherit from their biological father should be upheld. The court did not uphold the *woryokwe* custom on the basis that it was "unreasonable, and repugnant to natural justice, equity, and good conscience."[16] This ruling could have been a landmark legal case against harmful traditional practices, but while the court rightly ruled against the *woryokwe* system, a customary practice, in this instance, the report cited another case in which the court sided with elements of a customary practice, which in my view, should be labeled as harmful. In the case of *Tano v. Akosua Koko* (1974), the court upheld the punishment of being ostracized and liable to banishment reserved for Krobo women who become pregnant prior to undergoing the customary nubility rite of *dipo,* which is required of all Krobo women.

The decision of the court, according to the report, was based on the moral objective of the custom, which is basically the promotion of chastity, as opposed to promiscuity, among Krobo women.[17] The problem with the court's opinion is that if the test of the harmfulness of a customary practice depends on its moral objective, then should the court not have ruled in favor of *woryokwe*, or for that matter the *trokosi* system, whose moral objective is the pursuit of truth, righteous living, and deterrence from crime?[18] The intention of the ancestors of the Ewes who originated the practice was not to make slaves out of *trokosis*. In the purely traditional Ewe society, the practice served a moral purpose: it was considered a just and fair process of religious worship, sacrifice, doing justice, and holding families accountable for the crimes of their members (Ameh, 2001; Ame, 2010). A similar argument could be made for all harmful traditional practices in Ghana.

Further, in the *trokosi* system, it is parents and relatives who send the girls and women to the shrines, and the shrines are part of the religious and customary practices of the *trokosi* practicing areas and, thus, should legally be exempt from accusation of "slavery" as provided for by section 314 (2) of Criminal Code (Act 29). Hence, prior to the Criminal Code Amendment Act (1998), which specifically criminalized harmful traditional practices, the law could not effectively deal with ritual and other harmful traditional practices such as *trokosi*. Thus, at the beginning of the contemporary anti-trokosi campaign in the early 1990s, Ghanaian law was not adequate to address the problem, nor that of any other harmful traditional practice. It was in this vein that Amy Bilyeu (1999:485–487) argued that not only the CRC but also Ghanaian law was limited in its protection of *trokosi* children in respect to "abuses based on cultural tradition or bias" (1999:486) because both the international and domestic laws: (1) emphasize the need for the child to develop within the cultural framework and learn about community practices; (2) encourage strengthening the family unit, perhaps even to the subordination of children's rights; (3) do not protect the child from exploitation that takes place within the family; and (4) do not have an enforcement mechanism. The same could be said of all harmful traditional practices in Ghana. Thus, until Parliament made specific changes to the laws of Ghana starting from the 1990s that harmonized the laws on slavery, the concept and practice of *trokosi*, like any other harmful traditional practice in the country, was not necessarily illegal even if it was morally reprehensible in post-colonial Ghana.

Thus, proponents of the *trokosi* system may have been right in insisting that *trokosi* was not slavery at the beginning of the anti-*trokosi* campaign. The Afrikania Mission (2000), African Renaissance Mission (1999), Ameve (1999a, 1999b, 2000), Dartey-Kumordzie (n.d.), and Addo (1998) have consistently argued that the *trokosi* system is part of Ewe traditional religion, which is guaranteed by the 1992 Constitution. For example, Addo (1994, 1998) argued that *trokosi* is religion, which happens to have some elements of bondage in its practice. He may have been right to some extent.[19]

The Ghana Law Reform Commission report and human rights advocates such as the Federation of International Women Lawyers (FIDA), contributed greatly in calling for the amendment of section 314 of Act 29 and other relevant sections of the Criminal Code to include customs that enslave people and subject them to forced labor. This call, joined by a host of human rights NGOs such as International Needs Ghana; individuals; traditional leaders such as chiefs and queenmothers; and state institutions such as the Commission on Human Rights and Administrative Justice (CHRAJ) put pressure on Parliament, which led to the passage in June 1998 of what has since become known as the "*trokosi* law" (Ameh, 2001, 2004a). The "*trokosi* law," the Criminal Code 1960 Amendment Act 1998 (Act 554), criminalized *trokosi* and other ritual or customary practices by effectively amending section 314 (2) of the 1960 Criminal Code (Act 29) through the insertion of section 314A, which states:

> Whoever (a) sends to or receives at any place any person; or (b) participates in or is concerned in any ritual or customary activity in respect of any person with the purpose of subjecting that person to any form of ritual or customary ritual commits an offence and shall be liable on conviction to imprisonment to a term of not less than three years.

While nicknamed the "*trokosi* law," it is important to state that this amendment applies to all harmful customary practices, including but not limited to *trokosi* practice. While previous laws such as the Criminal Code Amendment Act 1994 (Act 484), which criminalized female circumcision, and PNDC Law 111, which sought to transform some negative widowhood and inheritance practices, targeted specific negative practices, the target of Criminal Code Amendment Act 1998, the so-called *trokosi* law, applies to all negative traditional practices in Ghana. Considering the fact that several harmful ritual and customary practices are found in Ghana, it is a shame that many Ghanaians construe this law as applying only to the *trokosi* system. The law was crafted to encompass all harmful traditional practices even if outcry against *trokosi* triggered its enactment.

It bears repeating that with this law, all harmful traditional practices, including *trokosi*, are now effectively criminalized, and the Criminal Code, which originally lent support to harmful customary practices and slavery-like acts perpetrated by families and communities, has now aligned itself with the relevant sections of the 1992 Ghanaian Constitution and related laws, both domestic and international that Ghana has ratified or signed. Today, Ghana boasts several child-friendly laws such as the Criminal Code Amendment Act 1994, the Children's Act 1998, Juvenile Justice Act 2003, the Human Trafficking Act 2005, the Disability Act 2006, and the Domestic Violence Act 2007, which together with Ghana's ratification of several relevant international treaties[20] should now enable a clearer and effective application of the law to harmful traditional practices such that cases related to slavery-like institutions such as forced labor, child maintenance, issues of dignity, denial of education and healthcare can now be more effectively pursued before the law courts.

Conclusion

With the Criminal Code now amended to fully align all sources of Ghanaian law with the international treaties Ghana is signatory to, especially the CRC, what next? Can the law "kill" harmful traditional practices? Almost twelve years after the Criminal Code Amendment effectively criminalized all harmful traditional practices, apart from the prosecution of a couple of people for engaging in female circumcision (Senaya, 1997), there is no record of anybody else being prosecuted for their role in any negative traditional practice in the country, and there is no sign that these practices have decreased. On the contrary, reports on victims of harmful traditional practices abound in the Ghanaian media. This demonstrates that the CRC obligation of states parties to abolish traditional practices prejudicial to the health of children is a complicated task as pointed out by scholars (Van Bueren, 1998; Tobin, 2009; Bilyeu, 1999) and illustrated by the difficulties presented by efforts to abolish *trokosi* practice as discussed in this chapter.

Recognition of traditional practices and religious rites in domestic law, acquiescence of parents and other close relatives, high patronage in practicing communities, and failure of governments, traditional councils, and civil society organizations to propose credible alternatives to these practices have all coalesced to complicate and muddle efforts to transform these practices. Equally complicating the attempts to transform these practices is the sanctimonious attitude of Ghanaians—the public and politicians alike—that the problem of harmful traditional practices apply to only specific practices and ethnic groups in the country and that whatever harmful practices pertain in their ethnic groups are untouchable by the laws of Ghana. As Tobin (2009:375–377) rightly pointed out, the CRC obligation goes beyond the bio-metric measurement of health and legal understanding and should encompass a deeper socio-cultural understanding of such practices. Ghanaian children will be better off if scholars and research institutions devote more time and other resources toward researching this problem, with the objective of seeking more effective means of transforming these practices beyond the legislative efforts of Parliament. An understanding of the social context of these practices and dialogue with key stakeholders can effectively help in transforming these practices at least.

Notes

1. For example, the Slavery Convention (1926), the Universal Declaration of Human Rights (1948), the Supplementary Convention on the Abolition of Slavery, the Slave

Trade, and Institutions and Practices Similar to Slavery (1956), and the Rome Treaty (1998), which are discussed later in this chapter.

2. UN document E/CN.4.1986/42.

3. Witch villages are designated villages to which people, usually old men and women, accused of witchcraft are banished in some parts of Northern Ghana.

4. The author did an in-depth and the first most comprehensive study of *trokosi* practice in Ghana for his doctoral dissertation (*Child bondage in Ghana: A contextual policy analysis of* trokosi, School of Criminology, Simon Fraser University, Burnaby, BC, Canada, 2001). A summary of the key findings of his doctoral dissertation (*Reconciling human rights and traditional practices: The anti-*trokosi *campaign in Ghana*) has been published in the *Canadian Journal of Law and Society* vol. 19, no. 2, 51–72. Prior to completing this study, his article, *Trokosi* (child slavery) in Ghana: A policy approach, was published in *Ghana Studies* (1998, vol. 1, 35–62), a refereed journal of the Ghana Study Group within the African Studies Association, US. He has also contributed a chapter, Human rights, gender, and traditional practices: The *trokosi* system in West Africa, in Anita Kalunta-Crumpton and Biko Agozino (eds.) (2004), *Pan-African Issues in Criminology*, 23–39. Aldershot, UK: Ashgate Press. He is currently working on a book titled, Trokosi *Politics: Reconciling Human Rights and Traditional Practices.*

5. It is a shame that due to ethnic bigotry, political expediency, and intellectual dishonesty, some in Ghana now seek to give the impression that the *trokosi* system is the only harmful traditional practice found in the country. The author partially addressed this issue in his paper, Traditional religion, social structure, and children's rights in Ghana: The making of a *trokosi* girl, that appeared as a chapter in D. L. Agbényiga, D. Johnson, and R. Hitchcock (eds.) (2010), *The Undefended Childhood in Global Context: Structural Challenges to Schooling, Health and Well-being Among the World's Children.* Berghahn Books, forthcoming.

6. See Robert Ame (2010). Traditional religion, social structure, and children's rights in Ghana: The making of a *trokosi* girl. In D. L. Agbényiga, D. Johnson, and R. Hitchcock (eds.), *The Undefended Childhood in Global Context: Structural Challenges to Schooling, Health and Well-being Among the World's Children,* Berghahn Books, forthcoming.

7. *Troxorvi* shrines are shrines (places of worship in Ewe traditional religion) that accept human beings (including children) as "objects" of atonement. Not all shrines within Ewe traditional religion accept human beings as sacrifice (Ameh, 2001).

8. David Weissbrodt and Anti-Slavery International's (1999) *Working Paper, Review of the Implementation of and Follow-up to the Conventions on Slavery,* presented to the Fifty-first Session of the Working Group on Contemporary Forms of Slavery, UN Commission on Human Rights, Sub-commission on Prevention of Discrimination and Protection of Minorities. UN Doc. E/CN.4/Sub.2/1999, May 24, 1999. Available at www.anti-slavery.org.

9. Available at the website of the Office of the United Nations High Commissioner for Human Rights. Retrieved February 5, 2010, from http://www2.ohchr.org/english/law/slavery.htm.

10. Available at the website of the Office of the United Nations High Commissioner for Human Rights. Retrieved February 5, 2010, from http://www2.ohchr.org/english/law/slavetrade.htm.

11. Available at the website of the Office of the United Nations High Commissioner for Human Rights. Retrieved February 5, 2010, from http://www2.ohchr.org/english/law/criminalcourt.htm.

12. The girls and women of a more humane variant of the *trokosi* system (Ameh, 1998, 2001; Greene, 1996).

13. In Ghana, it is not uncommon for children to be asked to accompany adults to undisclosed destinations. It is part of the obedience parents exact from their children in traditional societies in Ghana.

14. In fact, anyone who practices slavery is guilty of a second-degree felony as provided in section 314 of the Criminal Code. Article 28 of the 1992 Constitution guarantees children the right not to be subjected to treatment that detracts from their human dignity. Section 3 of this article states, "No child shall be subjected to torture or other cruel, inhuman or degrading treatment or punishment."

15. Ghana Law Reform Commission (1995). *The Impact of the Constitutional Provisions on the Customary Disabilities of Women in Ghana: Report on the Abolition of Ritual Slavery, Forced Labour and Other Related Practices.* Accra: Ghana. Anita Ababio (1995), representing both the GLRC and FIDA, restated some of the key findings of the report in her presentation at the First National Workshop on *Trokosi*. See Anita Ababio (1995), The legal basis for abolishing the *trokosi* system in International Needs *Report of the First National Workshop on* Trokosi *System in Ghana*, Accra: Ghana, 37–43.

16. *Atomo v. Tekpetey* (1980) cited in Ghana Law Reform Commission (1995:13–15).

17. *Tano v. Akosua Koko* [(1974) 1GLR 451 CA] cited in Ghana Law Reform Commission (1995:30).

18. One could respond to this question by arguing that the difference lies in the fact that whereas breaking the chastity law, as in the *dipo* rites, directly leads to the punishment of the perpetrator, *trokosi* practice punishes an innocent family member. However, this argument only leads to another controversial issue in human rights discourse: group versus individual rights. Space limitations will not permit a discussion of this in this chapter; but while many Western developed countries focus on individual to the exclusion of group rights, many cultures in developing countries recognize both individual and group rights. Suffice it to say here that, it was not for nothing that the Organization of African Union (now African Union) chose to title its key 1981 regional human rights convention: The African Charter of Human and *People's* Rights.

19. See a more detailed analysis of the question as to whether *trokosi* is religion or slavery in Robert Ame (2010), Traditional religion, social structure, and children's rights in Ghana: The making of a *trokosi* girl. In D. L. Agbényiga, D. Johnson, and R. Hitchcock (eds.), *The Undefended Childhood in Global Context: Structural Challenges to Schooling, Health and Well-being Among the World's Children,* Berghahn Books, forthcoming.

20. Ghana has either signed or ratified almost all major UN treaties. See the Office of the High Commissioner for Human Right's Ghana website at http://www2.ohchr.org/english/bodies/ratification/index.htm for the status of ratification of UN treaties by Ghana.

References

Ababio, A. (1995). The legal basis for abolishing the *trokosi* system. International Needs *Report of First National Workshop on* Trokosi *System in Ghana (Accra),* 37–43.

Ababio, A. M. H. (2000). Challenges to the application of international women's human rights in Ghana. *Canadian Woman Studies* 20 (3), 167–171.

Abotchie, C. (1997). *Social Control in Traditional Southern Eweland of Ghana: Relevance for Modern Crime Prevention.* Accra: Ghana Universities Press.

Addo VIII, T. (1994). Memorandum on inquiries into the *trokosi* system of Klikor (to CHRAJ) dated August 17.

———. (1998). *Trokosi* system: Religion or bondage with particular reference to *fiasidi* of Klikor shrines. International Needs *Report of the Second National Workshop on* Trokosi *System in Ghana (Accra),* 63–65.

African Renaissance Mission. (1999). *Resolution on Christian indoctrination of children in government funded schools.* December 10. Accra: Ghana.

Afrikania Mission. (1998). *Fact-finding mission to genuine* Troxovi *shrines: Report.* Accra: Ghana.

———. (2000). Speech delivered by His Holiness Osofo Komfo Kofi Ameve, leader of Afrikania, at a press conference held at the art centre on June 13, 2000, to explain the Afrikania position on the teaching of religion in the first cycle public schools in Ghana. *Daily Graphic,* Wednesday, June 21, p. 12.

Ame, R. (2010). Traditional religion, social structure, and children's rights in Ghana: The making of a *trokosi* girl. In D. L. Agbényiga, D. Johnson, and R. Hitchcock (eds.). *The Undefended Childhood in Global Context: Structural Challenges to Schooling, Health and Well-being Among the World's Children.* Berghahn Books, forthcoming.

Ameh, R. (1998). *Trokosi* (child slavery) in Ghana: A policy approach. *Ghana Studies* 1, 35–62.

———. (2001). *Child bondage in Ghana: A contextual policy analysis of* trokosi. Doctoral dissertation submitted to the School of Criminology, Simon Fraser University, Burnaby, BC, Canada.

———. (2004a). Reconciling human rights and traditional practices: The anti-*trokosi* campaign in Ghana. *Canadian Journal of Law and Society* 19 (2), 51–72.

———. (2004b). Human rights, gender, and traditional practices: The case of *trokosi* practice in West Africa. In A. Kalunta-Crumpton and B. Agozino (eds.). *Pan-African Issues in Crime and Justice,* 23–39. Aldershot, UK: Ashgate Press.

Ameve, O. K. (1999a). Address delivered at the meeting of the *troxovi* shrines held at Klikor Unity Park on April 10 (available from African Renaissance Mission).

———. (1999b). *Culture and Tradition.* Accra: Afrikania/Afrikan Renaissance Books Ltd.

———. (2000). Speech delivered at a press conference held at the Arts Centre on June 13. Accra: Ghana.

Anti-Slavery International. (1995). *Fetish slaves.* Report submitted to the Working Group on Contemporary Forms of Slavery Twentieth Session, April 19–28. United Nations Economic and Social Council Commission on Human Rights Sub Commission on Prevention of Discrimination and Protection of Minorities.

———. (1998). *Updates for the Working Group on Contemporary Form of Slavery on two issues in West Africa about which Anti-Slavery International has submitted information in the past.* Report submitted to the Working Group on Contemporary Forms of Slavery Twenty-third Session, May. United Nations Economic and Social

Council Commission on Human Rights Sub Commission on Prevention of Discrimination and Protection of Minorities. Available at http://www.antislavery.org/uns98up.htm.

Arendt, H. (1951). *The Origins of Totalitarianism.* New York: Harcourt Brace.

Bales, K. (2004). *Disposable People: New Slavery in the Global Economy.* Revised edition. Berkeley: California University of California Press.

Bibbio, N. (1996). *The Age of Rights.* Cambridge: Polity Press.

Bilyeu, A. S. (1999). *Trokosi*—The practice of sexual slavery in Ghana: Religious and cultural freedoms vs. human rights. *Indiana International and Comparative Law Review* 9 (2), 457–504.

Cardenas, S. (2009). Human rights in comparative politics. In Michael Goodhart (ed.). *Human Rights: Politics and Practice.* Oxford: Oxford University Press, 75–91.

Dartey-Kumordzie, S. (1995, July 15). *Trokosi* or *fiasidi*: Pillar of Africa's survival. *Weekly Spectator,* 5.

———. (2000, July 1). Re-defining hu-yehweh: The knowledge of Africa and the various organs for development of human resources (2). *The Ghanaian Times,* 14.

———. (n.d.). *Report on* fiasidi-*vestal virgins.* Accra: Hu-Yehweh Society.

———. (n.d.). *Origin and the importance of* troxovi *or* fiashidi *(*trokosi*) in modern Ghana.* Accra: Ghana. Available from the author.

———. (n.d.). *The relevance of* trokosi *(*fiasidi*) in modern Ghana.* Accra: Ghana. Available from the author.

Dovlo, E., and A. K. Adzoyi. (1995). *Report on* trokosi *institution.* Legon-Accra: Department for the Study of Religions, University of Ghana. Report commissioned by International Needs.

Ensalaco, M. (2005). The right of the child to development. In M. Ensalaco and L. C. Majka (eds.). (2005). *Children's Human Rights: Progress and Challenges for Children Worldwide.* Lanham, MD: Rowman and Littlefield Publishers, Inc., pp. 9-30.

Ghana Law Reform Commission. (1995). *The impact of the constitutional provisions on the customary disabilities of women in Ghana: Report on the abolition of ritual slavery, forced labour and other related practices.* Accra: Ghana.

Goodhart, M. (ed.). (2009). *Human Rights: Politics and Practice.* Oxford: Oxford University Press.

Greene, S. E. (1996). *Gender, Ethnicity, and Social Change on the Upper Slave Coast: A History of the Anlo-Ewe.* Portsmouth, NH: Heinemann.

Howard, R. E. (1986). Is there an African concept of human rights? In R. J. Vincent (ed.). *Foreign Policy and Human Rights: Issues and Responses.* Cambridge; New York: Cambridge University Press.

———. (1992). Dignity, community and human rights. In A. A. An-Na'im (ed.). *Human Rights in Cross-Cultural Perspectives: A Quest for Consensus.* Philadelphia: University of Pennsylvania Press.

———. (1993). Cultural absolutism and the nostalgia for community. *Human Rights Quarterly* 15, 315–338.

———. (1995). *Human Rights and the Search for Community.* Boulder, Colorado: Westview Press.

Howard, R. E., and J. Donnelly. (1986). Human dignity, human rights, and political regimes. *American Political Science Review* 80 (3), 801–817.

Langlois, A. (2009). Normative and theoretical foundations of human rights. In M. Goodhart (ed.). *Human Rights: Politics and Practice.* Oxford: Oxford University Press, 11–25.

Miers, S. (2000). Contemporary forms of slavery. *Canadian Journal of African Studies*

34 (3), 714–747. Special issue on slavery and Islam in African history: A tribute to Martin Klein.

Motala, Z. (1989). Human rights in Africa: A cultural, ideological, and legal examination. *Hastings International and Comparative Law Review* 12, 373–410.

Nhlapo, R. (1989). International protection of human rights and the family: African variations on a common theme. *International Journal of Law and the Family* 3, 1–20.

O'Byrne, D. (2003). *Human Rights: An Introduction.* Pearson Education Ltd.

Senaya, N. (1997). Law against female circumcision sends practice underground. *Public Agenda,* 22–28, December, 3, 5, 8.

Short, E. (2001). *Harmonizing the laws, policies, and programmes to transform ritual servitude in the West Africa sub-region.* Paper presented at the First Sub-regional Workshop on Ritual Servitude in Accra on February 7.

———. (2000). Keynóte address at *trokosi* liberation durbar at Akatsi on July 29.

Short, E. F. (1995). *Trokosi*—Legal or illegal? International Needs *Report on First National Workshop on* Trokosi *System in Ghana (Accra),* 22–8.

———. (1997). *Trokosi* Transformation. Unpublished speech delivered July 18 at *trokosi* liberation ceremony, Dzangpong Shrine, Tokpo. Copy obtained from a friend who attended the ceremony.

———. (1998a). Keynote address. International Needs *Report of the Second National Workshop on* Trokosi *System in Ghana (Accra),* 59–62.

———. (1998b). Securing the inalienable rights of *trokosi* women and children in bondage. International Needs *Report of the Second National Workshop on* Trokosi *System in Ghana (Accra),* 73–76.

———. (2001) *Harmonising the Laws, Policies, and Programmes to Transform Ritual Servitude in the West Africa Sub-region.* Paper presented at the First Sub-regional Workshop on Ritual Servitude in Accra on February 7.

Smith, R. (2005). *Textbook on International Human Rights* 2nd. ed. Oxford University.

Teeple, G. (2004). *The Riddle of Human Rights.* Aurora, Ontario: Garamond Press.

Tobin, J. (2009). The international obligation to abolish traditional practices harmful to children's health: What does it mean and require of states? *Human Rights Law Review* 9 (3), 373–396.

Turley, D. (2000). *Slavery.* Malden, Massachusetts: Blackwell Publishers Ltd.

United Nations Economic and Social Council. (1998). Updates for the Working Group on Contemporary Forms of Slavery on two issues in West Africa about which Anti-Slavery International has submitted information in the past. Twenty-third Session of the Working Group on Contemporary Forms of Slavery, Geneva, May. Available at http:www.antislavery.org/uns98up.htm.

Van Bueren, G. (1998). *The International Law on the Rights of the Child.* The Hague, Netherlands: Martinus Nijhoff Publishers.

Wa Mutua, M. (1995). The Banjul Charter and the African cultural fingerprint: An evaluation of the language of duties. *Virginia Journal of International Law* 35, 339–380.

Weissbrodt, D., and Anti-Slavery International (1999). *Review of the implementation of and follow-up to the conventions on slavery.* Working paper presented to the Fifty-first Session of the Working Group on Contemporary Forms of Slavery, UN Commission on Human Rights, Sub-commission on Prevention of Discrimination and Protection of Minorities. UN Doc. E/CN.4/Sub.2/1999, May 24, 1999. Available at www.anti-slavery.org/.

Chapter 9
Assessing the Progress of the 1998 Children's Act of Ghana: Achievements, Opportunities, and Challenges of the First Ten Years

By Afua Twum-Danso

Ghana was the first country to ratify the 1989 United Nations (UN) Convention on the Rights of the Child (CRC) in January 1990. The next step after ratification for countries committed to the Convention was the harmonization of national laws with the Convention. Thus, the Ghanaian government reviewed its policies and domestic legislation in the years that followed. This process was facilitated by the return to democracy in 1992 and the introduction of a new Constitution. From 1992 onward, key landmarks relating to children's rights and welfare were made in legislation. In 1995, the government initiated a comprehensive law reform process to ensure full compatibility between national laws and the Convention. The result of this process was the passage of the Children's Act (Act 560) in 1998 (Government of Ghana, 1998). The Act, which is now the major legislation protecting children in Ghana, entered into force in January 1999. It aims to ensure that children's rights to protection, development, and care are provided by families, communities, and by the state through its institutions and structures.

However, the reality of children's lives, eleven years after its passage, remains in stark opposition to the picture the legislation sought to draw. The reality on the ground points to a hostile environment for child protection and the implementation of children's rights. Therefore, this chapter seeks to explore the progress the Act has made in the past ten years and the challenges it has faced and, also, draw attention to opportunities available for more effective implementation of the Act for the next ten years and beyond. Data presented in this chapter is based on research undertaken in two communities in the capital of Ghana, Accra (Nima and Ga Mashie) between May 2005 and March 2006.

Background to the 1998 Children's Act

Passage of the Children's Act was closely linked to the CRC, which was ratified by the Government of Ghana in 1990, just three months after its adoption by the UN General Assembly, making Ghana the first country to ratify the treaty. In trying to explain its rapid ratification of the Convention, the Ghanaian government pointed to the various steps it had already taken to ensure the welfare of children and create an environment conducive to the implementation of the Convention in the country. Education, for example, had long been considered a birthright. Basic education, which was defined as the first nine years of school (from age six to age fifteen) by the 1987 Education Reform Program, was made compulsory and free for all in the 1961 Education Act. Following this lead, the Labor Decree Act of 1967 stipulated that until the age of fifteen, children may only be employed within their own families, undertaking light work of a domestic or agricultural nature. Although children between the ages of fifteen and eighteen were permitted to work, there were limits to the type of work they could undertake. In addition, government officials and other commentators pointed to the establishment of the Ghana National Commission on Children as early as 1979, the International Year of the Child, as another reason for enabling the government to ratify the Convention at this time. This is because the establishment of the Commission represented an important landmark in the collective effort to bring issues relating to children to the forefront of development policy and practice. As a result, some commentators have concluded that the combination of the above activities clearly demonstrated that Ghana "had a head start in appreciating the value of the Convention" (Tengey, 1998).

As ratification of the Convention required governments to take steps to ensure that all children within their national boundaries are able to enjoy the rights stipulated in the Convention, governments were not only expected to report their progress to the UN Committee on the Rights of the Child periodically, but also to harmonize their national laws with the Convention's standards. Hence, the Government of Ghana began to review its policies and legislation after 1990. The return to democracy in 1992 assisted in this process, as according to many government and civil society officials, its passage created a better climate for respecting and enforcing children's rights. Thus, from 1992 onward, key landmarks relating to children's rights and welfare were achieved in legislation. That same year, the Constitution, a product of the return to democracy, was passed by Parliament and included specific provisions relating to the rights of the child. Article 28 guarantees rights and freedoms for children in terms similar to the

Convention and enjoins Parliament to enact laws to ensure children's survival, development, and protection. Following this, the government initiated a comprehensive law reform process in 1995 to ensure full compatibility between national laws and the Convention. Central to this process was the establishment of the Child Law Reform Advisory Committee by the Ghana National Commission on Children to review the status of, and law regarding, children in the country. The Committee concluded that the interests of children would be best served by the enactment of a comprehensive law, which would ensure easy reference for the prompt and effective administration of justice for children. The result of this process was the passage in 1998 of the Children's Act (Act 560), which brought together all laws relating to children into a single, child-focused legislation that at the same time, incorporated the Convention into the national laws of the country. The Act entered into force in January 1999.

The passage of the Children's Act led many to hope that this would represent a real turning point in the progress of children's rights and welfare in the country. Indeed, it paved the way for the passage of other legislation and policies relating to children: the Juvenile Justice Act 2003 (Act 653), the Human Trafficking Act 2005 (Act 694), the Gender and Children's Policy (2002), and the Early Childhood Care and Development Policy. It also provided an environment conducive to the establishment of key institutions. Two are noteworthy. First, it facilitated the creation of the Domestic Violence and Victims Support Unit of the Ghana Police Service (formerly known as the Women and Juvenile Unit), which was initially established in Accra in November 1998 in an attempt to make the criminal justice system more responsive to the special needs of children and women who experience violence. The unit is now present in all ten administrative regions of the country as well as Tema, which is considered part of the Greater Accra Region. Steps are also underway to set up satellite offices in all 138 districts in the country.

Second, it led to the establishment of the Ministry for Women and Children's Affairs (MOWAC), which was set up in February 2001 with a mission to:

> Champion the cause of all women and children, through the promotion of gender equality and the survival, development, protection and participation of children, to achieve equal status, equal opportunities and equal rights for women, men and children in the development of Ghana (Ghana National Commission on Children, 2005).

Consequently, the Ministry was charged with coordinating, monitoring, and reviewing the formulation of gender- and child-responsive policies, as well as overseeing their implementation within the relevant sector ministries. As a result, it took over two interrelated organizations, the National Council on Women and Development and the National Commission on Children. With regard to the latter commission, its domestication into the Ministry changed its status from an independent policymaking body to a department under the Ministry responsible for implementation. As a result, as a department within the Ministry, the Ghana

National Commission on Children plays an essential coordination role and is paramount in coordinating the National Multi-Sectoral Committee and all inter-agency committees on children's rights and protection (UN & GOG, 2004). Finally, the Act led to the decentralization of other institutions of childcare and protection such as the District Assemblies, Family Tribunals, Circuit Courts, and the High Court.

The Children's Act: In Focus

The Act, in and of itself, is a good, comprehensive piece of legislation. As Woll claimed, the Act is the most visible outcome of the Convention and one of the strongest examples of the government's commitment to children's rights (Woll, 2000:61). For the very first time in the Ghanaian legal framework, laws relating to children's welfare and protection, which were hitherto scattered throughout the statutes, were now brought together into one single document that embodies all legal issues relating to children. This was intended to make them more accessible, easier to promote, and thereby easier to enforce.

As the architects of the Act were determined to identify the position of the child within the society, its provisions cover the protection of all children below the age of eighteen in all aspects of their life, thus providing a clear and unambiguous definition of who is perceived as a child in Ghana in legislation and policy. It also protects the family unit by outlining parental and governmental roles and responsibilities in order to clarify any ambiguity surrounding who is supposed to do what for the child.

It is worthwhile outlining the various components of the Act, which is divided into six parts, with each part being further divided into sub-parts. Part 1 focuses on the rights of the child, which are all in accordance with the Convention's principles, including the best interests of the child, the right to education and well-being, and the right to express an opinion on decisions affecting the child's welfare, the right to protection from torture, exploitative labor, and forced betrothal. In this part of the Act, the concept of the state as the parent of the child in need of care and protection not otherwise provided is introduced, with the implication that the state, in the form of the District Assembly, can assume custody of a child who is being abused or neglected within the home. Part 2 of the Act provides for a quasi-judicial body called the Child Panel, which has the potential, when fully operationalized, to absorb not only the civil issues pertaining to non-maintenance of children, child labor, parental neglect or maltreatment, and truancy/failure to send a child to school, but also minor crimes committed by children such as petty theft. Thus, this system will enable families and communities to seek their own way to resolve problems without recourse to the main judicial system, which is a costly and lengthy process.

Part 3 of the Children's Act deals with parentage, custody, access, and maintenance. The considerations that are now to be taken into account when making decisions regarding custody and access include the age of the child, the desire to keep siblings together, the need to maintain continuity, and the views of the child. With regard to the maintenance of children, the Act makes parents liable for educating their children up to the basic educational level. An additional duty to provide reasonable shelter was added to the maintenance responsibility, and action may now be brought to enforce the payment of existing maintenance arrears. Part 4 of the Act focuses on adoption and fosterage, which is also a first for the Ghanaian legal framework and is a result of the recognition that the traditional practice of families handing over their children to another who is willing to undertake the care and maintenance of the child (i.e., fosterage) is increasingly becoming commercialized and vulnerable to exploitation. Thus, its inclusion is an indication of the recognition by government that mechanisms need to be put in place to ensure that the rights of these children are not infringed in the process.

Part 5 deals with the employment of children. Children under age eighteen are prohibited from engaging in exploitative and hazardous labor, which is defined as any labor that deprives a child of its health, education, or development (moral and physical), all in line with Article 28 (2) of the Constitution and the Convention. However, they can be admitted into other types of employment and embark on apprenticeships from the age of fifteen, which coincides with the age of the completion of basic education. Part 6, the final part of the Act, makes provisions for institutionalized care such as the regulation of both state and privately run residential homes, which can now have their licences cancelled or suspended if they fail to maintain the required standard of care. This is another legal first for the country, as previously, private children's homes existed without any legal framework, and no provisions were made for their inspection and regulation, thus, the protection of children within these institutions was not assured.

The similarities between the Act and the Convention have led some in Ghana to talk of it as merely a domestication of the Convention in the country's legislative framework. Two of these are worth exploring in greater detail. Part 1 of the Children's Act makes provisions for the basic rights of children, including the right to grow up with parents, unless it is not in the best interests of the child, the right to parental property, the right to education and well-being (i.e., immunization, adequate diet, clothing, shelter, medical attention), the right to social activity, the right to express an opinion and participate in decisions affecting the child's well-being, and the right to protection from torture, degrading treatment, and forced betrothal—all of which are in line with the Convention. As any contravention of this part of the Children's Act is liable to a fine of not more than five million cedis or a term of imprisonment not beyond one year or both, the Act criminalizes the non-participation of children in decision-making in a culture where the government itself has admitted that child participatory rights are the most problematic of all rights stipulated in the Convention to implement in the Ghanaian social and cultural context. Therefore, in striving to harmonize national law with the Convention's standards, policymakers have overlooked or disregarded the resistance that this provision would engender.

Despite the similarities, it is important to note that the Act is not merely a domestication of the Convention in Ghana. It also takes into consideration the local context within which it is to operate. This further shows the flexibility inherent in the Convention that enables governments to incorporate its provisions into national law, and at the same time take into account the cultural values and belief systems of their own people. An example of this is the Child Panel provision, which is rooted in the Ghanaian cultural and administrative context. It is a community-based structure composed of well-respected and trusted members of a community who are trained in children's rights and have the capacity to educate and influence others. Because of their role in the community, panel members are charged with mediating minor civil and criminal matters at this level, including those involving the rights of children and parental duties and assisting victim-offender mediation in minor criminal matters such as petty theft and threatening offenses. In addition, the Act makes a distinction between work that is hazardous and exploitative and that which is considered as "light." Such work does not affect attendance at school or the capacity of the child to benefit from schoolwork and is undertaken between six o'clock in the morning and eight o'clock at night—for example, selling products either at a stall or hawking on the streets before or after school, which can be done by children as young as thirteen. This provision not only takes into consideration traditional and cultural beliefs that emphasize children's responsibilities towards their families and communities, but also takes into account the reality of the current socioeconomic context, which forces many impoverished families to rely on the labor of their children to supplement their income.

Enforcing the Act: Turning Legislation into Reality

Although it was envisaged that the Children's Act would represent a change in the lives of children in the country, the reality of children's lives ten years after its passage remains in stark contrast to the picture the legislation sought to draw. The reality on the ground points to a hostile environment for child protection and the implementation of children's rights. Children are subjected to various forms of physical, mental, and sexual abuse. While it is difficult to assess the exact nature and scope of this phenomenon due to lack of official data, information from the media, courts, and the Domestic Violence Victims Support Unit (DOVVSU) of the Ghana Police Service point to a number of violations of children's rights, including defilement or statutory rape (very often by people closest to children such as uncles, teachers, neighbors), incest and harassment, harmful corporal punishment, abandonment, child abduction or stealing, trafficking, intentional neglect, commercial exploitation for domestic servitude or sexual purposes, and labor that has now been deemed by the Children's Act as hazardous for children. With regard to the latter, information collected for the 2003 Ghana Child Labor Survey (Ghana Statistical Service, 2003) indicates that 2,474,545 children are engaged in usual economic activity, which is about two of every five children between ages five and seventeen (GSS, 2003:xvii). While approximately half of rural and one-fifth of urban children are engaged in economic activity, 40 percent of this group work for more than six months per year (many of those in Greater Accra, Central and Eastern regions). Therefore, children under the age of eighteen remain very visible as laborers, including in work that has now been defined by the Children's Act as exploitative and hazardous, namely, mining, quarrying and galamsey, fishing, agriculture, and the hotel industry, which altogether employ an estimated 242,074 children (2003). According to the survey, 57 percent of the 2,474,545 working children who participated in the study were engaged in agriculture/forestry/fishing; 21 percent worked as hawkers and street vendors, selling ice water and food; and 11 percent were engaged in general laborer chores, such as washing of cars, fetching firewood and water, pushing trucks, and carrying goods as porters. This latter occupation has received significant media attention in recent years. Many of these porters, also known as *kayaye,* are predominately young female migrants from the three northern regions of Ghana who migrate to Accra in order to raise capital to start more profitable ventures or acquire necessary items for marriage. On arrival in Accra, they work as porters and carry headloads of 30 kg over an average of 5 km a day for shoppers and traders, which has an impact on their physical development (GSS, 2003:xiv; UNICEF–Ghana, 2002). They also end up among the large numbers of street children who are found in large cities not only working, but also living, on the streets—sleeping at night at shop fronts, markets, office verandas, and other open places—which makes them vulnerable to sexual abuse and exploitation, as well as other types of violence.

While many children engage in economic activities in order to pay for their school-related expenses, it must be acknowledged that the continued engagement in this type of work—be it part-time or full-time—hinders their ability to participate fully in school work. In some parts of the country, families are so reliant on their children to assist them at certain times of the day or particular times of the year that children's attendance at school is at best irregular during these periods. In northern Ghana where most people are farmers, 80 percent of children do not attend school due to their commitments to generating income for the survival of the family (GSS, 2003).

Understanding the Reasons Behind the Limited Implementation of the Children's Act and Children's Rights

Agency Constraints

Central to the understanding of the limited implementation of the Children's Act and, as a result, the Convention, is the lack of resources—both human and financial—which has severely impeded the ability of key institutions charged with enforcing the Act to fulfill their mandates.[1] This section will explore the challenges facing two bodies that are key to the implementation of the Act.

The Children's Act (sub-part 2 of part 1) gives the responsibility for protecting the welfare of children, as well as promoting their rights, to the District Assemblies, which are charged with ensuring that the relevant sectors liaise with each other on matters concerning children. Therefore, much is expected of the decentralized local government system if the Children's Act is to be implemented effectively. However, studies have shown that an extremely limited proportion of the District Assembly Common Fund, which is allocated to District Assemblies by central government for the development of their districts, is used for the protection of vulnerable groups such as children, while the bulk goes to capital projects such as building roads (UN and GOG, 2004:42). This can largely be attributed to the fact that a large number of District Assemblies have yet to be sensitized or educated on the Convention and the Act. In an interview with Hon. Adjiri Barnor, Accra metropolitan assemblyman for Nlgeshi (Ga Mashie), he admitted that he had not read the Children's Act and, thus, did not know what it contained (Interview, Accra, March 8, 2006). As a result of this lack of knowledge that is widespread at the local authority level, it is difficult for the District Assemblies to appreciate the importance of children's rights, and this limits their ability to incorporate these principles into their medium-term plans. In addition, those members of the District Assemblies who have been sensitized often have difficulty in understanding and comprehending the law. Even when aware and willing, most District Assemblies lack the capacity to implement the law effectively due to the sheer magnitude of local government responsibilities that have been placed on them at a time when they are facing severe staff shortages and high personnel turnover. Therefore, they have difficulty apportioning their time and resources adequately and are unwilling to take on new assignments (Tengey, 1998; Woll, 2000).

The Department of Social Welfare, which is part of the Ministry of Manpower Development and Employment, works in three program areas—namely, justice administration, child rights promotion and protection, and community care. The Department is particularly responsible for children "in need of care and protection," who are defined in the Act as those who are neglected, ill-treated, abandoned, orphaned, and begging on the streets. However, the capacity of the Department to fulfill its mandate is restricted by a severe lack of both financial and human resources. Like the District Assemblies, conditions of service are poor, and this, in turn, further demoralizes the already disillusioned staff and results in a high turnover. Hence, there is a severe shortage of personnel to handle the workload of the Department, which has increased tremendously since the passage of the Children's Act in 1998. Many social welfare district offices are only able to employ one social worker, which limits the Department's ability to fulfill its mandate (Gagnon, 2005:35). As a result, instead of being able to investigate or follow up cases and monitor violations of children's rights, district social workers are reduced to their desks and forced to wait for cases to be brought to them. This is problematic in a context where state intervention in family affairs is not welcomed, and thus, families rarely take the initiative to report cases of abuse to social workers (Gagnon, 2005; Interview with Gifty Okine, Accra, March 2, 2006). The restrictions that the Department faces in its work are further compounded by the fact that district social welfare offices do not have vehicles at their disposal, restricting their mobility and making it difficult for them to reach families in more remote places.

Challenges in Cross-agency Coordination

Cross-agency coordination has also proved problematic for those working to enforce the Children's Act. There has been lack of clarity in oversight responsibilities, particularly between the Ministry of Manpower, Youth, and Employment, the sector ministry in which the Department of Social Welfare is based, and the Ministry of Women and Children's Affairs. The mandates of the two agencies regarding the protection of children overlap in several areas, leading to duplication of efforts and gaps in services (UN & GOG, 2004). Stephen Adongo, then deputy director of the Department of Social Welfare, raised the problem of coordination between the two agencies during my interview with him:

> MOWAC [the Ministry of Women and Children's Affairs] is meant to be the coordinating ministry—coordinating issues relating to women and children in all ministries, but now they are venturing into implementation, and that is where the problems are arising. MOWAC believes that they should do everything that is to do with children. There is an attitude that anyone can do social work, so MOWAC feels they can do our work. They do not try to encroach on women and children's issues in other Ministries, e.g., health, agriculture, but because they think social work can be done by anyone, they interfere in our work. . . . They have taken on child labor and maintenance cases. It won't work because they do not have the expertise. . . . At the political level they play it down. They say it is no problem. But it is. Just last week the Minister of MOWAC said there was no child labor in the cocoa industry. The next day, DSW [the Department of Social Welfare] was holding a workshop on child labor in the cocoa industry. . . . The Ministers of the sectors involved have to clarify the roles (Interview, Accra, February 21, 2006).

Lack of Resources

Financially, while the government provides budgetary support to the Department for the implementation of the Children's Act, it is seen to be severely inadequate. Government allocations (non-salary expenditures) to the Department of Social Welfare for 2002–2004 ranged from 184 million to 261 million cedis for operations in the entire country, and even this was only released after a long delay, hampering activities (UN & GOG, 2004). As a result, the Department has had to rely on financial support from international agencies such as UNICEF–Ghana. According to Stephen Adongo:

> There is no separate budget for children. It's always tied to MOWAC, and whatever allocation there is [it's] always late. Why? It is a matter of our concept of development. Successive governments think when you build roads, markets, toilets—that is development. Social welfare institutions are driven to the background because they are not providing revenue to the country. Governments think that when you improve education and health, then you have social development. So these ministries get a lot from the government and donors. Therefore, it is down to political orientation. They do not see the output of what we do. It is not so tangible (as building a market). DSW is just seen as a drainpipe. . . . Our institutions such as children's homes and correctional institutions have become so run down that they themselves can be considered as cases of 'abuse' (Interview, Accra, February 21, 2006).

As a result of the Department's inability to fulfill its mandate, some nongovernmental organizations (NGOs) have emerged to fill the resulting gap and take over part of the role of an institution that should be taking the lead in ensuring the provision of quality and standardized services for children in the country. Therefore, the credibility of the Department has been undermined, and its ability to undertake its work effectively has been impeded, as it is now competing with civil society for donor funds.

The problem of the limited implementation of children's rights is not merely due to insufficient budget allocation from central funds. Senior figures within the government itself have pointed to numerous external factors that have impeded their ability to fully implement children's rights instruments to which the government had committed itself. As Vice President Mahama explained at the UN Special Session on Children in New York in May 2002, in spite of the government's polices and programs and the fact that the government is "making every effort to mobilize resources locally to improve the situation of our children":

> Ghana . . . could not fully realize her desired goals for her children because of the lack of resources. Fluctuation on world prices of our export commodities, coupled with high petroleum prices on the international market, our growing external debt and dwindling official development assistance, have greatly lim-

> ited the amount of resources at the disposal of government for the care of our children. . . . Mr. President, we in Africa acknowledge that it is our responsibility to ensure the well-being of children on our continent. Unfortunately, we are unable to meet this all-important obligation (Mahama, 2002).

Due to these challenges, the responsibility to care for children is almost solely being held by parents who, more often than not, cannot afford to bear it in full. Some parents contend that they, as adults, also have economic and social rights, which are violated by bad economic policies pursued by the government. They argue that if their rights cannot be met, society cannot expect them to assure the very same rights for their children (Tengey, 1998). Furthermore, endemic poverty in Ghana, where 42 percent of the 18.9 million inhabitants live in acute poverty on less than $1 per day (Ghana Living Standards Survey, GSS, 2000), leads to children's rights becoming a low priority for many families and communities. The 1995 Ghana Living Standards Survey found a steady increase in school enrollment with rising levels of welfare (GSS, 1995), indicating that parents are willing to send their children to school as long as they have the resources to cover the costs. When these are not available, they will not only stop sending their children to school, but will also need to rely on their labor. This is further supported by Sylvester Kyei-Gyamfi of the Research Unit at the Ghana National Commission on Children:

> I am not trying to use poverty as an excuse, but in the situation that the people find themselves in, they have nothing else they can do other than fall on the assistance of children. There is no social safety net here in Ghana (Interview, Accra, January 26, 2006).

In some cases, parents have provided the initial capital for their children to set themselves up as street vendors (UNICEF–Ghana, 2002:135). Therefore, there is a need to recognize that very often parents make conscious decisions about using the labor of their children to ensure the survival of their family.

Lack of Awareness

While financial and human resources are certainly severe impediments to the implementation of the Act and the Convention, lack of awareness is also a critical factor as it is arguably directly linked to lack of political will, which in turn reinforces the lack of resources available for the effective implementation of children's rights. Most members of the public and even policymaking bodies do not know about the Children's Act and the Convention on the Rights of the Child. In cases where they do have knowledge of them, they do not know much about these legal instruments and their contents. Ruth Addison, program manager at the Ghana National Commission on Children, informed me that there are some Ministers of Parliament who do not even know what is in the country's Children's Act, which many of them voted into passage in 1998 (Interview, Accra, February 27, 2006). Even in cases where the public is aware of the Act, they do not recognize its importance or its relevance, given that traditionally, the extended family has played the role of caring for children, leading Gagnon to assert that, "public intervention is thus quite alien to Ghanaian society" (2005:4). Even civil society, which is very much aware of children's rights and the relevant instruments, has not developed a habit of reporting children's cases to the Department of Social Welfare. In their research on violence against women and children in Ghana, Cusak & Coker-Appiah noted that:

> Reporting to state agencies is rare even when there are medical injuries; cases are being arbitrarily referred back to the family and/or community, and cases are being closed as trivial, false, and lacking in evidence (1999).

Hence, there is a need to go beyond lack of awareness and resources as obstacles and acknowledge as a problem the concept and language of children's rights itself and its impact on the limited implementation of children's rights laws in Ghana. By focusing on the lack of awareness and resources as the key impediments to the implementation of the Convention and the Act, there is the assumption that once people know about children's rights, they will accept it as if they are passive receivers of information and knowledge, or that once resources are available, they will be used for children's rights, which has, hitherto, not been the case. Therefore, there is a need for policymakers to acknowledge that even once people have information about children's rights and have the resources to facilitate its implementation, they may still reject the concept, as it attacks and threatens the very premise on which Ghanaian cultural values are based—values centered on concepts such as respect and obedience, responsibility from an early age, and importantly, reciprocity, which is antithetical to the idea of inalienable rights for anyone, let alone children.[2]

Cultural Values

I will explore the implications one of these cultural values has on children's rights—reciprocity, which forms a central component of the socialization process in Ghana. Thus, children grow up very much aware that the caring that their parents provide for them is based on the belief of a payoff. By bringing forth a child and taking care of him or her during childhood, a parent is issuing a contract, for which he expects to be paid back once the child is in position to do this by fulfilling expected responsibilities and behaving in an appropriate manner. A child who does that will have his or her rights fulfilled. Mensa-Bonsu & Dowuona-Hammond supported this concept when they claimed that in Ghana "a child is obliged to render services to a parent which obligation is then reciprocated by the parent by care and maintenance" (1996:15). Furthermore, Nsamenang, writing of the broader African context, argued that it is because African parents expect their children to serve them and compensate for their disappointments and failures in life, that parents spare no effort to support and educate their children, especially during adolescence, in order to raise their status and increase their ability to improve the welfare and resource base of the family (2002:73). This payback is expected from a very early age. In fact, by simply being born, a child already begins to fulfill his part of the contract, as he is a source of prestige and respect for his parents. As soon as he is old enough, he is expected to participate in household duties and in the main income-generating activities of the family as discussed above. Because of the lack of any form of effective social welfare system in Ghana, children have also come to be regarded as a form of security for old age. Therefore, as adults, children are expected to support their parents in the same way their parents looked after them when they were young, weak, and dependent. According to Awedoba:

> The reciprocities between African parents and their children are life-long ones and are backed, not by legal requirements necessarily, but by moral and religious obligation. Society does not spare those African parents and children who fail in their reciprocal obligations. The recalcitrant child or parent may be ridiculed or gossiped about by concerned others. The aged parent may curse the negligent child who neglects that aged parent. Not only is this reciprocity life-long, it continues after the death of the parent and finds expression in religious prestations such as sacrifices and offerings at shrines erected to deceased parents in many African societies (2002:90).

Therefore, it is the expectation of a child's value—either as a child or in the future, as an adult—that obliges a parent to provide for that child. The centrality of reciprocity in intergenerational relationships and all social relationships in Ghana makes the concept of inalienable rights for anyone, especially children, difficult for many in different communities to accept.

Furthermore, in some sectors of the population, there is the belief that children's rights (in cases where they are aware of such a concept) means the right to empowerment only. According to Ruth Addison, "some see children's rights as giving too much power to children" (Interview, Accra, February 27, 2006). This viewpoint was further supported by a participant in an FGD with media professionals who said:

> When children know their rights, they may over do it. Some children are very rude, and this is because they know their rights. This is why some parents do not allow their children to know their rights (FGD with Media Professionals, September 14, 2005).

The anger felt toward the concept of children's rights in some sectors further became apparent in my interview with Nii Futa I, the chief of Nima, one of the two focus communities of this study:

> We have enough problems with children without giving them their rights. They should straighten up, go to school, and look after us when we are old. Children's rights are a luxury that only people in London and New York can enjoy.

> But in Nima, the basic things are not being taken care of. When you have provided basic things (costs of schooling, medicine), then you can sit down and ask them for their opinions. Because of poverty levels and problems, we do not have time to discuss these things. We do not have time to ask children their opinions unless they are going to be able to bring money. When I have to worry about where I am going to get my next pay from, I cannot be asking my child for his opinion. . . . Besides, you need to enforce things on children. If you leave them, they will do the wrong thing (Interview, Accra, December 16, 2005).

Thus, there is an element of confusion or misunderstanding about what children's rights mean within communities. As a result, much of the anger felt is based on the belief that the concept of children's rights is about children being empowered rather than about the provision of basic needs such as education and food, clothing, and shelter, which are also rights. According to Tine & Ennew, while there is much misunderstanding of what children's rights means, there is considerable willingness to promote the fulfillment of children's needs (1998). However, even with regard to the basic provisions to which children are entitled and which societies know they must provide, there is currently some anger and frustration felt within communities. This is because of the shift in language and policy from a focus on parental obligations and children's needs to an emphasis on children's rights. By criminalizing parental irresponsibility as the Children's Act does, the duty to maintain children is now perceived as a legal, not a moral issue. As a result, parental responsibility is now subject to sanctions and penalties for those parents who do not provide the necessities of life for their children. Hence, the anger and resistance felt towards the idea of children's rights is also based on the feeling that while parents may strive to do their best with the little resources they have available to them—very often without much support from the state—they are now subject to penalties if they fail to meet their obligations to their children (importantly, by the same state that does little to help them). Penalizing parents for doing what they consider their best causes anger and frustration toward the very concept of children's rights and contributes to the retreat from parenthood that is evident in Ghana today (Oppong, 2006).

Moving Beyond Challenges: Looking for Opportunities for the More Effective Implementation of the Children's Act and Children's Rights

Due to the centrality of cultural values in limiting the realization of children's rights and the enforcement of the Children's Act, it is, thus, necessary to explore strategies for engaging with local communities in Ghana in the interpretation of children's rights and the identification of avenues for the more effective implementation of the Children's Act and children's rights in Ghana today. Specifically, it is necessary to explore how international and national policymakers can make children's rights work for different and disparate communities and thereby legitimize it in the eyes of local communities in Ghana as well as elsewhere.

The importance of this strategy has been underscored repeatedly by Abdullahi An-Na'im, a Sudanese human rights academic, who has devoted a large part of his career to searching for a cultural legitimization of human rights within both African and Islamic contexts. He argued that efforts to promote respect for international human rights standards are often likely to remain superficial and ineffectual until such time as they relate directly to, and where possible are promoted through, local cultural, religious, and other traditional communities (An-Na'im, 1992; An-Na'im & Hammond, 2002). Specifically, he claimed that human rights stand a better chance of implementation if they are perceived to be legitimate within the various cultural traditions of the world (An-Na'im, 1992:3). This further emphasizes the fact that it is not enough to claim universality simply because governments have ratified relevant instruments.

As a result of this stand, An-Na'im proposed an approach that seeks to broaden consensus by exploring cultural reinterpretation and reconstruction through internal cultural discourse and cross-cultural dialogue as a means to enhance the universal legitimacy of human rights (1992:3). In his view, there may be "room for changing a cultural position from within, through *internal discourse* about the fundamental values of the culture and the rationale for these values" (1992:4). He suggested that this should be done by engaging the public and raising their awareness through intellectual and scholarly debate, artistic literary expression of alternative views on these issues, and political and social action furthering these views. Furthermore, since cultures are constantly changing and evolving internally, as well as through interaction with other cultures, it may be possible to influence the direction of that change and evolution from outside through cross-cultural dialogue (1992:4). However, he adds that this process:

> Must be both mutual between cultures and sensitive to the needs of internal authenticity and legitimacy. . . . Those of one cultural tradition who wish to induce a change in attitudes must also be respectful of the integrity of the other culture. . . . They must never even appear to be imposing external values in support of the human rights standards they seek to legitimize within the framework of the other culture (1992:5).

By advocating such an approach, An-Na'im was not seeking to repudiate existing international standards, but rather aimed to strengthen their implementation by legitimizing them in the eyes of those who would be most affected by them: the local communities. This theoretical approach is based on the belief that despite their apparent peculiarities and diversity, human beings and societies share certain fundamental interests, concerns, qualities, traits, and values that can be identified and articulated as the framework for a common culture of universal human rights (1992:21). Berger (1977) added to this viewpoint when he claimed that notions of respect for humans are common to all cultures and provide the basis for fundamental human rights. Above that basic level, different cultures may choose to establish different, additional norms that reflect their particular values (Silk, 1990:317–318).

The benefits of legitimizing human rights and specifically children's rights in the eyes of local communities cannot be dismissed. As An-Na'im & Hammond asserted, "Local acceptance enriches the universal idea by giving it meaning and relevance to people's lives" (2002:16). The logic of this new approach makes it possible to revise and reformulate existing standards through a process of cross-cultural dialogue and analysis.

Thus, this approach demonstrates the need to involve local communities in the interpretation and implementation of the Convention and domestic legislation by initiating dialogue about children's rights through local, cultural, and religious belief systems and understandings. As part of this process, it is vital that policymakers first uncover the views of local communities and how they understand and interpret concepts central to the children's rights debate. This dialogue process can take traditional forms such as village and community meetings or more modern technologically based forms such as media discussions, in particular. This process will ensure that laws that emerge as a result of harmonizing national legislation with the Convention are not simply imitative of such international standards but also take into account the peculiarities and features of a given society. Such dialogue would enable policymakers to search for a middle ground that could lead to compromises, which would mean that while the end goal is the protection of children, the strategy developed would be appropriately contextualized and supported by local communities.

Conclusion

This chapter has shown that despite the passage of the Children's Act in an attempt to harmonize national law with the Convention's standards, implementation has proved problematic in Ghana. Although lack of awareness and resources are important impediments to the implementation of the Act and thereby the Convention within this social and cultural context, inherent in analyses focusing on these factors is the assumption that once people have knowledge, or that once resources are available at the state, local government, and family levels, children's rights will be implemented. This has not, hitherto, been the case because even when communities were aware of children's rights and when resources have been available, the progress of children's rights has remained slow. A primary reason for the slow progress of the Act and the Convention is the community/public perception of children's rights as a concept. Many adults fear the implications such a concept will have for the cultural and social fabric of their societies. In particular, they worry about its impact on child rearing and socialization processes. Hence, it is not sufficient for those charged with implementing the Convention to identify a middle ground in the laws and policies of a particular country such as Ghana. Policymakers and others seeking to implement the Convention within this context must go further and explore the possibility of identifying a middle ground within local perceptions about children's position in their communities and their entitlements, as local communities are key to the effective implementation of the Convention and the national laws that it engenders. This can only be done by involving local communities in the interpretation of children's rights and engaging them in dialogue about what constitutes children's rights in their context. The dialogue that will emerge as a result will form the basis of a partnership for the implementation of rights that are not only recognized internationally but which are also valued locally.

Notes

1. The Committee on the Rights of the Child has also raised concerns about the lack of adequate human and financial resources, which is an impediment to an effective and systematic implementation of the Children's Act. In particular, the Committee raised concerns about the limited capacities of the District Assemblies, which hamper the implementation of the Convention on the Rights of the Child at the local level (United Nations, 2006).

2. The issue of cultural values as obstacles to children's rights is similar to the issues raised by women's rights activists with regard to the position of women in the country. The Committee for the Convention on the Elimination of Discrimination Against Women (United Nations, 2006) reported in its recent conclusion that the persistence of deep-rooted cultural norms, customs, and traditions remained a severe impediment for the situation of women's rights in Ghana.

References

An-Na'im, A. (1992). Towards a cross-cultural approach to defining international standards of human rights: The meaning of cruel, inhuman, or degrading treatment or punishment. In A. A. An-Na'im (ed.). *Human Rights in Cross-Cultural Perspectives: A Quest for Consensus*. Philadelphia: University of Pennsylvania Press.

An-Na'im, A., and J. Hammond. (2002). Cultural transformation and human rights in African societies. In A. A. An-Na'im (ed.). *Cultural Transformation and Human Rights in Africa*. London/New York: Zed Books.

Awedoba, A. K. (2002). *Culture and Development in Africa: With Special Reference to Ghana*. Accra: Institute of African Studies, University of Ghana, Legon.

Cusak, K., and D. Coker-Appiah. (1999). *Violence against women and children in Ghana*. Accra: Gender Studies and Human Rights Documentation Centre.

Gagnon, L. (2005). *Access to justice by children*. Accra: Judicial Service of Ghana, UNICEF–Ghana and CUSO.

Ghana National Commission on Children (GNCC). (2005). *Annual report 2004*. Accra: Ghana National Commission on Children.

Ghana Statistical Service. (1995). *Ghana Living Standards Survey.* Accra: Ghana Statistical Service.

———. (2000). *Ghana Living Standards Survey.* Accra: Ghana Statistical Service.

———. (2003). *Ghana Child Labor Survey.* Accra: Ghana Statistical Service.

Government of Ghana (GOG). (1998). The 1998 Children's Act of Ghana (Act 560). . Accra: Government of Ghana.

Mahama, A. A. (May 2002). Statement by H. E. Alhaji Aliu Mahama, vice president of the Republic of Ghana, at the 27th. Special Session of the United Nations General Assembly on Children. New York: www.un.org/ga/children/ghanaE.htm.

Mensa-Bonsu, H., and C. Dowuona-Hammond (1996). The child within the Ghanaian family. In E. Ardayfio-Schandorf (ed.). *The Changing Family in Ghana.* Accra: Ghana University Press.

Nsamenang, A. B. (2002). Adolescence in sub-Saharan Africa: An image constructed from Africa's triple inheritance. In B. Bradford Brown, R. W. Larson, and T. S. Saraswathi (eds.). *The World's Youth: Adolescence in Eight Regions of the Globe.* Cambridge University Press, Cambridge.

Oppong, C. (2006). Demographic innovation and nutritional catastrophe: Change, lack of change and difference in Ghanaian family systems. In G. Therborn (ed.). *African Families in a Global Context.* Uppsala: Nordiska Afrikainstitutet.

Silk, J. (1990). Traditional culture and the prospect for human rights in Africa. In A. A. An-Na'im and F. M. Deng (eds.). *Human Rights in Africa: Cross-Cultural Perspectives.* Washington, DC: The Brookings Institution.

Tengey, W. (1998). *The Convention on the Rights of the Child impact study: The study of Ghana.* Accra: Save the Children UK–Ghana.

Tine, N. D., and J. Ennew. (January 1998). *The African contexts of children's rights: Seminar report.* Harare: ANPPCAN–Zimbabwe, Childwatch International, CODESRIA, Redd Barna–Zimbabwe.

United Nations Children's Fund (UNICEF)–Ghana. (2002). *Situational analysis of children and women in Ghana 2000.* Accra: UNICEF–Ghana, revised version.

United Nations and the Government of Ghana (UN & GOG). (2004). *Common Country Assessment (CCA) Ghana.* Accra: United Nations and Government of Ghana.

United Nations Committee on the Rights of the Child. (March 2006). *Consideration of reports submitted by states parties under Article 44 of the Convention: Concluding observations, Ghana.* Geneva: United Nations.

United Nations Committee on the Elimination of Discrimination Against Women. (August 2006). *Concluding comments of the Committee on the Elimination of Discrimination Against Women: Ghana.* Geneva: United Nations.

Woll, L. (2000). *The Convention on the Rights of the Child: Impact study.* Stockholm: Save the Children Sweden.

Chapter 10

Situating CRC Implementation Processes in the Local Contexts of Correctional Institutions for Children in Conflict with the Law in Ghana

By Lilian Ayete-Nyampong

The United Nations (UN) Convention on the Rights of the Child (CRC), which commemorated its twentieth anniversary in 2009, is the most ratified treaty and one that addresses comprehensively social, economic, cultural, civil, and political rights as provided by the Universal Declaration of Human Rights (UDHR). Ghana demonstrated its commitment to promoting human rights of children by being the first country to ratify the CRC in 1990.

Ghana's efforts at instituting appropriate legislative, institutional, and policy initiatives in promoting the human dignity of the child are worthy of recognition. Nevertheless, there is more to be done for children in conflict with the law (juvenile and young offenders) in terms of implementing the CRC and relevant legislative instruments that derive from it.

While it may be easier to acknowledge the vulnerability of children who are usually victims of abuse such as ritual servitude (*trokosi*),[1] child trafficking, rape, defilement, etc., that of child offenders is perhaps difficult because of the criminal guilt associated with them. By being held in detention, children in conflict with the law are rendered additionally vulnerable;[2] they tend to suffer triple vulnerability: as children, as "criminals" or deviants, and as detainees. Consequently, issues regarding them are easily relegated to the very bottom of Ghana's priorities for vulnerable children[3] (DSW, 2005; UNDP, 2007[4]).

This chapter provides reflections based on preliminary fieldwork[5] undertaken by the author in 2009 in three correctional institutions for children in conflict with the law in Ghana. It aims at motivating discussions about promoting implementation of the CRC in practice for children in conflict with the law. The chapter has an added objective to establish a case for examining daily experiences of juvenile and young offenders while in detention and to inspire discussions that go beyond the role of the criminal justice system and the single definition of crime.

The pre-occupation of lawyers and human rights officers with compliance and implementation of human rights standards and laws as part of monitoring human rights observance in detention institutions prevents human rights professionals from seeing the social person(s) behind the legal label. As a result, the appreciation of real life experiences of children in conflict with the law and detainees relative to other vulnerable groups in Ghana, suffer from a lack of interest at both national and international levels.

Similarly, scholarly research seldom addresses real life experiences of young offenders in correctional institutions, notwithstanding studies on deviance, crime, gangsters, and related areas (Hobbs, 2001; Taylor, 1990), which provide invaluable information on day-to-day experiences in challenging settings. With the exception of a few studies such as Goldson's (2002, 2008),[6] which employ interviews and direct testimonies from young people—although like the others, such studies also aim at penal and criminal justice reform at the macro level and not fully situated within the context of active every day detention life—a greater proportion of these studies are survey based.

In Africa, studies on juvenile justice are relatively few, with South Africa being credited with a majority of these studies. Field studies employing participant observation in Africa's prisons and correctional institutions are scanty.[7] De Kock, in his study, Youth in Conflict with the Law, examined life stories of young people in Gauteng, South Africa, awaiting trial but not young offenders in detention (De Kock, 2005). In an eight-month ethnographic field study on prison officer training and practice in Nigeria, the author examined prison officer training, penal philosophy, and practice of the Nigerian Prisons Service (Jefferson, 2007). Despite his focus on prison officers in adult prisons, his study brought to the fore everyday dynamics of officer training and practice in Nigeria—his study being the only ethnographic field study in correctional institutions identified in West Africa. No ethnographic study in correctional institutions for juvenile offenders has as yet been identified in West Africa.

In light of this crucial deficiency of interest and information about the actual life experiences of juvenile offenders in correctional institutions, the following questions are addressed: Are human rights only words and laws on paper, with little meaning for actual lives of juvenile and young offenders? What relevance do monitoring mechanisms have for the day-to-day life of juveniles in detention? Do juveniles constitute a monolithic entity devoid of diversity and change? Can juvenile offenders claim their fundamental human rights in accordance with the provisions of the CRC? Are implementation processes of the CRC situated within specific day-to-day contexts for juvenile offenders? Are conventions, laws, and policies supreme; in other words, do they translate linearly? What type and level of commitment has Ghana shown to promoting the rights of children in conflict with the law?

Concluding discussions of this chapter provide a reflection on initiatives that assume that prisons and correctional institutions are monolithic and homogenous and should be subjected to standardized reforms, which in most cases are external to the context. It is not enough to advocate effective policy implementation and compliance with human rights conventions such as the CRC without respecting the human rights of children in conflict with the law enough to appreciate their narratives, real stories, ideas, and experiences. In other words, bridging the gap between rhetoric and practice requires policymakers and human rights professionals to approach implementation of human rights laws and policies with an open mind, creating space for day-to-day practicalities that are usually unpredictable.

Background on Juvenile Justice Administration in Ghana

Promoting human rights in practice for children in conflict with the law warrants an appreciation of the historical context of committing juvenile offenders to correctional institutions in Ghana.

Detention institutions have been utilized from the mid-nineteenth century through periods of Ghana's checkered political past, characterized by military and civilian rule as repressive instruments and weapons of punishment as well as means of ridding society of unsafe elements. In the process of consolidating its democratic efforts, Ghana like other states has tended to project a good reputation among its own citizenry and the international community through experimentation with different types of punitive and rehabilitative reforms that have not always yielded the desired outputs.

Ghana inherited an English Common Law tradition, which permeated various spheres of Ghana's social, economic, and political life since Britain assumed direct control[8] of the territory from the mid-nineteenth century to 1957 (Ellis, 1971; Goldschmidt, 1981). A Criminal Code, which was drafted in the 1870s, was based on the English Criminal Code; earlier, an ordinance created courts to handle criminal and civil issues[9] (Ellis, 1971). Prisons were established in forts during the same period (mid-nineteenth century) by the British Council of Merchants, and a Prisons Ordinance was adopted in 1860, which outlined regulations for the management and upkeep of prisoners. By the early 1900s, the British colonial administration managed the nation's prisons until the period after World War II when local officers began to assume oversight.[10]

No formal provision existed for juvenile delinquents during this period, although juvenile delinquency had been addressed informally through noncustodial processes such as restitution, compensation and fines, mediation (between the offender and the offended), apologies, and occasionally punishment, among others (DSW, 2005). This informal traditional system had survived the period spanning pre- and post-colonial administration through post-independence administration until the present and had been administered over the years by family and clan heads, chiefs, and councils of elders (Harvey, 1966). The early twentieth century marked the onset of non-state-initiated custodial systems or committals for juvenile offenders. These institutions such as the one established in Agona Swedru in the Central Region by the Salvation Army Church[11] trained delinquent youth in vocational and technical skills.

The government of the Gold Coast later established other industrial schools and institutions[12] and defined a juvenile as a person under 16 years.[13] Subsequently, social work commenced in the 1940s, and the Ghana Borstal Institution, as well as a remand and probation home in Accra and other regions, was established in the same period. The Ghana Borstal Institution was under the supervision of the Social Welfare Department until later when the Prisons Service took over its administration in the mid-1950s.[14]

After independence, the Criminal Procedure Code of 1960 was passed, which saw the repeal of earlier statutes and the incorporation of what was contained in previous ordinances. The period after 1970[15] realized the need to shift from committal to strengthening of noncustodial options such as probation and community service. This was partly on account of budgetary constraints in maintaining juvenile institutions and the realization that incarceration did not pose enough deterrence to juvenile crime (DSW, 2005). Within that period, the age of criminal responsibility was raised from age 7 to age 12 under section 4 of the Criminal Code Amendment Act (554) of 1998, while there were discussions about the need for greater emphasis on probation work and alternatives to custodial sentencing and rights-based approaches, which gave prominence to the best interest of the child. Subsequently in 2003, Ghana passed the Juvenile Justice Act 653, a comprehensive act that introduced innovative provisions[16] and incorporated relevant provisions of instruments that have existed since the 1940s. The Juvenile Justice Act, the Children's Act 560 of 1998 (that draws on the CRC), and other related instruments constitute the basis for promoting the human rights of juvenile and young offenders.

The following section discusses the broad framework of Ghana's commitment to promoting the rights of children in conflict with the law since ratifying the CRC, followed by the passage of a comprehensive Juvenile Justice Act.

Implementation of the CRC and Ghana's Commitment to the Rights of Children in Conflict with the Law

The CRC is the most ratified treaty and one that addresses comprehensively social, economic, cultural, civil, and political rights as provided for in the UDHR. Ghana being the first country to ratify the CRC in 1990, demonstrated its "official"[17] commitment to promoting and protecting the rights of children, including children in conflict with the law. Not long after ratification, the Republic of Ghana's Constitution of 1992 was promulgated, and this saw the entrenchment of children's rights in Ghanaian supreme law. In December 1998, an elaborate Children's Act (560) that draws extensively on the CRC was enacted. Five years later, the innovative Juvenile Justice Act 653 of 2003 was passed, which along with the Children's Act gave prominence to the best interests of the child. Subsequently, Ghana formulated relevant policies[18] and established state institutions[19] to demonstrate its "actual"[20] commitment to implementing requisite legislative provisions for children. In 2007, a National Social Protection Strategy (NSPS) that sought to promote specific programs for poor communities, including children, while contributing to achieving the Millennium Development Goals, was instituted. Similarly, the Ministry of Manpower, Youth, and Employment launched a program in March 2008 known as the Livelihood Empowerment Against Poverty, a component of the NSPS, a strategy that guarantees the implementation of specific programs for poor and vulnerable groups, including vulnerable children in Ghana.[21]

Undoubtedly, these legislative, institutional, and policy measures constitute commendable efforts toward promoting and protecting the rights and welfare of children in Ghana. Nevertheless, in the face of these strides, Ghana's laws, policies and programs over the years have not translated successfully in practice for children in conflict with the law. Issues regarding juvenile and young offenders are easily relegated to the very bottom of Ghana's priorities for vulnerable children[22] (DSW, 2005; UNDP, 2007) and are seldom targeted directly for human rights education programs' related intervention efforts. It is no wonder that interactions with juveniles and young offenders[23] revealed that a majority had little idea of what human rights were; about eight out of ten children had never heard of the national human rights institution, which is the Commission on Human Rights and Administrative Justice (CHRAJ) in Ghana. They tended to have their own ambivalent constructions of human rights such as punishment to the deserving, a voice for the vulnerable, and charitable acts to good people in need.

Prior to committal, most children had already suffered sustained neglect and deprivation of basic survival needs of food, clothing, and shelter. Many a child presently in detention, in an effort to survive and meet livelihood needs, got involved in acts considered unacceptable that led to their present demise (DSW, 2005). Social inquiry reports of juvenile and young offenders, coupled with responses from interviews held with a cross section of them, indicate that seven out of ten suffered some form of neglect from their parents in the form of deprivation of food, health, education, and medical care. Not surprising, complaints received by the CHRAJ as well as those filed with the Domestic Violence and Victims Support Unit of the Police Service (DOVVSU) and other human rights non-governmental organizations (NGOs) such as the Federation of International Women Lawyers (FIDA), indicate that a substantial proportion of such complaints relate to lack of maintenance of children.

The CRC and the Children's Act oblige parents to assume primary responsibility for the upbringing of the child, while giving consideration to the best interests of the child. The Children's Act (sections 47 and 48) imposes a duty on every parent (mother or father) and also any person legally liable to maintain a child, to provide the child with the necessaries of health, life, and reasonable education.

The effective implementation of the CRC requires that parents and families be strengthened and well equipped to offer the requisite support to children and, thus, prevent juvenile delinquency or ameliorate the incidence of child offending. Considering the number of children whose rights of maintenance have been abused, one wonders how many have had an application submitted on their behalf to a family tribunal. To what extent has the state rendered appropriate assistance to parents and legal guardians in the performance of child rearing responsibilities?

The CRC (Article 3), the Juvenile Justice Act 653 of 2003 (section 2) and the Children's Act refer to the best interests of children in conflict with the law, which should constitute the primary consideration in all situations concerning child offenders. Articles 3 and 4 of the CRC regarding the best interest principle of the child and the nondiscrimination principle in Article 2 of the same treaty emphasize the need for the state to make adequate allocation for children in conflict with the law. The CRC addresses responsibilities for promoting the best interests of the child not only to states but to parents, children, and to society.

In keeping with the best interest principle of the child, Article 40 of the CRC, as well as the Juvenile Justice Act and Children's Act, shifts from the punitive and retributive model to a reformative approach through emphasis on diversion and alternatives to custodial sentencing that reflect rights-based approaches. Thus, the use of committals to correctional centers as a last resort is consistent with this principle. Unfortunately, this principle has been undermined on account of juveniles, who spend lengthy periods of time (sometimes for committing minor offenses) in pre-trial detention and sometimes are kept in adult police cells. The welfare principle is further undermined when some juvenile offenders committed to junior correctional institutions stand the risk of being deprived of the requisite educational provision and training that promote reformation and reintegration.[24]

Sections 3–15 of the Juvenile Justice Act, pursuant to Articles 37 and 40 of the CRC, acknowledge rights of due process of children in conflict with the law and provide that juveniles shall not be arrested or detained arbitrarily. During arrest and pre-trial detention, the rights to privacy, use of reasonable force by the police, conduct of search of juveniles in decency, right to be informed of reason of arrest, and to be released by self recognizance or recognizance, the need to commit the juvenile detained in a police station with others of the same sex, and right to food, medical treatment, and visits from parents and relatives are provided for in the Juvenile Justice Act.

Sections 16–38 provide for informal court proceedings, determination of age, and assistance to juveniles in the form of legal representation and legal aid, remand orders, expeditious hearing (within six months), preparation of social inquiry report, the decision by the court as to appropriate treatment of juvenile such as payment of fine, probation, or committal to a correctional center.

Sections 39–59 relate to correctional centers, duration of detention, supervision of centers, and contributions by parents of juveniles, among other provisions. Section 42 mandates that the ministers responsible for the departments of Social Welfare and the Interior and also the CHRAJ must visit and inspect any correctional center for juvenile and young offenders.

In spite of the above-cited requirements, provision of facilities and services for the care of children in conflict with the law in Ghana has been inadequate. Ghana has only one senior correctional center, which has been in existence since the 1940s and serves only male offenders; there is no senior correctional center to house young females whom the court might consider in their best interest to be committed. In discussions with the head teacher and staff of the only female junior correctional institution, which also houses young offenders beyond the age of 18, they lamented the challenges and difficulties encountered as a result of committing both juvenile and young offenders to the same institution.

Other inadequacies include: committing juvenile offenders on charges of minor offenses to long periods of committals in poorly resourced correctional institutions, which tends to waste away the developmental and productive lives of these children; inability of probation officers, due to resources and other constraints, to conduct detailed investigations that would ensure the preparation of well-informed Social Inquiry Reports as required by section 50 of the Children's Act; ineffective functioning of probation services[25] and Child Panel[26] systems in various districts in Ghana; and the inability of District Assemblies to provide the required logistics or pay seating allowances for members of Child Panels[27] (DSW, 2005).

One wonders whether there is justification to deny children in conflict with the law their human rights on the basis of delinquent or criminal status. By virtue of being human, detainees have human rights, and the CRC guarantees rights of provision (of services to promote survival and development such as adequate nutrition, healthcare, education, etc.), protection (from abuse, neglect, violence, exploitation), and participation (in decisions about matters that affect the child) commonly referred to as the "three Ps" for children in conflict with the law (Marshall & Parvis, 2004). In practice, however, there seems to be a lack of sympathy expressed by various actors and the general public towards promoting the rights of the detained—on account of their criminal or alleged criminal status—and improving their living conditions. For many, child detainees are undeserving of their right to food, health, education, etc., and their interests and needs should not be privileged over that of impoverished children who are law abiding. Situating juvenile and young offenders as subjects of the rights of provision, protection, and participation and not merely beneficiaries or objects of charity acknowledges their entitlements to these rights.

Life in correctional institutions for most of these children offers them an opportunity to have the necessaries of life and some form of education for the first time, and it is worth recognizing efforts by relevant authorities and officers in charge of the respective institutions to provide these needs in spite of their resource constraints. Nevertheless, it was observed that provision of these necessaries of life still fall short of the requirements of Article 2 (sections 3 and 4) and Articles 24–29 of the CRC, section 8 of the Children's Act, and section 41 of the Juvenile Justice Act. As a consequence, the rights of provision, protection, and participation have not translated effectively for children in conflict with the law in Ghana.

Food

Interviews with detaining authorities of all three institutions revealed an insufficient budget for correctional institutions. The officer in charge of one of the correctional institutions indicated that the feeding ration was increased in January 2008 from 40 pesewas (28 cents) to 60 pesewas (42 cents)[28] per inmate, an amount woefully inadequate to provide for three square meals for young people. The head of the female junior correctional institution shared similar concerns and lamented about the inadequacy of funds and the fact that only a fraction of their budgetary request is met. The male junior correctional institution seemed to be the most starved of resources; according to the headmaster and assistant headmaster, the budgetary support was negligible, and there was virtually no support from philanthropists.

Participant observations revealed that young people in some junior correctional institutions go without food, and interviews with them indicate that the menu is unvaried, and the quantity and quality of food supplied leave much to be desired. It was observed at other correctional institutions that their strict regime did not permit inmates to decide whether or not to eat meals offered by the kitchen; it was possible, though, for young people who could afford to purchase food prepared for staff to do so in between meals.

Education

Education is both a human right and an indispensable means of realizing other human rights. It is the primary means by which children in conflict with the law in Ghana can access livelihood opportunities, thereby preventing engagement in unlawful acts upon discharge. But who holds the state accountable for failing to provide the relevant educational infrastructure and educational provision for the fulfillment of this right for children in conflict with the law? To what extent is the state obliged to ensure implementation of Article 19 of the CRC for children in conflict with the law, relative to other vulnerable and impoverished children?

Discussions with young people revealed that education was one of their major concerns compared with other basic needs such as health and food. They seemed highly enthusiastic about their educational needs and lamented bitterly about the short duration of educational provision they received.[29] Whereas few of them partake of mainstream education while in detention, most children miss out on regular education for the period of committal, which in most cases is between two and three years. The form of education provided by some institutions is usually wholesale and provides nearly the same content for varying ages and standards. For most institutions, the duration of teaching and learning is short; there is a lack of teachers and textbooks, and educational needs of young people are not provided for adequately.[30]

Article 28 (a) and (b) of the CRC enjoin the state to make primary education compulsory and available and free to all without discrimination on any grounds, and it is incumbent on the state to promote different forms of education, including general and vocational education, while ensuring the following features of educational provision for children in conflict with the law:[31] *availability* of functioning educational institutions and programs and facilities such as a library, computer facilities, and information technology; and *accessibility* of educational institutions and programs for children and young people in conflict with the law without discrimination. These provisions must be relevant given the local context of correctional institutions and should be of good quality (acceptability), within safe physical reach (physical accessibility), and adaptable to the diverse social and cultural needs of juvenile offenders in detention. In other words, any meaningful effort to promote this right must give due consideration and respect to the people for whom the educational provision is made. Subsequently, such provisions must be situated within the varying local contexts of correctional institutions, while respecting the diverse interests and views of young people in detention.

The principles of non-discrimination and best interests of human rights provided by the CRC and Ghana's Children's Act acknowledge specific needs of children in conflict with the law such as protection from abuse and neglect. By supporting a rights-based approach, the CRC affirms children as subjects of rights and rights holders, while making provision for the assessment of the child's specific needs within the framework of Article 3 about the best interests of the child. These rights provided for by the CRC impose an obligation on the state[32] to *respect* (not to take any measures to violate rights), *protect* (to ensure that enterprises or individuals do not violate these rights), and to *fulfill* (to consciously make budgetary and resource provision for the fulfillment of rights). Marshall & Parvis (2004) emphasized the interrelatedness of the three Ps in stating that:

> The importance of identifying them as rights rather than good practice is that it makes it less likely that the needs and voices of children and young people will be drowned by adults eagerly proclaiming their own rights, or rushing to meet timescales or budgets for which they will be called to account by other adults. Rights give children a stake in our society. The content of these rights is significant for the actual lives of children and for the well being of society in general (Marshall & Parvis, 2004:236).

Discussions so far stress the view that by virtue of being human, child detainees have human rights and must not suffer deprivation of their entitlements under the CRC on account of their criminal or alleged criminal status. The Juvenile Justice Act, in recognizing that children in conflict with the law are not criminals but are in the process of growth and development, seeks to promote correction and prohibits sentencing of juveniles to imprisonment (section 32:1). The non-discrimination principle based on Article 2 of the CRC requires the state to ensure implementation of the CRC, particularly for vulnerable and disadvantaged groups of children, while the best interests principle requires states to make adequate budgetary provision for these purposes (Article 4). By being held in detention, children in conflict with the law are most vulnerable, as they tend to suffer triple vulnerability—as children, as "criminals" or deviants, and as detainees—and issues regarding them should be accorded the utmost priority. Thus, the argument that child detainees are undeserving of the three Ps such as the right to food, health, education, etc., and whose interests and needs should not be privileged over that of law-abiding impoverished children, smacks of betrayal of the very principles of the best interests of the child and non-discrimination that underpin the implementation of the CRC.

On the basis that human rights are inherent in every human being and by virtue of that juvenile offenders and detainees have human rights, discussions in this section have shown that children in conflict with the law have benefited minimally from CRC implementation efforts.[33]

Reflections on Human Rights Monitoring Visits to Detention Institutions

Whereas historically, one primary aim of penal establishments has been to keep unsafe elements from society, there have also been attempts to prevent the development of further criminal behavior, resulting in experimentation of various criminal justice reforms and human rights interventions. With the onset of the international human rights movement, attention has been increasingly drawn to the human dignity of criminals and suspects previously considered undeserving of their rights. On the basis of this, conditions in detention and the human rights of detainees in correctional institutions have become a popular focus for human rights professionals and researchers. Ghana, as well as other states parties, is obliged by Article 3 (3) of the CRC to ensure that institutions, services, and facilities responsible for the care or protection of children conform to relevant standards by means of monitoring. Section 42 of the Juvenile Justice Act (653 of 2003) mandates the minister responsible for the departments of Social Welfare and the Interior and also the CHRAJ to visit and inspect any correctional center for juvenile and young offenders.

It is within this framework that the CHRAJ, in keeping with the CRC, relevant UN standards, the Children's Act, and the Juvenile Justice Act,[34] has since 1996 regularly monitored conditions in detention institutions, including the senior correctional institution for young offenders. In the following discussions, the author reflects on the relevance of such monitoring visits to promoting in practice the human rights of children in conflict with the law.

Prisons and correctional institutions have constituted a focal point for human rights intervention efforts that have sought to assess states' observance of human rights by promoting rights of detainees, advocating humane conditions, and preventing torture and ill treatment in correctional institutions.

As part of measures to promote the rights of detained persons and in keeping with international, regional, and domestic mechanisms, the CHRAJ,[35] which is the national human rights institution in Ghana, has since 1996 conducted monitoring visits to detention institutions.[36] The CHRAJ's monitoring mechanism as well as others such as those established by the Optional Protocol to the Convention Against Torture (OPCAT)[37] aim for regular visits to places of detention so as to prevent torture and other cruel, inhumane, or degrading treatment or punishment. The CHRAJ's process is designed to assess conditions of detention facilities relative to domestic, regional, and international standards for the treatment of detainees. It examines general living conditions of inmates, including their health, feeding, sanitation, and facility accommodations, as well as recreational activities. In 2009, for instance, the CHRAJ monitored twenty-five prisons and 355 police cells across the country.[38]

CHRAJ's monitoring visits are relevant for their preventive function and have created a heightened interest and awareness about conditions in these confinement sites, which otherwise would have remained unknown to the general public due to their inaccessibility. On account of these visits, conditions have improved, although mildly, and there have been efforts made to comply with CHRAJ's recommendations such as attempts by the Department of Social Welfare and the Ministry of Interior to ensure that juvenile offenders are not incarcerated in adult prisons.

Notwithstanding the usefulness of monitoring visits, the author observed that such mechanisms tended to give prominence to poor prison conditions such as issues of overcrowding, poor sanitation, and the situation of detainees such as overstay of remand prisoners, incarcerating juveniles in adult prisons, among others. These issues are commonly reported for most correctional institutions in Africa and elsewhere in the world:

> Prisons in many parts of the world are in crisis. . . . The penal crisis is not limited to poor countries or those in the south. . . . The problems are primarily attributed to those of high confinement, which results in a lack of resources and overcrowded, unsafe and squalid conditions (Sarkins, 2008:11).

CHRAJ's efforts, as well as other regional and international human rights monitoring mechanisms, though, serve as a preventive measure against torture and inhumane and degrading treatment (Muncie, 2008; Sarkin, 2008), yet seldom give attention to the actual life experiences of child detainees. On the basis of methods employed to gather information and the inability of monitors to establish their presence in correctional institutions over a prolonged period, monitoring mechanisms and visits tend to miss out on relevant details pertaining to everyday experience in detention, which reflect children's experiences in their entirety and totality. Yet, respect for the views of juveniles and lived experiences in their totality is relevant to determining the observance of human rights in these institutions' best interests of juvenile and young offenders in a particular situation. Not respecting juvenile offenders enough to appreciate their experiences in their entirety undermines the fundamental principles of human rights and the principle of best interests of the child in conflict with the law.

The perception that discussion and studies about prisons and correctional institutions in Africa do not go beyond the usual lament about poor conditions and the need for criminal justice and human rights interventions tends to give the impression that detainees, juvenile offenders, and correctional institutions constitute a monolithic and homogenous entity that should be subjected to universal reforms and interventions.

However, during preliminary fieldwork undertaken by the author in January and February 2009, juvenile offenders were differentiated immensely on account of their views, relationships, encounters, life experiences, delinquent history, and other structural differences such as family background, gender, etc. Such differences are reflected in the following statements made during interviews and focus group discussions with staff and young offenders in juvenile institutions:

- Felix dropped out of school at a tender age of 5. He started exhibiting offensive behavior following divorce of parents. Offender and siblings later lived with maternal grandmother. Relatives fed up with offender's behavior and stated, "For him to change, he needs to be controlled strictly."

- Stephen started smoking at the age of 6 and was involved in bad company. The father used to send him to buy cigarettes and alcohol for him. He threatened his friend with a gun, and it was assumed that he knew how to use it. He was also a bully at school.

- At the time of committing offense, Grace lived with father and stepmother, who reportedly did not like her. She was involved in theft cases and lived a promiscuous life.

- Others have absconded, but we have chosen to stay. We are only doing them a favor, we could have easily absconded, too.

- Our fathers never cared for us, and we are determined to revenge on our release. We shall jail them!

- Church activities services have been particularly helpful as we receive guidance as to how we can cope in difficult situations. The aspect we do not like is that we are forced to attend these services.

These diversities exhibited among juveniles are not necessarily in respect of structural factors stemming from socioeconomic and cultural factors as suggested in anecdotes cited above such as separation of parents, divorce, parental neglect, impoverished backgrounds, peer influence, age trends, type, and nature of offense, etc. On the contrary, they are socially and culturally constructed and stem from children's own understanding of experiences, situations, and relationships around them and how they relate to these experiences.

Juvenile offenders, in an attempt to cope in different situations, devise various strategies such as resorting to the use of language and jargons that have no bearing with ordinary usage (for instance, they would say "preaching" instead of "stealing"), but to them such jargons carried a sense of security, identity, belonging, and privacy against a context subjected to continuous surveillance. Such strategies and elements of everyday life are usually hidden from human rights professionals or researchers who visit to execute a questionnaire or conduct a two-hour focus group discussion, or ask some youth a few questions. Even the caretaker, teacher, or prison officer who has continuous interaction with children can seldom predict these strategies, as they are neither overtly manifested nor verbalized in detention routines of jogging, meal times, workshop and school sessions, church services, etc.

Interviews and observations during preliminary fieldwork revealed that among these children strategies are usually short-term, episodic, emergent rather than planned, and can change depending on a particular situation. They attribute this to a distrustful and suspicious environment in which they cannot enjoy sustained trust from anyone, not even their own friends.

Friendships and groups are not sustained but are opportunistic and thrive more on reciprocity than trust—though some proportion of the latter is still required for such relationships—which possibly implies that anyone who does not have anything to offer in terms of tactic, strategy, or resources may end up being a loner. Loners, however, are rare, as children seem to make every effort to forge friendships. According to them, though friendships are not sustained, they constitute one of their main lifelines in correctional institutions, particularly given that most do not receive visits from their parents or other acquaintances.

Unfortunately, policy interventions and attempts to bridge the gap between theory and practice rarely take cognizance of children's own constructions and understandings of their experiences in correctional institutions. In an effort to promote implementation of the CRC and relevant laws for children in conflict with the law, there has been an over reliance on statistical information and surveys that employ fully structured questionnaires devoid of open-ended questions which do not elicit practical details of detention life. Sometimes, one tends to draw on secondary information from reports and other sources about juveniles and detaining authorities; while in other cases, there is dependence on one's own assumptions or that of others about life in correctional institutions. Thus, children's experiences in correctional institutions are seldom an interpretation of their own, but instead, lend themselves to adults' own translations, preconceived thoughts, and suppositions, resulting in a gap between adult's assumptions and what pertains in practice for children. Consequently, policy implementation and interventions derive from children's needs and vulnerabilities on the basis of pre-determined categories such as gender, impoverished and disadvantaged backgrounds, religion, ethnicity, type of correctional institution, which in themselves may be relevant but are different from children's own constructions of vulnerability and experiences in detention.

Another issue worthy of consideration is that young offenders are usually perceived by the criminal justice system and other policing efforts as stubborn, unruly, rebellious, and deviant (Presdee, 2000; Blok, 2001; Trulson, 2007) and are targeted and monitored deliberately (Arts & Popovski, 2006). Such perceptions, which can be antagonistic, perceive crime as a lone or single occurrence without context, directed at juveniles as offenders. During the period of the author's preliminary fieldwork, there were reports of juvenile offenders being committed to two or three years of detention for petty pilfering such as stealing palm fruits. In one instance, a thirteen-year-old juvenile offender, who probably on account of the nature of offense, was committed to the senior correctional institute [section 46 (4) of the Juvenile Justice Act provides that a juvenile offender under the age of fifteen who commits a serious crime[39] shall be committed to a senior correctional center]. This particular child was unwilling to speak to anyone, including the warders and staff, and some staff attributed this to the child not being able to speak a comprehensible language. One could not, however, rule out the possibility of the child being traumatized, in view of being plunged into the midst of young offenders ages eighteen–twenty-one years. However, having visited the male junior correctional institution and witnessing the level of resource deprivation, the author would have—given the choice between the two—also recommended the senior correctional institute for this child. Yet such a decision would not have been in the best interest of the child, as the Juvenile Justice Act makes other choices available. The question that easily comes to mind is whether or not the social inquiry report for the child in question was detailed and informative enough and gave due regard to the best interest of the child and also to the social and real circumstances of the correctional institution. Were rules and laws, on the basis of the above discussions, merely being enforced devoid of a social context and without consideration to the best interest of the child as provided by the CRC?

Criminal justice reforms that aim at promoting the best interests of the child, rehabilitation, reformation, and prevention of juvenile crime and yet merely emphasize compliance and enforcement without appreciating the social construction of crime or the wider social context of juvenile offenders may end up reinforcing concepts of retribution and punishment and the taken-for-grantedness of the existence of correctional institutions.

The author does not, in view of the foregoing discussions, seek to privilege life at the micro level over the broader human rights situation of juvenile offenders in Ghana. Nor do these discussions seek to downplay the importance of human rights monitoring efforts. On the contrary, it is an acknowledgment of the invaluableness of realistic experiences of children in conflict with the law to normative human rights standards and the recognition that normative principles of human rights and local, everyday practices in correctional institutions are reciprocally constituted. It is pretense to advocate effective policy implementation and compliance with human rights standards without respecting human rights of detainees well enough to appreciate their narratives, real stories, ideas, and experiences.

Consequently, any effort to bridge the gap between rhetoric and practice in ensuring compliance with the CRC and relevant human rights standards for juvenile offenders must give recognition to the fact that by virtue of being human, juvenile offenders have human rights and deserve to be heard, and their real life experiences deserve attention and prominence by policymakers and human rights professionals.

The final section discusses yet another vital issue in connection with bridging the gap between rhetoric and practice for children in conflict with the law.

Mediating and Negotiating Laws?

Discussions in this section demonstrate how juvenile and young offenders as well as state and non-state agents are able to negotiate structures and processes, giving an indication that laws and policies are not supreme and do not translate linearly, with their implementation being met by unpredictable contexts characterized by multiple actors with contesting interests (James & Prout, 1990; Long, 2001; Jensen & Jefferson, 2009).

This section discusses a key determining factor with respect to committing an offender to one institution or the other. There have been frequent reports of juveniles being incarcerated in adult prisons and police cells, and these reports are usually attributable to inadequate facilities for juveniles, coupled with the difficulty in determining the age of juvenile offenders.[40]

In accordance with the Juvenile Justice Act, a juvenile offender is a child under age 18 who is in conflict with the law and who has been convicted of an offense for which the court may impose a sentence of imprisonment for one month or upward without the option of a fine. A juvenile offender, in keeping with the Act, should be detained in a junior correctional institute for a period of detention not exceeding three months for children below the age of sixteen. Juvenile offenders above age sixteen but below age eighteen should not be detained for a period exceeding six months in a junior correctional institute.

A young offender is one who is eighteen years or above but below twenty-one years, who has been convicted of an offense for which the court may impose a sentence of imprisonment for one month or upward without the option of a fine. Young offenders, in keeping with section 47 of Act 651, are to be detained in a senior correctional center but not beyond the date on which they attain twenty-one years. In accordance with the Juvenile Justice Act, the center can also house juvenile offenders below fifteen years of age who have committed serious crimes.[41]

Act 653 does not set a lower age limit nor make reference to the age of legal criminal accountability; however, in keeping with section 4 of the Criminal Code (Amendment) Act 1998 (Act 554), the legal age of criminal accountability is twelve years. Accordingly, discussions about juveniles and young offenders refer to age categories between twelve and twenty years.[42]

The Juvenile Justice Act provides that ages of juvenile offenders be determined medically in the absence of a birth or medical certificate:

> In the absence of a birth certificate or a baptismal certificate, a certificate signed by a medical officer as to the age of a person below 18 years of age shall be evidence of that age before a court without proof of signature unless the court directs otherwise. An order of a court shall not be invalidated by any subsequent proof that the age of the child has not been correctly stated. . . . Where it appears to the court that the person brought before it has attained the age of 18 years, the person shall for the purposes of this Part, be deemed not to be a juvenile. [Act 653, section 19 (2)–(4)].

Notwithstanding these provisions, age overlaps were observed in all the institutions visited;[43] there were a number of juvenile offenders (younger than eighteen years) in the senior correctional center who had apparently committed minor offenses.

Reports of the CHRAJ have consistently indicated that juveniles are usually advised to inflate their ages so as to spend shorter terms in adult prisons and avoid spending the mandatory three years in a juvenile correctional institute. Whereas prior to the passage of Act 653, juvenile and young offenders were in most cases committed to correctional institutions for three years, with the passage of the Juvenile Justice Act in 2003, juveniles can spend less time in detention depending on age, type of offense, and recommendation of social inquiry reports, in which case the argument of avoiding longer sentences does not hold.

Why, then, is age determination still problematic, and what accounts for inflation and reduction of age by juvenile and young offenders? Discussions reveal that both inflation and reduction of age contribute to the advantage of the offender, as the former and the latter result in spending less time in adult prisons and correctional institutions for juvenile offenders, respectively, and that state agents tend to recommend age inflation not necessarily on account of the benefit the juvenile will derive from it. During interview sessions,[44] it came to the fore that the process of committing and conveying juveniles to correctional centers is apparently more cumbersome than if juveniles were sentenced to adult prisons. The same reason was cited by the regional commander in the 2001 CHRAJ Report on Inspection of Prisons and Police Cells:

> According to him, the procedure at juvenile courts is cumbersome, and that accounts for the inflation of ages of juveniles on the recommendation of the police so as to avoid going through the process.

Thus, juveniles are reportedly advised to inflate their ages in order to attract a prison sentence instead of placement in an institution for juveniles.

In deciding whether or not to commit an offender to one institution or the other on the basis of age, magistrates and judges draw on social inquiry reports prepared by social workers. These reports, in keeping with the Juvenile Justice Act and the Children's Act, should provide all relevant details and processes in respect of age and committals; yet in practice, this is not always the case. Many a time, this is attributable to resource constraints, which make it difficult for social workers to conduct detailed investigations that feed these reports.

In interviews conducted by the author, questions about age usually incited laughter and giggles among juvenile and young offenders, as they tend to be doubtful and sometimes raise questions about one another's ages. In one instance, two different ages were cited, with the juvenile offender explaining without hesitation that one was for office records and the other was the actual age.

Uncertainty about one's age is also due to parents' inability to register their children at birth, although in a number of cases, there seems a deliberate attempt not to disclose actual ages. Discussions and interviews with staff and juvenile offenders revealed that parental interest and influence or the influence of other non-state agents and private persons could also result in juveniles being committed to a correctional institution that should normally admit juveniles younger or older. Similarly, young offenders are not helpless subjects of laws and interventions as they may seem, but they strategize actively and tend to negotiate these laws on their own terms (by altering their ages) as they relate to various actors, whether or not they are state or non-state actors.

Thus, in practice, the implementation of codified laws and pre-existing rules such as section 19 of Act 653 meets and intersects with actions by young offenders and state and private actors such as parents who intervene across the implementation process. Implementation of laws becomes problematic when these unpredictable day-to-day practicalities are either not taken into consideration or ignored by policymakers. Consequently, laws, policies, and logical frameworks are regarded as blueprints and already-made plans with neat boundaries without drawing on actors' actual day-to-day life interactions and strategies.

Conclusion

Discussions in this chapter are demonstrative of Ghana's official commitment to promoting and protecting the rights and welfare of children in conflict with the law by instituting relevant legislative, institutional, and policy measures. Nevertheless, Ghana's laws, policies, and programs over the years undoubtedly have not translated successfully into practice for children in conflict with the law, and implementation processes usually perceived as linear make little space for lived experiences in correctional institutions.

Concluding discussions beg a shift from outlining series of recommendations addressed to various state and non-state agencies and advocating state of the art monitoring and evaluation plans to track progress (as is usually the case). Having been an ardent adherent of the foregoing processes, the author admits that though such efforts can be useful, most often they are adept at contributing more to transformation of rhetoric than of reality, as they seldom take account of actual day-to-day experiences of groups targeted.

The way forward to implementing a treaty that has been in existence for more than twenty years is to acknowledge and make space for practicalities—these are sometimes written off under the guise of "non-compliance" or "failures" to meet relevant standards—which characterize actors' realm of practice. Such everyday practicalities are unpredictable and cannot be subjected to step-by-step and neatly bounded implementation processes.

These discussions do not by any means seek to propose an agenda that runs contrary to human rights principles, rather one that upholds human dignity and respects the totality life of various actors enough to listen to their perspectives and situate implementation processes within their local contexts.

Promoting human rights compliance, while pretending that there is no real life beyond the legal label of juveniles and young offenders and that state agents are perfect executors and implementers of state policy and agenda, results in implementation without context. Such disengagement takes out or denies the existence of actual life experiences in the name of noncompliance and only further widens the gap between human rights rhetoric and practice.

Promoting human rights in practice for children requires increased levels of reflexivity and self questioning among policymakers, human rights institutions, NGOs, and practitioners who seek to promote compliance with the CRC and related legislative instruments to create space for human lives to inform human rights (Jensen & Jefferson, 2009) and for local contexts to inform conventions, laws, and policies.

Notes

1. A *trokosi,* translated as wife of the gods, is a girl child who is made to atone for the sin of a relative by serving in a traditional shrine for some or most part of her life.

2. *Training Manual for Human Rights Monitoring*, chapter 9:43. Retrieved in September 2006 from http://www1.umn.edu/humanrts/monitoring/chapter9.html#C1. *Monitoring Places of Detention: A Practical Guide* by the Association for the Prevention of Torture, Geneva. Retrieved September 2007 from http://www.apt.ch/component/option,com_docman/task,cat_view/gid,58/Itemid,59/lang,en/.

3. Annual reports of the Commission on Human Rights and Administrative Justice (2000–2005).

4. 2007 Ghana Human Development Report–UNDP.

5. The author, in her capacity as deputy director, has oversight of one of four departments of the Commission on Human Rights and Administrative Justice, Headquarters, Ghana. The department has responsibility for human rights education, human rights monitoring and the promotion of collaborative efforts with human rights civil society organizations. She is currently on study leave, pursuing her doctoral studies in the Netherlands, and as part of her studies, she undertook this preliminary fieldwork in January and February 2009, during visits to Mamobi Boys Senior Correctional Institute in Accra (the only senior correctional institute in Ghana); Osu Girls Correctional Institute, also located in Accra (the only female correctional institute in Ghana, which also houses the girls' vocational school, a shelter for girls who have suffered some form of abuse, and the Osu boys' remand home), and finally the Swedru Boys Junior Correctional Institute (which also houses the Swedru vocational/technical school) located in the Central Region. She acknowledges the immense support and cooperation from the authorities in charge, staff, juvenile and young offenders, and all related actors during the preliminary stage. In an effort to ensure confidentiality, pseudo names of young offenders have been employed. A primary aim of the author's doctoral study was to put aside normative conceptualizations of human rights, her own assumptions, and those of others about the needs and claims of children in conflict with the law. By means of an ethnographic approach, she sought to penetrate the world of juvenile offenders and find out about their construction of needs and of human rights in their day-to-day lives and experiences in detention.

6. Goldson has done substantial work in the fields of youth justice and criminology for jurisdictions within the UK—England and Wales, Northern Ireland, and Scotland—and has to his credit many publications, including the *Dictionary of Youth Justice*.

7. Reports on prison conditions by NGOs and national human rights institutions are available; however, these reports provide little information in terms of day-to-day experiences and life stories of young offenders in detention.

8. Prior to British Royal African Company administration from the mid-eighteenth century to mid-nineteenth century.

9. *World Factbook of Criminal Justice Systems* by Obi N. I. Ebbe, State University of New York at Brockport. Retrieved December 2009 from http://bjs.ojp.usdoj.gov/content/pub/ascii/WFBCJGHA.TXT.

10. The Ghana prison system. Source: *The Library of Congress Country Studies, CIA World Factbook.* Retrieved in September 2009 from http://www.photius.com/countries/ghana/economy/ghana _economy_prison_system.html.

11. Interviews held (by the author) with the assistant headmaster of the present institution revealed a sharp contrast with the earlier institution manned by the Salvation Army

Church. The erstwhile institution boasted of well-equipped workshops, with school buildings that covered a vast expanse of land. Juveniles, on account of the educational provision offered them at the time, were always in high demand, and even while in detention, they engaged in paid employment, and their monies were kept for them in savings accounts. On completion, reintegration into society did not pose much challenge to them, as there was a high demand for their skills on the labor market. The current institution utilizes the same premises as the erstwhile one, except that it has only one dilapidated building allocated to the junior correctional institution as a dormitory; remaining buildings are for the predominant use of the vocational and technical institution.

12. There was widespread juvenile delinquency close to the end of World War II; the conscription of men into the Gold Coast army impacted on the care of children, resulting in school dropouts, streetism and rural-urban migration.

13. A secretary for social services was appointed in 1943, and provision was made for the establishment of a juvenile justice system pursuant to section 54 (b) of the court's ordinance (DSW, 2005). In keeping with the court's ordinance, the governor was empowered to constitute from time to time, special courts that exercised jurisdiction similar to those of District Magistrates' courts for hearing cases involving juveniles (*Treatment of Juvenile Offenders,* Justice Osafo Sampong, retrieved in December 2009 from http://www.judicial.gov.gh/JTI/jti_documents/Learing%20Materials/TREATMENT%20 OF%20JUVENILE%20OFFENDERS.pdf.

14. Interview with officer in charge, senior correctional center, February 2009.

15. Ghana reportedly experienced an increase in juvenile delinquency and the exposure of children to street life between the 1970s and the 1990s. This was due to parents' inability to provide properly for their children as a result of growing unemployment, stemming possibly from harsh economic policies that resulted in the privatization of state institutions and enterprises.

16. Such as the preparation of Social Inquiry Reports. These are detailed reports prepared by a social worker based on investigations conducted with respect to the family, school, and general environment in which the juvenile offender resides and other factors that must have influenced the committal of crime (DSW 2005; Act 653 of 2003, section 24) and the re-designation of industrial schools and the Borstal Institution as junior correctional centers, and the senior correctional center, respectively.

17. Stems from Howe & Covell's (2007) approach to evaluating compliance and commitment to the CRC.

18. Some of these policies include the formulation in 1992 of a ten-year National Program of Action based on the World Declaration on the Rights of the Child to Survival, Protection, Development, and Participation; Draft Street Children in Ghana Policy Framework, 1995; the launch of a Free, Compulsory and Universal Basic Education (FCUBE) program in 1996; Adolescent Reproductive Health Policy, 2000; National Health Insurance Scheme (NHIS) in 2003; Early Childhood Care and Development Policy, 2004; National Gender and Children Policy, 2004; ILO-IPEC Time Bound Program in 2004, which sets time frames for progress on the elimination of the Worst Forms of Child Labor in Ghana; Educational Decentralization and Management and Capitation Grant Scheme (resulting in school fees being abolished at the basic level of education in public schools) in 2005; Ghana School Feeding Program in 2005 and other related programs.

19. These include: the establishment of the Ghana National Commission on Children (GNCC) in 1979 to coordinate the activities of child-related agencies (the GNCC assumed the status of a department within the Ministry of Women and Children in 2001);

the establishment in 1993, pursuant to Act 456 of Ghana's 1992 Constitution, of the Commission on Human Rights and Administrative Justice (CHRAJ) to promote and protect the fundamental human rights of the citizenry, including children; the establishment in 1998 of the Women and Juvenile Unit of the Ghana Police Service (WAJU) to prevent, protect, investigate, and prosecute crimes against women and children, and later in 2005 was designated as the Domestic Violence and Victims Support Unit (DOVVSU).

20. Stemming from Howe & Covell's (2007) approach to evaluating compliance and commitment to the CRC.

21. Dr. Sonya M. Sultan (DFID Ghana), *Social protection for the poorest in Africa: Learning from experience*; Tamar T. Schrofer (UNICEF Ghana), *Building support to have targeted social protection interventions for the poorest—The case of Ghana.* September 8–10, 2008, Kampala, Uganda. Retrieved in May 2009 from http://www.unicef.org/socialpolicy/files/Social_Protection_for_the_Poorest_-_Ghana.pdf.

22. Annual reports of the Commission on Human Rights and Administrative Justice (2000–2005).

23. Preliminary fieldwork, 2009.

24. Preliminary fieldwork conducted in 2009.

25. When a juvenile is released on probation, the probation officer who is a social worker is expected to assume a supervisory role over all the activities of the juvenile offender in keeping with the probation order. See sections 22 and 23 of Act 560 of 1998.

26. Sections 27–32 of Act 560 of 1998.

27. Interview with a district-level social worker, who was a member of a Child Panel in the district.

28. At the rate of 1.00 dollar to 1.42 Ghana cedi.

29. About five out of ten expressed the desire to pursue further education upon discharge.

30. In spite of the poor educational provision, it is worth mentioning that there has been steady progress in educational provision over the past years.

31. In her preliminary report to the Commission on Human Rights, the special rapporteur on the right to education set out "four essential features that primary schools should exhibit—namely: availability, accessibility, acceptability, and adaptability" (E/CN.4/1999/49, para. 50).

32. In accordance with *General Comment No. 3* adopted by the Committee on Economic, Social and Cultural Rights.

33. *The 2008 African report on child well-being.* Retrieved in December 2009 from http://www.africanchildinfo.net/africanreport08/. The report was developed by the African Child Policy Forum (ACPF). It rated Ghana 29 out of 52 in its child friendliness index and 42 out of 52 in respect to legal protection for children.

34. Ghana's efforts to promote the rights and welfare of children and young people are also guided by the following UN rules: Standard Minimum Rules for the Administration of Juvenile Justice (the Beijing rules), Guidelines for the Prevention of Juvenile Delinquency (The Riyadh Guidelines), Rules for the Protection of Juveniles Deprived of Their Liberty, and the Robben Island Guidelines.

35. The CHRAJ is the only institution in Ghana that conducts regular monitoring visits annually to all detention institutions in the country.

36. Six years following the commencement of CHRAJ's annual monitoring visits to prisons, the Optional Protocol to the Convention Against Torture (OPCAT) was adopted in 2002 and came into force in 2006. The OPCAT establishes a system of regular visits by international and domestic bodies to detention institutions.

37. The OPCAT is unique as it establishes a system of regular visits to places of

detention and makes a wide range of institutions [see Article 4 (1) of the OPCAT] such as prisons, police cells, and other detention institutions where people are detained (includes both government-operated facilities and privately operated facilities) open to domestic and international visiting mechanisms, thus making state parties to the OPCAT accountable to both domestic and international communities. On account of various advocacy campaigns undertaken by the CHRAJ in Ghana in collaboration with the Association for the Prevention of Torture (APT) in Geneva, Ghana signed the OPCAT in November 2006 but has not as yet ratified the treaty.

38. Draft 2009 report on the state of detention institutions in Ghana, by the CHRAJ (unpublished).

39. Serious crimes according to section 46 of Act 653 include murder, rape, defilement, indecent assault involving unlawful harm, robbery with aggravated circumstances, drug offenses, and offenses related to firearms.

40. Department of Social Welfare (DSW) 2005; prisons reports of the Commission on Human Rights and Administrative Justice (1996–2005).

41. The definition of an infant under section 18 of the Ghana's Courts Act 459 of 1993 is a person under the age of twenty-one years.

42. See note 41.

43. Preliminary fieldwork in 2009.

44. Preliminary fieldwork in 2009.

References

Arts, K., and V. Popovski. (2006). *International Criminal Accountability and the Rights of Children.* The Hague: Hague Academic Press.

Ayete-Nyampong, L. (2009). *Juvenile offenders in Ghana making meaning of human rights in their day-to-day life in detention.* Unpublished notes on doctoral preliminary fieldwork.

Blok, A. (2001). *Honour and Violence*. USA: Blackwell Publishers.

De Kock, D. (2005). Youth in conflict with the law and socio-economic experiences in their childhood: A relationship. *Journal of Child and Youth Care Work* 20, 56–71.

Department of Social Welfare (DSW). (2005). *A report on the state of juvenile justice administration in Ghana, Department of Social Welfare*. Accra: UNICEF.

Ellis, A. B. (1971). *A History of Gold Coast of West Africa.* London: Curzon Press.

Goldschmidt, J. E. (1981). *National and Indigenous Constitutional Law in Ghana.* Accra: Ghana Publishing Corporation.

Goldson, B. (2002). *Vulnerable Inside: Children in Secure and Penal Setting.* London: The Children's Society.

———. (2008). *Child Incarceration: Institutional Abuse, the Violent State and the Politics of Impunity.* London: Routledge.

Harvey, W. B. (1966). *Laws and Social Change in Ghana.* Princeton: Princeton University Press.

Hobbs, D. (2001). Ethnography of deviance. In Atkinson et al. (ed.). *Handbook of Ethnography.* London: Sage.

Howe, R. B., and K. Covell. (2007). *A Question of Commitment: Children's Rights in Canada.* Waterloo, ON: Wilfrid Laurier University Press.

James, A., and A. Prout. (1990). *Constructing and Reconstructing Childhood: Contemporary Issues in the Sociological Study of Childhood.* London: Falmer Press.

Jefferson, A. M. (2007). Prison officer training and practice in Nigeria: Contention, contradiction and re-imagining reform strategies. *Punishment and Society* 9 (3), 253–269.

Jensen, S., and A. M. Jefferson (eds.). (2009). *State Violence and Human Rights: State Officials in the South.* Milton Park: Abingdon; New York: Routledge-Cavendish.

Long, N. (2001). *Development Sociology: Actor Perspectives.* London: Routledge.

Marshall, K., and P. Parvis. (2004). *Honouring Children: The Human Rights of the Child in Christian Perspective.* University of Edinburgh: Saint Andrew Press.

Muncie, J. (2008). The "punitive turn" in juvenile justice: Cultures of control and rights compliance in Western Europe and the USA. *Youth Justice* 8 (2), 107–121.

Presdee, M. (2000). *Cultural Criminology and the Carnival of Crime.* London: Routledge.

Sarkins, J. (2008). *Human Rights in African Prisons.* South Africa: HSCR Press.

Taylor, C. S. (1990). *Dangerous Society.* East Lansing: Michigan State University Press.

Trulson, C. R. (2007). Determinants of disruption: Institutional misconduct among state committed delinquents. *Youth Violence and Juvenile Justice* 5 (1), 7–34.

United Nations Development Program (UNDP). (2007). *Ghana Human Development Report: Towards a More Inclusive Society.* Accra: Combert Impression.

Chapter 11
Ghana's Education System: Where Rhetoric Meets Reform

By Leah McMillan

A book on children's rights without a chapter on education is nearly unfathomable. Education is not only a right itself but is a precursor to the achievement of many other rights. As the agent of socialization second only to that of the family, to educate is to create active, knowledgeable members of society. The data speaks for itself when correlating educational achievement to other rights: better education leads to greater employment opportunities; better education lessens maternal mortality rates; better education improves gender equality. Perhaps even more significantly, better education heightens one's awareness of all human rights attainable. Education builds knowledge, capabilities, esteem, and awareness.

A child's right to education, as the story above relays, seems so intuitively necessary that rarely do we adequately step far enough back from our education policies, grounded in international human rights, and question their relevance and progress. From a human capital perspective, Ghana is making progress with its education system—primary enrollment rates increased from 51 percent in 1991 to 72 percent in 2007, revealing a shared optimism among policymakers that this climate of change is working and that Ghana is progressing adequately (UNESCO Institute, 2008).

Yet when one shifts to perceiving these statistics through a human rights lens, this optimism dissipates. While enrollment rates may be on the rise, the Government of Ghana (GOG) is still failing to meet its obligations under the United Nations (UN) Convention on the Rights of the Child (CRC). With free, compulsory primary education for all not being met, secondary and higher education deteriorating, and a severe lack of mechanisms for monitoring attendance,

Ghana's education policies have been insufficient in implementing CRC Article 28. What is more, 28 percent of the Ghanaian population has still not had its right to education fulfilled.

Despite Ghana perpetually being praised as a "prize pupil," a "success story" amid the majority of western Africa plagued with war and turmoil, Ghana has still not fulfilled its obligations to the Convention (Hutchful, 2002). This chapter will journey through the accessibility issues challenging enrollment, the most recent educational reforms, and the involvement of the international community to argue that the GOG must adapt its policies to develop a strategy that is more in tune with the accessibility issues facing its citizens. Further, the government must commit fully to these policies to move these statements beyond mere rhetoric toward an actual commitment to fulfilling its obligations under CRC Article 28.

The History: From Colonization to the Convention

Much of the inaccessibility issues existing today trace their roots back to the time of British colonization. While Southern Ghana, particularly in today's Greater Accra, Brong-Ahafo, Volta, and Central regions, inherited both basic school infrastructure and the optimism behind the burgeoning higher institutions such as the University of Cape Coast or the University of Ghana, Northern Ghana did not receive similar treatment. Rather than developing its knowledge base, the British reserved the north for extracting cheap labor. The stark contrast between education in the north and south may have been introduced at the time of colonization, but fifty-one years after independence, the country is still plagued by the same dilemmas.

President Nkrumah's modernizing initiatives following independence were rampant with infrastructural plans. More schools were built, education was used as a means for promoting Ghanaian citizenship and national development, and enrollment rates were rapidly increasing. Not surprising given the socialist concerns of the Nkrumah government, public school was free. While Northern Ghana was still severely lagging behind, optimism was felt the country over. Unfortunately, this optimism was short-lived. Soon came an oil crisis that shook the world, and a decrease in development so severe that Ghana found itself implementing the Economic Recovery Plan prescribed by the International Monetary Fund (IMF) in 1982 (Boafo-Arthur, 2007). To recover economically, the country suffered educationally. The program decreased social spending, dropping Ghana's enrollment rate from 67 percent in 1982 to 45 percent by 1989 (UNESCO Institute, 2008).

By 1987, a decentralization strategy was implemented following the realization that a country without a solid education system had minimized its opportunity for achieving socioeconomic development. In 1992, the Ministry of Education (MOE) implemented the official decentralized education strategy. In between those years, Ghana ratified the CRC, which, according to Article 28, rendered the government legally obligated to provide schooling for all primary school-age children. Beyond this, secondary and higher education needed to be accessible, and attendance rates needed monitoring. These obligations were to all fall under the auspices of "international cooperation." Yet while Ghana implemented a Free Compulsory Universal Basic Education (FCUBE) program and updated its educational reforms in 2001, problems with inaccessibility persist.

Unquestionably, the GOG has attempted to improve its system of education. Since the ratification of the CRC, the GOG has made significant changes to its education policy, signaling motivation on the part of the government to improve the public school system. Basic education is a prioritized component of the Ghana Poverty Reduction Strategy (GPRS) and, as such, the government has allocated a significant amount of spending to this area. In 2001, of the 16.9 percent of gross national product (GDP) spent on the education sector, as determined by the GPRS, 60.6 percent was allocated for basic education; in 2004 this rose to 64.7 percent (Ministry of Finance, 2004, 2006).

It is clear the government has recognized there is a problem in its education sector; over a decade of changes illustrates this. That said, this book does not ask about motivations, desires, or intended results. The question this book asks is quite simple: Have the GOG's obligations to the CRC been met or not? More specific to this chapter, has the GOG fulfilled its obligations to the CRC articles pertaining to education, most notably Article 28? Irrespective of changes made, intentions apparent, or improvements envisaged, 28 percent of Ghanaian children are still not attending school. This clearly indicates that the right to education is not yet a reality in Ghana. However, the story does not end here. It is insufficient to simply state that the GOG is failing to meet its obligations under Article 28. What follows is an analysis as to why this is the case.

Three Vulnerable Groups

Article 28 (1) (a) of the CRC mandates that education be "free and compulsory for all." To fulfill this mandate, the international community has identified three groups that are most vulnerable to exclusion from education: girls, developmentally disabled persons, and the rural poor. In Ghana, these three categories represent the most disadvantaged in terms of access to education. The following will explain these groups' challenges, detailing the lack of commitment from the GOG to ensure that these groups receive adequate education. The GOG has demonstrated its commitment to achieving universal primary education (UPE) via its signing of the CRC. The Ministry of Education, Science and Sports states, "The overall goal of the Ministry is to provide relevant and quality education for all Ghanaians, especially the disadvantaged" (GOG, 2009). The government has expressed its commitment to vulnerable groups in writing; it is imperative that the government acts upon this statement, thereby ensuring that communities are able to implement relevant strategies in line with the overarching goal of this Ministry. If UPE is to be achieved, these three groups warrant more recognition and aid.

Girls

Globally, girls are disadvantaged in their opportunities to attend school; the situation in Ghana is no different. While 100 girls compared to 201 boys attend school, the ratio jumps to 100 girls for every 417 boys in the rural areas of the country. Forty-one percent of Ghanaian females have never been to school in comparison to 21 percent of males (IMF, 2003:21). In a study regarding the implementation of children's rights in Ghana, Asiegbor et al. found that "the classroom has been noted as being one of the sites where rights and equity issues are less likely to be enforced" (Asiegbor, Fincham, Nanang, Gala, & Britwum, 2001:8). They note that gender discrimination is evident in the curriculum itself (Asiegbor et al., 2001). As well, a shortage of female teachers limits the number of positive female role models in schools. Instead, girls must contend with male teachers and administrators, many who have been known to discriminate against female students (Fentiman, Hall, & Bundy, 1999). Although the new junior secondary school (JSS) curriculum includes human rights and gender equity in the updated syllabi, these changes are so recent that little to no real improvement has been made. Moreover, the lack of appropriate teacher training and funding for training manuals, particularly in remote areas, makes the appropriate implementation of these gender equity measures even more difficult (Asiegbor et al., 2001).

Article 28 (1) (a) specifies that education must be compulsory *for all.* The international community has been persistent in the need to develop specific means for ensuring that girls have access to education, in order for the "all" in the Convention to be achieved. Three percent of girls do not attend school owing to pregnancy. This not only connects with abuse but also with the tendency for rural girls to marry younger (Sussex, 2004:2). Yet while pregnancy creates numerous obstacles to attaining an education, it should not be a prevention.

In a 2004 report issued by the University of Sussex, 27 percent of Ghanaian girls surveyed had been sexually propositioned by a teacher. While the study was only conducted in one school in each of three selected regions, the authors concluded that these statistics were at least indicative of an obvious problem in the school system, even if the percentage cannot be generalized nationally. Forty-five of the forty-eight girls also reported having been beaten at least once by a teacher. Again, though these statistics cannot be assumed to be accurate nationally, it is undeniable that such occurrences are familiar throughout the country as a whole (Sussex, 2004:3). The Ghana non-governmental organization (NGO) Coalition on the Rights of the Child's report to the UN Committee on the Rights of the Child criticized the GOG for failing to collect data pertaining to the abuse of children, especially girls, in the school system. As abuse is a major deterrent and reason for girls not attending school, it is critical that data is collected in order to grasp the severity of the problem. By not adequately acknowledging the incidence of abuse at schools, the government is perpetuating the silence on the issue, thus encouraging the silent dropout of victims rather than encouraging an environment of dialogue (Ghana NGO, 2005). Though several legislative measures have come into effect that could potentially deter abusive situations, including the 1998 Children's Act and the 2003 Juvenile Justice Act (Ghana NGO, 2005) the Ghana Living Standards Survey and other national documentations do not adequately assess the extent of the problem (White, 2005). Acknowledging this is particularly important because girls are often not believed when reporting incidences; the lower status of women in society, coupled with the culture of authority prevalent, places the word of someone in authority, including a teacher, ahead of the girl child.

The UN Children's Education Fund (UNICEF) advises that "FCUBE and the research report on Synethsis of Research on Girls' Education in Ghana outline strategies and activities to address various forms of inequality between girls and boys in education" (Asiegbor et al., 2001). While FCUBE has outlined the need for equity education and equal opportunities for girls, these ideas have not translated into any concrete plan of action. A Girls' Education Unit and a Girl Child Education Project were introduced to oversee the implementation of equity education and equal opportunity, but the study indicates that such actions have not translated into practice. In particular, UNICEF recommends better teacher training to ensure that human rights are integrated into the classroom. While equity education appears to be a useful tool for ensuring that equality is taught in the classroom, without adequate training, teachers are unqualified to teach these ideas to the students (Asiegbor et al., 2001).

There are also practical reasons for girl child absenteeism. During their menstrual cycle, many girls must miss school owing to lack of proper sanitation, such as latrines and water resources. Girls in many rural households must awaken and travel before dawn to collect water and help the other women with kitchen duties. Many miss the opportunity to attend school due to inappropriate scheduling. The Ghanaian school day aligns with that of the formal Western 9-to-3 system, leaving these girls, and many farming children in general, unable to attend these regular school hours (Tanye, 2008). While there have been some cases of communities adapting their school day to match family needs, this is not true in most areas.

Developmentally Disabled Persons

A second category of children most likely to be disadvantaged by the Ghanaian education system is children with developmental disabilities, including physical and mental impairments. While these children are seemingly disadvantaged in all countries, it is in the developing world where such disadvantages are most exacerbated. There are two predominant reasons for this, both of which are demonstrated in the Ghanaian context. Although approximately 10 percent of the Ghanaian population is disabled (Dei, Asgharzadeh, Bahador, & Shahjahan, 2006:209), merely 2 percent of disabled persons are provided for by special institutions (Casely-Hayford & Lynch, 2003). Although there is no data available to indicate the number of disabled children in schools, interviews and observations in cross-country studies suggest that enrollment of this demographic is quite low (Dei et al., 2006). This lack of data collection signifies a problem in and of itself. If the government is to adequately address the lack of enrollment of disabled individuals, it needs to be identifying the number of students who fit this category. Throughout the country, a mere twenty-three schools operate specifically for students with disabilities (Casely-Hayford & Lynch, 2003). A Department for International Development (DFID) report states that the majority of these services and schools are located in urban areas, thus perpetuating the inequality of access felt by rural Ghanaians. Only 10 percent of visually impaired children attend a special school, indicative of the lack of accessibility of these special institutions (Casely-Hayford & Lynch, 2003:12). As well, these special schools are intended to only care for those with significant physical and mental disabilities. Other children with disabilities must enter the mainstream system. Although these students are considered to be more capable of entering the regular school program, these students still require specific schooling to meet their special needs. By forcing these children to enter the mainstream system, they are severely disadvantaged.

Disability has been one of the major ways in which children are significantly excluded from the education system. Dei et al. observed that schools reflect the society at large and, as such, incorporate the mores maintained in the larger societal setting. In Ghana then, the disadvantages and stigmas associated with disabled persons have transcended into the educational system (Dei et al., 2006). The negative labeling applied to persons with disabilities renders them automatically disadvantaged on account of their special needs (Agbenyega, 2003). Transportation costs can be a major obstacle, particularly for persons with physical disabilities. And while education might be "free," it is also likely to be in a classroom with one teacher to approximately fifty-eight students, as the average ratio in the north suggests. In this setting, students with a learning disability are, without doubt, disabled from learning. Teachers do not have the time or the training to assist with their special circumstances. In a culture that is already widely unaccepting of the developmentally disabled, those who actually do beat the odds and find their way into a classroom will be met with a mainstreamed, formal education system ill-suited to meet their learning needs (Fentiman et al., 1999).

Many teachers in Ghanaian schools reported in a 2007 study that the majority of their students who were disabled had visual impairments. Most teachers have received no disabilities education training and are inevitably unable to adequately meet the needs of these students. Bhasin & Obeng recommended that the Ghana Education Service institute disabilities education teaching at all teacher training schools in order to better meet the needs of disabled Ghanaian children (Bhasin & Obeng, 2007). Bhasin & Obeng's study indicated that many teachers felt as though these students should not be permitted to attend already crowded classrooms since they were not receiving appropriate education anyhow.

The Ministry of Education (MOE) does have a Special Education Division, but how well it has implemented its policies is questionable at best. For example, a mere eighty-seven children have actually been integrated into a Sight Saver program that is intended to help students with visual impairments (Casely-Hayford & Lynch, 2003:13). While the MOE has interesting strategies, none have been implemented effectively to date.

Resource deficiencies include appropriate reading material for the visually impaired, accessibility for children with physical disabilities, and appropriately trained staff to care for their special needs (Dei et al, 2006). As well, some policies are inadequate. For example, the JSS system regulations state that disabled children are simply given an additional year to complete the program. Schools designed for disabled students have instead had to tailor the curriculum to meet the needs of these students (Casely-Hayford & Lynch, 2003). One can imagine that schools without the appropriate time and resources would be unable to undertake such a commitment. Further, by simply giving children additional time to meet the mainstream program requirements, the government is failing to provide a curriculum that meets the special needs of these students. In fact, it is failing to even acknowledge that such special needs exist.

Indeed, Article 28 admonishes that all children are entitled to education. Article 29 stipulates that "education of the child shall be directed to (a) the development of the child's personality, talents, and mental and physical abilities to their fullest potential." The application of this particular right is especially relevant in the context of developmentally disabled children. Further, Article 23 states that children with disabilities should have "effective access to and receive education, training, healthcare service, rehabilitation services, preparation for employment and recreation opportunities in a manner conducive to the child's achieving the fullest possible social integration and individual development." Within this article, there is a clear mandate that children with disabilities are entitled to an accessible, quality education that is tailored to their specific needs. Primarily for reasons of resource deficiencies and cultural discrimination, this right is not being realized in Ghanaian schools.

Small steps should also be taken by the GOG to ensure that a concrete strategic plan is established. For example, there persists conflict regarding which dialect of sign language should be taught in schools. A national strategy could ensure that all children in need of this language instruction receive similar training. Less than 4 percent of the MOE budget is directed toward special needs education. With resource deficiencies being identified as a predominant reason for problems for these children, evidently more of the budget needs to be allocated for providing for these children (Kuyini & Desai, 2009).

The Rural Poor

The UN Educational, Scientific, and Cultural Organization (UNESCO) and UNICEF identified the most severely impoverished, girls, and the developmentally disabled as the three groups most vulnerable to being unable to access education. Indeed, these identified groups reflect the Ghanaian reality. Ensuring access to education is much more than simply building more schools and increasing numbers of teachers. The issues are complex and personal, cutting across gender, cultural, religious, and socioeconomic lines. In a 2005 survey undertaken in the Upper East and Upper West regions, 65 percent of parents with children not attending school stated that they would rather see their children attend, if possible; 88 percent of these children shared a marked preference for attending rather than staying at home (de Lange, 2007:33). While these parents would prefer to send their children to school, they must make a rational decision based on certain trade-offs. While the legal minimum working age is set by the Ministry of Employment and Social Welfare at fifteen years,[1] the unofficial, undocumented labor force is rampant. Many children must stay home to help with subsistence farming, household duties, or to supplement their family's employment by finding work in the informal labor force.

Many northern children report registering for school, yet they become less and less able to attend as domestic duties, farm work, or a family business interferes with their ability to complete homework. In the three northern regions where electricity is sparse, the number of hours in which a child can complete homework is already limited. Agricultural areas are traditionally more impoverished than urban areas, as seen throughout both sub-Saharan Africa and the developing world at large. In Ghana, the situation is no different, with 2 percent of the Urban Coastal and 2.9 percent of the Urban Forest localities being severely impoverished versus 45.4 percent in the Rural Savannah.[2] In the Upper East and Upper West regions, those in extreme poverty are 60.1 percent and 79 percent, respectively, in comparison to 6.2 percent, 6.6 percent, and 9.7 percent in the Greater Accra, Eastern, and Central regions, respectively (IMF, 2009). Suffice it to say, it is where rural areas flourish that poverty rates are highest. These populations are not only impacted owing to lack of industry, but they are disadvantaged in terms of geography and quality of life. One-third of Ghana's rural areas do not have access to safe drinking water. In fact, the sanitation is so poor that guinea worm is a struggle in many villages, with Ghana cited as having the greatest number of incidences of guinea worm in 2004.

A basic level of health is necessary for a child to be capable of mentally engaging in the learning process. Fentiman et al. observed that hunger and malaria are health issues that greatly influence both absence and dropout rates (Fentiman et al., 1999:345).

There has been some indication of improvements to Ghana's education system. The 2001 JSS reforms have worked toward ensuring that more students have the opportunity to attend this level of education. Furthermore, the Committee on the Rights of the Child affirmed the state report that the Capitation Grant and School Feeding Programs were leading to increased enrollment rates. Ghana's present ruling party, the National Democratic Congress, recently initiated a free school uniform policy intended to offset one of the leading causes of indirect school fees throughout the continent. While these efforts are certainly a step in the right direction, they have not been sufficient to ensure that all children have the opportunity to receive an education. As in Uganda where the elimination of school fees has been praised despite 18 percent of the population still not able to access education, the word "free" in Ghana's FCUBE system is quite relative. "Free" in the Ghanaian context implies the complete removal of any tuition costs associated with schooling. While using the rhetoric of "free" to suggest that education is now much more accessible, the government has not taken into account the many indirect costs associated with schooling, including textbooks, transportation, and intangible outputs such as time and lost labor. This report recommended that FCUBE actually be "implemented to the letter," criticizing that at present it is nothing more than rhetoric (Ghana NGO, 2005:13).

The Ghana Poverty Reduction Strategy Paper (GPRSP) cited almost one-third of children not attending school owing to their need to continue working. Another one-third of the population admitted that the cost of schooling was the predominant reason for their lack of attendance (IMF, 2003:23). The GPRSP then analyzed, quite appropriately, that this means that two-thirds of children out of school cite nonattendance for monetary reasons. The CRC Article 26 (1) (a) mandates that school be free. How, then, is this proportion of children not attending owing to the high cost of schooling? Although the GOG has sufficiently eliminated direct costs associated with schooling, the perpetuation of indirect costs has rendered schooling still inaccessible to a large portion of the population. Ghana's commitment to "free education" as outlined by the CRC is evidently not being fulfilled.

While the information presented thus far has focused on Northern Ghana, urban poverty in the south is growing as migration increases and city slums expand. Ghana's HIV/AIDS rate might be quite low in comparison to many African countries, but the phenomenon still forces many orphaned children to survive on the streets. With a sex tourist industry slowly emerging, and migration to the south resulting in street-ridden young people, urban poverty is a reality that is only getting worse. Yet, much like this chapter began by highlighting inaccessibility problems of the north, the majority of reports and NGO activities similarly emphasize these challenges. While the rural poor may be hugely disadvantaged and marginalized, their presence is at least acknowledged. While school feeding programs have been active in the north since 2002, and the majority of civil society organizations are working in these northern settings, impoverished children in the south are seemingly forgotten.

Despite the growth of urban poverty, currently, international development efforts to maintain cultural perceptions and prejudices deny the existence of poverty in cities. Although the rural areas have traditionally been more impoverished than cities, this has meant that in-country migration flows from village to town or city. Yet, more often than not, migration to the city-centers does not reap the desired benefits. Rather, the reality of living in poverty simply moves from a rural base to an urban base (Davis, 2006). And with this has come more challenges. Urban centers are now underequipped to handle the massive numbers of persons who have entered the cities. The cyclical effect of this reality is, then, that urban schools are known to have considerable constraints. This both decreases the quality of education at schools and increases the number of more well-off individuals in cities who send their children to private schools in hopes of their achieving an improved education.

Lastly, migration of children increases their chances of dropping out of school. The likelihood of a child returning to school after moving is quite small. Much depends on the reason for the migration. Children have been known to migrate in order to help pay for another sibling's education. This perpetuates their existence in work rather than in school (de Lange, 2007).

Unsuccessful Policies Revealed

The problem with Ghana's education system is not that it does not recognize the need to have policies in place to encourage access, but that these policies have been inadequately implemented and, thus, have been unsuccessful in meeting the needs of the country's most vulnerable citizens. While human rights are designed to reach even the most vulnerable, Ghana's education model has continued the legacy passed on from the colonial period—policies that benefit the south at the expense, or rather at the neglect, of the north.

In 1992, decentralized education reforms were beneficial to the districts in the south. By bringing decision-making down to the level of the local government, these communities could better address the needs of their citizens, thereby increasing enrollment. In the north, this meant that under-serviced and underfunded districts felt even more abandoned by the capital, and even further from realizing the goal of full enrollment (Naidoo, 2002). Although the Capitation Grant and School Feeding Program are beginning to improve potential enrollment in the north, the disparity between enrollment rates in the north and south still demonstrates a need for improved educational programming in the north to ensure that schooling is accessible to more children in this locality. In 2006, net enrollment sat at 65.4 percent, 69 percent and 70 percent in the Northern, Upper East, and Upper West regions, respectively. This was a dramatic improvement from 2004 rates, which were 52.4 percent, 55.5 percent and 54.5 percent in the same regions. Despite the apparent increases, more effort is needed should the CRC call for 100 percent enrollment to be realized.

In 2001, the secondary education reform instituted by the National Educational Reform Committee combined the previously separated junior secondary school (JSS) and senior secondary school (SSS) into "senior high school." While this decreased budgetary expenses in these two areas and encouraged a more fluid curriculum, these reforms brought little to no change in the north where JSS and SSS facilities are reserved for the most privileged citizens. Those living on the margins have not reaped the benefits of a system they were never able to access in the first place.

The Right to Education: Rhetoric, Reality . . . and Reason?

This chapter, thus far, has highlighted major considerations for inaccessibility. This discussion has emphasized the domestic reasons for inaccessibility: Why are some Ghanaian children not attending school? What policies has the GOG implemented in an attempt to address these issues? Where has the government clearly fallen short?

Yet in the post-Cold War era of globalization, characterized by deterritorialization and interconnection, social services cannot be regarded solely within a domestic lens (Scholte, 2005). Although it is still at the level of the nation-state that laws are developed and implemented, the influence of external actors has grown exponentially. The area of human rights illustrates this reality. As a signatory to the CRC, Ghana has indicated that its own national laws and policies will align with the dominant international system. CRC Article 28 (3) calls for an international effort for achieving the right to education. The very notion that education should be a basic human right is embedded within a global system of ethics that has transferred into the rights discourse. For Ghana, such international cooperation has come in the form of the Millennium Development Goals (MDG), the Education for All (EFA) initiative and, as noted previously, the GPRSP. While following these strategies helps Ghana maintain its international reputation and secure donor funding, it places the country within a general category of educational needs for the entirety of the developing world. Beginning with the 1987 decentralization strategy, Ghana has been adapting its education policies to match the objectives and policies of the international community. Unfortunately, these policies are not always adequately geared toward meeting the needs of Ghanaians.

Similar to many developing countries, Ghana's education system is heavily influenced by external actors, most notably the World Bank, UNICEF, and UNESCO. Ghana's education strategy lies within its Poverty Reduction Strategy Paper (PRSP). The paper not only indicates Ghana's place as part of the Highly-Indebted Poor Country initiative, but it also reflects the extent of influence of the major international financial institutions in the country. Although the World Bank has indicated its commitment to ensuring that PRSPs are country-driven and country-owned, certain criteria must still be met if governments are to remain a part of this program.

Since the introduction of the first Economic Recovery Plan in the 1980s, Ghana has maintained a reputation as a stable and peaceful country, one that has good relations with other institutions and governments. Ghana was lauded as the "prize pupil" during the era of structural adjustment, gaining a reputation as a country that would adequately adapt to meet the policies of its donors (Hutchful, 2002). This reputation has helped Ghana to be perceived a safe haven for foreign investment and, thus, a likely recipient for foreign aid and donor cooperation. This reputation has also meant that Ghana seems to always be swept up in whatever the popular "development initiative" or "poverty reduction strategy" exists at the time.

Over-emphasizing Primary Education

Despite FCUBE calling for the elimination of direct schooling costs, a predominant reason for parents opting to not send their children to school is the knowledge that they will not be able to afford higher years of learning, including secondary and tertiary education. Despite this, no Ghanaian education policy has addressed this concern. Instead, the focus of education remains at the primary level. Although the CRC itself makes note of all levels of education necessitating support, the GOG has emphasized primary education at the expense of these other levels.

Yet, while the GOG incorporates EFA policies into the GPRS in hopes of achieving the second MDG by 2015, any shortcomings of these internationally designed policies infiltrate into the Ghanaian educational system. Thus, while the EFA policy and MDGs have been criticized for focusing on Article 28 (1) at the expense of the other sections in the Article, this has translated into an increased focus on Ghana's primary education system at the expense of its secondary and tertiary levels. This is hindering the realization of Article 28 (2) and (3), which oblige the GOG to ensure that these two higher levels of education are accessible to all students based on merit. If the CRC defines a child as any person up to and including age 18, one must question the emphasis on schooling for those age 10 years and under.

The logic, according to UNESCO and UNICEF, is that building a solid primary basis of education first will provide secondary and tertiary levels with more prepared students, thereby improving Ghana's education system holistically. Yet insomuch as the dependency era of development initiatives observed that benefits trickling downward is not automatic, to presume that benefits will trickle upward is nearly impossible, both metaphorically and literally.

As Ghana's policies focus on the younger years of schooling, its limited number of universities and polytechnic institutions are scarcely funded, understaffed, and under-resourced. Ghana might be fulfilling its obligation of international cooperation and at least attempted free, compulsory primary education, but Article 28 is much broader than these policies suggest. Interestingly, the emphasis that current President Kufuor has placed on primary education enrollment is in contrast to the education system of Ghana's past. From the time of Ghana's independence in 1957 until former President Nkrumah's overthrow in 1966, education was free for primary, secondary, and tertiary levels of education. Following his time in office, primary and secondary school fees were introduced, while tertiary education remained free, reflecting policies that stressed the importance of higher levels of education. Thus, the FCUBE policy demonstrates for the first time since the Nkrumah era that primary education is of paramount value. This emphasis on primary education certainly reflects a desire on the part of the Ghanaian government to implement the suggestions of the international community to focus on primary education. That said, Ghana's deemphasis of the secondary and tertiary sectors could prove to be problematic in future years. While a basic level of education is critical for a child's initial development, secondary and tertiary education significantly adds to employment opportunities and life quality and choices (DFID, 2006). In fact, while the CRC stipulates that basic education be free and compulsory for all, it also urges states to "make high education accessible to all" and to "encourage the development of different forms of secondary education" [CRC Article 28 (1) (b) and (c)]. Undoubtedly, the CRC does not encourage emphasizing primary education at the expense of secondary and tertiary levels of learning.

By the end of the 1980s, Ghana's education sector had been weakened by the decline in social spending embedded within the Economic Reform Program. Similar to the majority of developing countries, nearing the end of the 1980s Ghana embarked on a decentralization program. This plan was intended to improve social service delivery by involving local governments, at both the district and regional levels, in the implementation and decision-making processes (Jeong, 2001). The GOG adopted a decentralized education policy in 1987. By the time the CRC was signed, major responsibility for education policy rested in the hands of the District Assemblies. The connection between a decentralized education system and the right to education was envisioned. The government argued that by increasing the influence held by local government, education would become more accessible. The local level is seen as being closer to community members and, thus, better able to understand the needs of local communities. Local communities would, thus, better understand reasons for inaccessibility of schools. The World Bank attributes decentralization policies as providing an "enabling environment." Much research has indicated, however, that decentralizing the education system has not achieved the desired results. Under resourced and incapacitated, the local government bodies are unable to provide the services intended. These weaknesses, inherent particularly within District Assemblies, have meant that they are unable to adequately provide for citizens.

The GPRSP has taken the majority of aid policies and service delivery and placed it in the overarching theme of "poverty reduction." For example, the 2003–2015 Education Strategic Plan was developed within the paper, outlining the strategy by which Ghana is to achieve UPE by 2015 (Adamu-Issah, Elden,

Forson, & Schrofer, 2007). Yet because poverty reduction is viewed as existing at the macroeconomic level, in turn, service delivery strategies have been moved to the macroeconomic level. The MOE is still responsible for education, but it has become part of a Core Team, primarily comprising the Ministry of Finance and the Ministry of Local Government, with the Central Bank also having a role. This arrangement has been criticized for focusing too heavily on economic gains rather than ensuring that schooling provides the ideal learning environment for children (Killick, 2001).

Child Labor and Accessing Education

While the legal working age in Ghana is fifteen years,[3] many children must begin work, especially in non-formal sectors, at a much earlier age. Many of these children must work to help provide for their families or to help pay for their school fees. The government should be more aggressive in its efforts to keep children out of the workplace. If primary education is really to be compulsory [CRC Article (1) (a)], it follows that child labor must be kept to a minimum. Kielland and Tovo argue that African governments do not adequately focus on the link between child labor and school absenteeism. This is certainly the case in Ghana (Kielland & Tovo, 2006).

Child labor is difficult to control, especially in agriculturally based communities where children must help with family farming duties. Moreover, until extreme poverty is overcome, child labor will persist. Most parents do not choose to send their child to work but have no other options (Kielland & Tovo, 2006). Rather than turning a blind eye to the existence of child labor, the GOG should develop strategies to both overcome the practice but to also aid those children who must work to attend school. To illustrate, school hours should be adjusted to meet the needs of the majority of children in the community. School hours at present still follow the traditional British school day, running from 9 a.m. to approximately 3 p.m. This practice began during colonization, reflecting a European timeframe (Dei, Asgharzadeh, Bahador, & Shahjahan, 2006). To better meet the needs of the child worker, a later morning start might be a more suitable alternative. Efforts to make changes to the school system have been apparent and need to continue. In 1989, the creation of the Non-formal Education Division under the MOE has helped encourage the learning of functional skills and literacy, even for children who are not able to enroll in the normal formal schooling program. A Literacy and Functional Skills Program, for example, rotates time throughout the ten regions, ensuring that more Ghanaians have an opportunity to learn in light of other responsibilities and challenges. Despite these efforts, the fact that many students are still unable to attend school signals a need for better policies that address problems of inaccessibility.

Moreover, homework should be kept to a minimum to ensure that children have ample time to both attend their classes and attend to their extra-curricular duties. While homework could provide extra aid to those students in need or with time, it should not be a necessary addition to attending class during the regular program. Students should be kept from falling behind as much as possible. The GOG could regulate both hours and amount of homework given. This could be a first step in not condoning child labor, but in recognizing that the present school hours and homework loads may be deterring some children from attending (Save the Children, 2008).

Quality vs. Quantity

The EFA initiative moves the discussion of the "right to education" beyond numbers. Instead, the EFA insists that the right to quality education and the right to respect within the learning environment are of value equal to the right of access to education. "Quality education is holistic and a prerequisite for education for sustainable development" (UNESCO, 2009). Although CRC Article 28 is taken as the dominant understanding of education as a human right, Article 29 is also relevant, especially when considering the quality versus quantity question. Weissbrodt & de la Vega argued that these articles must follow in sequence (Weissbrodt & de la Vega, 2007). It makes sense logically that education be accessed before discussing the content of education received. That said, the Convention makes no mention of a hierarchy of articles therein. The contents of Article 29, while qualitative in nature, must also be considered.

Ghana's National Plan of Action for Education is laid out in the Education Strategic Plan (ESP). Implementation of its second volume began in 2003 and will be carried out until 2015. The Ministry of Education, Youth and Sports is the major overseer of this strategy. The Plan sets out to ensure that the ten policy goals envisaged by the EFA are being realized in the Ghanaian context, including implementation. Careful analysis of the matrix, however, reveals much about Ghana's commitment to the CRC. First, while it is important that the ESP is identifying particular priorities, it is questionable why these were not prioritized previously. With the CRC having been signed eleven years prior to the ESP's inception, it calls to question why the GOG failed to implement many of these objectives until recently. What is more, the priorities, therefore, must be met with appropriate skepticism. For example, the document calls for "50 percent female share in primary enrollment rate by 2005," with this policy objective commencing in 2003. Yet the CRC's commitment to accessibility *for all* should have meant that this prioritization to gender equality began prior to 2003. And while 2005 was the year for achieving this objective, only 64 percent of primary school-aged girls were attending primary school that year. The number has merely risen to 71 percent to date. While the enrollment rate for boys is quite similar at 72 percent, the numbers remain dismal when placed into the holistic context of primary school enrollment (UNESCO, 2009).

Relying solely on quantitative indicators is also problematic in a country that has such low birth registration information. UNICEF advises that not only are such registrations "relatively low," but they are "still largely done by hand" (UNICEF, 2009). By not adequately registering births, the GOG is not fulfilling its obligations under CRC Article 7; as well, this is a major hindrance to documentation of enrollment rates as it skews the reality of enrollment. Tomasevski argued that this hinders local community members and governments from ensuring that best practices for improving accessibility can be endured (Tomasevski, 2003). Excluding children from birth registration is known to disadvantage them in terms of not providing access to social services, including education (UNICEF, 2005). In 2004, only 51 percent of Ghanaian childbirths were recorded, demonstrating a need to substantially improve this monitoring (United Nations, 2006:6).

Article 29 brings attention to the particular religious, language, and cultural requirements of children. A country with over fifty different ethnicities, at least seventy varying languages, and different religious practices (most notably Christianity, Islam, and different indigenous practices), curriculum should reflect this diversity (Dei, 2005). Insufficient teacher training, however, has limited the number of languages, religions, and ethnicities represented in the teaching profession.

Outbound mobility enrollment for primary and secondary school-aged Ghanaians is 8 percent. This has fluctuated somewhat over the past decade, with 12 percent outbound mobility enrollment in 2004 being the highest, and 7 percent in 2001 being the lowest. While some of this percentage can be accounted for by parental employment location changes, a portion of this percentage indicates that parents are sending their children to school elsewhere to gain a better quality of education. This reality becomes even more apparent when considering the enrollment percentage of children in private schools: 16 percent in primary school and 13 percent in secondary school, respectively (IMF, 2003).

The language of instruction has been a debated issue, particularly owing to the interconnection between language and culture (Owu-Ewie, 2006). By law, the first three years of primary school are in English. Since the 2001 reforms, incentives to encourage teachers to work in northern regions have been assessed. This has had modest results at best. First, although education is in English, it is not the mother tongue of the majority of students. Should confusion arise with a meaning or concept, the teacher and student are prevented from communicating in a language most comfortable to them, thus hindering the learning process. Second, while teachers are provided with incentives to work in the north, many do not realize the disadvantageous situation they are pursuing until their actual relocation. Placed in greatly under-resourced schools in remote locations, many of these teachers become frustrated with their situation and, consequently, stop coming to work, either because they have moved south once again, or because they are seeking another job. In either case, children must sit in a classroom with no teacher. Community members are reluctant to share this information with the District Education Office for fear of losing funding for a mismanaged school.

Parents, particularly in rural communities, are losing extra help and part of the family budget by putting a child through school. Thus, the relevance of the curriculum becomes very important to them. To make this trade off beneficial, they must render the long-term effects of their child's education worthwhile. For many in rural settings, practical skills given on the farm are of much greater benefit to the child than the abstract curriculum taught in the classroom. Parents argue that the Ghanaian school curriculum reflects a Western-biased curriculum best suited for employment opportunities in the south. The curriculum seems inapplicable for sustaining their rural lifestyle. Not only does this render school impractical, it heightens fears of continuing the southern migration already negatively impacting the rural north. While the northern curriculum does incorporate an agricultural component, it is often neglected and rarely reflects the many facets of farm life. Hashim notes that these are often viewed like apprenticeships, with women trained in such skills as sewing and cooking, rather than seen as necessitating literacy (Hashim, 2007).

If the GOG is to accurately follow its obligations to the CRC, it must demonstrate a heightened commitment to achieving quality education. Data collection for the Ghana Living Standards Survey (GLSS) should include statistics demonstrating teacher literacy, language of instruction, and student examination results and progress. There should be greater emphasis on the monitoring of the curriculum, perhaps by the Ghana Education Service. Heightened dialogue between parent teacher associations, local governments, and the ministries could better ensure that schooling is as quality-focused as possible.

Enrollment and Improved Data Collection

With an over-emphasis on enrollment numbers, the GOG has inadequately monitored dropout and absentee rates. Though the government suggests that parents enroll their children in school at the age of six, 60 percent of Ghanaian students begin school at a later age. Interestingly, it is within this demographic that the highest incidences of dropouts occur. If primary education is to be truly compulsory as called for in CRC Article (1) (a), the GOG should also make the age of enrollment compulsory. The government must do more to encourage earlier enrollment. Adopting better data collection processes is a first step to ensuring that the government can better address reasons for dropouts and absenteeism (Fentiman et al., 1999). Improved statistical data collection would not only reveal the age of enrollment, but would possibly bring to light other issues that have yet to be considered. Identifying the problem should be the first step in creating a solution.

Concluding Remarks

Twenty-eight percent of Ghanaian children are not receiving the right to education to which they are legally entitled. For a country that ratified the CRC eighteen years ago, this statistic is abysmal. Yet it is not enough to simply look at the statistic with pessimism. One must question the realities, obstacles, and challenges that are preventing the government from meeting its obligations. It is not that the government is not attempting policies to meet the commitments; rather, it is that these policies are inadequate in their efforts to overcome the obstacles that exist. While the policies might better address the challenges faced by a few, for the majority of the most vulnerable—girls, developmentally disabled, and the severely impoverished—these policies are a far cry from providing relevant solutions. It is apparent that more must be done if Ghana is to fulfill the education rights of its citizens as set out in CRC Article 28. While the government has demonstrated the will to implement effective policies to improve education, better resources and better understanding of policy measures are essential if the government is to effectively capture all that is mandated within Article 28.

UNESCO warns that an international education crisis is pending (UNESCO, 2009). With sub-Saharan Africa predicted to be among the worst hit in the long term by the global financial crisis, resources for social services are expected to decline. With remittances and foreign direct investment decreasing, external aid diminishing, and Ghana's export commodities devaluing on the world scale, Ghana's education sector could be in jeopardy (Naude, 2009). Of essence is a sound strategy to education that commits the government to achieving UPE despite predictable obstacles. It is imperative that the GOG work toward improving the sector immediately before the economic crisis worsens.

Article 28 (4) was not addressed throughout the text of this chapter, as it is better suited for its conclusion. The CRC obliges its signatories to track progress—enrollment rates, dropout rates, attendance rates—in order for the government to realize the effects of its policies. While Ghana may have instituted educational reforms in 1992 and again in 2001, actual monitoring of the progress, which would reveal the true outcomes of those reforms, is nonexistent. Ghana must institute a monitoring and evaluation mechanism to best ensure that its educational policies are reaping the benefits intended. Otherwise, the rhetoric of the "right to education" will remain as far from becoming a reality as it is now.

Notes

1. Age 15 is also the age for children's work indicated by the 1998 Children's Act. Section 90 of this same act permits light work at age 13.

2. Rural savannah in this case includes the Northern, Upper West, and Upper East regions. The Urban Coastal and Urban Forest are localities defined by the Ghana Statistical Service to site geographical incidence of poverty.

3. The legal working age is 15, according to section 89 of Act 560, the 1998 Children's Act. Section 90 of the same act permits light work at the age of thirteen.

References

Adamu-Issah, M., L. Elden, M. Forson, and T. Schrofer. (2007). Achieving universal primary education in Ghana by 2015: A reality or a dream? *UNICEF Division Policy and Planning Working Paper.* New York: UNICEF.

Agbenyega, J. (2003). The power of labeling discourse in the construction of disability in Ghana. *AARE Conference Papers.* P. L. Jeffery (ed.). Retrieved March 4, 2009, from http://www.aare.edu.au/03pap/abs03.htm.

Asiegbor, I., K. Fincham, M. Nanang, E. E. K. Gala, and A. O. Britwum. (2001). *Rights and equity in the classroom: A case study of classroom interactions in basic schools in Ghana.* Accra: UNICEF.

Bhasin, Vijay K., and C. K. Obeng. (2007). Disparities of education and poverty among households in Ghana. *Icfai University Journal of Applied Economics* 0 (6), 77–93.

Boafo-Arthur, K. (ed.). (2007). *Ghana: One Decade of the Liberal State.* Zed Books: London.

Casely-Hayford, L., and P. Lynch. (2003). *ICT based solutions for special education needs in Ghana.* UK Department for International Development. Retrieved on March 4, 2009, from http://www.dfid.gov.uk/pubs/files/imfundo/Educational-needs-Ghana.pdf.

Davis, M. (2006). *Planet of Slums.* New York: Verso Press.

Dei, G. J. S. (2005). The challenge of inclusive schooling in Africa: A Ghanaian case study. *Comparative Education* 41 (3), 267–289.

Dei, G. J. S., A. Asgharzadeh, S. E. Bahador, and R. A. Shahjahan. (2006). *Schooling and Difference in Africa: Democratic Challenges in a Contemporary Context.* Toronto: University of Toronto Press.

de Lange, A. (2007). Child labor migration and trafficking in rural Burkina Faso. *International Migration* 45 (2), 147–167.

Department for International Development, UK (DFID). (2006). *The importance of secondary, vocational and higher education to development.* Briefing paper. July 2006. Retrieved September 16, 2009, from http://webarchive.nationalarchives.gov.uk/+/http://www.dfid.gov.uk/pubs/files/postprimary.pdf.

Fentiman, A., A. Hall, and D. Bundy. (1999). School enrollment patterns in rural Ghana: A comparative study of the impact of location, gender, age and health on children's access to basic schooling. *Comparative Education* 35 (3), 331–349.

Ghana NGO Coalition on the Rights of the Child. (2005). *The Ghana NGO report to the UN Committee on the Rights of the Child on implementation of the Convention of the Rights of the Child by the Republic of Ghana.* UNICEF. Retrieved February 5, 2009, from www.crin.org/docs/Ghana_GNCRC_ngo_report.doc.

Government of Ghana (GOG). (2009). Ministry of Education, Science and Sports website. Retrieved September 22, 2009, from http://ghana.gov.gn/ministry_of_education_science_and_sports.

Hashim, I. M. (2007). *Exploring linkages between children's independent migration and education: Evidence from Ghana.* Development Research Centre on Migration, Globalization, and Poverty.

Hutchful, E. (2002). *Ghana's Adjustment Experience: The Paradox of Reform.* Oxford: James Curry.

International Monetary Fund (IMF). (2003). Ghana Poverty Reduction Strategy Paper. *IMF Country Report No. 03/56.* Washington: International Monetary Fund.

———. (2009). Ghana: Poverty Reduction Strategy Paper. *IMF Country Report No. 09/237.* Washington: International Monetary Fund.

Jeong, H. (2001). Ghana: Lurching toward economic rationality. *World Affairs* 159 (2), 64–71.

Kielland, A., and M. Tovo, (2006). *Children at Work: Child Labor Practices in Africa.* Boulder: Lynne Rienner Publishers.

Killick, T, (2001). Poverty-reducing institutional change and PRSP processes: The Ghana case. *Discussion Paper No. 2001/70,* United Nations University.

Kuyini, A. B., and I. Desai. (2009). Providing instruction to students with special needs in inclusive classrooms in Ghana: Issues and challenges. *International Journal of Whole Schooling* 4 (1), 1–39.

Ministry of Finance (2004, 2006). Ministry of Finance national budget statements. Retrieved September 20, 2009, from http://www.mofep.gov.gh/budget.cfm.

Naidoo, J. P. (2002). *Education decentralization in sub-Saharan Africa—Espoused theories and theories in use.* Paper presentation at CIES Annual Conference: 2002—The Social Construction of Marginality: Globalization's Impact on the Disenfranchised. March 6–9, University of Central Florida, Orlando.

Naude, W. (2009). The financial crisis of 2008 and the developing countries. *UNU-WIDER Discussion Paper No. 2009/01.* Helsinki: UNU-WIDER.

Owu-Ewie, C. (2006). The language policy of education in Ghana: A critical look at the English-only language policy of education. In J. Mugana et al. (eds.). *Selected Proceedings of the Thirty-fifth Annual Conference on African Linguistics.* Somerville, MA, 76–85.

Save the Children. (2008). *Making schools inclusive: How change can happen.* London: Save the Children Fund.

Scholte, J. A. (2005). *Globalization: A Critical Introduction.* New York: Palgrave-MacMillan.

Sussex, University of. (2004). Gender violence in schools: Ghana. *Gender in Schools* 3. Retrieved March 25, 2009, from http://www.sussex.ac.uk/education/documents/ghana_.pdf.

Tanye, M. (2008). Access and barriers to education for Ghanaian women and girls. *Interchange* 39 (2), 167–184.

Tomasevski, K. (2003). *Education Denied: Costs and Remedies.* London: Zed Books.

United Nations. (2006). *Committee on the Rights of the Child: Concluding observations Ghana.* CRC/C/GHA/CO/2, March 17. Retrieved September 16, 2009, from http://www.unhchr.ch/tbs/doc.nsf/0/ba9ccae3e901b5f4c125716200435cea/$FILE/G0640957.pdf.

United Nations Children's Fund (UNICEF). (2005). *The state of the world's children 2006: Excluded and invisible.* New York: UNICEF.

———. (2009). *Country at a glance: Ghana.* Retrieved March 5, 2009, from http://www.unicef.org/infobycountry/ghana.html.

United Nations Educational, Scientific, and Cultural Organization (UNESCO). (2009). Education for all by 2015. *EFA Homepage.* Retrieved September 24, 2009, from http://portal.unesco.org/education/en/ev.php.

———. (2009). Education for sustainable development. *UNESCO Decade Homepage.* Retrieved January 6, 2009, from http://portal.unesco.org/education/en/ev.php-URL_ID=27542&URL_DO=DO_TOPIC&URL_SECTION=201.html.

United Nations Educational, Scientific, and Cultural Organization (UNESCO) Institute for Statistics. (2008). Online statistical database. Retrieved January 15, 2009, from http://www.uis.unesco.org/ev.php?ID=2867_201&ID2=DO_TOPIC.

Weissbrodt, D., and C. de la Vega. (2007). *International Human Rights Law: An Introduction.* Philadelphia: University of Pennsylvania Press.

White, H. (2005). Using household survey data to measure educational performance: The case of Ghana. *Social Indicators Research* 74, 395–422.

Chapter 12
Conclusion: The Future of Children's Rights in Ghana

By Robert Kwame Ame, Nana Araba Apt, and DeBrenna LaFa Agbényiga

As noted in this book, Ghana ratified the 1989 United Nations (UN) Convention on the Rights of the Child (CRC) on Febuary 5, 1990, making it the first country to do so. One of the challenges faced after ratifying the CRC was to bring domestic law into line with the standards set in the Convention. This book discussed several laws, policies, and programs put into place since Ghana's ratification of the CRC, in addition to signing several UN human rights instruments, including the CRC Optional Protocols on Children in Armed Conflicts and the Trafficking of Women and Children for the Purpose of Prostitution and Sexual Trade. The enactment of the numerous legislative instruments, policies, and programs discussed in this book highlights Ghana's commitment under the CRC. Furthermore, these efforts represent significant progress of children's rights issues within the relatively short period of twenty years! These legal and policy actions constitute a sign of Ghana's commitment to the CRC and, by implication, to children's rights issues. This level of commitment can be described as an "expanding commitment" based on Brian Howe and Katherine Covell's (2007:1–2) classification model in the implementation of the CRC, whereby a country experiences increases in policies, programs, and institutions related to children's issues and, hence, the government's commitment to children's rights over time.[1]

But what do all these laws and policies mean in terms of creating opportunities for children and youth in Ghana? Do they translate into a brighter future for

Ghanaian children? Are their rights better protected than prior to the enactment of these laws?

The preceding chapters have shown a huge implementation gap to be filled, whether it is the implementation of most recently enacted laws or older laws seeking to protect the rights of children to their identity and their protection from exploitation and many of the dangerous circumstances that confront children in Ghana in both traditional and modern contexts. Common to all the laws, policies, and programs, as discussed in the previous chapters in this book, is an acute lack of resources from a human capital, material, or financial perspective. It appears that the human and budgetary infrastructures that necessarily accompany the enforcement of social policy instruments and programs are usually missing in the drawing board of policy planning in Ghana (Apt, 2007). These challenges imply a huge gap between rhetoric and reality.

Despite these challenges, it is not out of place to argue that the passage of these laws and the introduction of new policies and programs constitute a good first step toward children's rights in Ghana and providing a brighter future for their welfare. While laws per se cannot secure a better future for children anywhere in the world nor create all the opportunities for them to successfully thrive, law does provide legitimacy that strengthens the hands of child agencies and organizations, both governmental and non-governmental, to boldly carry out their missions of protecting the rights and interests of children. For example, although there is evidence that the Criminal Code Amendment Acts of 1994 and 1998, which criminalized female circumcision and female ritual servitude, respectively, have not been implemented effectively, the mere existence of these laws provides human rights advocates, NGOs, and child protection agencies with the ability to pursue violators of children's rights in these realms (Ameh, 1998, 2001, 2004). Without these laws, their work would lack legitimacy, and they could be accused of participating in illegal acts for trying to protect the rights of children. In chapter 8, it was shown how prior to the passage of the *trokosi* law (Act 554), the courts arrived at mixed decisions in cases involving customary practices, which are recognized by the 1992 Constitution and the 1960 Criminal Code. However, with the enactment of the *trokosi* law, the influence of NGOs such as International Needs Ghana was strengthened to continue with the work they began prior to the passage of the law. Furthermore, law has become an essential and effective tool by which governments express social policy. In fact, laws constitute an integral part of any policy in modern states (Ameh, 1993; Twumasi, 1985). Thus, these child-friendly laws introduced since Ghana's ratification of the CRC indicate the government's policy direction and intention to act in the matter of children's rights. For this, the government can be viewed in a positive light.

It is also important to note that the CRC itself (Article 4 of the CRC) acknowledges that its goals would not be attained in a day and definitely not in twenty years. Rather, it is reasonable to interpret the CRC from a "progressive achievement" of goals perspective. It is a gradual but progressive process that will take several years, if not decades, to attain (Tobin, 2009). Hence, the apparent delay in advancing children's rights in Ghana subsequent to the enormous challenges encountered in implementing the law and polices should not render children's rights in Ghana a hopeless case. We should, instead, perceive the enactment of these laws as one very important first step in the long and arduous process of tackling children's rights issues.

Concern has, however, been raised about the confusion related to the overlap of several of the child-friendly laws that have been enacted by Parliament.[2] For example, sections of the Children's Act, Juvenile Justice Act, Anti-Human Trafficking Act, and Domestic Violence Act each address similar issues. There should not be too many unmanageable problems caused by the overlap between these Acts. There is a Ghanaian saying that literally goes like this: "Plenty meat does not spoil soup." That is, if you use too much meat in preparing soup, it does not necessarily affect the quality of the soup adversely. This proverb alludes to the fact that too much of a good thing does not necessarily become something detrimental. In a similar vein, too many good laws that overlap should not necessarily become detrimental for advancing children's rights in Ghana. The overlap, in this instance, rather serves to reinforce the laws and buttress the point that the state is really concerned about children's issues. While potentially there could arise a problem of blame-shifting regarding what ministries, departments, and agencies (MDAs) are responsible for implementation and protection of specific aspects of children's rights, especially when things do not go well, the Ghanaian Parliament has been good at explicitly stating the responsibilities of specific MDAs and institutions in the implementation of each of the children's rights-related laws discussed in this book. What appears to be a problem is the obvious lack of coordination and integration among government agencies charged with the responsibility for the protection of children (Apt & Akuffo-Amoabeng, 2007).

Further, it is important to note that where these laws seem to overlap, they rather tend to emphasize different aspects of the same issue. For example, while the Children's Act addresses the problem of child labor and apprenticeship, it does not speak to the issue of trafficking, which is an equally exploitative act of child labor. Also, whereas the overarching aim of the Children's Act is child protection in general, the Domestic Violence Act focuses exclusively on the protection of children from violence perpetrated within the family/domestic context. Again, while there is an overlap between the Children's Act and the Juvenile Justice Act regarding alternative measures, the former defines the functions, composition, and methods of the Child Panels which administer alternative measures, while the latter speak to the overall purpose and minimum standards of diversion. Essentially then, there is hardly any conflict between these laws even if they sometimes seem to overlap. What should be of concern, rather, is the political will and ability of government to implement laws. Evidence shows that there is a tendency on the part of governments generally to relax and deem their work is completed once they manage to put laws in place (Ameh, 2001; Shaffer, 1999). Of importance also is the willingness of the various government child protection agencies to relate and consult with each other on the common task of child protection (Apt, 2007:93).

Hence, the next stage in the process of protecting children's rights as we see it is for stakeholders and development partners to start lobbying the Government of Ghana and challenging her to implement her own domestic laws, now that Parliament has passed all these laws. This stage, like others, has a role carved out for both indigenous and international stakeholders interested in enhancing children's rights in Ghana.

Role of the People of Ghana

The people of Ghana must take a proactive role in the process of moving forward in enhancing children's rights in the country. NGOs, civil society organizations, parents, and traditional councils should champion the cause of children's rights and challenge the government to live up to its responsibilities with regard to the children's laws, policies, and programs it has put into place over the last twenty years. NGOs such as International Needs Ghana, the Ark Foundation, Children's Rights Foundation, College for Ama Foundation, Catholic Action on Street Children, Street Girls Aid, and a host of others should be commended for the great work they are doing on behalf of children and women in Ghana and should be supported to continue with their good deeds. The problem of parental neglect and irresponsibility is real in Ghana (Apt 2006, 2007:70–72) and so are cruelties meted out to children as punishment by parents and school teachers as shown in chapter 5 on corporal punishment. Parents should take their parental responsibilities more seriously and take advantage of some of the new programs such as the Livelihood Empowerment Against Poverty (LEAP) of the National Social Protection Strategy. As discussed in the introductory chapter, LEAP and related programs provide cash grants to extremely poor individuals, households, and communities, including those who need special care but lack access to basic social services.

There is need for attitudinal change on the part of Ghanaians at all levels of the social strata. Ghanaians need to start seeing children as individuals in their own capacity who are entitled to being treated with dignity and respect while moving away from the perspective that they are property of their parents and family. Raising awareness within traditional councils regarding aspects of child rights can help them initiate policies that would effectively change the "image of childhood" (Veerman, 1992) held by traditional Ghanaian society as outlined in chapter 2 addressing the meaning and context of childhood.

Role of International Organizations and Funding Agencies

Due to acute resource problems as made manifest in this book, the people and the Government of Ghana cannot all by themselves transform Ghanaian society into a society in which children's rights flourish. International stakeholders, especially rich nations, and funding agencies should live up to their obligations under the CRC (e.g., Articles 4 and 45 of the CRC) and other international development responsibilities (Ensalaco, 2005) by providing necessary aid and assistance for the implementation of the laws and by so doing help to protect children's rights in the country. They could, for example, as some already do, provide budgetary support and resource assistance to the Government of Ghana in aid of specific child programs such as the current popular School Feeding Program and Capitation Grant that have led to increased school enrollment figures (Apt, 2007; Ghana's State Report to the CRC 2005; United Nations, 2006; and Leah McMillan's chapter in this book). Development partners could provide the necessary financial and material support that is needed by in-country partners to ensure that they are able to effectively carry out their activities.

Apart from financial and other material aid, acting alone and also in collaboration with its partner organizations in Ghana, international funding agencies could play a lead role in holding the Government of Ghana accountable in the implementation of its own Ghanaian child rights laws. Ghanaian governments of any ideological tradition are prone to act quickly when foreign governments, development partners, and other international institutions raise concerns about any issue than when Ghanaian organizations and citizens who vote them into power do. Ameh (1993) calls this the "Western approval" factor in Ghanaian politics. This should be fully exploited in advancing children's rights in Ghana whereby international development partners constantly are seen as advocates of children's rights in the country.

Future Prospects: Where Do We Go from Here?

Beyond lobbying the government to implement its own laws and asking Ghanaians and development partners to play their part, cutting-edge research is needed to assess the impact of the various laws and policies created in response to the CRC. Contributors to this volume have set the pace in offering an assessment of several of these laws, including the 1998 Children's Act (see, for example, Afua Twum-Danso's chapter in this volume). Other researchers should follow suit and offer their assessment of the same Act. Ten years is usually considered a reasonable period after which the impact of new laws should take effect. For example, the Juvenile Justice Act and the Child Rights Regulations will have been in operation for ten years in 2013; the Human Trafficking Act in 2015; the

National Disability Act in 2016; and the Domestic Violence Act in 2017. This offers child rights scholars a window of opportunity to embark on timely and important comprehensive evaluation research on the impact of these laws. Universities in Ghana and other child rights scholars can contribute to enhancing the protection of children's rights in Ghana by producing scientifically sound knowledge, which could be used by policymakers, state child protection agencies, NGOs, and development partners in enhancing the quality of life of Ghanaian children. Any takers?

Notes

1. R. Brian Howe & Katherine Covell (eds.). (2007). *A Question of Commitment: Children's Rights in Canada.* Waterloo, ON: Wilfrid Laurier University Press.

2. Amy Chow, personal e-mail to Robert Ame. February 3, 2010. Amy, a student of Northwestern Law School, is participating in a project on children's rights in Ghana involving Northwestern Law School and UNICEF.

References

Ameh, R. (1993). *Juvenile delinquency control policy in Ghana: An evaluation study.* MPhil thesis submitted to the Department of Sociology, University of Oslo, Norway.

———. (1998). *Trokosi* (child slavery) in Ghana: A policy approach. *Ghana Studies* 1, 35–62. (*Ghana Studies* is a refereed journal of the Ghana Study Group within the African Studies Association, US).

———. (2001). *Child bondage in Ghana: A contextual policy analysis of* trokosi. Doctoral dissertation submitted to the School of Criminology, Simon Fraser University, Burnaby, BC, Canada.

———. (2004). Reconciling human rights and traditional practices: The anti-*trokosi* campaign in Ghana. *Canadian Journal of Law and Society* 19 (2), 51–72.

Apt, N. A. (2006). *Child domestic work and fosterage in Northern and Upper East regions.* UNICEF, Accra.

———. (2007) *Learning How to Play to Win. What Has 50 Years of Independence Brought Ghana? A Personal View of a "Returnee."* London, UK: Mot Juste Ltd.

Apt, N. A., and B. Akufo-Amoabeng. (2007). Department of Social Welfare assessment report, Ministry of Manpower Youth and Employment, Accra.

Ensalaco, M. (2005). The right of the child to development. In M. Ensalaco and L. C. Majka (eds.). *Children's Human Rights: Progress and Challenges for Children Worldwide.* Lanham, MD: Rowman and Littlefield Publishers, Inc.

Ghana's Second State Report to the Committee on the Rights of the Child (2005). (CRC/C/65/Add.34, July 14, 2005). Retrieved April 17, 2010, from http://daccess-dds-ny.un.org/doc/UNDOC/GEN/G05/427/38/PDF/G0542738.pdf?OpenElement.

Howe, R. B., and K. Covell (eds.). (2007). *A Question of Commitment: Children's Rights in Canada.* Waterloo, ON: Wilfrid Laurier University Press.

Shaffer, M. (1999). Criminal responses to hate-motivated violence: Is bill C-41 tough enough? In N. Larsen and B. Burtch. *Law in Society: Canadian Readings.* Toronto: Harcourt Brace Canada, 302–332.

Twumasi, P. K. (1985). *Criminal Law in Ghana.* Tema-Accra: Ghana Publishing Corporation.

Tobin, J. (2009). The international obligation to abolish traditional practices harmful to children's health: What does it mean and require of states? *Human Rights Law Review* 9 (3), 373–396.

United Nations. (2006). *Committee on the Rights of the Child: Concluding observations: Ghana.* CRC/C/GHA/CO/2, March 17. Retrieved April 17, 2010, from http://www.unhchr.ch/tbs/doc.nsf/(Symbol)/CRC.C.GHA.CO.2.En?Opendocument.

Veerman, P. (1992). *The Rights of the Child and the Changing Image of Childhood.* Martinus Nijhoff Publishers.

Appendices

Appendix A
United Nations Convention on the Rights of the Child 1989

Adopted and opened for signature, ratification and accession by General Assembly resolution 44/25 of 20 November 1989
Entry into force 2 September 1990, in accordance with article 49

Preamble

The States Parties to the present Convention,

Considering that, in accordance with the principles proclaimed in the Charter of the United Nations, recognition of the inherent dignity and of the equal and inalienable rights of all members of the human family is the foundation of freedom, justice and peace in the world,

Bearing in mind that the peoples of the United Nations have, in the Charter, reaffirmed their faith in fundamental human rights and in the dignity and worth of the human person, and have determined to promote social progress and better standards of life in larger freedom,

Recognizing that the United Nations has, in the Universal Declaration of Human Rights and in the International Covenants on Human Rights, proclaimed and agreed that everyone is entitled to all the rights and freedoms set forth therein, without distinction of any kind, such as race, colour, sex, language, religion, political or other opinion, national or social origin, property, birth or other status,

Recalling that, in the Universal Declaration of Human Rights, the United Nations has proclaimed that childhood is entitled to special care and assistance,

Convinced that the family, as the fundamental group of society and the natural environment for the growth and well-being of all its members and particularly children, should be afforded the necessary protection and assistance so that it can fully assume its responsibilities within the community,

Recognizing that the child, for the full and harmonious development of his or her personality, should grow up in a family environment, in an atmosphere of happiness, love and understanding,

Considering that the child should be fully prepared to live an individual life in society, and brought up in the spirit of the ideals proclaimed in the Charter of the United Nations, and in particular in the spirit of peace, dignity, tolerance, freedom, equality and solidarity,

Bearing in mind that the need to extend particular care to the child has been stated in the Geneva Declaration of the Rights of the Child of 1924 and in the Declaration of the Rights of the Child adopted by the General Assembly on 20 November 1959 and recognized in the Universal Declaration of Human Rights, in the International Covenant on Civil and Political Rights (in particular in articles 23 and 24), in the International Covenant on Economic, Social and Cultural Rights (in particular in article 10) and in the statutes and relevant instruments of specialized agencies and international organizations concerned with the welfare of children,

Bearing in mind that, as indicated in the Declaration of the Rights of the Child, "the child, by reason of his physical and mental immaturity, needs special safeguards and care, including appropriate legal protection, before as well as after birth",

Recalling the provisions of the Declaration on Social and Legal Principles relating to the Protection and Welfare of Children, with Special Reference to Foster Placement and Adoption Nationally and Internationally; the United Nations Standard Minimum Rules for the Administration of Juvenile Justice (The Beijing Rules); and the Declaration on the Protection of Women and Children in Emergency and Armed Conflict, Recognizing that, in all countries in the world, there are children living in exceptionally difficult conditions, and that such children need special consideration,

Taking due account of the importance of the traditions and cultural values of each people for the protection and harmonious development of the child, Recognizing the importance of international co-operation for improving the living conditions of children in every country, in particular in the developing countries,

Have agreed as follows:

PART I

Article 1

For the purposes of the present Convention, a child means every human being below the age of eighteen years unless under the law applicable to the child, majority is attained earlier.

Article 2

1. States Parties shall respect and ensure the rights set forth in the present Convention to each child within their jurisdiction without discrimination of any kind, irrespective of the child's or his or her parent's or legal guardian's race, colour, sex, language, religion, political or other opinion, national, ethnic or social origin, property, disability, birth or other status.

2. States Parties shall take all appropriate measures to ensure that the child is protected against all forms of discrimination or punishment on the basis of the status, activities, expressed opinions, or beliefs of the child's parents, legal guardians, or family members.

Article 3

1. In all actions concerning children, whether undertaken by public or private social welfare institutions, courts of law, administrative authorities or legislative bodies, the best interests of the child shall be a primary consideration.

2. States Parties undertake to ensure the child such protection and care as is necessary for his or her well-being, taking into account the rights and duties of his or her parents, legal guardians, or other individuals legally responsible for him or her, and, to this end, shall take all appropriate legislative and administrative measures.

3. States Parties shall ensure that the institutions, services and facilities responsible for the care or protection of children shall conform with the standards established by competent authorities, particularly in the areas of safety, health, in the number and suitability of their staff, as well as competent supervision.

Article 4

States Parties shall undertake all appropriate legislative, administrative, and other measures for the implementation of the rights recognized in the present Convention. With regard to economic, social and cultural rights, States Parties shall undertake such measures to the maximum extent of their available resources and, where needed, within the framework of international co-operation.

Article 5

States Parties shall respect the responsibilities, rights and duties of parents or, where applicable, the members of the extended family or community as provided for by local custom, legal guardians or other persons legally responsible for the child, to provide, in a manner consistent with the evolving capacities of the child, appropriate direction and guidance in the exercise by the child of the rights recognized in the present Convention.

Article 6

1. States Parties recognize that every child has the inherent right to life.

2. States Parties shall ensure to the maximum extent possible the survival and development of the child.

Article 7

1. The child shall be registered immediately after birth and shall have the right from birth to a name, the right to acquire a nationality and, as far as possible, the right to know and be cared for by his or her parents.

2. States Parties shall ensure the implementation of these rights in accordance with their national law and their obligations under the relevant international instruments in this field, in particular where the child would otherwise be stateless.

Article 8

1. States Parties undertake to respect the right of the child to preserve his or her identity, including nationality, name and family relations as recognized by law without unlawful interference.

2. Where a child is illegally deprived of some or all of the elements of his or her identity, States Parties shall provide appropriate assistance and protection, with a view to re-establishing speedily his or her identity.

Article 9

1. States Parties shall ensure that a child shall not be separated from his or her parents against their will, except when competent authorities subject to judicial review determine, in accordance with applicable law and procedures, that such separation is necessary for the best interests of the child. Such determination may be necessary in a particular case such as one involving abuse or neglect of the child by the parents, or one where the parents are living separately and a decision must be made as to the child's place of residence.

2. In any proceedings pursuant to paragraph 1 of the present article, all interested parties shall be given an opportunity to participate in the proceedings and make their views known.

3. States Parties shall respect the right of the child who is separated from one or both parents to maintain personal relations and direct contact with both parents on a regular basis, except if it is contrary to the child's best interests.

4. Where such separation results from any action initiated by a State Party, such as the detention, imprisonment, exile, deportation or death (including death arising from any cause while the person is in the custody of the State) of one or both parents or of the child, that State Party shall, upon request, provide the parents, the child or, if appropriate, another member of the family with the essential information concerning the whereabouts of the absent member(s) of the family unless the provision of the information would be detrimental to the well-being of the child. States Parties shall further ensure that the submission of such a request shall of itself entail no adverse consequences for the person(s) concerned.

Article 10

1. In accordance with the obligation of States Parties under article 9, paragraph 1, applications by a child or his or her parents to enter or leave a State Party for the purpose of family reunification shall be dealt with by States Parties in a positive, humane and expeditious manner. States Parties shall further ensure that the submission of such a request shall entail no adverse consequences for the applicants and for the members of their family.

2. A child whose parents reside in different States shall have the right to maintain on a regular basis, save in exceptional circumstances personal relations and direct contacts with both parents. Towards that end and in accordance with the obligation of States Parties under article 9, paragraph 1, States Parties shall respect the right of the child and his or her parents to leave any country, including their own, and to enter their own country. The right to leave any country shall be subject only to such restrictions as are prescribed by law and which are necessary to protect the national security, public order (ordre public), public health or morals or the rights and freedoms of others and are consistent with the other rights recognized in the present Convention.

Article 11

1. States Parties shall take measures to combat the illicit transfer and non-return of children abroad.

2. To this end, States Parties shall promote the conclusion of bilateral or multilateral agreements or accession to existing agreements.

Article 12

1. States Parties shall assure to the child who is capable of forming his or her own views the right to express those views freely in all matters affecting the child, the views of the child being given due weight in accordance with the age and maturity of the child.

2. For this purpose, the child shall in particular be provided the opportunity to be heard in any judicial and administrative proceedings affecting the child, either directly, or through a representative or an appropriate body, in a manner consistent with the procedural rules of national law.

Article 13

1. The child shall have the right to freedom of expression; this right shall include freedom to seek, receive and impart information and ideas of all kinds, regardless of frontiers, either orally, in writing or in print, in the form of art, or through any other media of the child's choice.

2. The exercise of this right may be subject to certain restrictions, but these shall only be such as are provided by law and are necessary:

(a) For respect of the rights or reputations of others; or

(b) For the protection of national security or of public order (ordre public), or of public health or morals.

Article 14

1. States Parties shall respect the right of the child to freedom of thought, conscience and religion.

2. States Parties shall respect the rights and duties of the parents and, when applicable, legal guardians, to provide direction to the child in the exercise of his or her right in a manner consistent with the evolving capacities of the child.

3. Freedom to manifest one's religion or beliefs may be subject only to such limitations as are prescribed by law and are necessary to protect public safety, order, health or morals, or the fundamental rights and freedoms of others.

Article 15

1. States Parties recognize the rights of the child to freedom of association and to freedom of peaceful assembly.

2. No restrictions may be placed on the exercise of these rights other than those imposed in conformity with the law and which are necessary in a democratic society in the interests of national security or public safety, public order (ordre public), the protection of public health or morals or the protection of the rights and freedoms of others.

Article 16

1. No child shall be subjected to arbitrary or unlawful interference with his or her privacy, family, or correspondence, nor to unlawful attacks on his or her honour and reputation.

2. The child has the right to the protection of the law against such interference or attacks.

Article 17

States Parties recognize the important function performed by the mass media and shall ensure that the child has access to information and material from a diversity of national and international sources, especially those aimed at the promotion of his or her social, spiritual and moral well-being and physical and mental health.

To this end, States Parties shall:

(a) Encourage the mass media to disseminate information and material of social and cultural benefit to the child and in accordance with the spirit of article 29;

(b) Encourage international co-operation in the production, exchange and dissemination of such information and material from a diversity of cultural, national and international sources;

(c) Encourage the production and dissemination of children's books;

(d) Encourage the mass media to have particular regard to the linguistic needs of the child who belongs to a minority group or who is indigenous;

(e) Encourage the development of appropriate guidelines for the protection of the child from information and material injurious to his or her well-being, bearing in mind the provisions of articles 13 and 18.

Article 18

1. States Parties shall use their best efforts to ensure recognition of the principle that both parents have common responsibilities for the upbringing and development of the child. Parents or, as the case may be, legal guardians, have the primary responsibility for the upbringing and development of the child. The best interests of the child will be their basic concern.

2. For the purpose of guaranteeing and promoting the rights set forth in the present Convention, States Parties shall render appropriate assistance to parents and legal guardians in the performance of their child-rearing responsibilities and shall ensure the development of institutions, facilities and services for the care of children.

3. States Parties shall take all appropriate measures to ensure that children of working parents have the right to benefit from child-care services and facilities for which they are eligible.

Article 19

1. States Parties shall take all appropriate legislative, administrative, social and educational measures to protect the child from all forms of physical or mental violence, injury or abuse, neglect or negligent treatment, maltreatment or exploitation, including sexual abuse, while in the care of parent(s), legal guardian(s) or any other person who has the care of the child.

2. Such protective measures should, as appropriate, include effective procedures for the establishment of social programmes to provide necessary support for the child and for those who have the care of the child, as well as for other forms of prevention and for identification, reporting, referral, investigation, treatment and follow-up of instances of child maltreatment described heretofore, and, as appropriate, for judicial involvement.

Article 20

1. A child temporarily or permanently deprived of his or her family environment, or in whose own best interests cannot be allowed to remain in that environment, shall be entitled to special protection and assistance provided by the State.

2. States Parties shall in accordance with their national laws ensure alternative care for such a child.

3. Such care could include, inter alia, foster placement, kafalah of Islamic law, adoption or if necessary placement in suitable institutions for the care of children. When considering solutions, due regard shall be paid to the desirability of continuity in a child's upbringing and to the child's ethnic, religious, cultural and linguistic background.

Article 21

States Parties that recognize and/or permit the system of adoption shall ensure that the best interests of the child shall be the paramount consideration and they shall:

(a) Ensure that the adoption of a child is authorized only by competent authorities who determine, in accordance with applicable law and procedures and on the basis of all pertinent and reliable information, that the adoption is permissible in view of the child's status concerning parents, relatives and legal guardians and that, if required, the persons concerned have given their informed consent to the adoption on the basis of such counselling as may be necessary;

(b) Recognize that inter-country adoption may be considered as an alternative means of child's care, if the child cannot be placed in a foster or an adoptive family or cannot in any suitable manner be cared for in the child's country of origin;

(c) Ensure that the child concerned by inter-country adoption enjoys safeguards and standards equivalent to those existing in the case of national adoption;

(d) Take all appropriate measures to ensure that, in inter-country adoption, the placement does not result in improper financial gain for those involved in it;

(e) Promote, where appropriate, the objectives of the present article by concluding bilateral or multilateral arrangements or agreements, and endeavour, within this framework, to ensure that the placement of the child in another country is carried out by competent authorities or organs.

Article 22

1. States Parties shall take appropriate measures to ensure that a child who is seeking refugee status or who is considered a refugee in accordance with applicable international or domestic law and procedures shall, whether unaccompanied or accompanied by his or her parents or by any other person, receive appropriate protection and humanitarian assistance in the enjoyment of applicable rights set forth in the present Convention and in other international human rights or humanitarian instruments to which the said States are Parties.

2. For this purpose, States Parties shall provide, as they consider appropriate, co-operation in any efforts by the United Nations and other competent intergovernmental organizations or non-governmental organizations co-operating with the United Nations to

protect and assist such a child and to trace the parents or other members of the family of any refugee child in order to obtain information necessary for reunification with his or her family. In cases where no parents or other members of the family can be found, the child shall be accorded the same protection as any other child permanently or temporarily deprived of his or her family environment for any reason, as set forth in the present Convention.

Article 23

1. States Parties recognize that a mentally or physically disabled child should enjoy a full and decent life, in conditions which ensure dignity, promote self-reliance and facilitate the child's active participation in the community.

2. States Parties recognize the right of the disabled child to special care and shall encourage and ensure the extension, subject to available resources, to the eligible child and those responsible for his or her care, of assistance for which application is made and which is appropriate to the child's condition and to the circumstances of the parents or others caring for the child.

3. Recognizing the special needs of a disabled child, assistance extended in accordance with paragraph 2 of the present article shall be provided free of charge, whenever possible, taking into account the financial resources of the parents or others caring for the child, and shall be designed to ensure that the disabled child has effective access to and receives education, training, health care services, rehabilitation services, preparation for employment and recreation opportunities in a manner conducive to the child's achieving the fullest possible social integration and individual development, including his or her cultural and spiritual development

4. States Parties shall promote, in the spirit of international cooperation, the exchange of appropriate information in the field of preventive health care and of medical, psychological and functional treatment of disabled children, including dissemination of and access to information concerning methods of rehabilitation, education and vocational services, with the aim of enabling States Parties to improve their capabilities and skills and to widen their experience in these areas. In this regard, particular account shall be taken of the needs of developing countries.

Article 24

1. States Parties recognize the right of the child to the enjoyment of the highest attainable standard of health and to facilities for the treatment of illness and rehabilitation of health. States Parties shall strive to ensure that no child is deprived of his or her right of access to such health care services.

2. States Parties shall pursue full implementation of this right and, in particular, shall take appropriate measures:

(a) To diminish infant and child mortality;

(b) To ensure the provision of necessary medical assistance and health care to all children with emphasis on the development of primary health care;

(c) To combat disease and malnutrition, including within the framework of primary health care, through, inter alia, the application of readily available technology and through the provision of adequate nutritious foods and clean drinking-water, taking into consideration the dangers and risks of environmental pollution;

(d) To ensure appropriate pre-natal and post-natal health care for mothers;

(e) To ensure that all segments of society, in particular parents and children, are informed, have access to education and are supported in the use of basic knowledge of child health and nutrition, the advantages of breastfeeding, hygiene and environmental sanitation and the prevention of accidents;

(f) To develop preventive health care, guidance for parents and family planning education and services.

3. States Parties shall take all effective and appropriate measures with a view to abolishing traditional practices prejudicial to the health of children.

4. States Parties undertake to promote and encourage international co-operation with a view to achieving progressively the full realization of the right recognized in the present article. In this regard, particular account shall be taken of the needs of developing countries.

Article 25

States Parties recognize the right of a child who has been placed by the competent authorities for the purposes of care, protection or treatment of his or her physical or mental health, to a periodic review of the treatment provided to the child and all other circumstances relevant to his or her placement.

Article 26

1. States Parties shall recognize for every child the right to benefit from social security, including social insurance, and shall take the necessary measures to achieve the full realization of this right in accordance with their national law.

2. The benefits should, where appropriate, be granted, taking into account the resources and the circumstances of the child and persons having responsibility for the maintenance of the child, as well as any other consideration relevant to an application for benefits made by or on behalf of the child.

Article 27

1. States Parties recognize the right of every child to a standard of living adequate for the child's physical, mental, spiritual, moral and social development.

2. The parent(s) or others responsible for the child have the primary responsibility to secure, within their abilities and financial capacities, the conditions of living necessary for the child's development.

3. States Parties, in accordance with national conditions and within their means, shall take appropriate measures to assist parents and others responsible for the child to implement this right and shall in case of need provide material assistance and support programmes, particularly with regard to nutrition, clothing and housing.

4. States Parties shall take all appropriate measures to secure the recovery of maintenance for the child from the parents or other persons having financial responsibility for the child, both within the State Party and from abroad. In particular, where the person having financial responsibility for the child lives in a State different from that of the child, States Parties shall promote the accession to international agreements or the conclusion of such agreements, as well as the making of other appropriate arrangements.

Article 28

1. States Parties recognize the right of the child to education, and with a view to achieving this right progressively and on the basis of equal opportunity, they shall, in particular:

(a) Make primary education compulsory and available free to all;

(b) Encourage the development of different forms of secondary education, including general and vocational education, make them available and accessible to every child, and take appropriate measures such as the introduction of free education and offering financial assistance in case of need;

(c) Make higher education accessible to all on the basis of capacity by every appropriate means;

(d) Make educational and vocational information and guidance available and accessible to all children;

(e) Take measures to encourage regular attendance at schools and the reduction of drop-out rates.

2. States Parties shall take all appropriate measures to ensure that school discipline is administered in a manner consistent with the child's human dignity and in conformity with the present Convention.

3. States Parties shall promote and encourage international cooperation in matters relating to education, in particular with a view to contributing to the elimination of ignorance and illiteracy throughout the world and facilitating access to scientific and technical knowledge and modern teaching methods. In this regard, particular account shall be taken of the needs of developing countries.

Article 29

1. States Parties agree that the education of the child shall be directed to:

(a) The development of the child's personality, talents and mental and physical abilities to their fullest potential;

(b) The development of respect for human rights and fundamental freedoms, and for the principles enshrined in the Charter of the United Nations;

(c) The development of respect for the child's parents, his or her own cultural identity, language and values, for the national values of the country in which the child is living, the country from which he or she may originate, and for civilizations different from his or her own;

(d) The preparation of the child for responsible life in a free society, in the spirit of understanding, peace, tolerance, equality of sexes, and friendship among all peoples, ethnic, national and religious groups and persons of indigenous origin;

(e) The development of respect for the natural environment.

2. No part of the present article or article 28 shall be construed so as to interfere with the liberty of individuals and bodies to establish and direct educational institutions, subject always to the observance of the principle set forth in paragraph 1 of the present article and to the requirements that the education given in such institutions shall conform to such minimum standards as may be laid down by the State.

Article 30

In those States in which ethnic, religious or linguistic minorities or persons of indigenous origin exist, a child belonging to such a minority or who is indigenous shall not be denied the right, in community with other members of his or her group, to enjoy his or her own culture, to profess and practice his or her own religion, or to use his or her own language.

Article 31

1. States Parties recognize the right of the child to rest and leisure, to engage in play and recreational activities appropriate to the age of the child and to participate freely in cultural life and the arts.

2. States Parties shall respect and promote the right of the child to participate fully in cultural and artistic life and shall encourage the provision of appropriate and equal opportunities for cultural, artistic, recreational and leisure activity.

Article 32

1. States Parties recognize the right of the child to be protected from economic exploitation and from performing any work that is likely to be hazardous or to interfere with the child's education, or to be harmful to the child's health or physical, mental, spiritual, moral or social development.

2. States Parties shall take legislative, administrative, social and educational measures to ensure the implementation of the present article. To this end, and having regard to the relevant provisions of other international instruments, States Parties shall in particular:

(a) Provide for a minimum age or minimum ages for admission to employment;

(b) Provide for appropriate regulation of the hours and conditions of employment;

(c) Provide for appropriate penalties or other sanctions to ensure the effective enforcement of the present article.

Article 33

States Parties shall take all appropriate measures, including legislative, administrative, social and educational measures, to protect children from the illicit use of narcotic drugs and psychotropic substances as defined in the relevant international treaties, and to prevent the use of children in the illicit production and trafficking of such substances.

Article 34

States Parties undertake to protect the child from all forms of sexual exploitation and sexual abuse. For these purposes, States Parties shall in particular take all appropriate national, bilateral and multilateral measures to prevent:

(a) The inducement or coercion of a child to engage in any unlawful sexual activity;

(b) The exploitative use of children in prostitution or other unlawful sexual practices;

(c) The exploitative use of children in pornographic performances and materials.

Article 35

States Parties shall take all appropriate national, bilateral and multilateral measures to prevent the abduction of, the sale of or traffic in children for any purpose or in any form.

Article 36

States Parties shall protect the child against all other forms of exploitation prejudicial to any aspects of the child's welfare.

Article 37

States Parties shall ensure that:

(a) No child shall be subjected to torture or other cruel, inhuman or degrading treatment or punishment. Neither capital punishment nor life imprisonment without possibility of release shall be imposed for offences committed by persons below eighteen years of age;

(b) No child shall be deprived of his or her liberty unlawfully or arbitrarily. The arrest, detention or imprisonment of a child shall be in conformity with the law and shall be used only as a measure of last resort and for the shortest appropriate period of time;

(c) Every child deprived of liberty shall be treated with humanity and respect for the inherent dignity of the human person, and in a manner which takes into account the needs of persons of his or her age. In particular, every child deprived of liberty shall be separated from adults unless it is considered in the child's best interest not to do so and shall have the right to maintain contact with his or her family through correspondence and visits, save in exceptional circumstances;

(d) Every child deprived of his or her liberty shall have the right to prompt access to legal and other appropriate assistance, as well as the right to challenge the legality of the deprivation of his or her liberty before a court or other competent, independent and impartial authority, and to a prompt decision on any such action.

Article 38

1. States Parties undertake to respect and to ensure respect for rules of international humanitarian law applicable to them in armed conflicts which are relevant to the child.

2. States Parties shall take all feasible measures to ensure that persons who have not attained the age of fifteen years do not take a direct part in hostilities.

3. States Parties shall refrain from recruiting any person who has not attained the age of fifteen years into their armed forces. In recruiting among those persons who have attained the age of fifteen years but who have not attained the age of eighteen years, States Parties shall endeavour to give priority to those who are oldest.

4. In accordance with their obligations under international humanitarian law to protect the civilian population in armed conflicts, States Parties shall take all feasible measures to ensure protection and care of children who are affected by an armed conflict.

Article 39

States Parties shall take all appropriate measures to promote physical and psychological recovery and social reintegration of a child victim of: any form of neglect, exploitation, or abuse; torture or any other form of cruel, inhuman or degrading treatment or punishment; or armed conflicts. Such recovery and reintegration shall take place in an environment which fosters the health, self-respect and dignity of the child.

Article 40

1. States Parties recognize the right of every child alleged as, accused of, or recognized as having infringed the penal law to be treated in a manner consistent with the promotion of the child's sense of dignity and worth, which reinforces the child's respect for the human rights and fundamental freedoms of others and which takes into account the child's age and the desirability of promoting the child's reintegration and the child's assuming a constructive role in society.

2. To this end, and having regard to the relevant provisions of international instruments, States Parties shall, in particular, ensure that:

(a) No child shall be alleged as, be accused of, or recognized as having infringed the penal law by reason of acts or omissions that were not prohibited by national or international law at the time they were committed;

(b) Every child alleged as or accused of having infringed the penal law has at least the following guarantees:

(i) To be presumed innocent until proven guilty according to law;

(ii) To be informed promptly and directly of the charges against him or her, and, if appropriate, through his or her parents or legal guardians, and to have legal or other appropriate assistance in the preparation and presentation of his or her defence;

(iii) To have the matter determined without delay by a competent, independent and impartial authority or judicial body in a fair hearing according to law, in the presence of legal or other appropriate assistance and, unless it is considered not to be in the best interest of the child, in particular, taking into account his or her age or situation, his or her parents or legal guardians;

(iv) Not to be compelled to give testimony or to confess guilt; to examine or have examined adverse witnesses and to obtain the participation and examination of witnesses on his or her behalf under conditions of equality;

(v) If considered to have infringed the penal law, to have this decision and any measures imposed in consequence thereof reviewed by a higher competent, independent and impartial authority or judicial body according to law;

(vi) To have the free assistance of an interpreter if the child cannot understand or speak the language used;

(vii) To have his or her privacy fully respected at all stages of the proceedings.

3. States Parties shall seek to promote the establishment of laws, procedures, authorities and institutions specifically applicable to children alleged as, accused of, or recognized as having infringed the penal law, and, in particular:

(a) The establishment of a minimum age below which children shall be presumed not to have the capacity to infringe the penal law;

(b) Whenever appropriate and desirable, measures for dealing with such children without resorting to judicial proceedings, providing that human rights and legal safeguards are fully respected. 4. A variety of dispositions, such as care, guidance and supervision orders; counselling; probation; foster care; education and vocational training programmes and other alternatives to institutional care shall be available to ensure that children are dealt with in a manner appropriate to their well-being and proportionate both to their circumstances and the offence.

Article 41

Nothing in the present Convention shall affect any provisions which are more conducive to the realization of the rights of the child and which may be contained in:

(a) The law of a State Party; or

(b) International law in force for that State.

PART II

Article 42

States Parties undertake to make the principles and provisions of the Convention widely known, by appropriate and active means, to adults and children alike.

Article 43

1. For the purpose of examining the progress made by States Parties in achieving the realization of the obligations undertaken in the present Convention, there shall be established a Committee on the Rights of the Child, which shall carry out the functions hereinafter provided.

2. The Committee shall consist of eighteen experts of high moral standing and recognized competence in the field covered by this Convention.[1] The members of the Committee shall be elected by States Parties from among their nationals and shall serve in their personal capacity, consideration being given to equitable geographical distribution, as well as to the principal legal systems.

3. The members of the Committee shall be elected by secret ballot from a list of persons nominated by States Parties. Each State Party may nominate one person from among its own nationals.

4. The initial election to the Committee shall be held no later than six months after the date of the entry into force of the present Convention and thereafter every second year. At least four months before the date of each election, the Secretary-General of the United Nations shall address a letter to States Parties inviting them to submit their nominations

within two months. The Secretary-General shall subsequently prepare a list in alphabetical order of all persons thus nominated, indicating States Parties which have nominated them, and shall submit it to the States Parties to the present Convention.

5. The elections shall be held at meetings of States Parties convened by the Secretary-General at United Nations Headquarters. At those meetings, for which two thirds of States Parties shall constitute a quorum, the persons elected to the Committee shall be those who obtain the largest number of votes and an absolute majority of the votes of the representatives of States Parties present and voting.

6. The members of the Committee shall be elected for a term of four years. They shall be eligible for re-election if re-nominated. The term of five of the members elected at the first election shall expire at the end of two years; immediately after the first election, the names of these five members shall be chosen by lot by the Chairman of the meeting.

7. If a member of the Committee dies or resigns or declares that for any other cause he or she can no longer perform the duties of the Committee, the State Party which nominated the member shall appoint another expert from among its nationals to serve for the remainder of the term, subject to the approval of the Committee.

8. The Committee shall establish its own rules of procedure.

9. The Committee shall elect its officers for a period of two years.

10. The meetings of the Committee shall normally be held at United Nations Headquarters or at any other convenient place as determined by the Committee. The Committee shall normally meet annually. The duration of the meetings of the Committee shall be determined, and reviewed, if necessary, by a meeting of the States Parties to the present Convention, subject to the approval of the General Assembly.

11. The Secretary-General of the United Nations shall provide the necessary staff and facilities for the effective performance of the functions of the Committee under the present Convention.

12. With the approval of the General Assembly, the members of the Committee established under the present Convention shall receive emoluments from United Nations resources on such terms and conditions as the Assembly may decide.

Article 44

1. States Parties undertake to submit to the Committee, through the Secretary-General of the United Nations, reports on the measures they have adopted which give effect to the rights recognized herein and on the progress made on the enjoyment of those rights

(a) Within two years of the entry into force of the Convention for the State Party concerned;

(b) Thereafter every five years.

2. Reports made under the present article shall indicate factors and difficulties, if any, affecting the degree of fulfilment of the obligations under the present Convention. Reports shall also contain sufficient information to provide the Committee with a comprehensive understanding of the implementation of the Convention in the country concerned.

3. A State Party which has submitted a comprehensive initial report to the Committee need not, in its subsequent reports submitted in accordance with paragraph 1 (b) of the present article, repeat basic information previously provided.

4. The Committee may request from States Parties further information relevant to the implementation of the Convention.

5. The Committee shall submit to the General Assembly, through the Economic and Social Council, every two years, reports on its activities.

6. States Parties shall make their reports widely available to the public in their own countries.

Article 45

In order to foster the effective implementation of the Convention and to encourage international co-operation in the field covered by the Convention:

(a) The specialized agencies, the United Nations Children's Fund, and other United Nations organs shall be entitled to be represented at the consideration of the implementation of such provisions of the present Convention as fall within the scope of their mandate. The Committee may invite the specialized agencies, the United Nations Children's Fund and other competent bodies as it may consider appropriate to provide expert advice on the implementation of the Convention in areas falling within the scope of their respective mandates. The Committee may invite the specialized agencies, the United Nations Children's Fund, and other United Nations organs to submit reports on the implementation of the Convention in areas falling within the scope of their activities;

(b) The Committee shall transmit, as it may consider appropriate, to the specialized agencies, the United Nations Children's Fund and other competent bodies, any reports from States Parties that contain a request, or indicate a need, for technical advice or assistance, along with the Committee's observations and suggestions, if any, on these requests or indications;

(c) The Committee may recommend to the General Assembly to request the Secretary-General to undertake on its behalf studies on specific issues relating to the rights of the child;

(d) The Committee may make suggestions and general recommendations based on information received pursuant to articles 44 and 45 of the present Convention. Such suggestions and general recommendations shall be transmitted to any State Party concerned and reported to the General Assembly, together with comments, if any, from States Parties.

PART III

Article 46

The present Convention shall be open for signature by all States.

Article 47

The present Convention is subject to ratification. Instruments of ratification shall be deposited with the Secretary-General of the United Nations.

Article 48

The present Convention shall remain open for accession by any State. The instruments of accession shall be deposited with the Secretary-General of the United Nations.

Article 49

1. The present Convention shall enter into force on the thirtieth day following the date of deposit with the Secretary-General of the United Nations of the twentieth instrument of ratification or accession.

2. For each State ratifying or acceding to the Convention after the deposit of the twentieth instrument of ratification or accession, the Convention shall enter into force on the thirtieth day after the deposit by such State of its instrument of ratification or accession.

Article 50

1. Any State Party may propose an amendment and file it with the Secretary-General of the United Nations. The Secretary-General shall thereupon communicate the proposed amendment to States Parties, with a request that they indicate whether they favour a conference of States Parties for the purpose of considering and voting upon the proposals. In the event that, within four months from the date of such communication, at least one third of the States Parties favour such a conference, the Secretary-General shall convene the conference under the auspices of the United Nations. Any amendment adopted by a majority of States Parties present and voting at the conference shall be submitted to the General Assembly for approval.

2. An amendment adopted in accordance with paragraph 1 of the present article shall enter into force when it has been approved by the General Assembly of the United Nations and accepted by a two-thirds majority of States Parties.

3. When an amendment enters into force, it shall be binding on those States Parties which have accepted it, other States Parties still being bound by the provisions of the present Convention and any earlier amendments which they have accepted.

Article 51

1. The Secretary-General of the United Nations shall receive and circulate to all States the text of reservations made by States at the time of ratification or accession.

2. A reservation incompatible with the object and purpose of the present Convention shall not be permitted.

3. Reservations may be withdrawn at any time by notification to that effect addressed to the Secretary-General of the United Nations, who shall then inform all States. Such notification shall take effect on the date on which it is received by the Secretary-General.

Article 52

A State Party may denounce the present Convention by written notification to the Secretary-General of the United Nations. Denunciation becomes effective one year after the date of receipt of the notification by the Secretary-General.

Article 53

The Secretary-General of the United Nations is designated as the depositary of the present Convention.

Article 54

The original of the present Convention, of which the Arabic, Chinese, English, French, Russian and Spanish texts are equally authentic, shall be deposited with the Secretary-General of the United Nations. In witness thereof the undersigned plenipotentiaries, being duly authorized thereto by their respective Governments, have signed the present Convention.

---

[1] The General Assembly, in its resolution 50/155 of 21 December 1995, approved the amendment to article 43, paragraph 2, of the Convention on the Rights of the Child, replacing the word "ten" with the word "eighteen." The amendment entered into force on 18 November 2002 when it had been accepted by a two-thirds majority of the States parties (128 out of 191).

Appendix B
The Children's Act, 1998 (Act 560)

ARRANGEMENT OF SECTIONS

Section

PART 1 – THE RIGHTS OF THE CHILD

Sub-Part 1 – Rights of the child and parental duty

1. Definition of child
2. Welfare principle
3. Non-discrimination
4. Right to name and nationality
5. Right to grow up with parents
6. Parental duty and responsibility
7. Right to parental property
8. Right to education and well-being
9. Right to social activity
10. Treatment of the disabled child
11. Right of opinion
12. Protection from exploitative labour
13. Protection from torture and degrading treatment
14. Right to refuse betrothal and marriage
15. Penalty for contravention

Sub-Part II – Care and protection

16. District Assembly to protect children
17. Persons to report child abuse and protection cases
18. Meaning of care and protection
19. Investigation by Department
20. Care order of Family Tribunal
21. Supervision order of Family Tribunal

22. Duties of probation officer and social worker
23. Home visits
24. General provisions on orders
25. Discharge of orders
26. Care order and adoption

PART II – QUASI-JUDICIAL AND JUDICIAL CHILD ADJUDICATION

Sub-Part I – Child Panels

27. Establishment of Child Panels
28. Functions of Child Panels
29. Composition of Child Panel
30. Meetings of Child Panel
31. Child Panel in civil matters
32. Child Panel in criminal matters

Sub-Part II – Family Tribunals

33. Family Tribunals
34. Composition of Family Tribunal
35. Jurisdiction of Family Tribunal
36. Family Tribunal sittings
37. Procedure at Family Tribunal
38. Rights of the child at Family Tribunal
39. No publication of information on child

PART III – PARENTAGE, CUSTODY, ACCESS AND MAINTENANCE

Sub-Part 1 – Parentage

40. Application for Parentage
41. Evidence of Parentage
42. Medical test

Sub-Part II – Custody and Access

43. Custody
44. Access
45. Consideration for custody or access
46. Unlawful child removal

Sub-Part III – Maintenance

47. Duty to maintain a child
48. Application for maintenance order
49. Consideration for maintenance orders
50. Request for social enquiry report
51. Form of maintenance order
52. Persons entitled to maintenance order
53. Duration of order
54. Continuation of maintenance orders in certain cases
55. Variation of discharge of orders
56. Enforcement of order
57. Non-custodial parent to have access to the child

58. Duplicity of maintenance applications
59. Offences under this part
60. Procedure for application
61. Waiver of fees

PART IV – FOSTERAGE AND ADOPTION

Sub-Part I – Fosterage

62. Person who can foster
63. Definition of foster-parent
64. Foster-care placement

Sub-Part II – Adoption application

65. Jurisdiction and procedure for adoption
66. Application for adoption
67. Restrictions on making adoptions orders
68. Consent of parents and guardians
69. Other consent
70. Conditions for adoption order
71. Interim order
72. Knowledge of adoption by child
73. Application by non-citizen
74. Children previously adopted
75. Effect of adoption on parental rights

Sub-Part III – Devolution of property on adoption

76. Devolution of property on intestacy
77. Testamentary disposition
78. Supplementary provisions on intestacy and testamentary disposition

Sub-Part IV – Miscellaneous adoption provisions

79. Adoption order and customary law
80. Adoption order and citizenship
81. Effect of adoption order on fit person order
82. Adopted children register
83. Offences related to adoption
84. Notice to be given to send child abroad
85. Inter-country adoption
86. Procedure rules for adoption

PART V – EMPLOYMENT OF CHILDREN

Sub-Part I – Child Labour

87. Prohibition of exploitative child labour
88. Prohibition of child labour at night
89. Minimum age for child labour
90. Minimum age for light work
91. Minimum age for hazardous employment
92. Application

93. Registration of children and young persons in industrial undertakings
94. Offences under this sub-part
95. Enforcement in formal sector
96. Enforcement in informal sector

Sub-Part II – Apprenticeship

97. Act to apply to apprenticeship in formal sector
98. Minimum age for apprentices
99. Responsibilities of craftsman
100. Apprenticeship agreement
101. Duties of apprentice
102. Release of apprentice
103. Resolution of disputes
104. Application of Sub-Part I of this Part

PART VI – INSTITUTIONALISED CARE AND MISCELLANEOUS MATTERS

Sub-Part I – Approved residential homes

105. Approval of residential homes
106. Department to monitor homes
107. Power of Minister to give directives to homes
108. Inspection
109. Admission of children to homes
110. Parental responsibility of staff of approved homes
111. Power of Family Tribunal to order contribution
112. Approved home and adoption
113. Regulations and homes
114. Offences under this Sub-part

Sub-Part II – Day Care Centres

115. Application to operate day care centres
116. Inspection
117. Bye-laws and guidelines
118. Policy directives
119. Existing operators
120. Offences under this Sub-part

Sub-Part III – Miscellaneous Provisions

121. Registration of births
122. Determination of age of a child
123. Regulations
124. Interpretation
125. Amendment and repeals
126. Savings

SCHEDULE

THE FIVE HUNDRED AND SIXTIETH
ACT
OF THE PARLIAMENT OF THE REPUBLIC OF GHANA ENTITLED
THE CHILDREN'S ACT, 1998

AN ACT to reform and consolidate the law relating to children, to provide for the rights of the child, maintenance and adoption, regulate child labour and apprenticeship, for ancillary matters concerning children generally and to provide for related matters.

DATE OF ASSENT: 30th December, 1998.

BE IT ENACTED by Parliament as follows –

PART I – THE RIGHTS OF THE CHILD

Sub-Part I – Rights of the child and parental duty

Definition of child
1. For purposes of this Act, a child is a person below the age of eighteen years.

Welfare principle
2. (1) The best interest of the child shall be paramount in any matter concerning a child.

(2) The best interest of the child shall be the primary consideration by any court, person, institution or other body in any matter concerned with a child

Non-discrimination
3. No person shall discriminate against a child on the grounds of gender, race, age, religion, disability, health status, custom, ethnic origin, rural or urban background, birth or other status, socio–economic status or because the child is a refugee.

Right to name and nationality
4. No person shall deprive a child of the right from birth to a name, the right to acquire a nationality or the right as far as possible to know his natural parents and extended family subject to the provisions of Part IV, Sub-Part II of this Act.

Right to grow up with parents
5. No person shall deny a child the right to live with his parents and family and grow up in a caring and peaceful environment unless it is proved in court that living with his parents would –

(a) lead to significant harm to the child; or
(b) subject the child to serious abuse; or
(c) not be in the best interest of the child.

Parental duty and responsibility
6. (1) No parent shall deprive a child his welfare whether – a) The parents of the child are married or not at the time of the child's birth; or b) The parents of the child continue to live together or not.

(2) Every child has the right to life, dignity, respect, leisure, liberty, health, education and shelter from his parents.

(3) Every parent has rights and responsibilities whether imposed by law or otherwise towards his child which include the duty to –

(a) protect the child from neglect, discrimination, violence, abuse, exposure to physical and moral hazards and oppression;

(b) provide good guidance, care, assistance and maintenance for the child and assurance of the child's survival and development;

(c) ensure that in the temporary absence of a parent, the child shall be cared for by a competent person and that a child under eighteen months of age shall only be cared for by a person of fifteen years and above except where the parent has surrendered his rights and responsibilities in accordance with law.

(4) Each parent shall be responsible for the registration of the birth of their child and the names of both parents shall appear on the birth certificate except if the father of the child is unknown to the mother.

Right to parental property

7. No person shall deprive a child of reasonable provision out of the estate of a parent whether or not born in wedlock.

Right to education and well-being

8. (1) No person shall deprive a child access to education, immunisation, adequate diet, clothing, shelter, medical attention or any other thing required for his development.

(2) No person shall deny a child medical treatment by reason of religious or other beliefs.

Right to social activity

9. No person shall deprive a child the right to participate in sports, or in positive cultural and artistic activities or other leisure activities.

Treatment of the disabled child

10. (1) No person shall treat a disabled child in an undignified manner.

(2) A disabled child has a right to special care, education and training wherever possible to develop his maximum potential and be self-reliant.

Right of opinion

11. No person shall deprive a child capable of forming views the right to express an opinion, to be listened to and to participate in decisions which affect his well-being, the opinion of the child being given due weight in accordance with the age and maturity of the child.

Protection from exploitative labour

12. No person shall subject a child to exploitative labour as provided under section 87 of this Act.

Protection from torture and degrading treatment

13. (1) No person shall subject a child to torture or other cruel, inhuman or degrading treatment or punishment including any cultural practice which dehumanises or is injurious to the physical and mental well-being of a child.

(2) No correction of a child is justifiable which is unreasonable in kind or in degree according to the age, physical and mental condition of the child and no correction is justi-

fiable if the child by reason of tender age or otherwise is incapable of understanding the purpose of the correction.

Right to refuse betrothal and marriage
14. (1) No person shall force a child –
(a) to be betrothed;
(b) to be the subject of a dowry transaction; or
(c) to be married.
(2) The minimum age of marriage of whatever kind shall be eighteen years.

Penalty for contravention
15. Any person who contravenes a provision of this Sub-Part commits an offence and is liable on summary conviction to a fine not exceeding ¢5 million or to a term of imprisonment not exceeding one year or to both.

Sub-Part II – Care and protection

District Assembly to protect children
16. (1) A District Assembly shall protect the welfare and promote the rights of children within its area of authority and shall ensure that within the district, governmental agencies liaise with each other in matters concerning children.

(2) The Social Welfare and Community Development Department of a District Assembly referred to in this Act as "the Department" shall investigate cases of contravention of childrens rights.

Persons to report child abuse and protection cases
17. Any person with information on –
(a) child abuse; or
(b) a child in need of care and protection shall report the matter to the Department.

Meaning of care and protection
18. (1) For purposes of this Act, a child is in need of care and protection if the child –
(a) is an orphan or is deserted by his relatives;
(b) has been neglected or ill-treated by the person who has the care and custody of the child;
(c) has a parent or guardian who does not exercise proper guardianship;
(d) is destitute;
(e) is under the care of a parent or guardian who, by reason of criminal or drunken habits, is unfit to have the care of the child;
(f) is wandering and has no home or settled place of abode or visible means of subsistence;
(g) is begging or receiving alms, whether or not there is any pretence of singing, playing, performing, offering anything for sale or otherwise, or is found in any street, premises or place for the purpose of begging or receiving alms;
(h) accompanies any person when that person is begging or receiving alms, whether or not there is any pretence of singing, playing, performing, offering anything for sale or otherwise:
(i) frequents the company of any reputed thief or reputed prostitute;

(j) is residing in a house or the part of a house used by any prostitute for the purpose of prostitution, or is otherwise living in circumstances calculated to cause, encourage or favour the seduction or prostitution of or affect the morality of the child;

(k) is a person in relation to whom an offence has been committed or attempted under section 314 of the Criminal Code, 1960 (Act 29) on slave dealing;

(l) is found acting in a manner from which it is reasonable to suspect that he is, or has been, soliciting or importuning for immoral purposes;

(m) is below the age of criminal responsibility under the Criminal Code, 1960 (Act 29) and is involved in an offence other than a minor criminal matter, or

(n) is otherwise exposed to moral or physical danger.

(2) A child shall not be considered to come within the scope of paragraphs (i) and (j) of subsection (1) if the only reputed prostitute that the child associates with is his mother and if it is proved that she exercises proper guardianship and care to protect the child from corrupt influences.

Investigation by Department

19. (1) If the Department has reasonable grounds to suspect child abuse or a need for care and protection, it shall direct a probation officer or social welfare officer accompanied by the police to enter and search the premises where the child is kept to investigate.

(2) The Department shall direct the probation officer or the social welfare officer to refer the matter to a Child Panel established under section 27 of this Act if the child is not in immediate need of care and protection.

(3) If after investigation it is determined that the child has been abused or is in need of immediate care and protection the Department shall direct a probation officer or social welfare officer accompanied by the police to remove the child to a place of safety for a period of not more than seven days.

(4) The child shall be brought before a Family Tribunal by the probation officer or social welfare officer before the expiry of the seven day period for an order to be made.

(5) Until the Family Tribunal determines the order, the Family Tribunal may commit the child to an approved residential home or to the care of a probation officer, social welfare officer or other suitable person.

Care order of Family Tribunal

20. (1) A Family Tribunal may issue order to the Department on an application by a probation officer or social welfare officer under section 19(4).

(2) The care order shall remove the child from a situation where he is suffering or likely to suffer significant harm and shall transfer the parental rights to the Department.

(3) The probation officer or social welfare officer shall take custody of the child and shall determine the most suitable place for the child which may be –

(a) an approved residential home

(b) with an approved fit person; or

(c) at the home of a parent, guardian or relative.

(4) The maximum duration of a care order shall be three years or until the child attains eighteen years which ever is earliest and the Family Tribunal may make an interim order or may vary the order.

(5) The Family Tribunal may make a further order that the parent, guardian or other person responsible for the child shall pay for the cost of maintaining the child.

(6) A Family Tribunal shall not designate the manager of an institution as an approved fit person to whom the care of a child can be entrusted unless the institution is one

which the Minister responsible for Social Welfare has approved by notice published in the Gazette or the institution is assigned that function by or under an Act of Parliament.

Supervision order of Family Tribunal

21. (1) A Family Tribunal may issue a supervision order to the Department on an application by a probation officer or social welfare officer under section 19(4).

(2) The supervision order shall be aimed at preventing any significant harm being caused to a child whilst he remains at his family home in the custody of his parent, guardian or relative.

(3) The supervision order shall place a child under the supervision of the probation officer or social welfare officer while he remains in the custody of his parent, guardian or relative.

(4) The maximum duration for a supervision order shall be one year or until the child attains eighteen years.

Duties of probation officer and social worker

22. The duties of a probation officer or social welfare officer with respect to a care or supervision order are to –

(a) advise and help the child and his family;

(b) take reasonable steps to ensure that the child is not subjected to harm; and

(c) hold regular reviews to plan for the future of the child.

Home visits

23. A probation officer or social welfare officer shall be permitted by a parent, guardian or relative of the child to visit the child at his family home.

General provisions on order

24. (1) A child who contravenes an order from the Family Tribunal and runs away may be apprehended without warrant by the police and returned to the place of the care or supervision order.

(2) The Family Tribunal may make another order where the child has run away in order to place the child elsewhere if the approved fit person is not willing to take the child.

Discharge of orders

25. A care or supervision order may be discharged in the best interest of the child by the Family Tribunal on the application of –

(a) the child;

(b) a probation officer;

(c) a social welfare officer; or

(d) a parent, guardian or relative of the child.

Care order and adoption

26. A child under a care order whose parent, guardian or relative does not show an interest in the welfare of the child within a period stipulated by a Family Tribunal may be put up for adoption.

PART II – QUASI-JUDICIAL AND JUDICIAL CHILD ADJUDICATION

Sub-Part I – Child Panels

Establishment of Child Panels

27. There shall be established in each district such number of Child Panels as the District Assembly may consider necessary.

Functions of Child Panels

28. A Child Panel shall have non-judicial functions to mediate in criminal and civil matters which concern a child prescribed under this Act.

Composition of Child Panel

29. (1) A child Panel shall consist of the following persons in the relevant district –

(a) the Chairman of the Social Services Sub-Committee of a District Assembly who shall be the chairman;

(b) a member of a women's organisation;

(c) a representative of the Traditional Council;

(d) the district social worker, who shall be the secretary;

(e) a member of the Justice and Security Sub-Committee of the District Assembly; and

(f) two other citizens from the community of high moral character and proven integrity one of whom shall be an educationalist.

(2) The members of a Child Panel shall be appointed by the Minister.

(3) The tenure of office of a Child Panel shall be the same as that of the District Assembly.

Meetings of Child Panel

30. (1) A Child Panel shall meet as often as may be necessary except that a Child Panel shall meet at least once in every three months.

(2) The quorum at any meeting of a Child Panel shall be four and in the absence of the Chairman shall be chaired by a member elected by the members present from their number.

(3) Any agreement made between the parties shall be recorded by the secretary to the Child Panel.

(4) Any person with a significant interest in a matter before a Child Panel may be invited to attend and participate in its deliberations.

(5) A Child Panel shall permit a child to express his opinion and participate in any decision which affects the child's well being commensurate with the level of understanding of the child concerned.

(6) Except as otherwise provided in this Sub-Part a Child Panel shall regulate the procedure at its meetings.

Child Panel in civil matters

31. A Child Panel may mediate in any civil matter concerned with the rights of the child and parental duties.

Child Panel in criminal matters

32. (1) A Child Panel shall assist in victim-offender mediation in minor criminal matters involving a child where the circumstances of the offence are nor aggravated.

(2) A Child Panel shall seek to facilitate reconciliation between the child and any person offended by the action of the child

(3) A child appearing before a Child Panel shall be cautioned as to the implications of his action and that similar behavior may subject him to the juvenile justice system.

(4) A Child Panel may decide to impose a community guidance order on a child with the consent of the parties concerned in the matter.

(5) A community guidance order means placing the child under the guidance and supervision of a person of good standing in the local community for a period not exceeding six months for purposes of his reform.

(6) A Child Panel may in the course of mediation propose an apology, restitution to the offended person or service by the child to the offended person.

Sub-Part II – Family Tribunals

Family tribunals

33. (1) There shall be Family Tribunals which shall exercise the jurisdiction provided under section 35 and any other provisions of this Act.

(2) Any reference to a Family Tribunal in this Act shall be construed to mean a Community Tribunal established under the Courts Act, 1993 (Act 459).

Composition of Family Tribunal

34. A Family Tribunal shall be duly constituted by a panel consisting of a Chairman and not less than two or more than four other members including a social welfare officer appointed by the Chief Justice on the recommendation of the Director of Social Welfare.

Jurisdiction of Family Tribunal

35. A Family Tribunal shall have jurisdiction in matters concerning parentage, custody, access and maintenance of children and shall exercise such other powers as are conferred on it by this Act or under any other enactment.

Family Tribunal sittings

36. (1) A Family Tribunal shall sit either in a different building or room from that in which sittings of other courts are held, or on different days from those on which sittings of other courts are held and no person shall be present at any sitting of a Family Tribunal except –

(a) members and officers of the Family Tribunal;

(b) parties to the case before the Family Tribunal, their counsel, witnesses and other persons directly concerned in the case;

(c) the parent or guardian of the child before the Family Tribunal;

(d) probation and social welfare officers; and

(e) any other person whom the Family Tribunal authorises to be present.

(2) The Chairman of a Family Tribunal shall arrange for its sitting as often as possible to dispose of cases expeditiously.

Procedure at Family Tribunal

37. The proceedings at a Family Tribunal shall be as informal as possible and shall be by enquiry and not by adversarial procedures.

Rights of the child at Family Tribunal

38. (1) A child shall have a right to legal representation at a Family Tribunal.

(2) A child shall have a right to give an account and express an opinion at a Family Tribunal.

(3) A child's right to privacy shall be respected throughout the proceedings at a Family Tribunal.

(4) The right of appeal shall be explained to the child, guardian and parents.

No publication of information on child

39. (1) No person shall publish any information that may lead to the identification of a child in any matter before a Family Tribunal except with the permission of the Family Tribunal.

(2) Any person who contravenes this section commits an offence and is liable on summary conviction to a fine not exceeding ¢5 million or imprisonment for a term not exceeding one year or to both.

PART III – PARENTAGE, CUSTODY, ACCESS AND MAINTENANCE

Sub-Part I – Parentage

Application for parentage

40. (1) The following persons may apply to a Family Tribunal for an order to confirm the parentage of a child –

(a) the child;

(b) the parent of a child;

(c) the guardian of a child;

(d) a probation officer;

(e) a social welfare officer; or

(f) any other interested person.

(2) The application to the Family Tribunal may be made –

(a) before the child is born; or

(b) within three years after the death of the father or mother of a child; or

(d) before a child is eighteen years of age or after the child has attained that age with special leave of the Family Tribunal.

Evidence of parentage

41. The following shall be considered by a Family Tribunal as evidence of parentage –

(a) the name of the parent entered in the register of births;

(b) performance of customary ceremony by the father of the child;

(c) refusal by the parent to submit to a medical test;

(d) public acknowledgement of parentage; and

(e) any other matter that the Family Tribunal may consider relevant.

Medical test

42. The Family Tribunal may order the alleged parent to submit to a medical test and the Tribunal shall on the basis of the evidence before it make such order as it considers appropriate.

Sub-Part II – Custody and Access

Custody
43. A parent, family member or any person who is raising a child may apply to a Family Tribunal for custody of the child.

Access
44. A parent, family member or any person who has been caring for a child may apply to a Family Tribunal for periodic access to the child.

Considerations for custody or access
45. (1) A Family Tribunal shall consider the best interest of the child and the importance of a young child being with his mother when making an order for custody or access.

(2) Subject to subsection (1) a Family Tribunal shall also consider –

(a) the age of the child;

(b) that it is preferable for a child to be with his parents except if his rights are persistently being abused by his parents;

(c) the views of the child if the views have been independently given;

(d) that it is desirable to keep siblings together;

(e) the need for continuity in the care and control of the child; and

(f) any other matter that the Family Tribunal may consider relevant.

46. **Unlawful child removal –**
No person shall unlawfully remove a child from another person who has the lawful custody of the child.

Sub-Part III – Maintenance

47. **Duty to maintain a child –**

(1) A parent or any other person who is legally liable to maintain a child or contribute towards the maintenance of the child is under a duty to supply the necessaries of health, life, education and reasonable shelter for the child.

(2) For the purpose of this section, education means basic education.

48. **Application for maintenance order –**

(1) The following persons who have custody of a child may apply to a Family Tribunal for a maintenance order for the child –

(a) a parent of the child;

(b) the guardian of the child; or

(c) any other person.

(2) The following may also apply to a Family Tribunal for a maintenance order –

(a) the child by his next friend;

(b) a probation officer;

(c) a social welfare officer; or

(d) the Commission on Human Rights and Administration Justice.

(3) The application for maintenance may be made against any person who is liable to maintain the child or contribute towards the maintenance of the child.

49. **Considerations for maintenance orders –**
A Family Tribunal shall consider the following when making a maintenance order –

(a) the income and wealth of both parents of the child or of the person legally liable to maintain the child;

(b) any impairment of the earning capacity of the person with a duty to maintain the child;

(c) the financial responsibility of the person with respect to the maintenance of other children;

(d) the cost of living in the area where the child is resident;

(e) the rights of the child under this Act; and

(f) any other matter which the Family Tribunal considers relevant.

Request for social enquiry report

50. (1) A Family Tribunal may request that a probation officer or social welfare officer prepare a social enquiry report on the issue of maintenance before it for consideration.

(2)The Family Tribunal shall in making any order consider the social enquiry report prepared by the probation officer or social welfare officer.

Form of maintenance order

51. (1) A Family Tribunal may award maintenance to the mother of a child whether married to the father or not where the father has been identified, and the maintenance shall include the following –

(a) medical expenses for the duration of her pregnancy, delivery or death of the child;

(b) a periodic allowance for the maintenance of the mother during her period of pregnancy and for a further period of nine months after the delivery of the child; and

(c) the payment of a reasonable sum to be determined by the Family Tribunal for the continued education of the mother if she is a child herself.

(2) A Family Tribunal may order a periodic payment or lump sum payment for the maintenance of a child and the earnings or property of the person liable may be attached.

(3) The attachment order should be applicable in all cases of failure to pay maintenance.

(4) When considering an application for maintenance, a Family Tribunal may make a maintenance order which it considers reasonable for any child in the household.

(5) A Family Tribunal may make an order for arrears of maintenance against any person liable to pay the maintenance.

Persons entitled to maintenance order

52. (1) Any person who has custody of a child who is the subject of a maintenance order is entitled to receive and administer the maintenance order of the Family Tribunal.

(2) If the parent, guardian or whoever has custody of the child should cease to be a fit person, the Family Tribunal of the area where the child is resident may appoint another person to have custody of the child and administer the maintenance order and that person shall act as if originally appointed by the Family Tribunal.

Duration of order

53. (1) A maintenance order issued by a Family Tribunal shall expire when the child attains the age of eighteen years or dies before that age.

(2) A maintenance order shall lapse before the child attains the age of eighteen years if before that age the child is gainfully employed.

Continuation of maintenance orders in certain cases

54. (1) Notwithstanding section 53 a Family Tribunal may continue a maintenance order after a child has attained eighteen years if the child is engaged in a course of continuing education or training after that age.

(2) An application under this section may be brought by a parent of the child, any person who has the custody of the young person or the young person concerned.

Variation or discharge of orders

55. A Family Tribunal may if satisfied vary or discharge a maintenance order on the application of a parent, the person who has the custody of the child or young person or any other person legally liable to maintain the child.

Enforcement of order

56. An action may be brought by any person to enforce a maintenance order thirty days after the order is made or due.

Non-custodial parent to have access to child

57. A non-custodial parent in respect of whom an application is made to a Family Tribunal for an order of parentage, custody, access or maintenance under this Part shall have access to the child who is the subject of the order.

Duplicity of maintenance applications

58. The provisions of this Act are subject to the Matrimonial Causes Act, 1971 (Act 367) and no action may be brought for a maintenance order if an application for maintenance is pending in matrimonial proceedings.

Offences under this Part

59. Any person who –

(a) unlawfully removes a child from another person who has lawful custody of the child contrary to section 46; or

(b) fails to supply the necessaries of health, life, education, and reasonable shelter for a child when legally liable to do so contrary to section 47; or

(c) brings an action for a maintenance under this Part while an application

for maintenance is pending in matrimonial proceedings commits an offence and is liable on summary conviction to a fine not exceeding ¢2 million or a term of imprisonment not exceeding six months or to both.

60. **Procedure for application –**

The forms to be used and the procedure for applications under this Part shall be provided for by regulations made under this Act.

61. **Waiver of fees** – The Chief Justice may by legislative instrument waive part or all of the filing fees or other fees payable for an application under this Part.

PART IV – FOSTERAGE AND ADOPTION

Sub-Part I – Fosterage

62. **Person who can foster –**

Any person above the age of twenty-one years of high moral character and proven integrity may be a foster-parent to a child.

63. **Definition of foster-parent –**
A foster parent is a person who is not the parent of a child but is willing to undertake the care and maintenance of the child.

64. **Foster-care placement –**
(1) Where –
(a) a child has been committed to an approved residential home under a care order;
(b) a recommendation has been made by a probation officer or social welfare officer that an approved residential home is the most suitable place for a child; or
(c) a child has been placed in an approved residential home by any person, a committee comprising a probation officer, social welfare officer, person in charge of the approved residential home and two other people from the community with interest in the welfare of children selected by the Department may place the child with a foster parent.
(2) An application to foster a child shall otherwise be made to a probation officer, social welfare officer or to the person in charge of the approved residential home who shall forward the application to the Department.
(3) A foster-parent in whose care a child is placed or committed shall have the same responsibilities in respect of the child's maintenance as the parent of the child while the child remains in his care.
(4) A foster-parent is liable for contravention of any of the provision under Part I of this Act.
(5) The Minister may by legislative instrument make regulations on fosterage.

Sub-Part II – Adoption application

65. **Jurisdiction and procedure for adoption** – An application for an adoption order may be made to the High Court, Circuit Court or to any Family Tribunal within the jurisdiction where the applicant or the child resides at the date of the application.

66. **Application for adoption –**
(1) An application for an adoption order may be made jointly by a husband and his wife to adopt a child.
(2) An application for an adoption order may be made by the mother or father of the child alone or by either of them jointly with a spouse.
(3) An application for an adoption order may be made by a single person subject to the provisions of this Sub-Part except that this shall only apply to a citizen of Ghana and with due regard to the best interest of the child.

67. **Restrictions on making adoption orders –**
(1) An adoption order shall not be made unless the applicant or, in the case of a joint application, one of the applicants –
(a) is twenty-five years of age and is at least twenty-one years older than the child; or
(b) is a relative of the child and is twenty-one years of age.
(2) A male applicant shall only be granted an adoption order if the application is in respect of his son or the court is satisfied that special circumstances warrant the order.
(3) An adoption order shall not be made for a child unless –
(a) the applicant and the child reside in Ghana but this shall not apply if the applicant is a citizen of Ghana resident abroad;

(b) the child has been continuously in the care and possession of the applicant for at least three consecutive months immediately preceding the date of the order; and

(c) the applicant has notified the Department of his intention to apply for an adoption order for the child at least three months before the date of the order.

(4) Except as provided under section 66 an adoption order shall not be made to authorise more than one person to adopt a child.

Consent of parents and guardians

68. (1) An adoption order shall only be made with the consent of the parents or guardian of the child.

(2) The court may dispense with the consent of any parent or guardian of the child if satisfied that the parent or guardian has neglected or persistently ill-treated the child, or that the person cannot be found or is incapable of giving consent or that the consent is unreasonably withheld.

(3) Any consent under this section may be given without the knowledge of the identity of the applicant for the order and where the consent is subsequently withdrawn only because the identity of the applicant was not known, the consent shall be considered to have been unreasonably withheld.

(4) Any parent or guardian of a child the subject of an application for adoption who has given consent for the adoption order shall not be entitled to remove the child from the care and possession of the applicant except with the permission of the court and in the best interest of the child.

Other consent

69. (1) The court may require the consent of any person for an adoption order if it considers that the person has any rights or obligations in respect of the child such as under an agreement, court order or under customary law.

(2) Subject to subsection (2) of section 66, where a married person is the sole applicant, the court may require the consent of the spouse of that person before the adoption order is made.

Conditions for adoption order

70. (1) Before a court makes an adoption order it shall be satisfied that –

(a) the consent required under this Sub-Part for the adoption order has been obtained and that the parent or guardian of the child understands that the effects of the adoption order will mean permanent deprivation of parental rights;

(b) it is in the best interest of the child and that the wishes of the child have been considered if the child is capable of forming an opinion;

(c) if the child is at least fourteen years of age, his consent to the adoption has been obtained unless it is impossible for the child to express an opinion; and

(d) the applicant has not received or agreed to receive any payment and that no person has made or agreed to make any payment or given or agreed to give any reward to the applicant for the adoption except such as the court may order.

(2) The court may impose conditions when granting an adoption order and may require the applicant to enter a bond to make such provision in respect of the child as the court considers necessary.

(3) The adoption order shall include the following particulars the –

(a) date and place of birth of the child;

(b) name, gender and surname of the child before and after adoption;

(c) name, surname, address, citizenship and occupation of the adopter; and

(d) date of the adoption order, unless the court directs otherwise.

Interim order

71. (1) Subject to the provisions of this section, the court may postpone the determination of the application and make an interim order giving the custody of the child to the applicant for a period not exceeding two years by way of probation and may attach such terms including provision for the maintenance, education and supervision of the child as it thinks fit.

(2) When making an interim order the court shall impose conditions that –

(a) the child shall be under the supervision of a probation officer or a social welfare officer, and

(b) the child shall not be taken out of Ghana without the permission of the court.

(3) The consent and the power to dispense with consent shall be the same for an interim order of adoption as for an adoption order.

(4) No interim order shall be made unless section 67 (3) has been complied with.

(5) An interim order shall not be considered to be an adoption order under this Sub-Part.

Knowledge of adoption by child

72. (1) An adoptive parent shall inform the adopted child of the fact that the child is adopted and his parentage but this disclosure shall only be made if it is in the best interest of the child and if the child is at least fourteen years of age.

(2) No person other than the adoptive parent shall disclose adoption to the adopted child.

(3) Any person who contravenes this provision commits an offence and is liable on summary conviction to a fine not exceeding ¢2 million or to a term of imprisonment not exceeding six months or to both.

73. **Application by non-citizen –**

In an application for adoption by an applicant who is not a citizen of Ghana or where there is a joint application and one applicant is not a citizen of Ghana, the court shall make an interim order for a period of not less than two years and shall postpone the determination of the application.

74. **Children previously adopted –**

An adoption order or an interim order may be made for a child who has already been adopted and the adopter under the previous adoption shall, if alive, be considered as the parent or guardian of the child for the purpose of the subsequent adoption.

75. **Effect of adoption on parental rights –**

(1) When an adoption order is made –

(a) the rights, duties, obligations and liabilities including those under customary law of the parents of the child or of any other person connected with the child of any nature whatsoever shall cease; and

(b) the adopter of the child shall assume the parental rights, duties, obligations and liabilities of the child with respect to custody, maintenance and education as if the child were born to the adopter.

(2) Where an adoption order is made jointly to a husband and wife, they shall assume the parental responsibilities jointly and the child shall relate to them as parents as if born naturally by them as husband and wife.

Sub-Part III – Devolution of property on adoption

76. **Devolution of property on intestacy –**

(1) Where an adopter dies intestate, his property shall devolve in all respects as if the adopted child is the natural child of the adopter.

(2) For the avoidance of doubt an adopted child is not entitled to inherit from his natural parents on intestacy.

77. **Testamentary disposition –**

(1) In a testamentary disposition of property, whether or not in writing made after the date of an adoption order –

(a) any reference whether express or implied to the child of the adopter shall unless the contrary intention appears be constructed as a reference to the adopted child;

(b) where a disposition made by the adopter prior to the adoption order makes no provision for the adopted child, the adopted child may apply to court to vary the disposition to provide for the adopted child from the estate of the adopter;

(c) any reference to a child of the adopted child's natural parents in a will shall not be construed as including a reference to the adopted child unless the contrary intention appears.

(d) Any reference to a person related to the adopter shall unless the contrary intention appears be construed as a reference to the person as if he were the relative of the child who is adopted.

(2) A disposition by will executed before the date of the adoption order shall not be treated for the purpose of this section as if made after that date by a codicil giving retrospective effect to the will.

78. **Supplementary provisions on intestacy and testamentary disposition –**

(1) The administrators or executors of an estate may distribute the estate of a deceased person to persons entitled under the estate without incurring any liability where at the time of the distribution they had no notice of an adoption order by virtue of which the adopted person is to benefit under the estate but this shall not prejudice the right of any entitled person to trace the property except against a purchaser in good faith.

(2) The previous adoption order of a child that has been adopted for a second time shall be disregarded for the purpose of devolution of property on the death of the previous adopter.

Sub-Part IV – Miscellaneous adoption provisions

79. **Adoption order and customary law –**

(1) An adopted child shall be subject to customary law as if he were the natural child of the adopter only if the adopter is subject to customary law.

(2) Where there is joint adoption by husband and wife references to the adopter in this section shall be taken as a reference to the husband and wife.

80. **Adoption order and citizenship –**

(1) A child need not be a citizen of Ghana to be adopted.

(2) A child of not more than sixteen years of age neither of whose parents is a citizen of Ghana shall be a citizen of Ghana if adopted by a citizen of Ghana.

81. **Effect of adoption order on fit person order** – Where an adoption order is made in respect of a child under a fit person care order of a Family Tribunal, the fit person care order shall cease to apply.

82. **Adopted Children Register –**

(1) The Registrar-General shall maintain at his office an Adopted Children Register in which shall be recorded particulars of the adoption order or interim order as the court may direct to be made under this Part.

(2) Notwithstanding the provision made in any regulations under the Adoption Act, 1962 (Act 104), every adoption order or interim order made by a court shall be served on the Registrar-General by the registrar of the court concerned within 30 days of the making of the order.

(3) The Registrar-General may by executive instrument make rules with respect to the Adopted Children Register particularly rules –

(a) for the admission in evidence of a certified copy of an entry in the Adopted Children Register;

(b) as to searches in that Register and the fees to be charged for service in connection with that Register.

(4) The Registrar-General shall keep other records that relate to entries in the Register of Births on adoption together with entries in the Adopted Children Register but these records shall not be available to the public and shall not be given to any person except under a court order.

Offences related to adoption

83. (1) No person shall give any payment or reward in respect of an adoption order except with approval of the court.

(2) No person shall receive any payment or reward in respect of any arrangement that may or may not lead to an adoption order.

(3) Any person who contravenes this section commits an offence and is liable on summary conviction to a fine not exceeding ¢5 million or to a term of imprisonment not exceeding one year or to both.

Notice to be given to send child abroad

84. (1) The Department shall be notified by the adopter when the adopted child is being sent out of the country permanently after the adoption order has been made by the court.

(2) This notice shall be given to the Department 30 days before the departure of the adopter and the adopted child from the country.

(3) Any person who contravenes this provision commits an offence and is liable on summary conviction to a fine not exceeding ¢2 million or to a term of imprisonment not exceeding six months or to both.

Inter-country adoption

85. (1) Subject to the provisions of this Part, the Department may investigate an application for inter-country adoption as an alternative means of child care, if a child cannot be placed in a foster or an adoptive family in Ghana or cannot in any suitable manner be cared for in Ghana.

(2) A court may grant an inter-country adoption order if it is in the best interest of the child.

Procedure rules for adoption

86. (1) For the purpose of adoption applications, the Rules of Court Committee may by constitutional instrument make rules for the procedure of adoption.

(2) The rules shall provide for –

(a) the proceedings to be held in camera except under exceptional circumstances;

(b) the admission of documentary evidence relating to the consent required for the order;

(c) requiring a probation officer or social welfare officer to represent the interest of the child in proceedings relating to an adoption order or an interim order;

(d) requiring a probation officer or social welfare officer to prepare a social enquiry report to assist the court to determine whether the adoption order is in the best interest of the child or not; and

(e) any other matter that the Committee may determine.

(3) For the purposes of this Part "court" means the High Court, Circuit Court and Family Tribunal within the jurisdiction where the applicant or the child resides at the time of the application.

PART V – EMPLOYMENT OF CHILDREN

Sub-Part I – Child Labour

Prohibition of exploitative child labour

87. (1) No person shall engage a child in exploitative labour.

(2) Labour is exploitative of a child if it deprives the child of its health, education or development.

Prohibition of child labour at night

88. (1) No person shall engage a child in night work.

(2) Night work constitutes work between the hours of eight o'clock in the evening and six o'clock in the morning.

Minimum age for child labour

89. The minimum age for admission of a child to employment shall be fifteen years.

Minimum age for light work

90. (1) The minimum age for the engagement of a child in light work shall be thirteen years.

(2) Light work constitutes work which is not likely to be harmful to the health or development of the child and does not affect the child's attendance at school or the capacity of the child to benefit from school work.

91. **Minimum age for hazardous employment –**

(1) The minimum age for the engagement of a person in hazardous work is eighteen years.

(2) Work is hazardous when it poses a danger to the health, safety or morals of a person.

(3) Hazardous work includes –

(a) going to sea;

(b) mining and quarrying;

(c) porterage of heavy loads;

(d) manufacturing industries where chemicals are produced or used;

(e) work in places where machines are used; and

(f) work in places such as bars, hotels and places of entertainment where a person may be exposed to immoral behavior.

92. **Application –**
For the avoidance of doubt, this Sub-Part shall apply to employment in the formal and informal sector.

93. **Registration of children and young persons in industrial undertakings –**

(1) An employer in an industrial undertaking shall keep a register of the children and young persons employed by him and of the dates of their births if known or of their apparent ages if their dates of birth are not known.

(2) An industrial undertaking is an undertaking other than one in commerce or agriculture and includes –

(a) mines, quarries and other works for the extraction of minerals from the earth;

(b) undertakings in which articles are manufactured, altered, cleaned, repaired, ornamented, finished, adopted for sale, broken up or demolished, or in which materials are transformed including undertakings engaged in ship building or in the generation, transformation or transmission of electricity or motive power of any kind;

(c) undertakings engaged in the transport of passengers or goods by road or rail including the handling of goods at docks, quays, wharves, warehouses and airports.

94. **Offences under this Sub-Part –**

(1) Any person who contravenes the provisions of this Sub-Part commits an offence and is liable on summary conviction to a fine not exceeding ¢10 million or to imprisonment for a term not exceeding two years or to both.

(2) Notwithstanding subsection (1) of this section, any person who contravenes section 93 (1) commits an offence and is liable on conviction to a fine not exceeding ¢500,000.00.

95. **Enforcement in formal sector –**

(1) A district labour officer shall carry out any enquiry he may consider necessary in order to satisfy himself that the provisions of this Sub-Part with respect to labour by children and young persons in the formal sector are being strictly observed.

(2) For purposes of this section any person may be interrogated by a district labour officer.

(3) If a district labour officer is reasonably satisfied that the provisions of this Sub-Part are not being complied with he shall report the matter to the police who shall investigate the matter and take the appropriate steps to prosecute the offender.

96. **Enforcement in the informal sector –**

(1) The Social Services Sub-Committee of a District Assembly and the Department shall be responsible for the enforcement of the provisions of this Sub-Part in the informal sector.

(2) For purposes of this section any person may be interrogated by a member of the Social Services Sub-Committee or by a member of the Department.

(3) If the member of the Social Services Sub-Committee or the Department is reasonably satisfied that the provision of this Sub-Part are not being complied with he shall report the matter to the police who shall investigate the matter and take the appropriate steps to prosecute the offender.

(4) Where the offender is a family member of the child whose rights are being infringed under this Sub-Part, the Social Services Sub-Committee or the Department shall request a probation officer or social welfare officer to prepare a social enquiry report on the matter.

(5) The social enquiry report prepared under subsection (4) of this section shall be considered by the police before any action is taken against the offender.

Sub-Part II – Apprenticeship

97. **Act to apply to apprenticeship in the informal sector –**
This Act applies to child apprentices in the informal sector.

Minimum age for apprentices
98. The minimum age at which a child may commence an apprenticeship with a craftsman is fifteen years or after completion of basic education.

Responsibilities of craftsman
99. The responsibilities of a craftsman towards an apprentice under his care shall be as follows to –

(a) train and instruct the apprentice in a trade to the best of the ability, skill and knowledge of the craftsman and to the best ability of the apprentice or cause the apprentice to be trained in a trade under the supervision of the craftsman;

(b) be responsible for any harm caused to the apprentice in the course of his training;

(c) provide food for the apprentice unless otherwise agreed;

(d) provide a safe and healthy environment for the apprentice;

(e) be responsible for the moral training of the apprentice; and

(f) protect the best interest of the apprentice generally.

Apprenticeship agreement
100. (1) The parent, guardian or relative of an apprentice shall enter into an apprenticeship agreement with the craftsman.

(2) The agreement shall be in accordance with the custom which pertains to the specific trade but shall not include the performance of any induction ceremony which may conflict with the rights of the child contained in Sub-Part I of Part I of this Act.

(3) The agreement shall contain such matters as may be agreed between the parties and may include –

(a) provision that the parent, guardian or relative shall bear the cost of protective clothing and the basic tools for the training of the apprentice;

(c) a duty that the craftsman is to provide shelter for the apprentice; and

(d) a provision that the craftsman is to give the apprentice an allowance of not less than half the minimum national daily wage for his daily sustenance.

(4) The agreement shall be in writing and shall contain provisions in the best interest of the parties and the apprentice.

(5) Should either party to the agreement contravene its terms, the agreement shall immediately lapse unless there is a contrary intention in the agreement.

Duties of apprentice

101. An apprentice shall diligently and faithfully obey and serve the craftsman and shall agree –

(a) that he will not absent himself from the apprenticeship without permission;

(b) to prevent any deliberate damage to the property of the craftsman; and

(c) not to conceal any damage to the property of the craftsman.

Release of apprentice

102. (1) The conditions for the release of an apprentice upon the completion of his training shall not be exploitative and shall be in accordance with the best interest of the child under Sub-Part I of Part I of this Act.

(2) The craftsman shall on completion of a period of apprenticeship issue a certificate of release to the apprentice which shall indicate that the apprentice has completed his training.

(3) If the craftsman refuses to issue the certificate of release without just cause he commits an offence and is liable on summary conviction to a fine not exceeding ¢2 million or six months imprisonment or both.

Resolution of disputes

103. Disputes related to an apprenticeship agreement shall be referred to the district labour officer of the district concerned by the parties to the apprenticeship agreement or the apprentice.

Application of Sub-Part I of this Part

104. The provisions of Sub-Part I of this Part on Child Labour shall apply to this Sub-Part.

PART VI – INSTITUTIONALISED CARE AND MISCELLANEOUS MATTERS

Sub-Part I – Approved residential homes

Approval of residential home

105. (1) The Government may establish a home referred to this Act as "a home" for the care of children in such areas as the Minister may determine.

(2) Any person or an NGO may also establish and operate a home for the care of children subject to the approval of the Minister.

(3) An application for the approval of a home shall be submitted to the Minister

(4) The Minister shall cause the home to be inspected by the Department and if the home meets the required standard it shall be approved by notice published in the Gazette.

(5) Upon approval by the Minister, the home shall obtain a license to operate issued by the Minister after payment of the prescribed fee but this provision shall not apply to a government home.

(6) Any non-governmental home in existence at the commencement of this Act shall apply to the Minister for approval and the issue of a license within a period of six months from the commencement of the Act.

106. **Department to monitor homes —**
The Department of a District Assembly shall monitor homes within its district.

107. **Power of Minister to give directives to homes** – The Minister may give such orders and directions to a home as may be expedient in the public interest.

108. **Inspection** – The Minister may authorise the inspection of a home by the Department at any time to ensure that the home is being maintained at the required standard.

109. **Admission of children to homes –**

(1) A child may be admitted to a home –

(a) Pending the determination by a Family Tribunal of an order under Sub-Part II of Part I of this Act;

(b) on the recommendation of a probation officer or social welfare officer who has determined that the approved home is the most suitable place for the child: or

(c) If the child is an orphan and family care and fosterage are not available.

(2) If a home fails to maintain the required standard its license to operate may be cancelled or suspended by the Minister and alternative arrangements shall be made by the Department for the children in the home

(3) It shall be the responsibility of the staff of a home, the probation and social welfare officer and any other person to assist a child resident in the home to become reunited with its parents, guardian or relatives.

(4) After a child has been returned to his family home from a home, the probation and social welfare officer shall keep in regular contact with the child and his family to ensure that the best interest of the child is sustained

(5) Where a child is unable to return to his parents or go to foster parents or has no parent or foster parent, he shall be encouraged and assisted by the home and the probation and social welfare officer to become independent and self reliant.

110. **Parental responsibility of staff of approved homes –**

(1) While a child is in a home the staff of the home shall assume parental responsibility for the child and ensure that the rights of the child in Sub-Part I of Part I of this Act are protected

(2) Notwithstanding subsection (1) of this section, the parents, guardian or relatives of a child in a home shall supplement the efforts of the home to safeguard and promote the welfare of the child by visiting the child and other wise protecting the interest of the child.

(3) Parental responsibility of a child in a home shall include an application to a Family Tribunal to protect the best interest of the child where necessary.

Power of Family Tribunal to order contribution

111. (1) A Family Tribunal may order that the parent, guardian or relative of a child in a home shall contribute towards the maintenance of the child in the home.

(2) Any amount to be contributed shall be reasonable and may be varied by the Family Tribunal if there is a change in circumstances of the contributor.

Approved home and adoption

112. (1) Subject to the provisions of this Act a child in a home shall be put up for adoption if it is in the best interest of the child.

(2) The decision for the adoption of a child in a home shall be taken by the Department in consultation with the management of the home.

Regulations and homes

113. The Minister may by legislative instrument make regulations for homes.

Offences under this Sub-Part

114. (1) The penalty for contravention in respect of the rights of the child and parental duty in section 15 of this Act shall apply to any person in a home who fails to uphold the rights of the child.

(2) Any person who ¬

(a) operates a home without a licence issued by the Minister, or

(b) continues to operate a home in contravention of this Sub-Part; or

(c) obstructs or hinders any person conducting an inspection under this

Sub-Part Commits an offence and is liable on summary conviction to a fine not exceeding ¢5 million or to a term of imprisonment not exceeding one year or to both and in the case of a continuing offence to a further fine not exceeding ¢100,000 for each day on which the offence continues.

Sub-Part II – Day-Care Centres

Application to operate day-care centre

115. (1) An application for a permit to operate a day-care centre shall be submitted by the applicant to the Department.

(2) The application shall be accompanied by such fee as may be prescribed in a bye-law of a District Assembly.

(3) The Department shall inspect the proposed day-care centre and if it meets the required standard it shall approve the application and grant a permit upon payment of the fee for the permit prescribed in a bye-law.

(4) Any day-care centre in operation without a permit granted by a Department shall be closed on fourteen days notice to the owner or operator by the Department.

Inspection

116. (1) The Department shall inspect the premises, books, accounts and other records of a day-care centre at least once in every six months and shall submit a report of the inspection to the Social Services Sub-Committee of a District Assembly.

(2) If the inspection reveals that the day-care centre is not being managed efficiently in the best interest of the children, the Department shall suspend the permit and the owner or operator shall be ordered to make good any default within a stipulated time.

(3) If the owner or operator fails to make good the default within the stipulated time, the permit shall be cancelled.

Bye-laws and guidelines

117. A District Assembly shall issue such bye-laws and guidelines as it may determine for the operation of day-care centres within its district.

Policy directives

118. The Ministry for Social Welfare and the Ministry for Education may issue such policy directives as may be necessary for the operation of day-care centres.

Existing operators

119. Any person who owns or operates a day-care centre before the commencement of this Act who intends to continue to operate the day-care centre shall apply to the Department for a permit within six months of the commencement of this Act.

Offences under this Sub-Part

120. Any person who –

(a) operates a day-care without a permit issued by the Department; or

(b) continues to operate a day-care centre in contravention of this Part; or

(c) obstructs or hinders any person conducting an inspection under this

Sub-Part commits an offence and is liable on summary conviction to a fine not exceeding ¢5 million or to a term of imprisonment not exceeding one year or to both and in the case of continuing offence to a further fine not exceeding ¢100,000 for each day on which the offence continues.

Sub-Part III – Miscellaneous Provisions

Registration of births

121. (1) The District Health Department of a District Assembly shall in consultation with the Department of the District Assembly be responsible for registration of births in the district.

(2) The registration of births shall form part of the district primary health care programme.

(3) The District Assembly may delegate any of its functions under this section to a Unit Committee or to such other person as it may determine to be appropriate.

Determination of age of a child

122. (1) In the absence of a birth certificate or a baptismal certificate a certificate signed by a medical officer as to the age of a child below eighteen years of age shall be evidence of that age before a Family Tribunal without proof of signature unless the court directs otherwise.

(2) An order of a Family Tribunal shall not be invalidated by any subsequent proof that the age of the child has not been correctly stated to the Family Tribunal and the age presumed or declared by the Family Tribunal to be the age of that child shall be deemed to be the true age for the purpose of any proceedings under this Act.

(3) A statutory declaration issued and certified by the High Court of Justice or person authorised by law to authenticate same as to the age of a child upon an application by a parent or guardian of the child shall be evidence of the age of that child.

Regulations

123. (1) Without limiting the power to make regulations under any Part of this Act, the Minister may by legislative instrument make regulations –

(a) in respect of care and protection under Sub-Part II of Part I;

(b) on fosterage under Sub-Part I and Part IV;

(c) on child labour under Sub-Part I of Part V;

(d) on apprenticeship under Sub-Part I of Part V;

(e) on homes under Sub-Part I of Part VI;

(f) on day-care centres under Sub-Part II of Part VI; and

(g) generally for the implementation of the provisions of this Act.

(2) Regulations made under this Act may provide for the charging of fees for anything to be done under this Act.

Interpretation

124. In this Act unless the context otherwise requires –
"approved residential home" means a residential home for children which is run by Government or a non-governmental home licensed by the Minister where children are given temporary substitute family care; "child abuse" means contravention of the rights of the child which causes physical or mental harm to the child; "craftsman" means a person who can train and instruct an apprentice in a trade; "day-care centre" means any early childhood development establishment where children below compulsory school going age are received and looked after for the day or a substantial part of the day with or without a fee; "Department" means the Social Welfare and Community Development Department of a District Assembly; "disabled child" means a child who suffers from abnormalities or loss of physiological functions, anatomic structure or psychological state and has lost in part or wholly the ability to engage in activities in a normal way and is as a result hampered in his normal functions in certain areas of social life; "district" means the area of authority of a District Assembly and includes a municipality and metropolis; "District Assembly" includes Municipal and Metropolitan Assembly; "District Chief Executive" includes Municipal and Metropolitan Chief Executives; "fit person" means a person of full age who is of high moral character and integrity and of sound mind capable of looking after a child, is not a relative of the child and has been registered by a probation officer or social welfare officer as being able to provide a caring home for a child; "home" means a residential place where a child is given temporary substitute family care; "informal sector" means the area of economy other than industry; "institution" means an approved residential home; "inter-country adoption" means the adoption of a child by a person who is not a citizen of Ghana who resides outside Ghana and the removal of the adopted child from the jurisdiction; "minor criminal matter" means a minor offence such as petty theft, petty assault and threatening offences; "Minister" means the Minister responsible for Social Welfare; "next friend" means a person who intervenes to assist a child to bring a legal action; "NGO" means a non-governmental organisation; "parent" means natural parent and includes a person acting in whatever way as parent; "young person" means a person of or above eighteen years who is under twenty-one.

Amendments and repeals

125. The enactments specified in the first column of the Schedule to this Act are amended or repealed in the manner specified in the second column of that Schedule.

Savings

126. (1) Notwithstanding the repeal of the enactments specified in the Schedule to this Act –

(a) the Day-Care Centres Regulations, 1979 (L.I. 1230);

(b) the Adoption (High Court) Rules, 1963 (L.I. 276); and

(c) any other rules or regulations

made under the repealed enactments and in force immediately before the commencement of this Act are hereby continued in force until amended or revoked or otherwise dealt with under this Act.

(2) Family Tribunals in existence immediately before the commencement of this Act by virtue of an enactment repealed by this Act are hereby continued in existence subject to the provisions of this Act.

Consequential Amendments and Repeals

Enactment	How affected
1. Marriage Ordinance (cap 127)	Subsection (2) of section 14 repealed. Section 27 is repealed.
2. Adoption Act, 1962 (Act 104)	Act is repealed.
3. Labour Decree, 1967 (N.L.C.D. 157)	(a) Section 16(1) is amended by the deletion of "sixteen" and the insertion of "fifteen"; (b) Section 16(2) is amended by the deletion of "sixteen" and the insertion of "fifteen"; (c) Section 32 is amended by the deletion of "sixteen" and the insertion of "fifteen"; (d) Sub-Part 2 of Part V – Children and Young Persons, section 44-46 is repealed; and (e) The following definitions in section 47 are deleted – i. "child"; ii. "night work" paragraph (b); and iii. "young person".
4. Scouts and Guides Decree, 1969 (N.L.C.D. 399)	(a) Subsection (2) of section 1 amended as follows – i. in paragraph (b) by the insertion of "courtesy, home craft" after "observation"; and ii. in paragraph (b) by the insertion of "love of nature, traditional arts and customs" after "others". (b) Paragraph (b) of subsection (2) of section 2 amended by the insertion of "observation, self-reliance", after "of".
5. Maintenance Decree, 1977 (S.M.C.D. 133)	Decree is repealed.
6. Day-Centres Decree, 1978 (S.M.C.D. 144)	Decree is repealed.

Continued on next page

Enactment	How affected
7. Intestate Succession Law, 1985 (P.N.D.C.L. 111)	(a) Section 5 is amended as follows- i. by the renumbering the section as subsection (1); ii. by the repeal of the proviso after paragraph (d); iii. by the insertion after paragraph (d) of the following proviso – "Provided that where there is a child who is a minor undergoing educational training, reasonable provision shall be made for the child before distribution." iv. by the insertion of a new subsection (2) as follows: "(2) Where there is no surviving parent one-fourth of the residue of the estate shall devolve in accordance with customary law"; (b) Section 12 is amended in paragraph (a) and (b) by the deletion of "¢50,000.00" and the insertion of "¢10 million"; and (c) Section 18 on interpretation is amended as following – i. in the definition of "child" by the insertion of "whether or not born in wedlock" after " child"; ii. by the insertion after "estate" of the following "house" includes an immovable property for dwelling purposes".
8. Social Security Law, 1991 (P.N.D.C.L. 247)	Section 40 is amended by – i. the insertion in subsection (6) of "shall review his nomination once every five years"; after "and"; and ii. the addition of a new subsection as follows – "(8) Notwithstanding subsection (7) if a member of the Scheme has a child of school going age 60% of the contribution shall be distributed to the child and 40% to the person nominated by the member".

Continued on next page

Enactment	How affected
9. Courts Act, 1993 (Act 459)	Subsection (2) of section 47 is repealed and the following inserted "A Community Tribunal shall also have jurisdiction to hear and determine any action arising under the Childrens Act, 1998 (Act 556) and shall for purpose of that enactment be the Family Tribunal".
10. Maintenance of Children Act, 1965 (Commencement) Instrument, 1965 (L.I. 477).	Instrument is revoked.
11. Maintenance of Children Decree, 1977, (Commencement) Instrument, 1978 (L.I. 1137).	Instrument is revoked.
12. Day-care Centre Regulations, 1979 (L.I. 1230).	(a) Regulation 1 is amended by the insertion of "and" after paragraph (c) and the insertion of a new paragraph as follows – "(e) a telephone if telephone service is available". (b) Regulation 3(1) is amended by the insertion of "and a reasonable quantity of toys made from wood and other non-toxic materials after "sandpit". (c) Regulation 8(4) is amended by the deletion of "twenty-five" and the insertion of "fifteen".

Date of Gazette notification: 5th February, 1999.

Index

Ababio, Anita, 146n15
Abangana v. Akologo, 47
Accelerated Development Plan for Education, 21, 23
access to education. *See* education, access to
access to health care. *See* health care, access to
Accra, Ghana: mobility strategies in, 115–17; poverty levels in, 5
ACPF. *See* African Child Policy Forum
ACRWC. *See* African Charter on the Rights and Welfare of the Child
Adali-Mortti, Geormbeeyi, 19–20
Addison, Ruth, 161, 163
adolescence, during colonial era, as concept, 22
Adolescent Reproductive Health Policy, 188n18
Adongo, Stephen, 159–60
adoption: under Children's Act, 155, 260–65; devolution of property on, 263; miscellaneous provisions, 263–65; paternity status and, 37
Adoption Act (1962), 273
adultery, legal status of children and, 45–48, 55n1; *Abangana v. Akologo*, 47; fees for, 46; among Frafra, 47–48; *Ibrahim v. Amalibini*, 47–48; inheritance rights and, 52; *Nyarkoa v. Mansu*, 46–47; status of women and, 45–46; as transaction between two males, 46
African Charter on the Rights and Welfare of the Child (ACRWC), 27, 41; child labor under, 100; child rights provisions in, 42; paternity status and, 38
African Child Policy Forum (ACPF), 189n33
African Renaissance Mission, 142
Afrikania Mission, 142
"ahenahene" game, 18
Akan people: childhood for, 16–18; corporal punishment against young girls, 81–82, 95n3
Amedzofe-Avatime people, paternity status among, 44
An-Na'im, Abdullahi, 165
Anti-Human Trafficking Act, 217
Anti-Slavery International, 137, 139–40
APT. *See* Association for the Prevention of Torture
Arendt, Hannah, 133
Ark Foundation, 218
Asantehene people, 20
Asante people, childhood among, 24
Ashanti people: childhood for, 20; paternity status among, 44
Association for the Prevention of Torture (APT), 189n37
Atomo v. Tekpetey, 141

Bales, Kevin, 139
bana ka dikgora (children whose fathers had crept surreptitiously

through the fence), 44
Barnor, Adjiri, 158
Bibbio, Norberto, 132
Bilyeu, Amy, 142
bogadi (bride wealth), 43
Buduburam Refugee Settlement, 60–69; child rights legislation and, 62–63, *63–64*; conflict experiences in, 68; under Constitution of Ghana, 64–65; coping strategies in, 65–69; economic role reversals in, 68; under Ghana Refugee Law, 65; health care access in, 63; illegal activities in, among young, 67; intergenerational roles within, 67–69; IRC, 62; labor opportunities within, 66–67; NGO involvement in, 61–62; peer support within, 65; repatriation from, 62; sex work in, 67–68; "vulnerable groups" in, 62

CAN. *See* Child Abuse Network
caning: at home, 83; in schools, 85
capitation grant programs, 108, 219; for education access, 202; for rural poor, 201
Case Book on the Rights of Women in Ghana, 38
cash crops: cocoa, 42; influence on family networks, 42
cash transfer programs, 108

Catholic Action for Street Children, 28
Catholic Action on Street Children, 218
CBOs. *See* community-based organizations
CEDAW. *See* Convention on the Elimination of All Forms of Discrimination Against Women
chastity laws, 146n18
chattel slavery, 140
Child Abuse Network (CAN), 92
childcare, by siblings, 18
childhood, 15–31; ACRWC guidelines, 27; age definitions for, 99; for Akan people, 16–18; for Asante people, 24; for Ashanti people, 20; child-naming, 17; child rights and, 28; during colonial era, 20–24; for Fante people, 18; for girls, end of, 17; globalized notion of, 99; ILO guidelines, 15; during post-colonial era, 24–27; during pre-colonial era, 16–20; social protections for, 26–27; spirit-child, 17, 30; termination of, 17; Western notions of, 101; WFCL and, 15. *See also* Children's Act; colonial era, childhood during; pre-colonial era, childhood during
child labor, 6, 99–109; African Charter on the Rights and Welfare of the Child, 100; age determination for, 211n3; apprenticeship and, 267–68; capitation grant programs, 108, 110n8; cash transfer programs, 108, 110n7; under Children's Act, 105, 155, 157, 265–68; cocoa as cash crop and, 101–2; under CRC, 99; in domestic work, 102, 106; education access and, 105, 116, 206–7; education policies and, 108–9; in fishing, 102–3; ILO guidelines, 6, 100; internationalization of, 100–101; *kayaye*, 157; LEAP program and, 108; parental decision-making about, 105–6; pension programs and, 107–8; poverty reduction as influence on, 107, 127n4; prosecution for, 109; in prostitution, 104; among rural poor, education access and, 206; in sales, 104–5; in small-scale mining, 103–4; WFCL, 6; under WFP, 110n9
child marriages, 131; as harmful traditional practice, 135–36
Child Panels, 154, 217, 254–55
child porterage work, 113
child prostitution, 104; under Children's Act, 156; as slavery, 140
Children and Youth in Broadcasting. *See* DOC/CURIOUS MINDS program
Children's Act (1998), 8, 15, 143, 151–67, 217, 219, 245–75; adoption un-

der, 155, 260–65; age determination of juvenile offenders under, 185, 210n1; agency constraints under, 158–59; amendments to, 273–75; appeals to, 273–75; apprenticeship under, of children, 267–68; approved residential homes under, 268–70; background to, 152–54; benefits of, 166; care and protection guidelines, 251–53; CEDAW and, 167n2; child labor under, 105, 155, 157, 265–68; child maintenance under, 257–59; Child Panels, 154, 217, 254–55; child prostitution under, 156; child rights under, 154, 249–54; child trafficking under, 156; corporal punishment under, 59, 88–90, 93, 156; CRC and, 152, 156; criminalization of child nonparticipation in decision-making under, 155; criminalization of parental irresponsibility under, 164; cross-agency coordination under, 159; cultural values as influence on, 162–64, 167n2; custody under, 154, 257; daycare centers under, 270–71; dialogue process with, 166; domestic labor under, 156; DOVVSU and, 156; education access for girls under, 197; educational access under, 157; enforcement of, 156–57; Family Tribunals, 252–53, 255–56; fosterage under, 155, 259–60; future implementation strategies, 164–66; global economic influences on implementation of, 160–61; goals of, 217; incest under, 156; institutionalized care under, 155, 268–72; internal cultural discourse over, 165; lack of resources for, 160–61; limited implementation of, 158–64; miscellaneous provisions of, 271–72; MOWAC and, 159; NGOs and, 160; parentage under, 154, 256; parental duty under, 249–51; parental responsibility under, 174; paternity status under, 45, 48, 50–51, 53; probation officers under, 253; public lack of awareness of, 161–62; rape treatment under, 156; social workers under, 253; UNICEF and, 160; universal rights under, 165–66

Children's Rights Foundation, 218

child rights: under ACRWC, 42; analysis of, 4–10; benefits of, 166; in Buduburam Refugee Settlement, 62–63, *63–64*; childhood and, 28; under Children's Act, 154, 249–54; children's views on, 107; citizen's role in, 218; under Constitution of Ghana, 40; CRC and, 38; cultural views on, 106–7; Declaration of the Rights of the Child (1924), 134; Declaration of the Rights of the Child (1959), 134–35; DSW and, 7; family size and, 5; funding agencies for, 219; future of, 215–20; future prospects for, 219–20; government's role in, 7–10; identity as, 30; institutional infrastructure for, 29–30; in international law, 134; international organizations and, 219; legislative role in, 15–16; paternity and, 38–41; population growth and, 6; poverty trends and, 4; refugees status and, 59–71; state mandates for, 29–30; universalization of, 99–100. *See also* Convention on the Rights of the Child

Child Rights International (CRI), 91

Child Rights Regulations, 219

The Child Rights Regulations (2003), 8

child trafficking, 113, 169; under Children's Act, 156

CHRAJ. *See* Commission on Human Rights and Administrative Justice

Christian Council, 61–62

Coalition on the Rights of the Child, 39, 196–97

cocoa cash crops, 42; child labor and, 101–2

College for Ama Foundation, 218

colonial era, childhood during, 20–24; Accelerated Development Plan for Education, 21; adolescence as concept and, 22; for Asante people, 24; education programs during, 21–22; on Gold Coast, 21; labor migration and, 22; for sex-education, 23–24

Commission on Children, 39
Commission on Human Rights and Administrative Justice (CHRAJ), 173, 179–80, 187n5, 188n19; age determination guidelines, 184–85; torture guidelines for, preventive measures in, 180; *trokosi* law under, 143
Committee on the Rights of the Child, 167n1
community-based organizations (CBOs): health care access and, 113; in mobility and transport strategies, 127n1
compulsory marriage, 140
consent: for harmful traditional practices, 136; for *trokosi* practices, 139–40
Constitution of Ghana: Buduburam Refugee Settlement under, 64–65; child rights under, 40; corporal punishment under, 89; definition of discrimination under, 52; harmful traditional practices under, 140; laws under, definition of, 39–40; paternity status under, 45
Constitution of Namibia, 52
contract slavery, 140
Convention on the Elimination of All Forms of Discrimination Against Women (CEDAW), 8, 41; Children's Act and, 167n2; paternity status under, 49, 53
Convention on the Rights of the Child (CRC), 41, 135, 215–20, 225–44; child labor under, 99; Children's Act and, 152, 156; child rights and, 38; corporal punishment under, 78; correctional institutions and, for children in, 169–86; education access under, 119, 193–94; Ghana ratification of, 3, 151; MOWAC and, 153; parental responsibility under, 174; paternity status under, 48–49; ratification of, 152–53; refugee status under, 59; rights guarantees under, 3–4. *See also* Children's Act
corporal punishment, 77–95; among Akan people, 81–82, 95n3; by caning, 83; under Children's Act, 59, 88–90, 93, 156; community views on, 82–83; under Constitution of Ghana, 89; under CRC, 78; under Criminal Code Amendment Act, 89; under Daycare Center Decree, 90; definition of, 78; DOVVSU and, 77, 79; DSW and, 79; by education authorities, 80; FBOs and, 91–92; forms of, 78; future policy changes for, 94–95; GES and, 79; GNCC study on, 83; government agencies and, 92, 96n18; *Head Teacher's Handbook* and, 85, 88, 90, 92–93; in home, 80–84; under Juvenile Justice Act (2003), 89; legislation on, 88–90; media and, 90–91; ministries and, 92; MOWAC and, 79; national response to, 88–92; NGOs and, 91; NGOs as information source, 79; in orphanages, 90; parameters of, 77; public debate over, 80; in schools, 85–90; study methodology on, 79; in Sweden, legal ban of, 78; UNICEF and, 92; UN studies on, 77; by women, 81–82. *See also* homes, corporal punishment in; schools, corporal punishment in
correctional institutions, children in, 169–86; age determination of offenders in, 183–85; CHRAJ guidelines, 173, 179–80; under CRC, 169–86; criminal justice reforms and, 183; cultural factors in, 181; cultural perception of offenders, 182; education access in, 176–78; food in, 176; friendships in, 181; Ghana Borstal Institution, 172; human right monitoring in, 178–83; inadequacies of, 175; under Juvenile Justice Act (2003), 173–75, 179; juvenile justice administration, 171–72; language use in, 181; legal

negotiations and, 183–86; mediation and, 183–86; NGO studies, 187n7; non-discrimination principles in, 177–78; Prisons Ordinance and, 171; socioeconomic factors in, 181; studies, 170. *See also* Commission on Human Rights and Administrative Justice
Courts Act (1993), 275
Covell, Katherine, 215
Covenant on Civil and Political Rights, 133
Covenant on Economic, Social, Cultural Rights (1966), 133
CRADLE-The Children Foundation, 50
CRC. *See* Convention on the Rights of the Child
CRI. *See* Child Rights International
Criminal Code Amendment Act (1994), 8, 143, 216
Criminal Code Amendment Act (1998), 8, 89, 172; age limits under, 184; harmful traditional practices under, 142
Criminal Procedure Code (1960), 172

Dangme peoples, *woryokwe* practices among, 131–32
DANIDA. *See* Danish International Development Agency
Danish International Development Agency (DANIDA), 92
Daycare Center Decree (1978), 273; corporal punishment under, 90
Daycare Center Regulations (1979), 275
daycare centers, 270–71
debt bondage, 140
Declaration of Rights (US), 132
Declaration of the Rights of Man and the Citizen (France), 132
Declaration of the Rights of the Child (1924), 134
Declaration of the Rights of the Child (1959), 48, 134–35; additional rights under, 135; NGOs and, 135; paternity status under, 48
Department for International Development (DFID), 198
Department of Social Welfare (DSW), 7; corporal punishment and, 79; development of, 188n13
DFID. *See* Department for International Development
dignity, human rights and, 133
dipo rites, 141–42; chastity laws and, 146n18
disability: education access and, 197–99; as life-cycle risk factor, 4; mobility and transport strategies and, 122; social stigma for, 198; teacher training and, 198–99; transportation costs, 198; visual impairment as, 198
Disability Act (2006), 143
discrimination: under Constitution of Ghana, definitions of, 52; against girls, 126
DOC/CURIOUS MINDS program, 80–81, 85, 91
domestic labor: children as, 102, 106; under Children's Act, 156; as slavery, 140
Domestic Violence Act (2007), 8, 15, 143, 217, 220
Domestic Violence Victims Support Unit (DOVVSU), 77, 79, 174; Children's Act and, 156
DOVVSU. *See* Domestic Violence Victims Support Unit
DSW. *See* Department of Social Welfare

Early Childhood Care and Development Policy, 153, 188n18
Economic Reform Program, 205
education, 119–22, 193–210; availability of, 177; capitation grants for, 202; child labor and, 105, 116, 206–7; child poverty and, 121–22; under Children's Act, 157, 197; as compulsory, 177, 196; in correctional institutions, 176–78; costs of, 120; under CRC, 119, 193–94; cultural requirements and, 208; data collection, 209; decentralization strategy for, 194–95, 202–3, 205; denial of rights for, 210; DFID, 198; for disabled persons, 197–99; Education Reform Program, 152;

EFA initiative, 203, 207; enrollment collection, 209; enrollment rates, 193; ESP, 207; FCUBE program, 25, 188n18, 195; gendered, 119–20; for girls, 196–97; GLSS, 161, 209; GPRS and, 195; history of, in Ghana, 194–95; as human right, 193, 203–4; IMF support of, 194; JSS, 119, 196, 202; under Juvenile Justice Act (2003), 197; language requirements and, 208; MDG for, 203; mobility and transport strategies, 114; outbound mobility enrollment, 208; parental responsibility and, 209; in primary schools, 120, 204–6; PRSP and, 113, 201, 203, 205–6; public schools, 194; quality v. quantity in, 207–9; religious requirements and, 208; School Feeding Programs for, 202; school shifts and, 116; sexual abuse and, 196; transport-related issues with, 120; UNESCO and, 210; UNICEF and, 197, 208; UPE as goal, 195; for vulnerable groups, 195–202. *See also* rural poor, education access for

Education Act (1961), 152

Education for All (EFA) initiative, 203, 207

education programs, 21–24, 203–4; during colonial era, 21–22; Economic Reform Program, 205; external influences on, 203; FCUBE, 25; for females, 23–24; gender gap in, 22; under Nkrumah, 25; World Bank on, 205

Education Reform Program, 152

Education Strategic Plan (ESP), 207

EFA initiative. *See* Education for All initiative

English Bill of Rights, 132

English Common Law, in Ghana, 171

EPI. *See* Expanded Program on Immunization

ESP. *See* Education Strategic Plan

Ewe peoples, *trokosi* practices among, 131

Expanded Program on Immunization (EPI), 26; health care access and, 116

facial scarification, as harmful traditional practice, 135–36

faith-based organizations (FBOs), corporal punishment and, 91–92

family networks, 41–45; cash crop economies and, 42; kinship networks, 41–42; literature on, 41–42; roles and responsibilities, 42

family planning services, 118–19

family size, child rights and, 5

Family Tribunals, 252–53, 255–56

Fante people, childhood for, 18

FBOs. *See* faith-based organizations

FCUBE. *See* Free Compulsory Universal Basic Education

Federation of International Women Lawyers (FIDA), 143, 174

female circumcision, as harmful traditional practice, 131; criminalization of, 143

fiasidis, 139

FIDA. *See* Federation of International Women Lawyers

fishing, child labor in, 102–3; risks of, 103; trafficking for, 103

forced feeding, as harmful traditional practice, 135

fosterage: under Children's Act, 155, 259–60; mobility and transport strategies and, 122; paternity status and, 37

Frafra people, adultery and, 47–48

Frans v. Paschke and Others, 44, 51–52

Free Compulsory Universal Basic Education (FCUBE), 25, 188n18, 195

Futa, Nii, 163–64

Ga people, paternity status among, 45

gender: access to education by, 119–20; education programs and, 22, 196–97; power for children and, 124–25

Gender and Children's Policy (2002), 153
genital mutilation, 38
GES. *See* Ghana Education Service
Ghana: Accelerated Development Plan for Education, 23; adultery in, legal status of children and, 45–48, 55n1; changing family perspectives in, 41–45; child labor in, 6; child malnutrition in, 25; child marriages in, 131; child population demographics in, 6; citizen's role in, for children's rights, 218; Commission on Children in, 39; Constitution, 39–40; controversial traditional practices in, 131–32; corporal punishment in, 77–95; CRC ratification by, 3; criminal code in, development of, 171; disabled population in, 198; DSW in, 7; education in, access to, 119–22, 193–210; English Common Law in, 171; female circumcision in, 131; GOG in, 192, 194–96, 199, 201; Gomoa District, 70; GPRS in, 8; health care access in, 116–19; health research in, 116; infant mortality rates in, 25; Interstate Succession Law, 43; juvenile delinquency in, history of, 188n12, 188n15; juvenile justice administration, 171–72; LEAP in, 9; life-cycle risk factors in, 4; MDG in, 8; mobility and transport strategies in, 113–17, 122–24; National Commission on Children, 15, 26; National Road Safety Strategy in, 123; NGOs in, 28; NSPS in, 8–10; OVC policy in, 6; paternity status in, 37–55; Poverty Reduction Strategy in, 113; poverty trends in, 4–5, 161; reciprocity as cultural value in, 162–63; Refugee Law in, 65; rural demographics for, 5; *trokosi* practices in, 131–32, 136–44; urbanization in, 20; widowhood rites, 131. *See also* child labor; Children's Act; colonial era, childhood during; corporal punishment; education, access to; paternity, legal status for; post-colonial era, childhood during; pre-colonial era, childhood during; refugee status, children's rights and; *trokosi* practices; specific legislative acts
Ghana Borstal Institution, 172
Ghana Education Code of Discipline, 85
Ghana Education Service (GES), 79; *Head Teacher's Handbook* and, 90
Ghana Interest Group, 4
Ghana Law Reform Commission, 141, 146n15
Ghana Living Standards Survey (GLSS), 161, 209
Ghana Media Advocacy Program (G-MAP), 88
Ghana National Commission on Children (GNCC), 83, 161, 188n19
Ghana News Agency (GNA), 88
Ghana Private Road Transport Union (GPRTU), 125
Ghana Refugee Law (1992), 65
Ghana Road Fund, 123
Girl Child Education Project, 197
girls: corporal punishment against, 81–82; discrimination against, 126; education access for, 196–97; end of childhood for, 17; as *kayaye*, 157; mobility and transport strategies for, 126; power for children and, 124–25
A Girl's Education Unit, 197
Global Road Safety Partnership (GRSP), 123
GLSS. *See* Ghana Living Standards Survey
G-MAP. *See* Ghana Media Advocacy Program
GNA. *See* Ghana News Agency
GNCC. *See* Ghana National Commission on Children
GOG. *See* Government of Ghana
Goodhart, Michael, 132
Government of Ghana (GOG), 192, 194–96, 199, 201
GPRS. *See* Growth and Poverty Reduction Strategy
GPRTU. *See* Ghana Private Road Transport Union
grounded theory, 60–61

Growth and Poverty Reduction Strategy (GPRS), 8, 195
GRSP. *See* Global Road Safety Partnership
Guinea worm, incidence rates for, 118

harmful traditional practices, 135–44; abolishment of, state obligations for, 136; under Constitution of Ghana, 140; under Criminal Code Amendment Act (1998), 142; *dipo* rites, 141–42; family consent for, 136; *woryokwe* practices as, 141. *See also trokosi* practices
Head Teacher's Handbook, 85, 88, 90, 92–93; GES and, 90
health care, access to, 116–19; in Buduburam Refugee Settlement, 63; CBOs and, 113; child poverty and, 121–22; EPI and, 116; family planning services, 118–19; Guinea worm incidence rates, 118; with home herbal remedies, 118; NGOs and, 113; with patent medicines, 118; preventive, 118–19; primary, 118; purposes of, 117; vaccinations, 118
HIV/AIDS. *See* Human Immunodeficiency Virus/Acquired Immune Disease Syndrome
homes, corporal punishment in, 80–84; by act, 81–82; appropriateness of, *84*; DOC/CURIOUS MINDS program, 80–81; by family member, *81*; MICS, 80; types of, *84*; for young women, 81–82
Howe, Brian, 215
Human Immunodeficiency Virus/Acquired Immune Disease Syndrome (HIV/AIDS), orphanhood and, 6
human rights: concept of, 132; definition of, 132; dignity and, 133; education as, 193, 203–4; harmful traditional practices and, 135–44; historical antecedents to, 132–33; legal compliance for, 170; modern elements of, 133; as moral standard, 133–34; paternity status and, 48–52; state role in, 133. *See also* UN Declaration on Human Rights
Human Trafficking Act (2005), 8, 15, 143, 153, 219

Ibrahim v. Amalibini, 47–48
ICCPR. *See* International Covenant on Civil and Political Rights
ICESCR. *See* International Covenant on Economic, Social, and Cultural Rights
identity, as right, 30
ILO. *See* International Labor Organization; International labor Organization
IMF. *See* International Monetary Fund
incest, under Children's Act, 156
inheritance rights: adultery and, legal status of children and, 52; paternity and, 43
International Bill of Rights, 40–41, 133; legal status of paternity under, 48
International Covenant on Civil and Political Rights (ICCPR), 41
International Covenant on Economic, Social, and Cultural Rights (ICESCR), 41
International Labor Organization (ILO), 92; childhood definitions, 15; child labor programs, 6, 100; child social protections under, 26; Time Bound Program, 188n18
International Monetary Fund (IMF), 26; education access support by, 194
International Needs Ghana, 216, 218
International Rescue Committee (IRC), 62
International Year of the Child, 38, 152
Interstate Succession Law of Ghana, 43
Intestate Succession Law (1985), 274
IRC. *See* International Rescue Committee
Isaac v. Isaac, 50

JSS. *See* junior secondary schools
junior secondary schools (JSS), 119, 196, 202; for rural poor, 200–201
juvenile delinquency, history of, in Ghana, 188n12, 188n15; Social Inquiry reports on, 188n16
Juvenile Justice Act (1998), 172–73
Juvenile Justice Act (2003), 8, 15, 143, 153, 173–75, 179, 217, 219; age limits under, 184; corporal punishment under, 89; education access for girls under, 197; juvenile offenders under, 182–84; medical determination of age under, 184–85
juvenile justice studies, 170

kayaye (porters), 157
kinship networks, 41–42
Kormazu, Morris, 71n1
Krobo people, paternity status among, 43
Kyei-Gyamfi, Sylvester, 161

The Labor Act (2003), 8
Labor Decree Act (1967), 152
labor migration, during colonial era, for children, 22
Labour Decree (1967), 273
Langlois, Anthony, 133
Law On Children (2002), 50–51
LEAP program. *See* Livelihood Empowerment Against Poverty program
Legesse, Asmorom, 26
Liberia. *See* Buduburam Refugee Settlement
Liberia Welfare Council, 71n1
Livelihood Empowerment Against Poverty (LEAP) program, 9, 173, 218; child labor and, 108; subprograms under, 9

Magna Carta, 132
Maintenance Decree (1977), 273
Maintenance of Children Act (1965), 275
Maintenance of Children Decree (1978), 275
Malnutrition Rehabilitation Centers (NRCs), 26
marriage. *See* child marriages; compulsory marriage
Marriage Ordinance, 273
MDG. *See* Millennium Development Goals
MICS. *See* Multiple Indicator Cluster Survey
Miers, Suzanne, 140
Millennium Development Goals (MDG), 8; for education access, 203; mobility strategies and, 114; for primary schools, 204
Miller, Kester, 71n1
Ministry of Women and Children's Affairs (MOWAC), 79; Children's Act and, 159; CRC and, 153
mobility and transport strategies, 113–17, 122–24; accident fatality rates and, 122–23; accident safety measures in, 123–24; with bicycles, 121–22; CBOs role in, 127n1; children's physique as factor in, 114, 122–24; children's power and, 115, 124–25; children's voice and, 115, 124–25, 127n1; constraints in, 126; for disabled, 122; for education, 114, 208; fostering and, 122; Ghana Road Fund and, 123; for girls, 126; GRSP and, 123; for health, 114; key literature for, 115–17; MDG and, 114; National Road Safety Strategy, 123; NGOs' role in, 127n1; physical, 114; poverty and, 114; traffic accidents and, 114–15; traffic education in, 123; walking, 122. *See also* education, access to; health care, access to
"The Mosquito and the Young Ghanaian," 25
MOWAC. *See* Ministry of Women and Children's Affairs
Multiple Indicator Cluster Survey (MICS), 80
mutilation, as harmful traditional practice, 135

Nagbe, Penny, 71n1
Namibia, 52
naming, of children, 17

National Commission on Children, 15, 26, 153
National Council on Women and Development, 153
National Disability Act (2006), 8, 220
National Gender and Children Policy, 188n18
National Health Insurance Scheme (NHIS), 188n18
National Program of Action, 188n18
National Road Safety Strategy, 123
National Social Protection Strategy (NSPS), 8–10, 173, 218; LEAP program under, 9, 173
"new" slavery, 139–40
NHIS. *See* National Health Insurance Scheme
Nkrumah, Kwame, 21; education programs under, 25
non-governmental organizations (NGOs): Children's Act and, 160; child social protections under, 26; corporal punishment and, as information source, 79, 91; correctional institutions and, studies on, 187n7; Declaration of the Rights of the Child (1959) and, 135; in Ghana, 28; health care access and, 113; in mobility and transport strategies, 127n1
NRCs. *See* Malnutrition Rehabilitation Centers
NSPS. *See* National Social Protection Strategy
Nyarkoa v. Mansu, 46–47

OAU. *See* Organization of African Unity
O'Byrne, Darren, 132
OPCAT. *See* Optional Protocol to the Convention Against Torture
Optional Protocol to the Convention Against Torture (OPCAT), 179, 189n36, 189n37
Organization of African Unity (OAU), 27
orphanages: corporal punishment in, 90; as life-cycle risk factor, 4
orphans and vulnerable children (OVC), 6; HIV/AIDS and, 6
OVC. *See* orphans and vulnerable children

Palm leaves of childhood (Adali-Mortti), 19–20
patent medicines, 118
paternity, legal status for, 37–55; ACRWC and, 38; adoption and, 37; adultery and, 45–48; among Amedzofe-Avatime, 44; among Ashanti, 44; under CEDAW, 49, 53; under Children's Act, 45, 48, 50–51, 53; child rights and, 38–41; under common law, 50–51; under Constitution of Ghana, 45; under CRC, 48–49; under Declaration of the Rights of the Child (1959), 48; fosterage and, 37; *Frans v. Paschke and Others*, 44, 51–52; among Ga, 45; human rights implications for, 48–52; inheritance rights, 43; International Bill of Rights and, 48; judicial influences on, 53–54; among Krobo, 43; under Law On Children, 50–51; reproduction issues and, 37; sexuality and, 37; as transaction between two males, 49; under *trokosi*, 38; among Tswana, 43–44; under UNHDR, 45; UNICEF and, 51
pension programs, 107–8
Plan Ghana, 91
population growth, child rights and, 6
post-colonial era, childhood during, 24–27; ILO protections, 26; intervention for, 26; in literature, 25; NGOs and, 26; social protection development during, 26–27
poverty: in Accra, 5; child labor and, 107, 127n4; education access and, 121–22; in Ghana, trends in, 4–5, 161; health care access and, 121–22; mobility strategies and, 114; women and, 5–6
Poverty Reduction Strategy Program

(PRSP), 113, 201, 203, 205–6
power, for children, 115, 124–25; gender and social hierarchy and, 124–25
pre-colonial era, childhood during, 16–20; "ahenahene" game, 18; for Akan people, 16–18; for Asantehene people, 20; for Ashanti people, 20; for Fante people, 18; social games, 18–19; socialization as "becoming" during, 19; termination of, economic factors for, 20
preventive care, 118–19
primary schools, 120, 204–6; MDGs, 204
Prisons Ordinance (1860), 171
probation officers, 253
prostitution. *See* child prostitution
Protocol to the African Charter on Human Rights on the Rights of Women, 41
PRSP. *See* Poverty Reduction Strategy Program

rape, 169; under Children's Act, 156
reciprocity, 162–63
refugee status, children's rights and, 59–71; within Buduburam Refugee Settlement, 60–69; coping strategies, 65–69; under CRC, 59; methodological approaches to, 60–61; policy implications for, 70–71; under UNHCR, 59. *See also* Buduburam Refugee Settlement
reproduction, paternity status and, 37
ritual killings, as harmful traditional practice, 135–36
ritual slavery, 140
Rome Final Act (1998), 138
rural poor, education access for, 200–202; capitation grants for, 201; child labor among, 206; child migration as influence on, 202; JSS reform, 200–201; PRSP, 201; School Feeding Programs for, 201; UNESCO, 200; urban v., 200

sales, child labor in, 104–5
Salvation Army, 187n11
Save The Children, 92
Save the Children International Union (SCIU), 22–23
School Feeding Programs, 201–2, 219; for education access, 202
schools, corporal punishment in, 85–90; in Apowa, 87; appropriateness of, *84*; caning, 85; consequences for, 87–88; DOC/CURIOUS MINDS program, 85; in Dwomo, 87; under Ghana Education Code of Discipline, 85; *Head Teacher's Handbook*, 85; learning as benefit of, 85; by perpetrator, *86*; reasons for, *86*; severity of, 87; types of, *84*, 85. *See also* junior secondary schools; primary schools; senior secondary schools
SCIU. *See* Save the Children International Union
Scouts and Guides Decree (1969), 273
senior secondary schools (SSS), 202
sexual abuse, education access and, 196
sex work: in Buduburam Refugee Settlement, 67–68. *See also* child prostitution
slavery, 137–38; child prostitution as, 140; definition of, 137; domestic labor and, 140; legal consequences for, 146n14; "new," 139–40; *trokosi* practices as, 137–44
Slavery Convention of 1926, 138
small-scale mining, child labor in, 103–4; age range of, 103
Social Security Law (1991), 274
social workers, 253
spirit-child, 17, 30
SSS. *See* senior secondary schools
Street Girls Aid, 28, 218
Supplementary Convention on the Abolition of Slavery, the Slave Trade, and Institutions and Practices Similar to Slavery (1956), 138–39
Sweden, corporal punishment bans in, 78

Tano v. Akosua Koko, 141
teacher training, for persons with disabilities, 198–99
Teeple, Gary, 132
Time Bound Program, 188n18

Tobin, John, 136
Torday, Emily, 23
trokosi practices, 131–32, 136–44, 169, 216; Anti-Slavery International, 137, 139–40; arguments in favor of, 142–43; under CHRAJ, 143; consent and, 139–40; control over personal belongings and, 138–39; among Ewes, 131; *fiasidis* and, 139; girls under, 187n1; group v. individual rights under, 146n18; paternity status under, 38; restriction of freedom of movement and, 138; as slavery, 137–44; *troxorvi* shrines, 137; women and, 141–42
troxorvi shrines, 137, 145n7
Tswana people: *bana ka dikgora* and, 44; *bogadi* and, 43; paternity status among, 43–44

UDHR. *See* Universal Declaration on Human Rights
UN Covenant on Economic, Social and Cultural Rights, 7
UN Declaration on Human Rights (UNHDR), 7; paternity status under, 45
Undefended Childhood Conference, 4
UNDP. *See* United Nations Development Program
UN Educational, Scientific, and Cultural Organization (UNESCO), 200, 208; education access and, 210
unemployment, as life-cycle risk factor, 4
UNESCO. *See* UN Educational, Scientific, and Cultural Organization
UNHCR. *See* United Nations High Commission for Refugees
UNHDR. *See* UN Declaration on Human Rights
UNICEF. *See* United Nations Children's Fund
UN International Convention on People's Rights, 7
United Nations Children's Fund (UNICEF): Children's Act and, 160; corporal punishment and, 92; education access for girls, 197; paternity status and, 51
United Nations Development Program (UNDP), 92
United Nations High Commission for Refugees (UNHCR), 59
United States Agency for International Development (USAID), 92
Universal Declaration on Human Rights (UDHR), 132, 169
universal primary education (UPE), 195
universal rights: for children, 99–100; under Children's Act, 165–66
UPE. *See* universal primary education
USAID. *See* United States Agency for International Development

vaccinations, 118
Van Bueren, Geraldine, 134
voice, for children, 115, 124–25, 127n1; gender and social hierarchy and, 124–25
"vulnerable groups," 62
vulnerable groups, education access for, 195–202; disabled persons as, 197–99; girls as, 195–97; rural poor as, 200–202

WAJU. *See* Women and Juvenile Unit of the Ghana Police Service
walking, as mode of transport, 122
war slavery, 140
Weissbrodt, David, 137
WFCL. *See* Worst Forms of Child Labor
WFP. *See* World Food Program
widowhood rites, as harmful traditional practice, 131, 136
witch villages, as harmful traditional practice, 136, 145n3
women: adultery and, legal status of, 45–46; corporal punishment by, 81–82; divorce rights for, 49–50; legal discrimination towards, 49; poverty trends for, 5–6; *trokosi*

practices and, 141–42. *See also* girls
Women and Juvenile Unit (WAJU) of the Ghana Police Service, 188n19
World Declaration on the Survival, Protection and Development of Children, 29, 188n18
World Food Program (WFP), 110n9
World Relief, 61
World Vision International, 92
Worst Forms of Child Labor (WFCL), 6; childhood and, 15
woryokwe practices: among Dangme, 131–32; as harmful traditional practice, 141–42

Youth in Conflict with the Law, 170

About the Contributors

Albert Abane is a professor of transport geography in the Department of Geography and Regional Planning at the University of Cape Coast, Ghana. Presently, he is the dean of the Faculty of Social Sciences at the University of Cape Coast.

Frank Owusu Acheampong assisted on a series of Durham University-led, Department for International Development-funded research projects in Ghana. He is currently a doctoral student at Durham University Business School, investigating the effect of financial liberalization on SME financing in sub-Saharan Africa, with Ghana as a case study. This includes assessment of the demand and supply of SME financing, equity issues in SMEs, access to external finance, with specific emphasis on geographic and gender equity and technological orientation. The final objective examined the effectiveness of government interventions that seek to enhance SMEs' access to finance.

Michael Kwodwo Adjaloo is a research fellow at the Technology Consultancy Center of the Kwame Nkrumah University of Science and Technology in Kumasi, Ghana. He has specialized in apiculture but has been involved in various studies across different disciplines, including refugee and other social science studies. He has been involved in diverse development work and has undertaken both local and international consultancy assignments. His publications have appeared in journals such as *Human Organization, Journal of Refugee Studies,* and *Fondazione Eni Enrico Mattei*. He is completing his PhD research on the pollination ecology of cocoa in Ghana.

DeBrenna LaFa Agbényiga, PhD, LMSW, is an assistant professor in the School of Social Work and assistant dean for equity, diversity and inclusive academic affairs in the College of Social Science at Michigan State University in East Lansing, Michigan, USA. As a part of the School of Social Work faculty, she teaches Advanced Human Behavior and Social Environment, Organizational and Community Practice, Social Development, and Administrative Skills Practice courses in the graduate program. She has worked in West Africa (Ghana and Togo) for over ten years as a researcher, consultant, and visiting lecturer, working on women's and children's rights issues, with an emphasis on their ability to access systems of care, education, health, and services. Dr. Agbényiga has consulted with ministries, NGOs, and private organizations in Ghana to build organizational and community capacity. She has played a key role in creating mutual, collaborative, university-to-university partnerships between her home university, the University of Ghana, and the Kwame Nkrumah University of Science and Technology. Dr. Agbényiga is currently co-editing a book addressing issues impeding children's access to health, education, and development from a global perspective. She is also working with organizations to facilitate the creation of competent service delivery systems for working with African refugees while creating sustainable community support structures. Currently, she serves as the co-principal investigator on a project addressing international perspectives of child rights from a multi-disciplinary perspective.

Robert Kwame Ame is assistant professor of human rights and criminology at Wilfrid Laurier University in Brantford, Ontario, Canada. He earned a PhD from the School of Criminology at Simon Fraser University in Burnaby, British Columbia. His research interests in human rights include the implementation of international human rights norms in non-Western cultures, transitional justice, truth and reconciliation commissions, and children's rights. His work in criminology focuses on the youth justice system in Ghana, the sociology of law, and restorative justice. Dr. Ame's publications have appeared in academic journals such as the *Canadian Journal of Law and Society*; *Criminal Justice Studies: A Critical Journal of Crime, Law and Society; Contemporary Justice Review*; *Canadian Journal of African Studies; Ghana Studies;* and as chapters in books. He is working on a book manuscript, *Trokosi Politics: Reconciling Human Rights and Traditional Practices,* which is at an advanced stage of completion.

George Oppong Ampong, PhD (UK), Msc. (Ghana), BA Hons. (Ghana), Cert. (Belgium), Cert. (Hungary), is chief executive officer of the Youth Development Foundation, executive secretary of Defense for Children International in Ghana, part-time lecturer of University College of Management Studies, and coordinator of the Kumasi Study Support Center of the McGrath Institute of Business Australia. He has also held a number of international positions, including temporary advisor to UNAIDS, and he ran numerous internationally funded projects of the International Labor Organization, African Development Foundation, and the International Development Research Center. His current interests include sustainability, children's rights, and youth development.

Nana Araba Apt, PhD, MSW, is a sociology professor and currently dean of academic affairs at Ashesi University College in Accra, Ghana. She is an expert on human development issues in Africa and a frequent consultant to many international human development organizations, including United Nations organizations and the African Union's Commission on Social Development. Before her position as dean at Ashesi, she taught at the University of Ghana and headed the departments of Sociology and Social Work. She was the founding director of the Center for Social Policy Studies at the same university. Professor Apt has published widely. Her research and publication record bridges disciplinary applications in gerontology, family relations, child development, and women's education.

Lilian Ayete-Nyampong, in her capacity as deputy director, has oversight of one of four departments of the headquarters of the Commission on Human Rights and Administrative Justice, with responsibility for human rights education, human rights monitoring, and the promotion of collaborative efforts with human rights civil society organizations. She has represented the Commission at various local, regional, and international fora and presented papers in connection with the Commission's human rights monitoring and promotional efforts. She graduated from the University of Aberdeen, Scotland, UK, in 1996, with a master's degree in educational studies and is currently on study leave, pursuing her doctoral studies in the Netherlands.

Kathrin Blaufuss undertook her PhD research at Durham University, UK. Currently, she works for the German NGO Forum on Environment and Development. She coordinates the political activities of German NGOs regarding the United Nations Convention on Biological Diversity.

George Clerk is a visiting lecturer in sociology at the University of Westminster in the UK. He received his PhD in sociology from the University of Sheffield and holds an MA in sociology of law from the International Institute for Sociology of Law, Onati, Spain. His research interests include children, poverty, ethnic minorities, and crime. He is currently working on an intergenerational project, bringing black and minority ethnic elders and children in London together.

Beatrice Akua Duncan currently works with UNICEF New York as a Human Rights Specialist and prior to that UNICEF Ghana as Child Protection Officer. Her general work interests have been in the promotion of women and children's rights and in support of this cause has written on a number of issues related to women and children among which have included children and legislative and constitutional reform, gender and land access and inheritance rights.

Kate Hampshire is a senior lecturer in anthropology at Durham University in the UK. Most of her research is in sub-Saharan Africa, on health, well-being, and mobility, with a particular focus on children and youth. She began working mainly in Francophone West Africa. Her PhD thesis (at UCL 1994–98) explored the social and demographic consequences of changing mobility patterns among Fulani agro-pastoralists in northern Burkina Faso, and in subsequent years, she worked with pastoralist populations in Chad and Niger. More recently, her research has diversified and expanded geographically. Her recent work in Africa includes a large project on child mobility in Ghana, Malawi, and South Africa, with Dr. Gina Porter; work among refugee youth in Ghana; and work in Niger regarding intra-household allocation of resources and impacts on child health.

Currently, she is also working on a few UK-based research projects, including one on the management and social consequences of infertility among British Pakistani Muslims and another looking at the social capital impact of children's participation in community arts projects.

Kate Kilpatrick has worked with humanitarian programs in Southern and West Africa. She is currently policy manager for conflict and low-income countries with the Fairtrade Labelling Organization in Bonn, Germany.

Peter Ohene Kyei is currently the rector of Pentecost University College, a faith-based institution in Accra, Ghana. He was a lecturer in the Department of Geography and Rural Development for many years at the Kwame Nkrumah University of Science and Technology in Kumasi, Ghana. His research interest is in decentralization and poverty alleviation in rural Ghana. He has worked with NGOs on their strategies of poverty alleviation in Northern Ghana, for which he obtained his doctorate at the University of Durham, UK. He is co-author of *NGOs and the State in the Twenty-first Century Ghana and India* and is a member of the research team on the resilience of Liberia youth in Budumburam refugee camp in Ghana, a Nuffield Foundation-funded research.

Sylvester Kyei-Gyamfi holds an MA degree in development studies and a BA degree in sociology/history. He has worked as a researcher and child rights advocate for fifteen years. He has had rich field experience, trained many young researchers in the use of field tools, and co-authored a number of national reports. As a researcher, he has assisted students and researchers in compiling comprehensive academic reports, dissertations, and theses, with a focus on child rights. Sylvester has also been part of various Ghanaian delegations to present issues on behalf of the Ghanaian child. He has served on many specialized government committees and is presently a member of the Inter-Ministerial Committee on Migration. He is currently the head of the Information Research and Advocacy Division of the Department of Children, Ministry of Women and Children's Affairs in Ghana.

Leah McMillan is a PhD candidate in global governance with the Balsillie School of International Affairs in Waterloo, Ontario, Canada. Her dissertation research analyzes the effect of global education policy on national education provision, with a particular emphasis on the role of the state as provider of human rights given the increasing involvement of global and non-state actors. She has worked in Ghana and Tanzania on participatory governance projects and undertook her doctoral field research in Tanzania, Zambia, and Malawi. Leah is a Balsillie Fellow at the Center for International Governance Innovation, Waterloo, Canada, where she is involved in the Center's African Initiative.

Gina Porter is senior research fellow in the Department of Anthropology, Durham University, UK. Her research combines ethnographic approaches, with a strong interest in spatial perspectives, reflecting her training as a geographer. Uneven power relationships and associated issues of exclusion are linking themes through her work, much of which has a strong gender component. She has undertaken field research in diverse contexts but considers herself primarily an Africanist. She is currently leading an interdisciplinary research project on children, transport, and mobility in three African countries—Ghana, Malawi, and South Africa. This builds on her long-standing research interest in daily mobilities in sub-Saharan Africa.

Afua Twum-Danso is a lecturer in the sociology of childhood at the University of Sheffield in the UK and was previously a visiting lecturer in children's rights at Roehampton University, UK. She holds a PhD from the Center of West African Studies at the University of Birmingham (UK). Her thesis was entitled, *Searching for a Middle Ground in Children's Rights: The Implementation of the Convention on the Rights of the Child in Ghana*. Building on this research, she has now embarked on a new research project that aims to elicit children's perceptions of physical punishment in Ghana, funded by the Nuffield Foundation Small Grants Scheme. Examples of her research interests include: implementation of international children's rights standards; the role of cultural values such as reciprocity, respect, and responsibility in limiting the impact of international children's rights standards; and children's right to express their opinions and participate in decision-making in non-Western societies. Her work has been published in a number of edited collections as well as in peer-reviewed journals such as *International Journal of Children's Rights*, *Children's Geographies*, and *Journal for the History of Childhood and Youth*.

www.ingramcontent.com/pod-product-compliance
Lightning Source LLC
LaVergne TN
LVHW101445200926
848483LV00001B/52
* 9 7 8 0 7 3 9 1 4 8 0 0 6 *